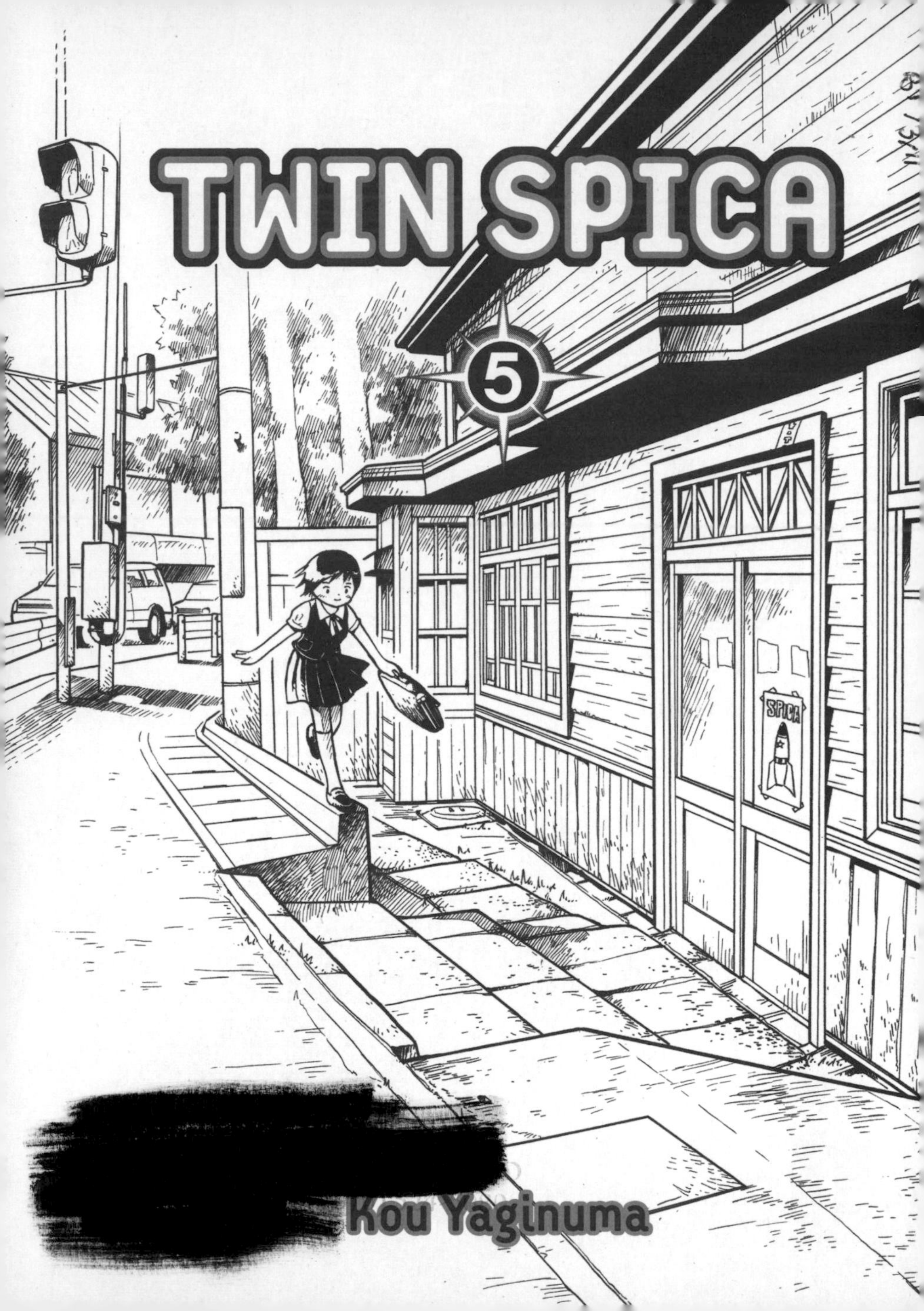
TWIN SPICA
5
SPICA
[redacted]
Kou Yaginuma

CONTENTS

MISSION:19...003

MISSION:20...033

MISSION:21...063

MISSION:22...093

MISSION:23...123

MISSION:24...153

●

ANOTHER SPICA.....................................183

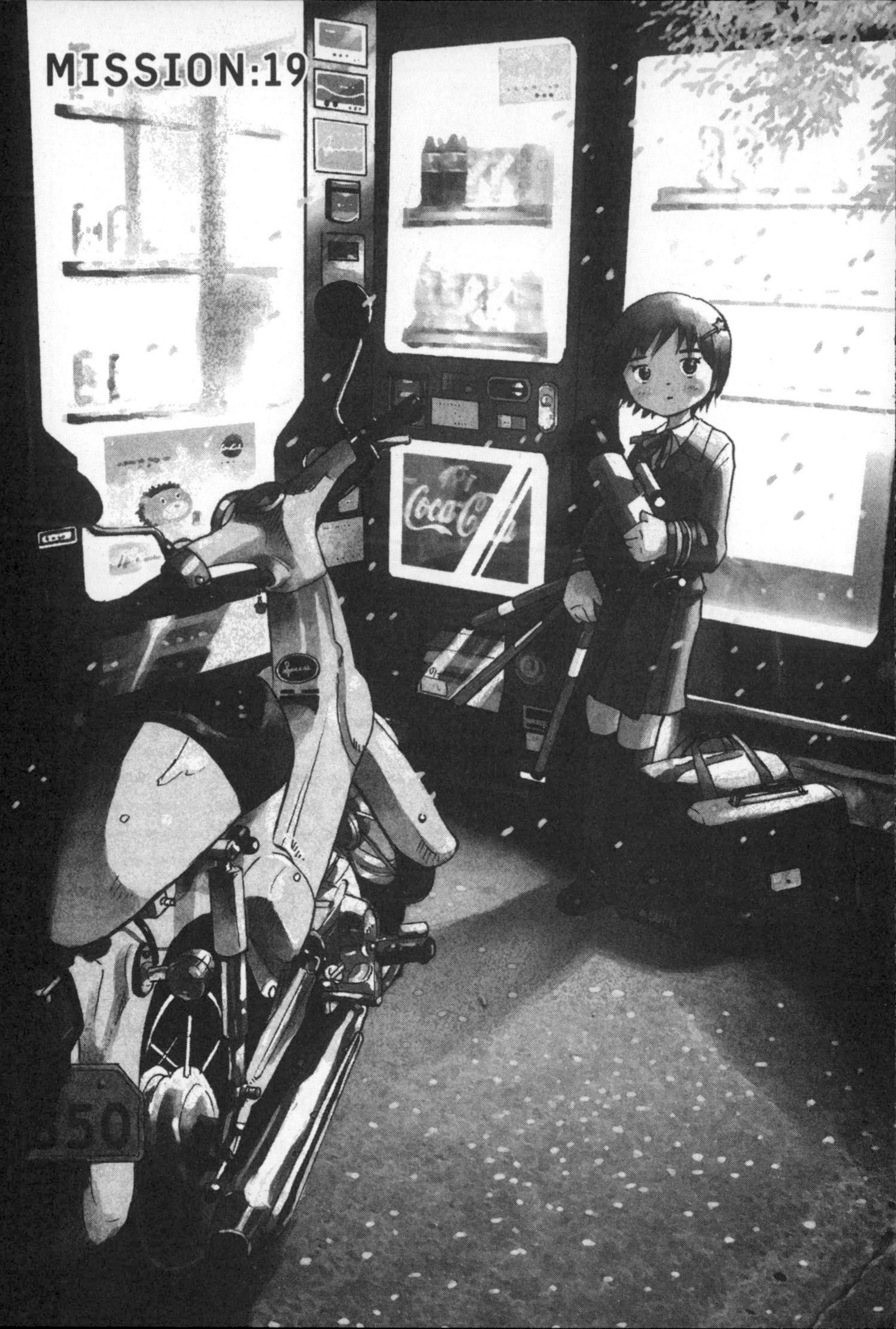
MISSION:19
Coca-Cola

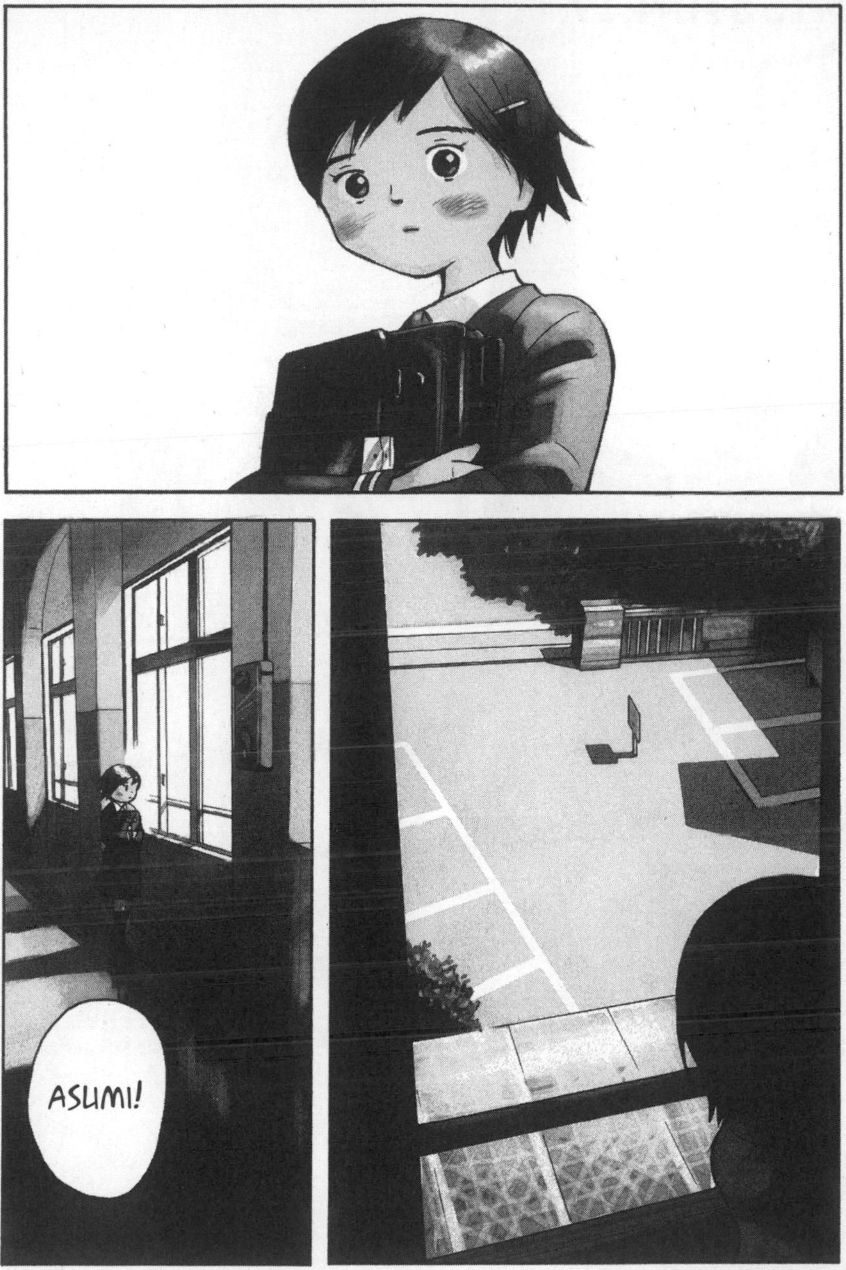
ASUMI!

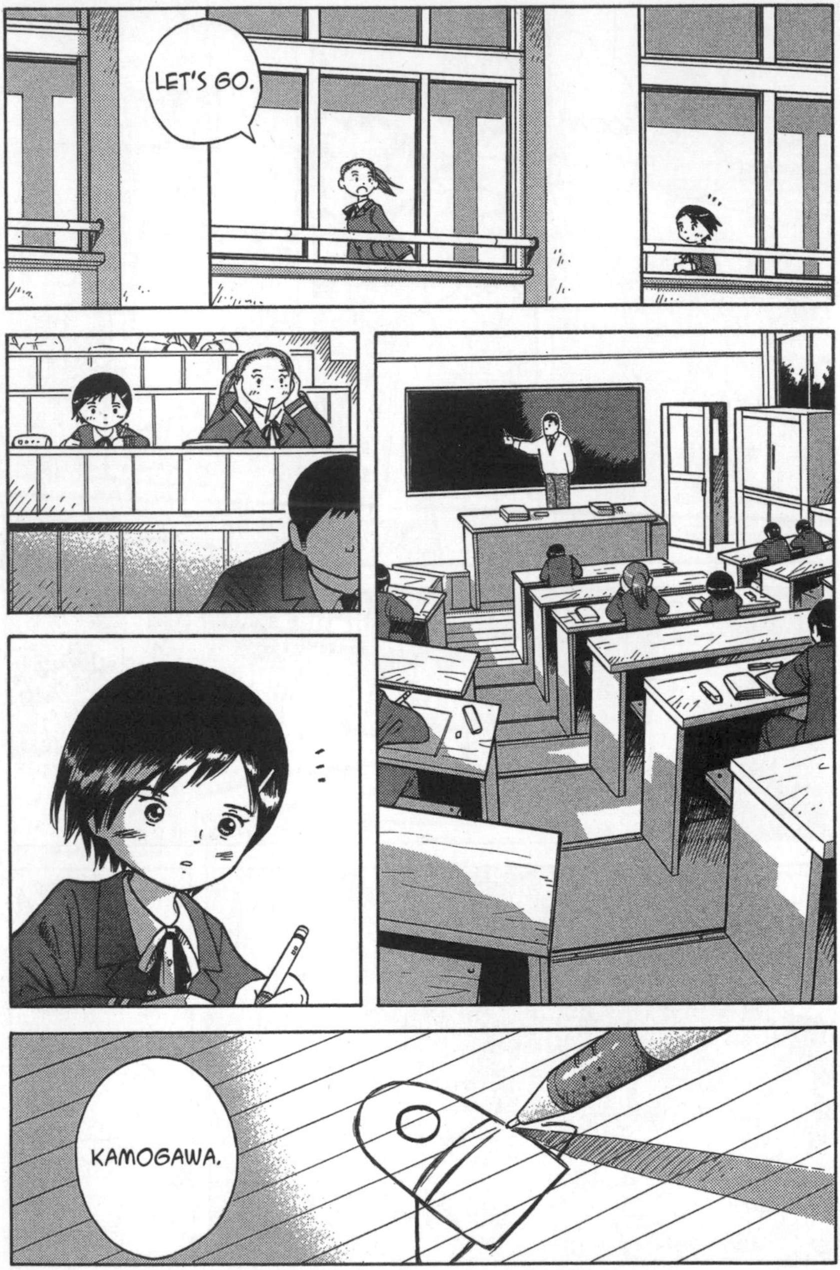
LET'S GO.
KAMOGAWA.

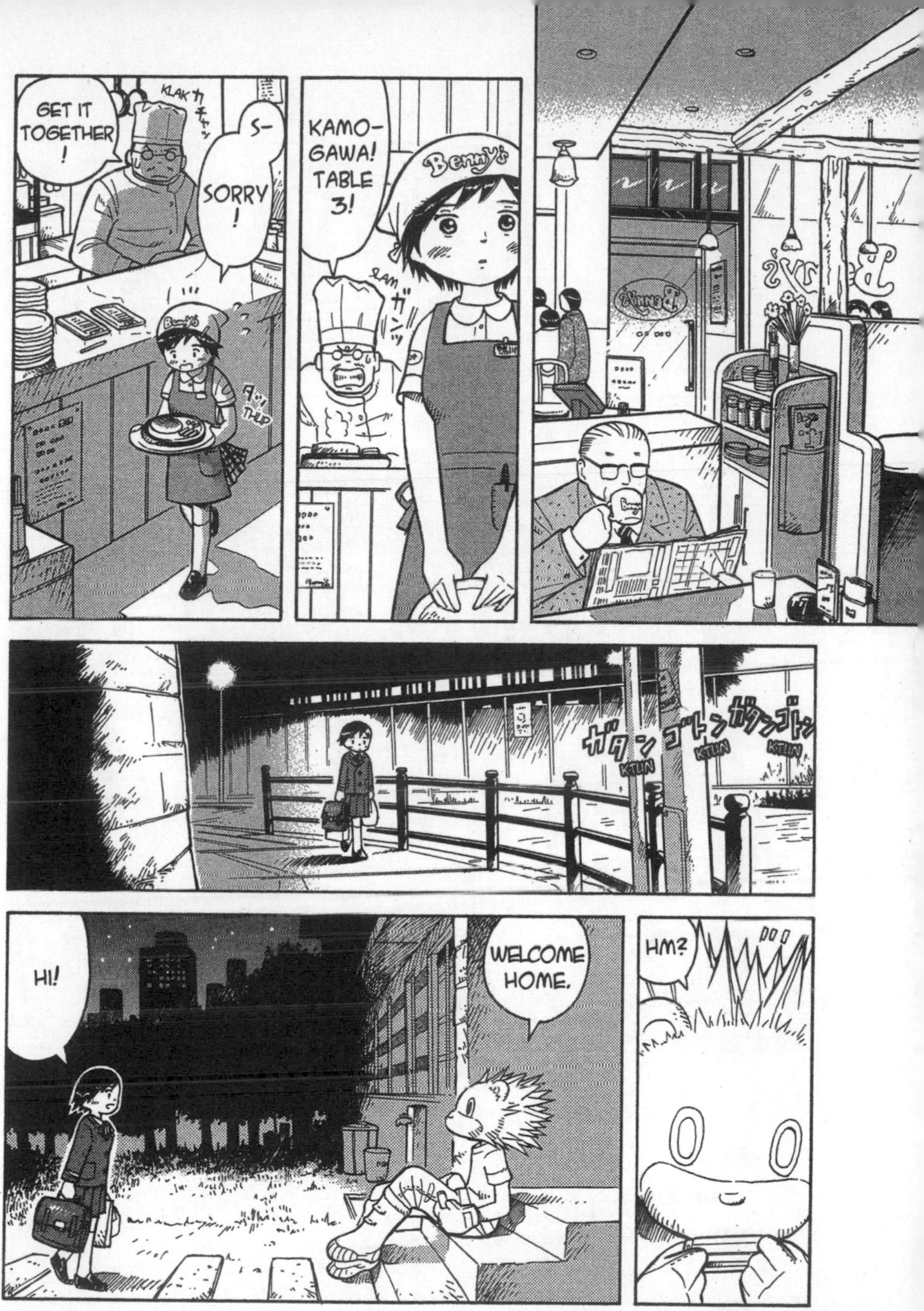

KAMO-GAWA! TABLE 3!
SLAM ガンッ
S- SORRY!
KLAK カチャッ
GET IT TOGETHER!
タッ THUP
ガタンゴトンガタンゴトン
KTUN KTUN KTUN
HM?
WELCOME HOME.
HI!

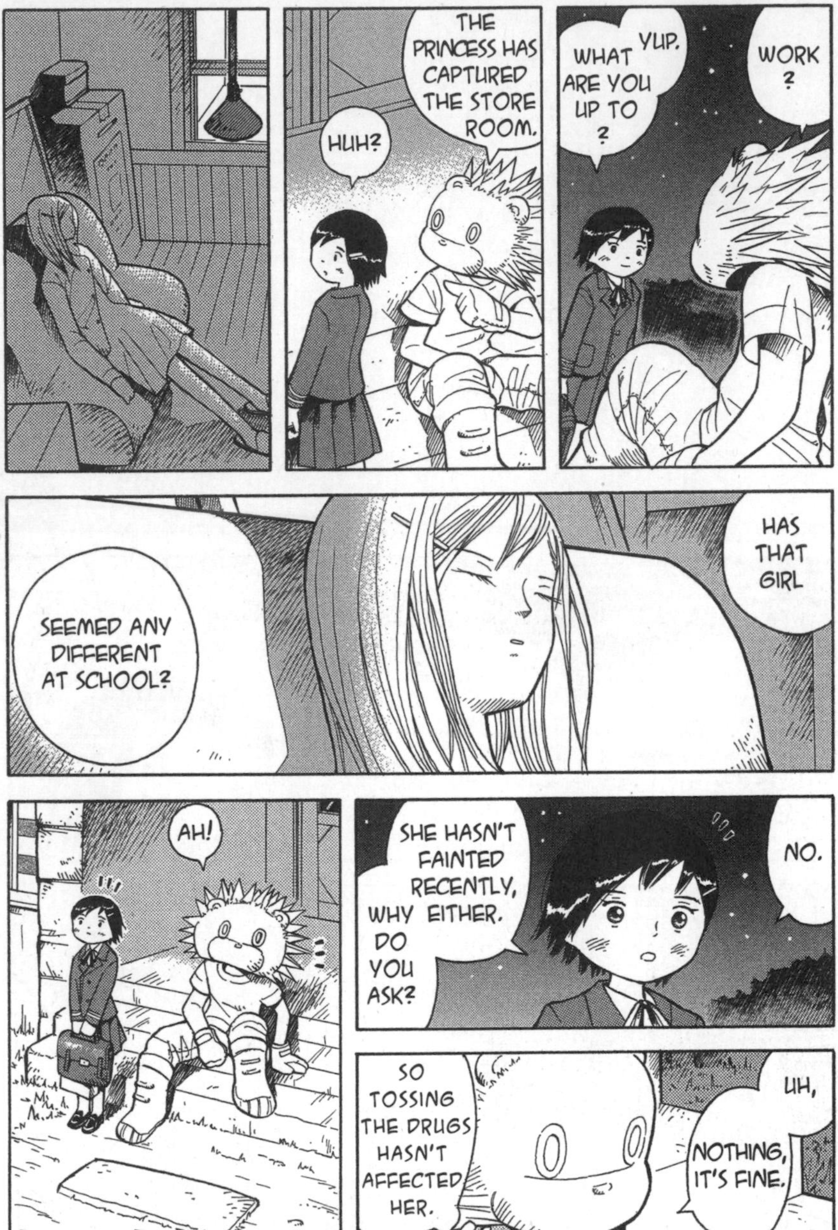
WORK?
YUP.
WHAT ARE YOU UP TO?
THE PRINCESS HAS CAPTURED THE STORE ROOM.
HUH?
HAS THAT GIRL
SEEMED ANY DIFFERENT AT SCHOOL?
NO.
SHE HASN'T FAINTED RECENTLY, EITHER.
WHY DO YOU ASK?
UH,
NOTHING, IT'S FINE.
SO TOSSING THE DRUGS HASN'T AFFECTED HER.
AH!

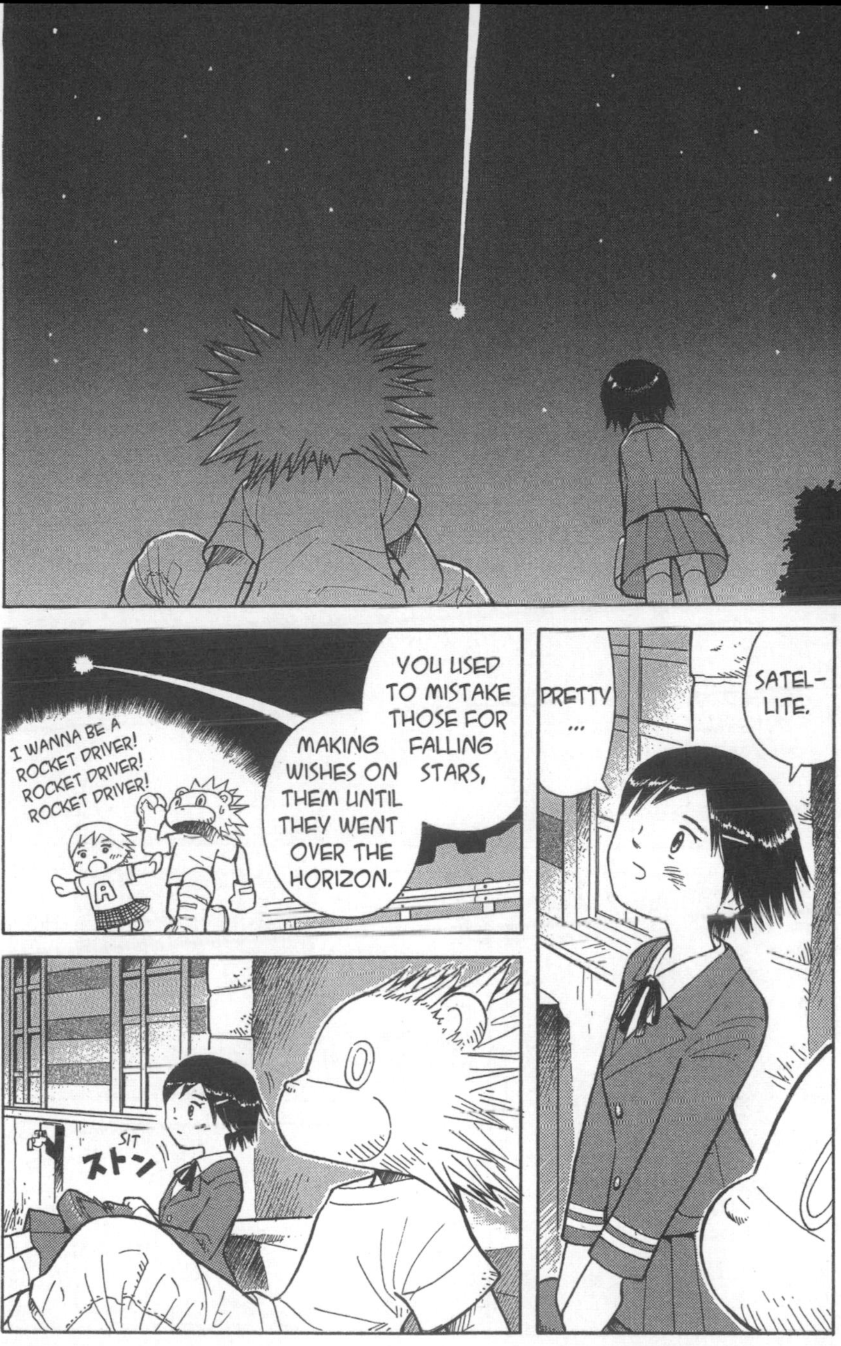
SATEL-LITE.
PRETTY ...
YOU USED TO MISTAKE THOSE FOR FALLING STARS, MAKING WISHES ON THEM UNTIL THEY WENT OVER THE HORIZON.
I WANNA BE A ROCKET DRIVER! ROCKET DRIVER! ROCKET DRIVER!
SIT
ストン

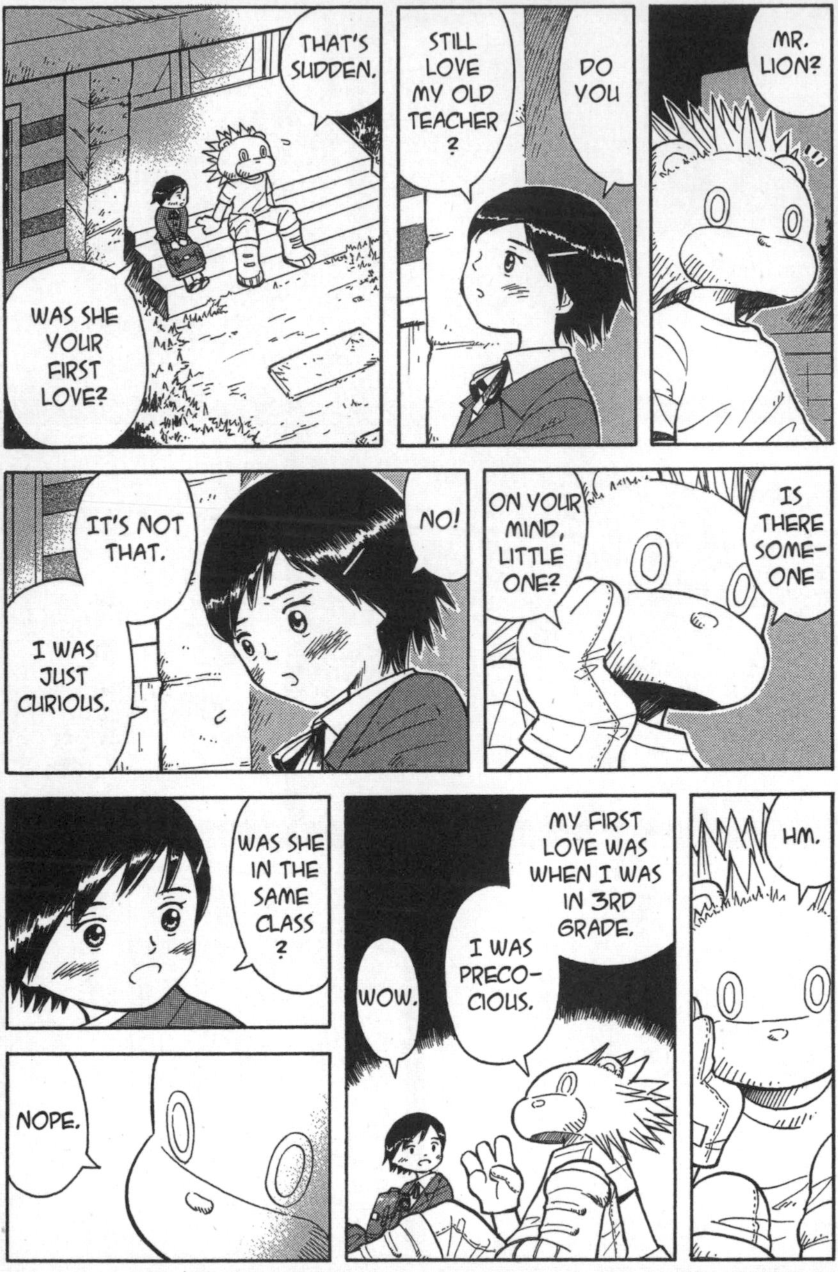
MR. LION?
DO YOU
STILL LOVE MY OLD TEACHER?
THAT'S SUDDEN.
WAS SHE YOUR FIRST LOVE?
IS THERE SOMEONE
ON YOUR MIND, LITTLE ONE?
NO!
IT'S NOT THAT.
I WAS JUST CURIOUS.
HM.
MY FIRST LOVE WAS WHEN I WAS IN 3RD GRADE.
I WAS PRECOCIOUS.
WOW.
WAS SHE IN THE SAME CLASS?
NOPE.

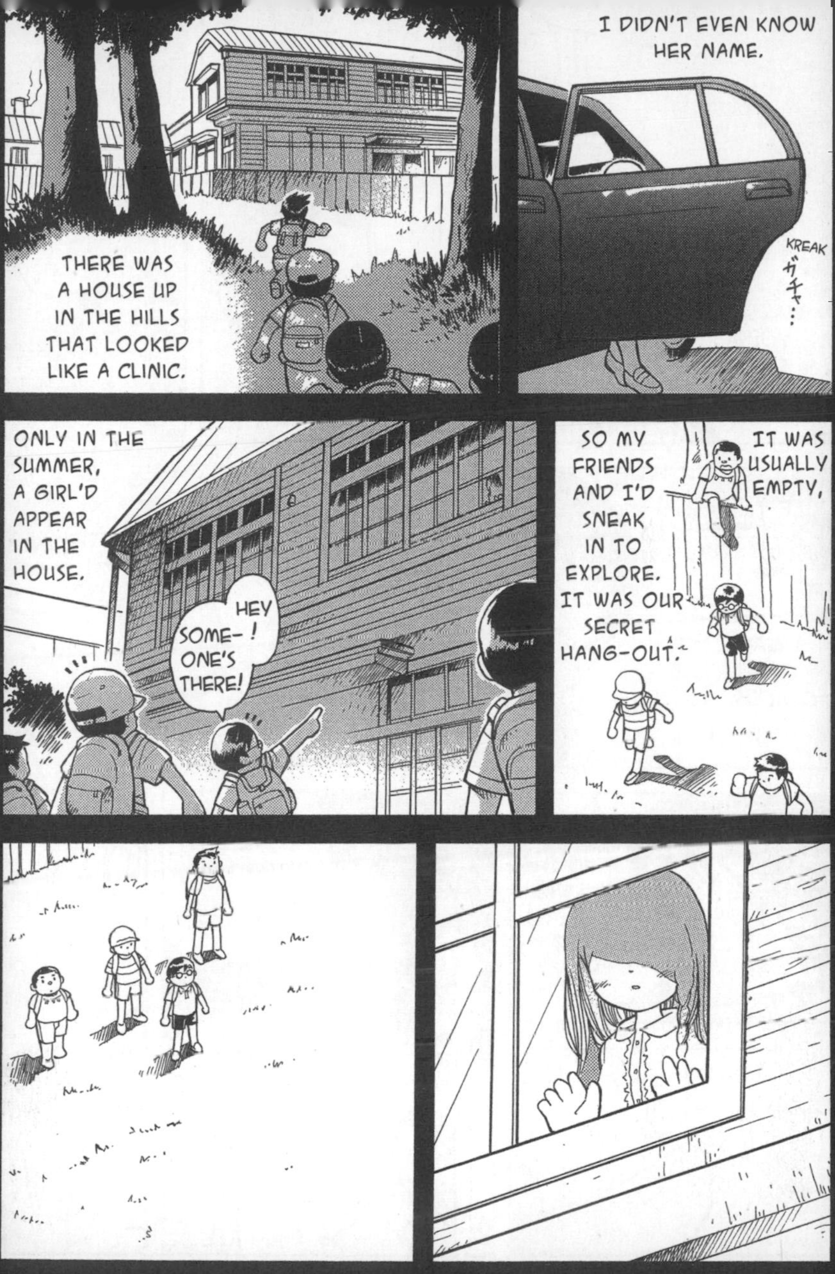
I DIDN'T EVEN KNOW HER NAME.
KREAK
ガチャ…
THERE WAS A HOUSE UP IN THE HILLS THAT LOOKED LIKE A CLINIC.
IT WAS USUALLY EMPTY,
SO MY FRIENDS AND I'D SNEAK IN TO EXPLORE. IT WAS OUR SECRET HANG-OUT.
ONLY IN THE SUMMER, A GIRL'D APPEAR IN THE HOUSE.
HEY SOME-ONE'S THERE!

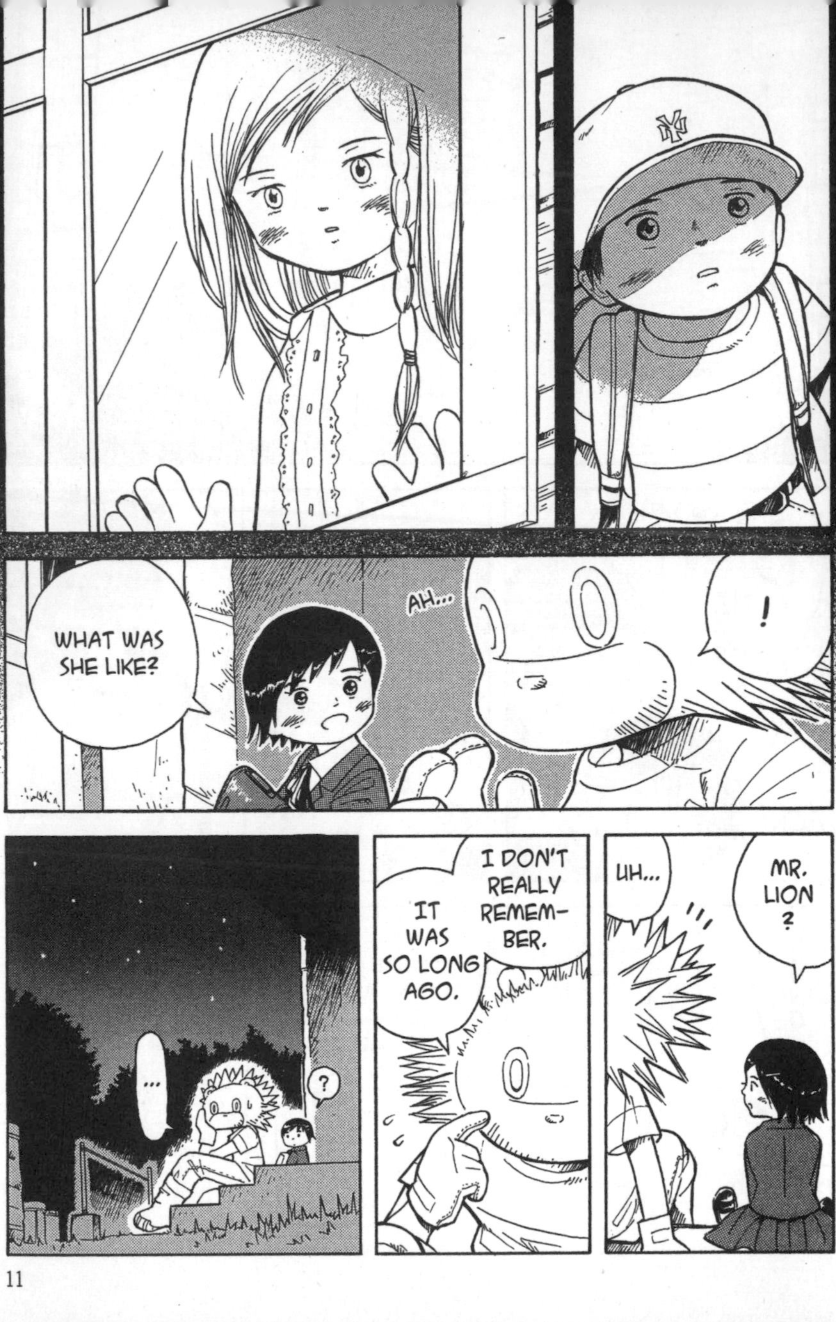
!
AH...
WHAT WAS SHE LIKE?
MR. LION ?
UH...
I DON'T REALLY REMEM- BER.
IT WAS SO LONG AGO.
...
?

DING DONG
キーンコーン
カーンコーン
SWOOP
ひょいっ
BAH!!
ACK!
CENTRAL, BACK, EAST AND NORTH.
YOU'VE BEEN STARING AT ALL THE ENTRANCE GATES. WHY?
UH,
DUNNO

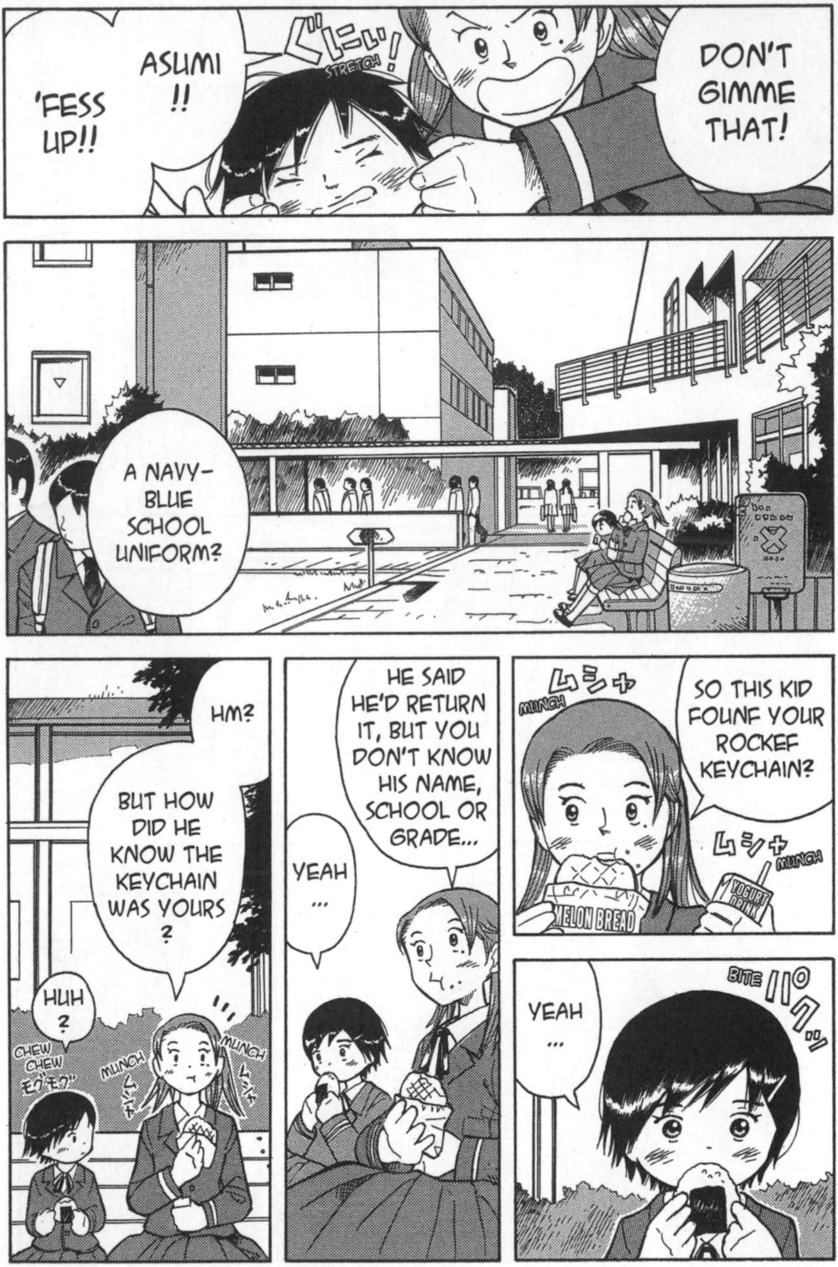
DON'T GIMME THAT!
STRETCH
ASUMI !!
'FESS UP!!
A NAVY-BLUE SCHOOL UNIFORM?
MUNCH
SO THIS KID FOUNF YOUR ROCKEF KEYCHAIN?
MUNCH
YOGURT DRINK
MELON BREAD
BITE
YEAH ...
HE SAID HE'D RETURN IT, BUT YOU DON'T KNOW HIS NAME, SCHOOL OR GRADE...
YEAH ...
HM?
BUT HOW DID HE KNOW THE KEYCHAIN WAS YOURS ?
HUH ?
MUNCH
MUNCH
CHEW CHEW

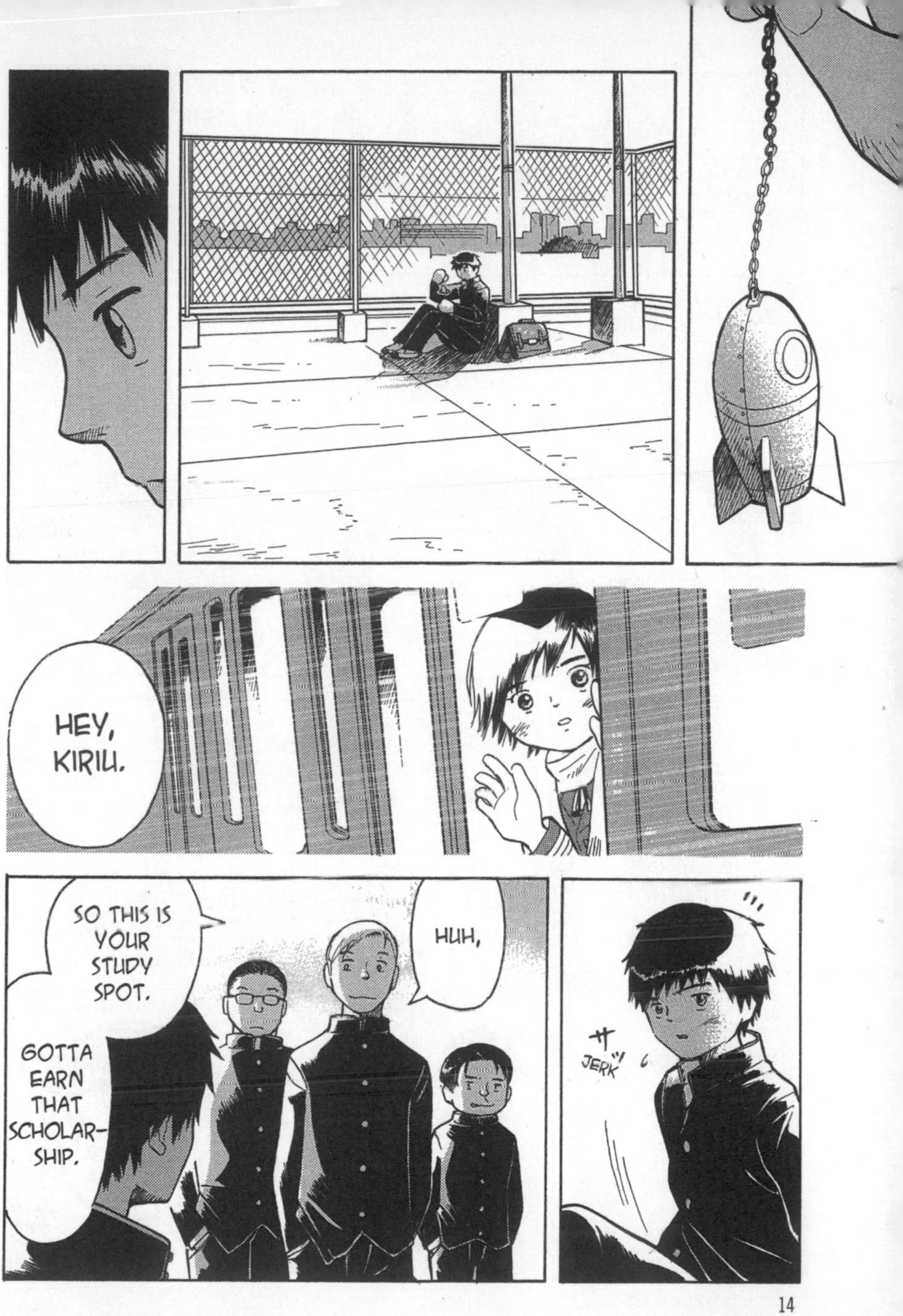
HEY, KIRIU.
サッ
JERK
HUH,
SO THIS IS YOUR STUDY SPOT.
GOTTA EARN THAT SCHOLAR-SHIP.

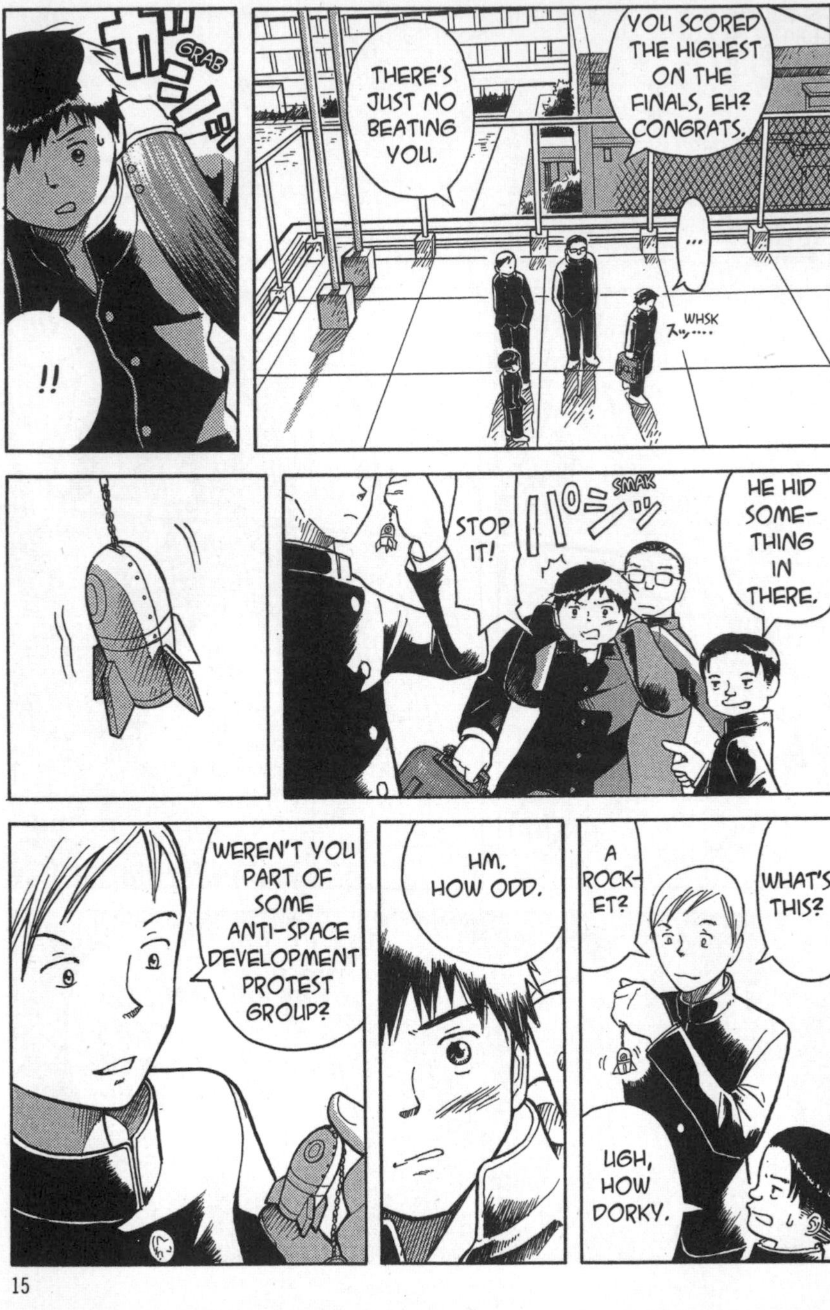
YOU SCORED THE HIGHEST ON THE FINALS, EH? CONGRATS.
THERE'S JUST NO BEATING YOU.
...
WHSK
スッ....
GRAB
!!
HE HID SOME-THING IN THERE.
SMAK
STOP IT!
WHAT'S THIS?
A ROCK-ET?
UGH, HOW DORKY.
HM. HOW ODD.
WEREN'T YOU PART OF SOME ANTI-SPACE DEVELOPMENT PROTEST GROUP?

KLANK
カコン/,,

OOH, THEN YOU'RE BAD TO HAVE THIS AT ALL.

THE ROCKET THAT LOOKED LIKE THIS.

WHAT WAS IT?

"THE LION."

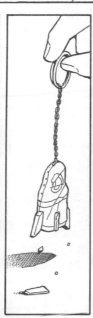

!!

ペ
キ,,
CRUNCH

AND NOW IT LOOKS EVEN MORE LIKE IT!

!!

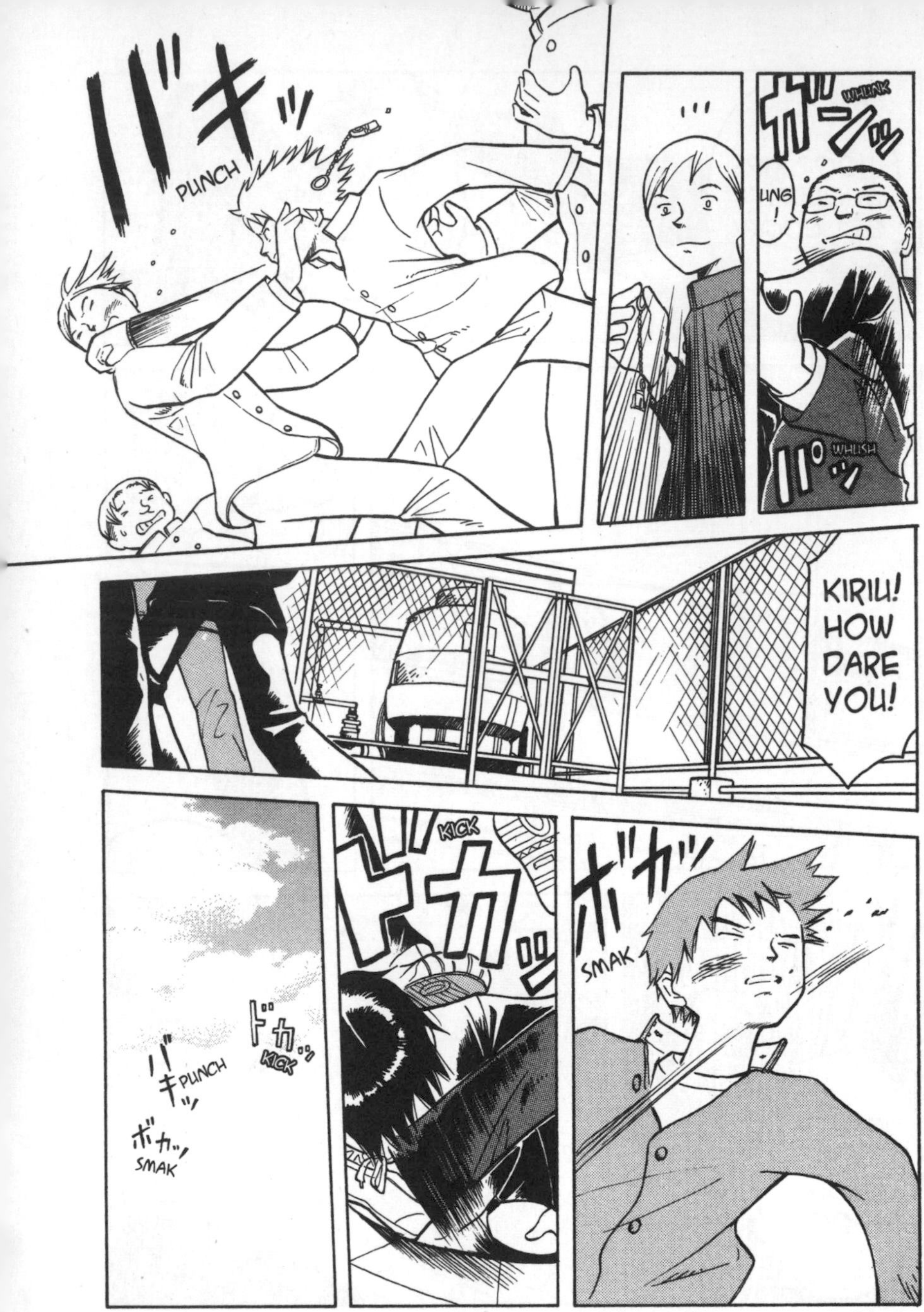

ガーンッ
WHUNK
UNG!
パッ
WHUSH
...
バキッ
PUNCH
KIRIU! HOW DARE YOU!
ボカッ
SMAK
ドカッ
KICK
ドカッ
KICK
バキッ
PUNCH
ボカッ
SMAK

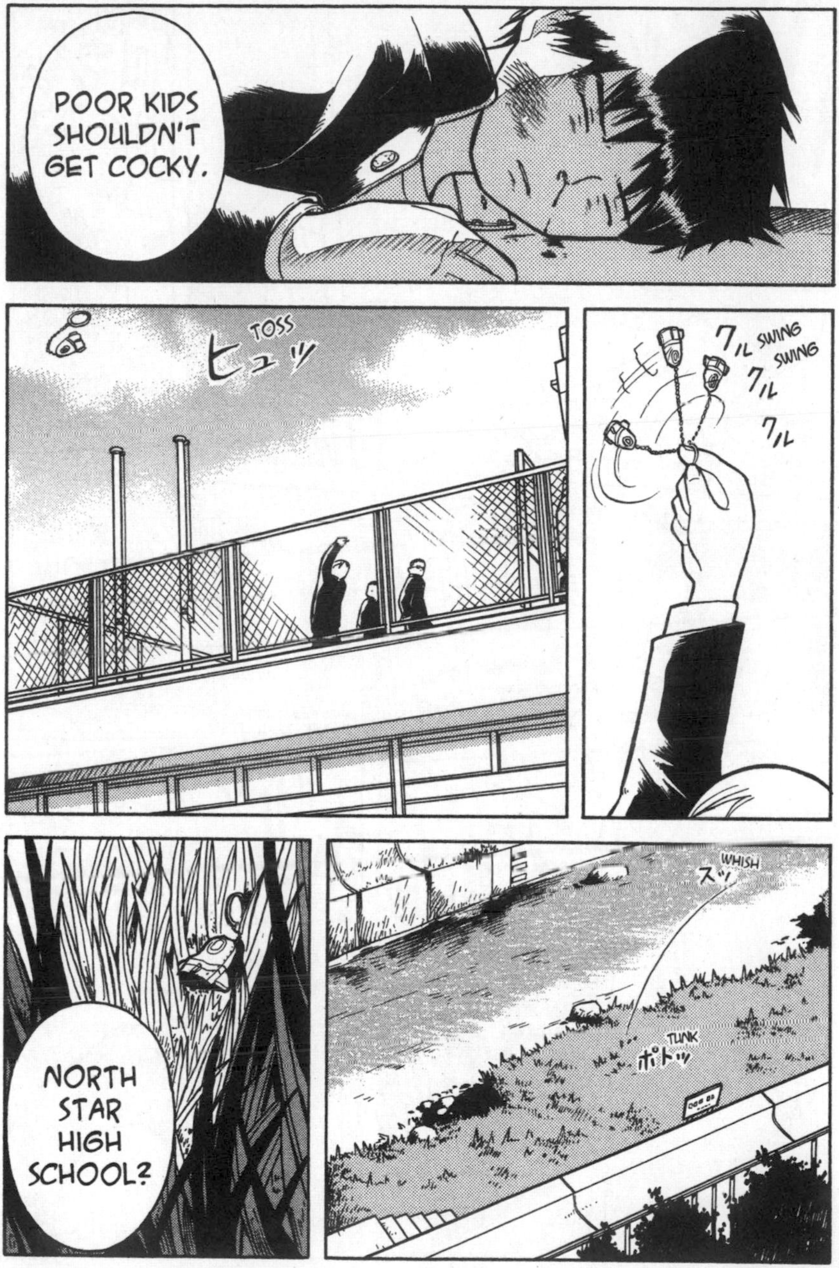
POOR KIDS SHOULDN'T GET COCKY.
クル SWING
クル SWING
クル
ヒュッ TOSS
ズッ WHISH
ポトッ TUNK
NORTH STAR HIGH SCHOOL?

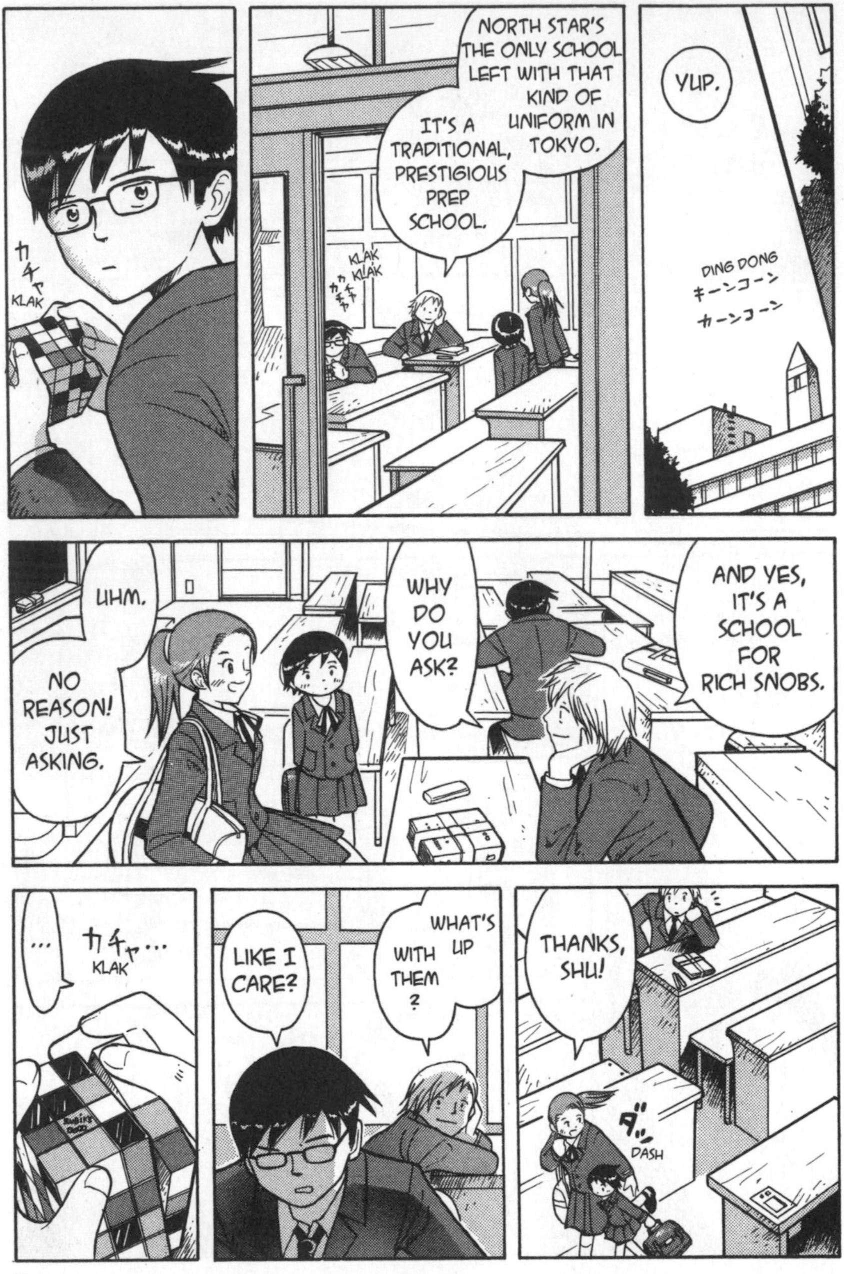
YUP.
DING DONG
キーンコーン
カーンコーン
NORTH STAR'S THE ONLY SCHOOL LEFT WITH THAT KIND OF UNIFORM IN TOKYO.
IT'S A TRADITIONAL, PRESTIGIOUS PREP SCHOOL.
KLAK KLAK
カチャカチャ
カチャ
KLAK
AND YES, IT'S A SCHOOL FOR RICH SNOBS.
WHY DO YOU ASK?
UHM.
NO REASON! JUST ASKING.
THANKS, SHU!
ダッ
DASH
WHAT'S UP WITH THEM?
LIKE I CARE?
...
カチャ...
KLAK

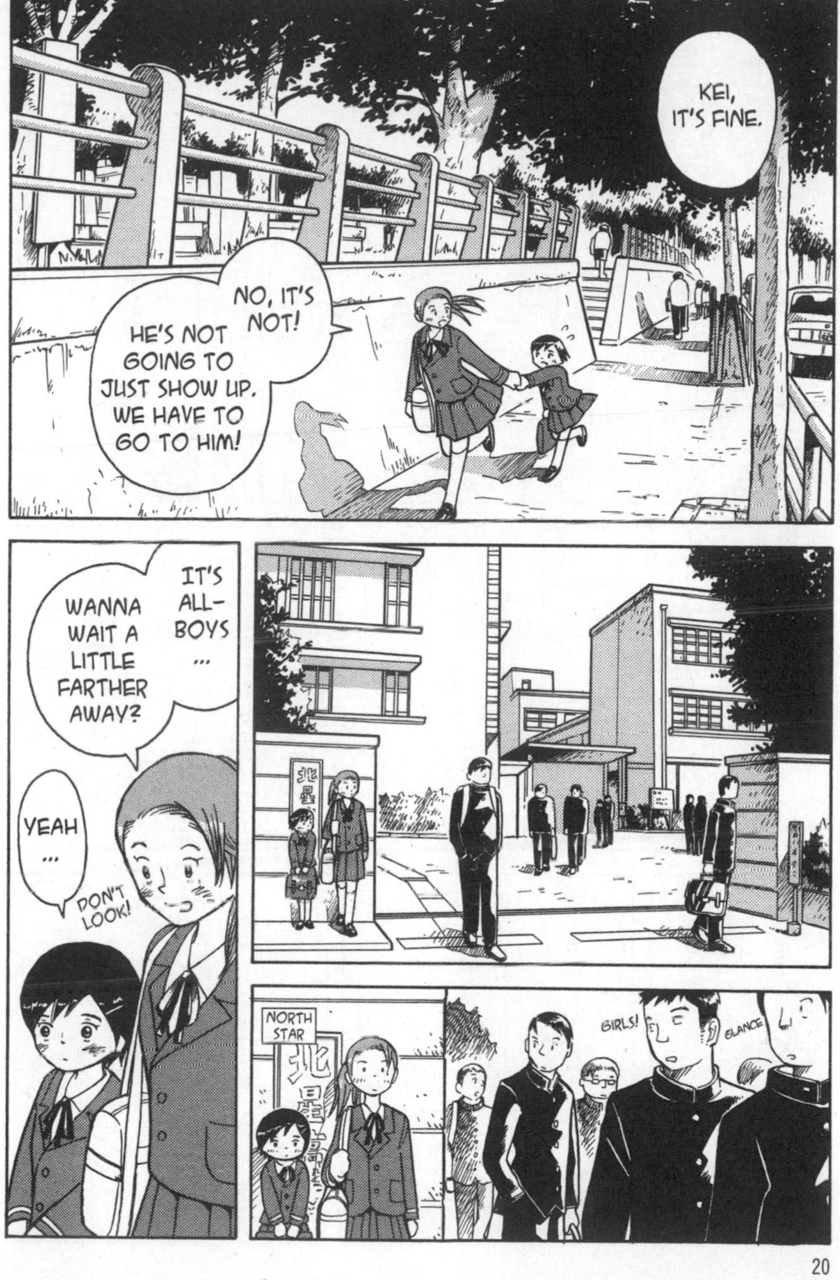
KEI, IT'S FINE.
NO, IT'S NOT!
HE'S NOT GOING TO JUST SHOW UP. WE HAVE TO GO TO HIM!
GLANCE
GIRLS!
NORTH STAR
IT'S ALL-BOYS ...
WANNA WAIT A LITTLE FARTHER AWAY?
YEAH ...
DON'T LOOK!

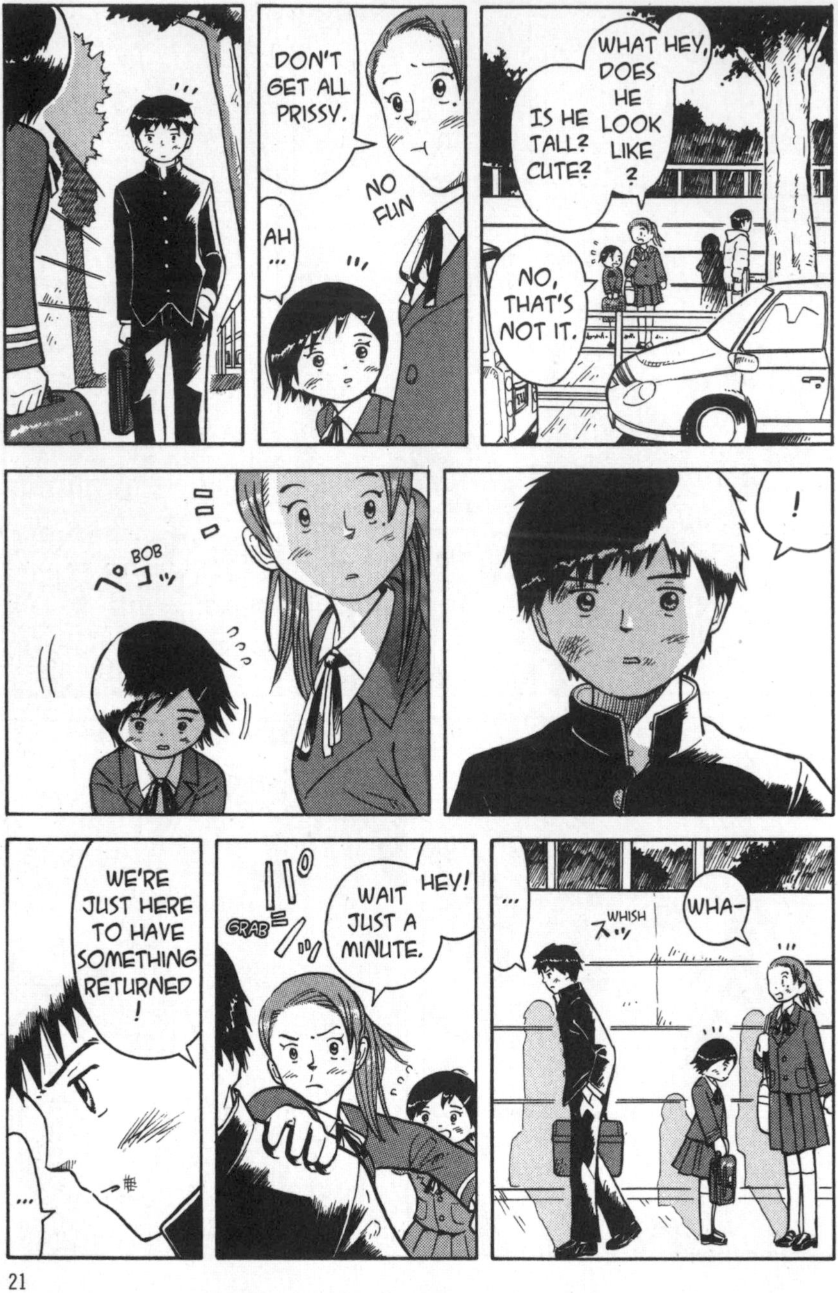
HEY, WHAT DOES HE LOOK LIKE? IS HE TALL? CUTE?
NO, THAT'S NOT IT.
DON'T GET ALL PRISSY.
NO FUN
AH ...
!
BOB
ペコッ
WHA-
WHISH
スッ
...
...
HEY! WAIT JUST A MINUTE.
GRAB
WE'RE JUST HERE TO HAVE SOMETHING RETURNED!
...

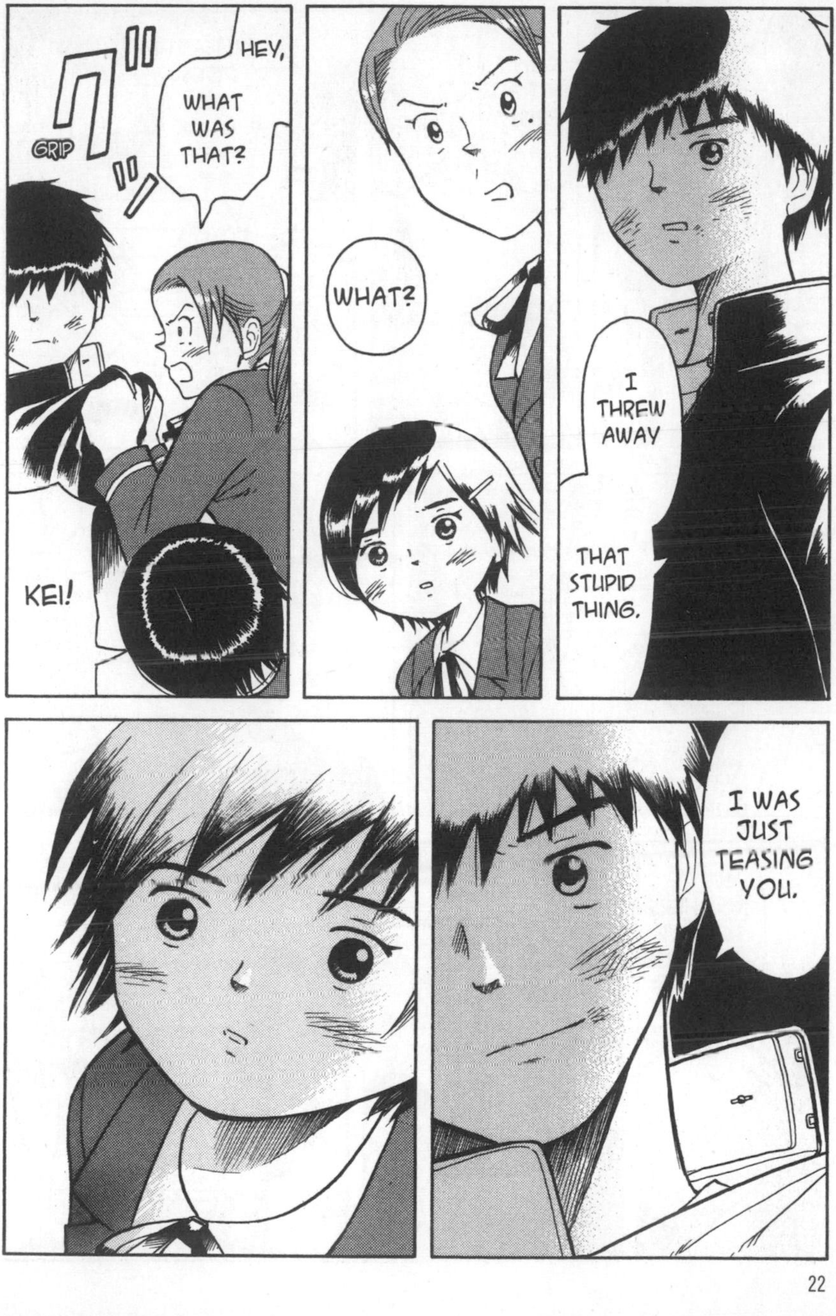
I THREW AWAY
THAT STUPID THING.
WHAT?
HEY,
WHAT WAS THAT?
GRIP
KEI!
I WAS JUST TEASING YOU.

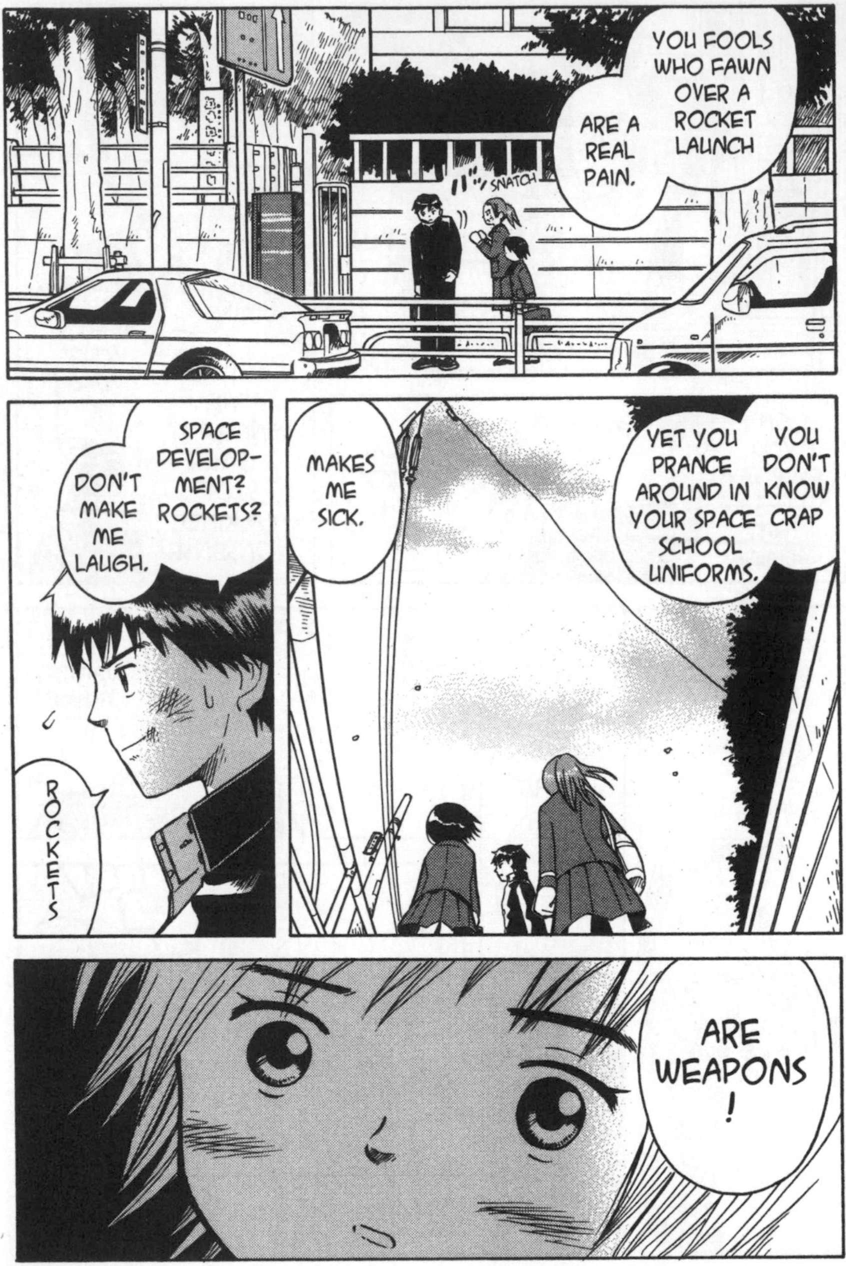
YOU FOOLS WHO FAWN OVER A ROCKET LAUNCH
ARE A REAL PAIN.
SNATCH
YOU DON'T KNOW CRAP
YET YOU PRANCE AROUND IN YOUR SPACE SCHOOL UNIFORMS.
MAKES ME SICK.
SPACE DEVELOPMENT? ROCKETS?
DON'T MAKE ME LAUGH.
ROCKETS
ARE WEAPONS!

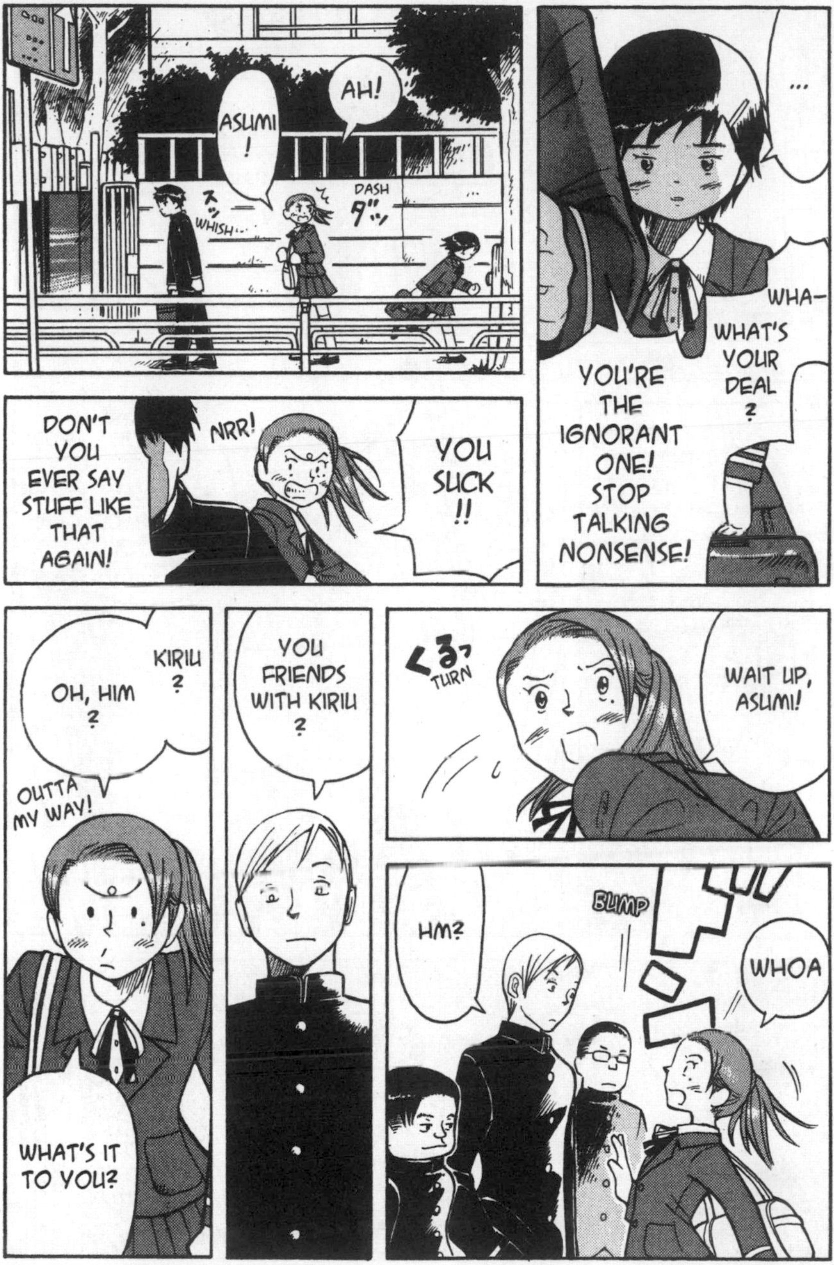
...
WHA-
WHAT'S YOUR DEAL?
YOU'RE THE IGNORANT ONE! STOP TALKING NONSENSE!
AH!
ASUMI!
DASH
ダッ
...
スッ
WHISH
YOU SUCK!!
NRR!
DON'T YOU EVER SAY STUFF LIKE THAT AGAIN!
WAIT UP, ASUMI!
くるっ
TURN
WHOA
BUMP
HM?
YOU FRIENDS WITH KIRIU?
KIRIU?
OH, HIM?
OUTTA MY WAY!
WHAT'S IT TO YOU?

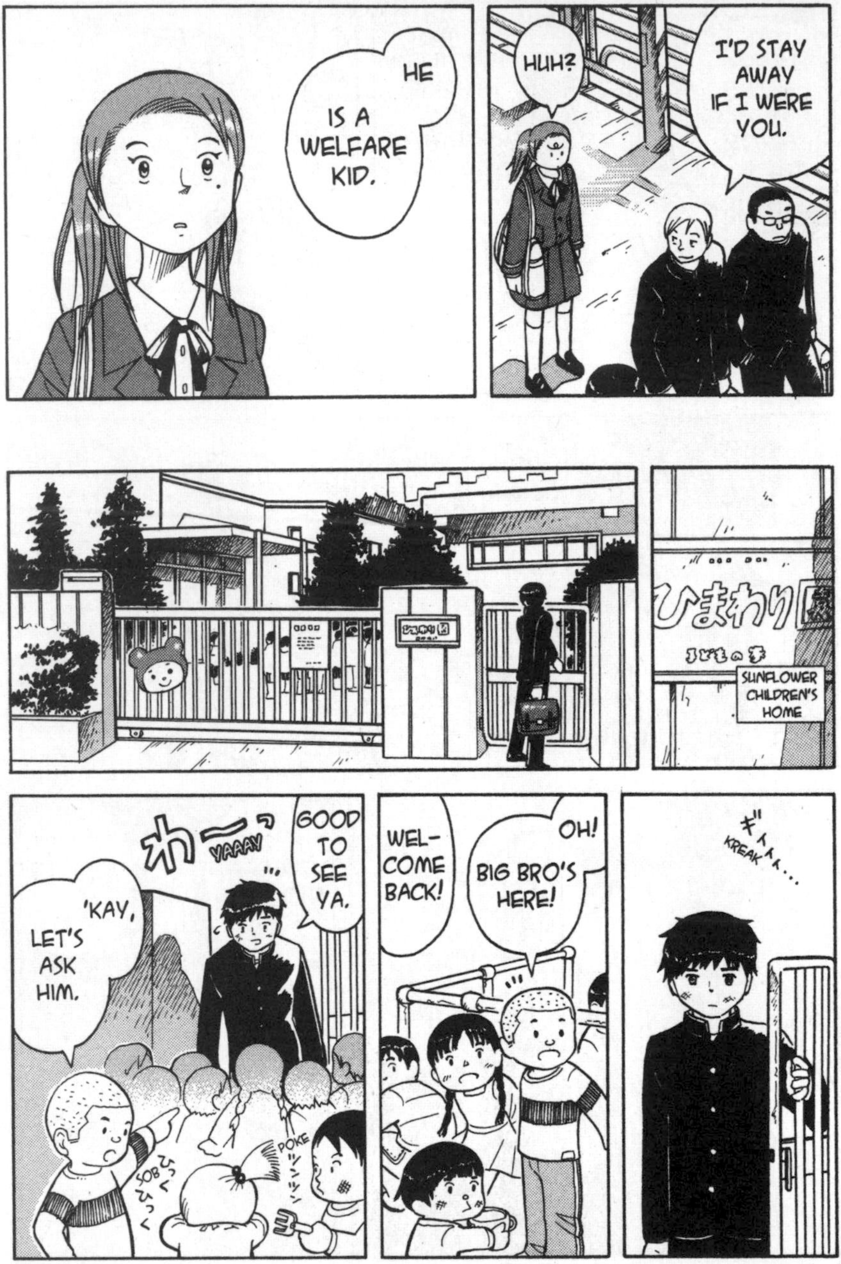
I'D STAY AWAY IF I WERE YOU.
HUH?
HE IS A WELFARE KID.
ひまわり園
こどもの家
SUNFLOWER CHILDREN'S HOME
ギィィ…
KREAK…
OH!
BIG BRO'S HERE!
WEL-COME BACK!
GOOD TO SEE YA.
わ〜っ
YAAAY
'KAY, LET'S ASK HIM.
ひっく ひっく
SOB
ツンツン
POKE

BRO, AKANE SAYS SHE SAW A MAJOR SHOOTING STAR LAST NIGHT.
A MAJOR SHOOT-ING STAR?
HEY ワイ
HEY ワイ
SNIFFLE
IT MUST HAVE BEEN A PLANE OR SOMETHING.
IT'S TRUE!
IT KEPT GOING RIGHT ACROSS THE SKY!
HMM. I THINK IT WAS A SATEL-LITE.
WHAT'S A SATELLITE?
PAT ポン
PAT ポン
SATELLITE?
YOU COULD SAY
IT'S A KIND OF STAR.
REALLY?
YUP.
TSK, THEN IT WAS A SHOOTING STAR.
BIG BRO KNOWS ALL ABOUT STARS.
HEY, IT'S GETTING COLD. GO INSIDE.
はーい
OKAY!
...

WHAT'S THAT LITTLE IDIOT DOING THERE?

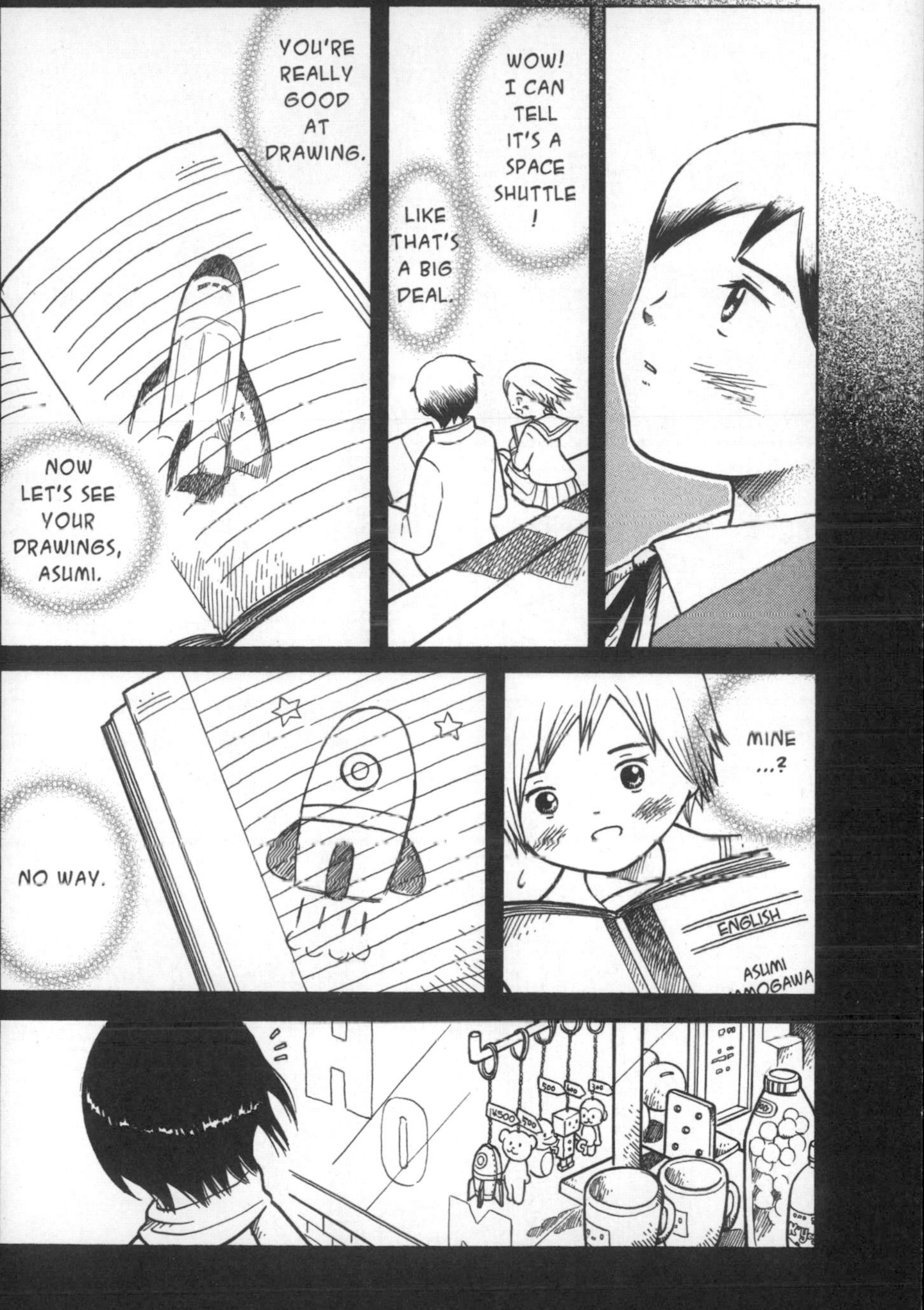
WOW! I CAN TELL IT'S A SPACE SHUTTLE!
LIKE THAT'S A BIG DEAL.
YOU'RE REALLY GOOD AT DRAWING.
NOW LET'S SEE YOUR DRAWINGS, ASUMI.
MINE ...?
ENGLISH
ASUMI
NO WAY.

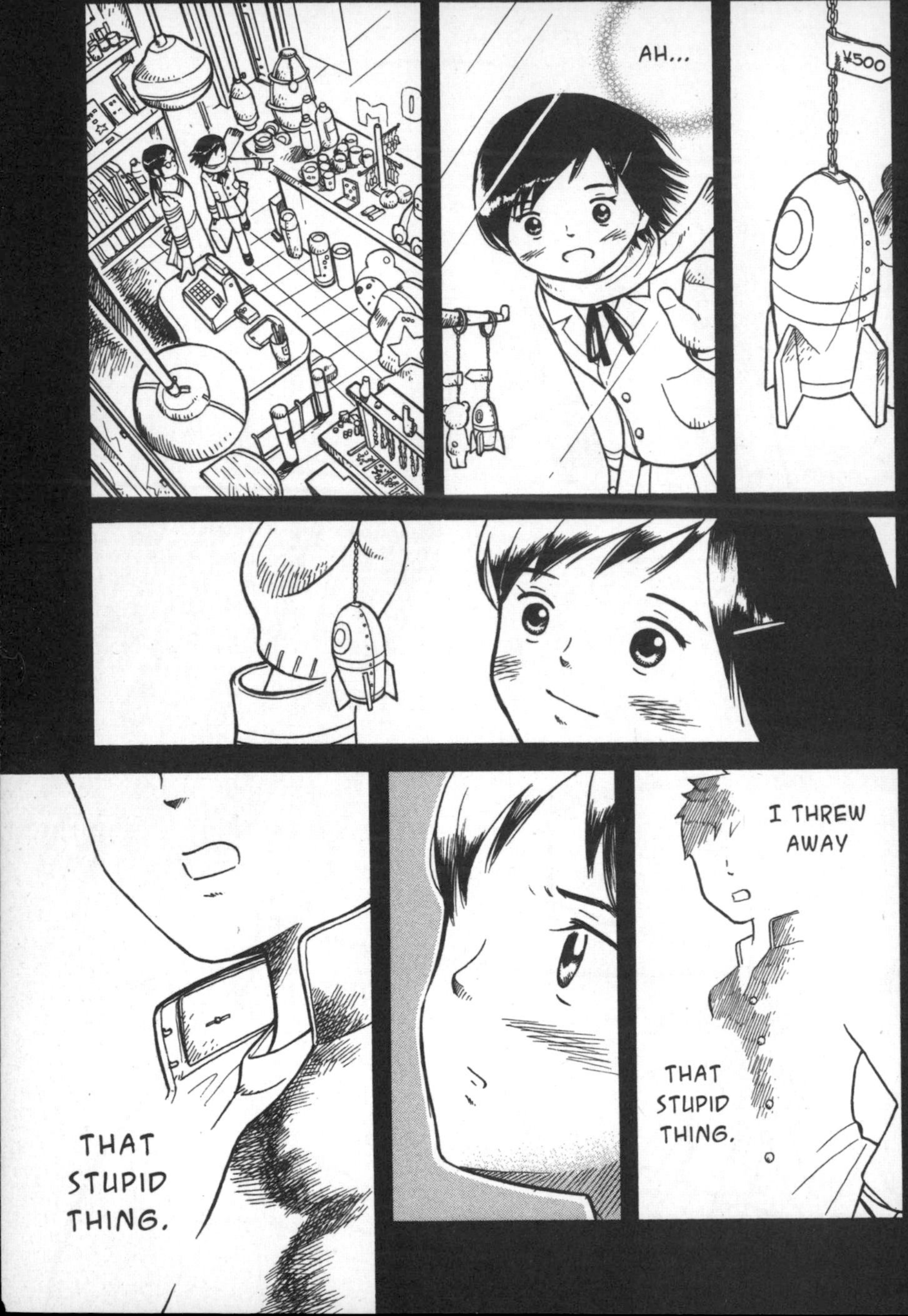
¥500
AH...
I THREW AWAY
THAT STUPID THING.
THAT STUPID THING.

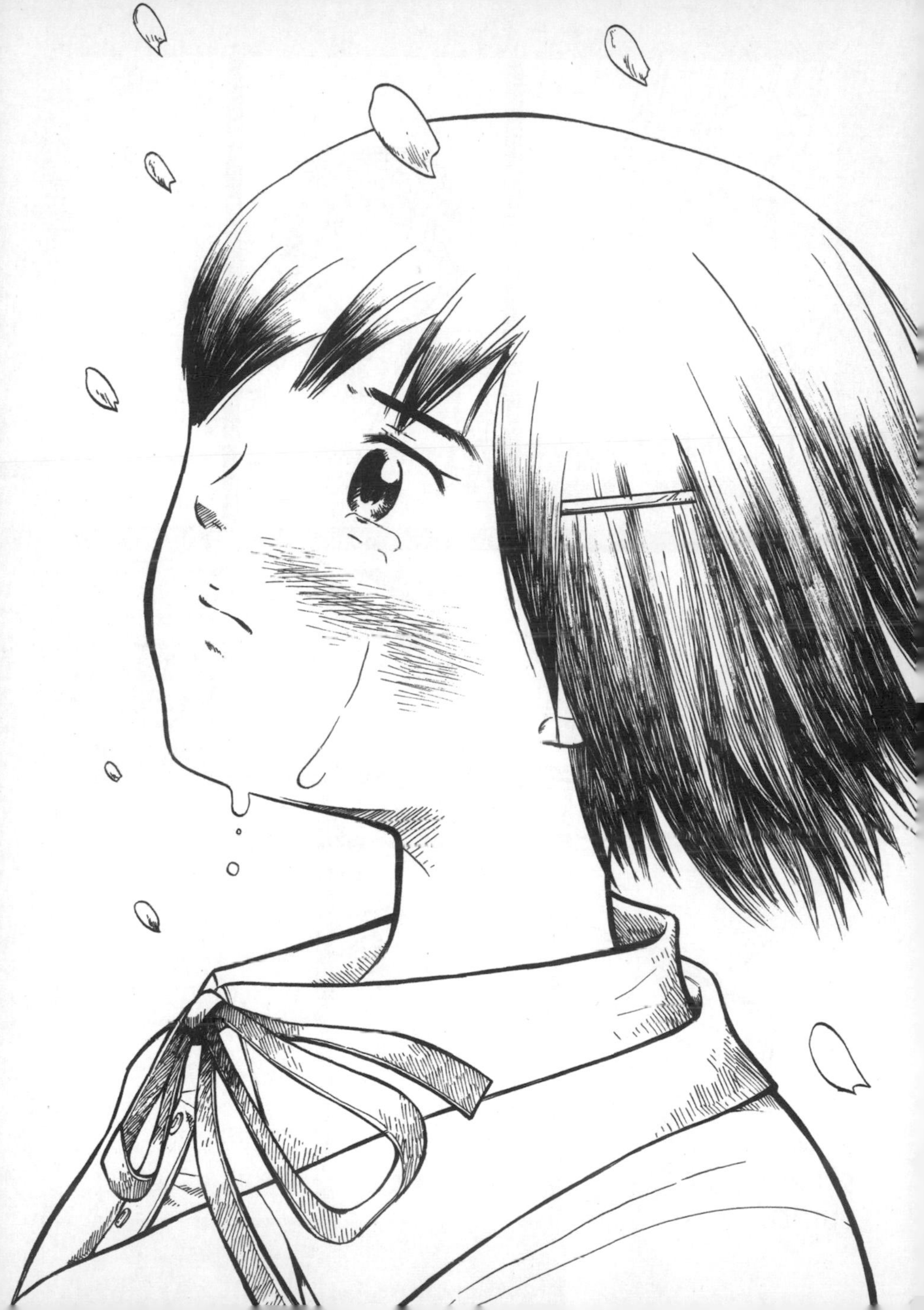

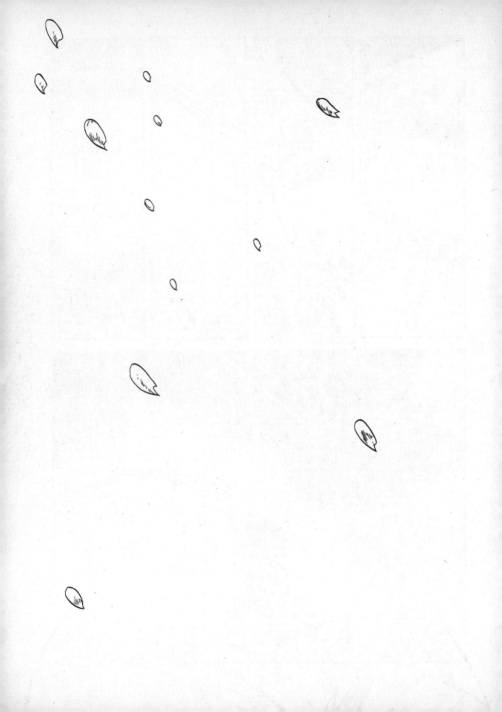

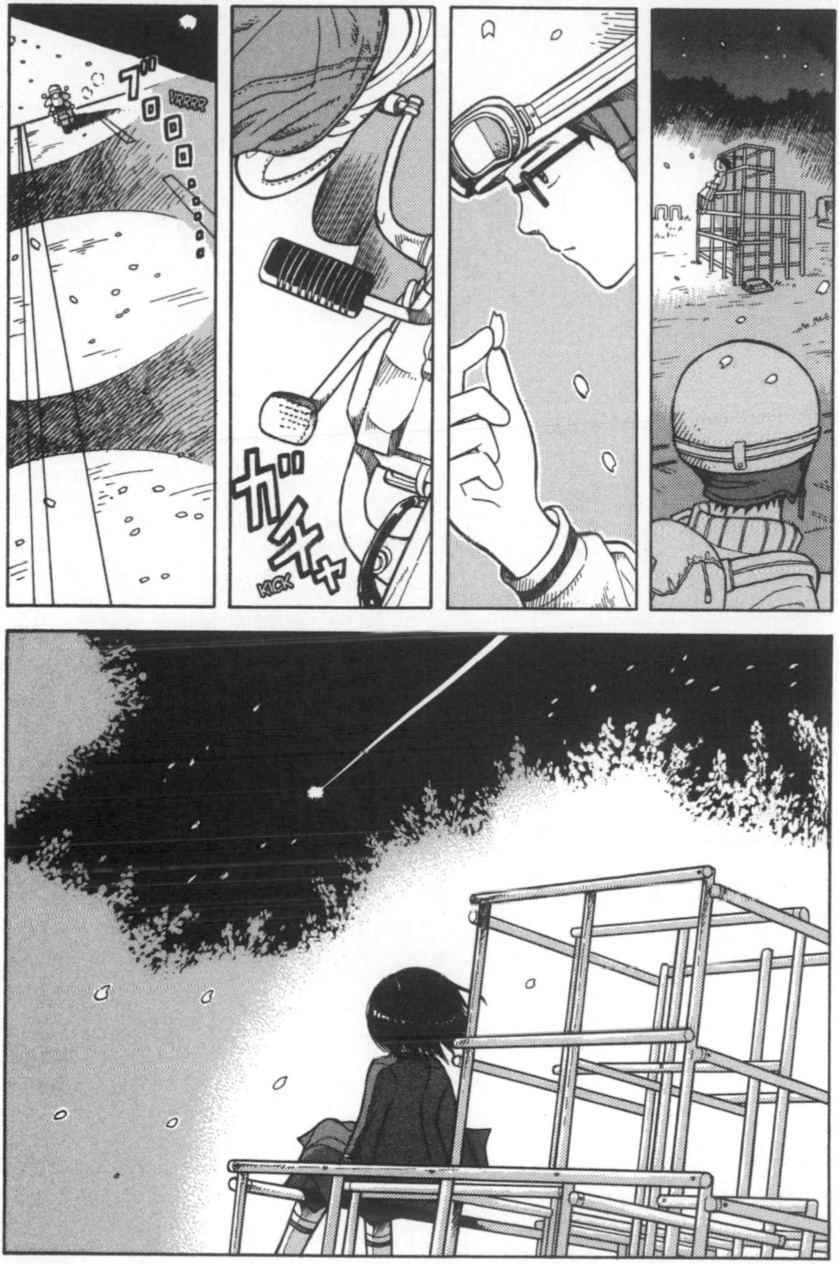
ガチャ
KICK
ブロロロ
VRRRR

MISSION:20

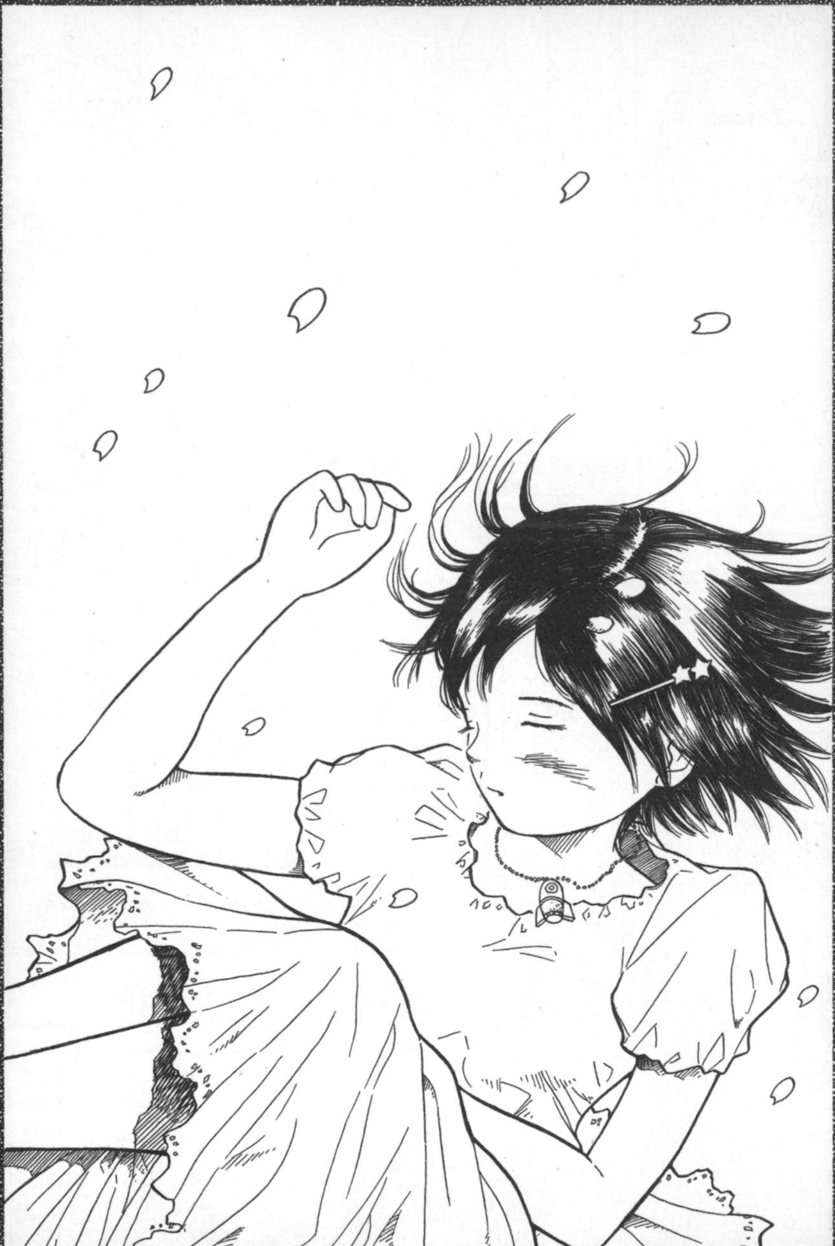

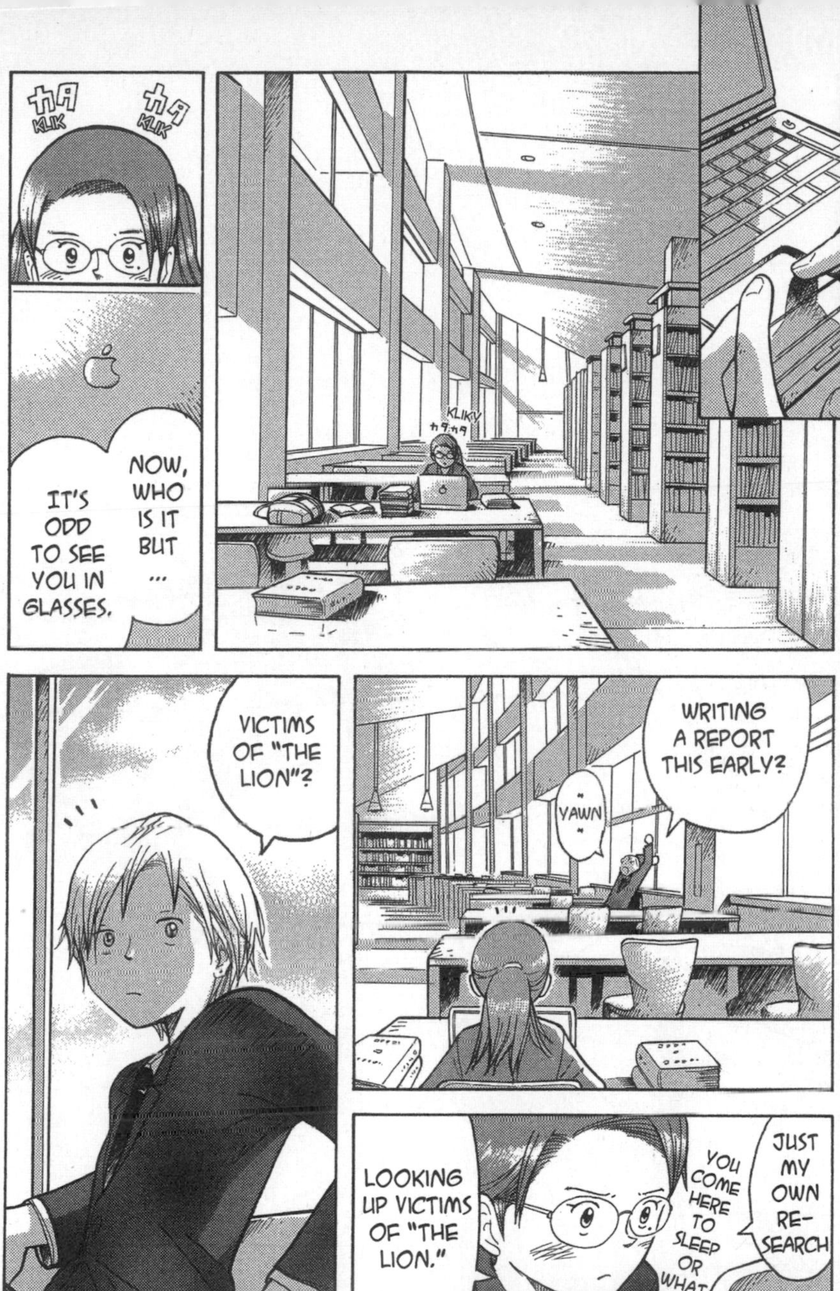
KLIK
カタカタ
カタ KLIK
カタ KLIK
NOW, WHO IS IT BUT ...
IT'S ODD TO SEE YOU IN GLASSES.
WRITING A REPORT THIS EARLY?
" YAWN "
JUST MY OWN RE-SEARCH
YOU COME HERE TO SLEEP OR WHAT?
LOOKING UP VICTIMS OF "THE LION."
VICTIMS OF "THE LION"?

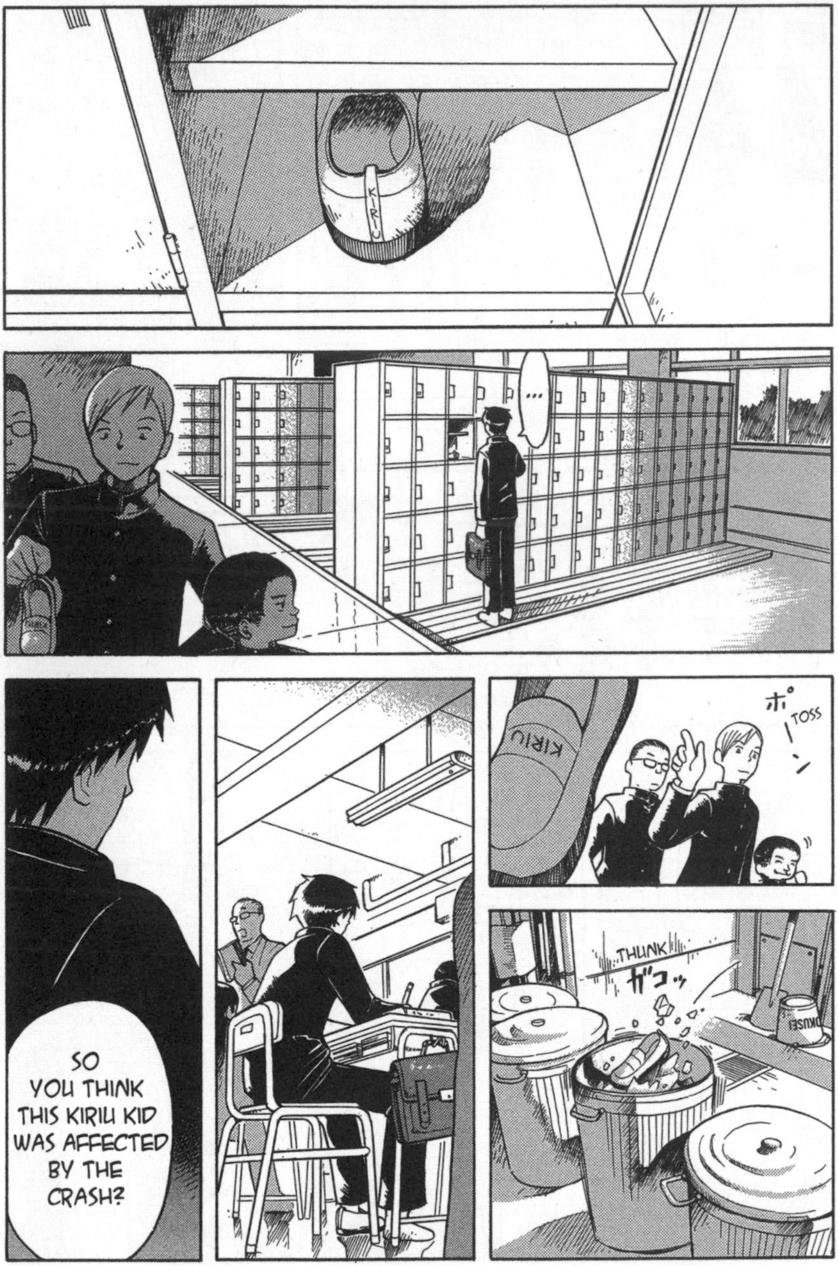
KIRIU
...
KIRIU
ポーン
TOSS
THUNK
ガコッ
SO YOU THINK THIS KIRIU KID WAS AFFECTED BY THE CRASH?

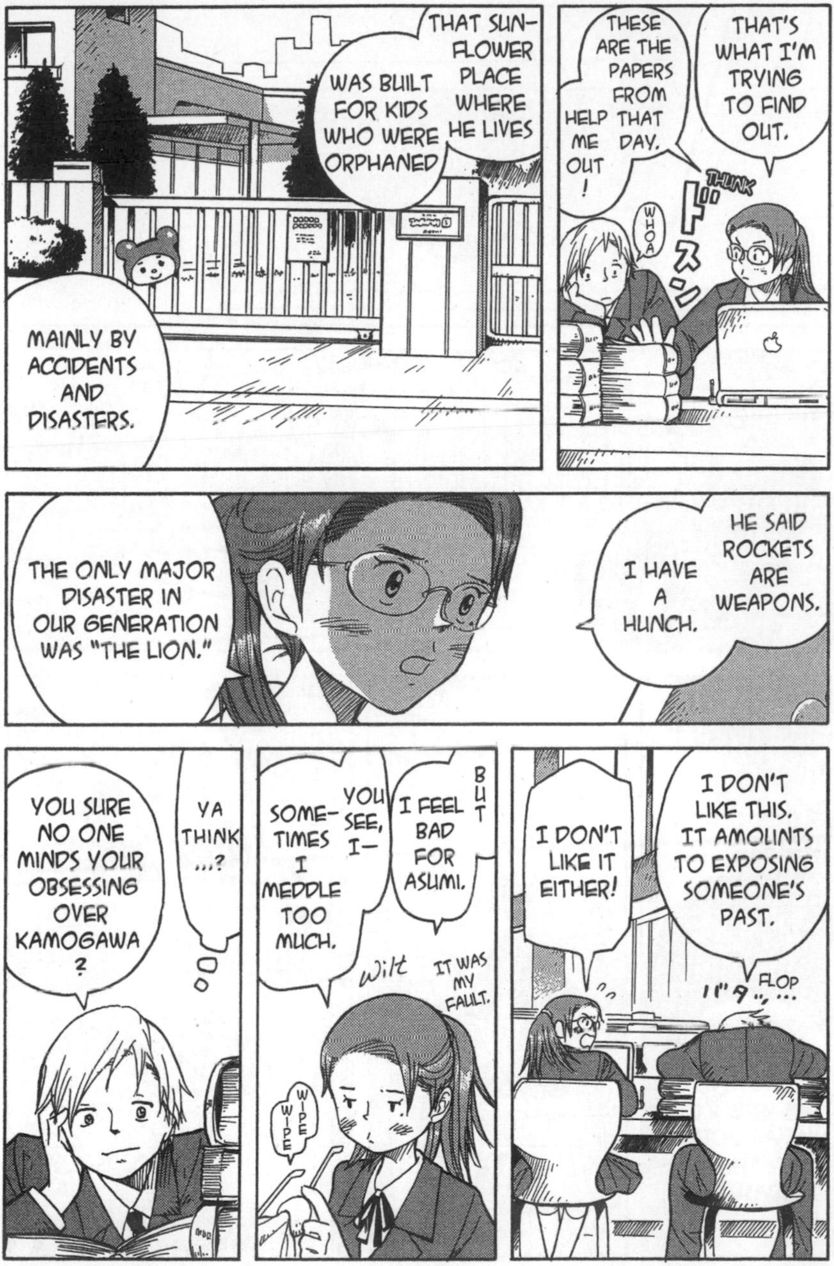
THAT'S WHAT I'M TRYING TO FIND OUT.
THESE ARE THE PAPERS FROM THAT DAY.
HELP ME OUT!
THINK
WHOA
THAT SUN-FLOWER PLACE WHERE HE LIVES
WAS BUILT FOR KIDS WHO WERE ORPHANED
MAINLY BY ACCIDENTS AND DISASTERS.
HE SAID ROCKETS ARE WEAPONS.
I HAVE A HUNCH.
THE ONLY MAJOR DISASTER IN OUR GENERATION WAS "THE LION."
I DON'T LIKE THIS. IT AMOUNTS TO EXPOSING SOMEONE'S PAST.
FLOP
I DON'T LIKE IT EITHER!
BUT I FEEL BAD FOR ASUMI.
YOU SEE, I—
SOMETIMES I MEDDLE TOO MUCH.
IT WAS MY FAULT.
Wilt
WIPE WIPE
YA THINK ...?
YOU SURE NO ONE MINDS YOUR OBSESSING OVER KAMOGAWA?

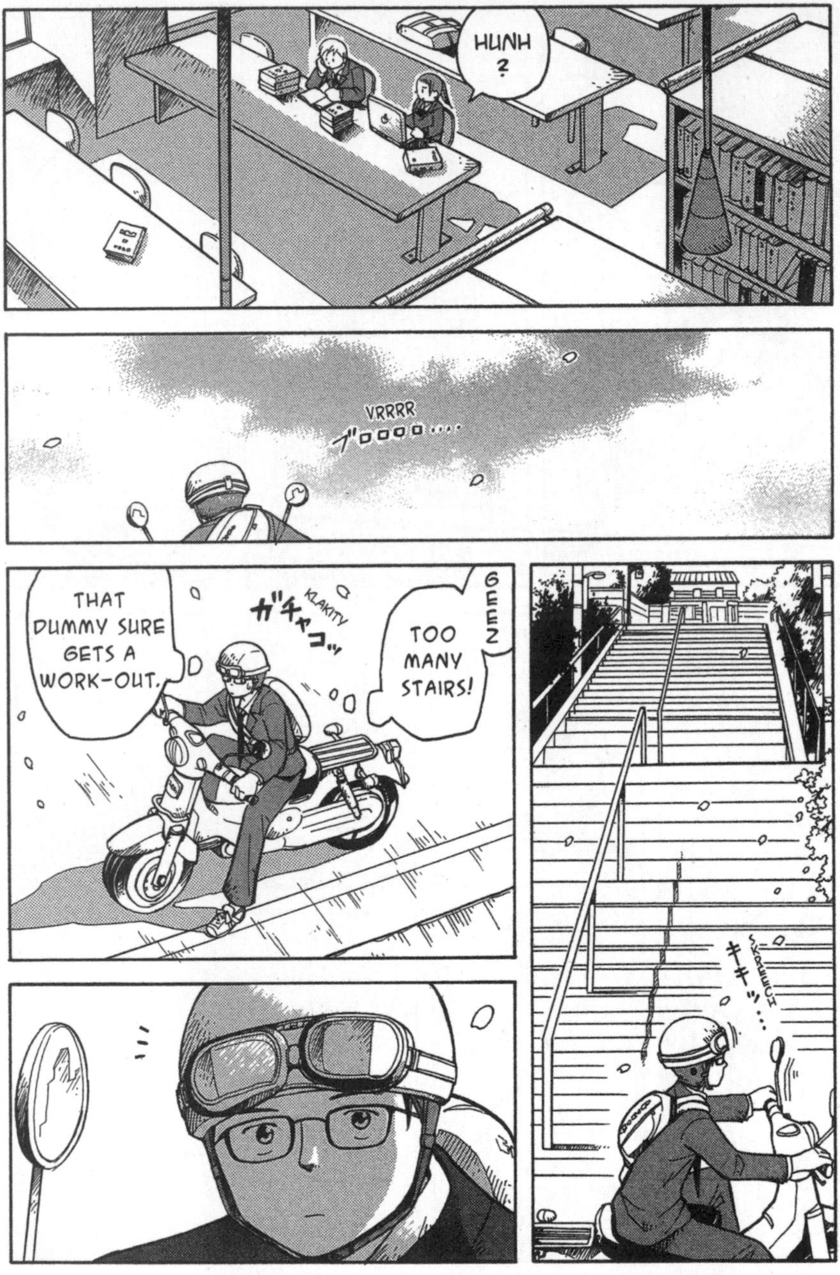
HUNH ?
VRRRR
ブロロロロ....
SKREECH
キキッ...
GEEZ
TOO MANY STAIRS!
KLAKITY
ガチャコッ
THAT DUMMY SURE GETS A WORK-OUT.

MISS KAMO-GAWA ALREADY LEFT.

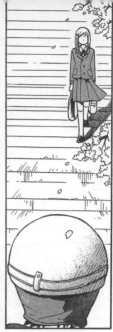

WANT A RIDE

TO SCHOOL ?

ブルルン
BRMM

I JUST HAPPENED TO PASS BY.

SURE.

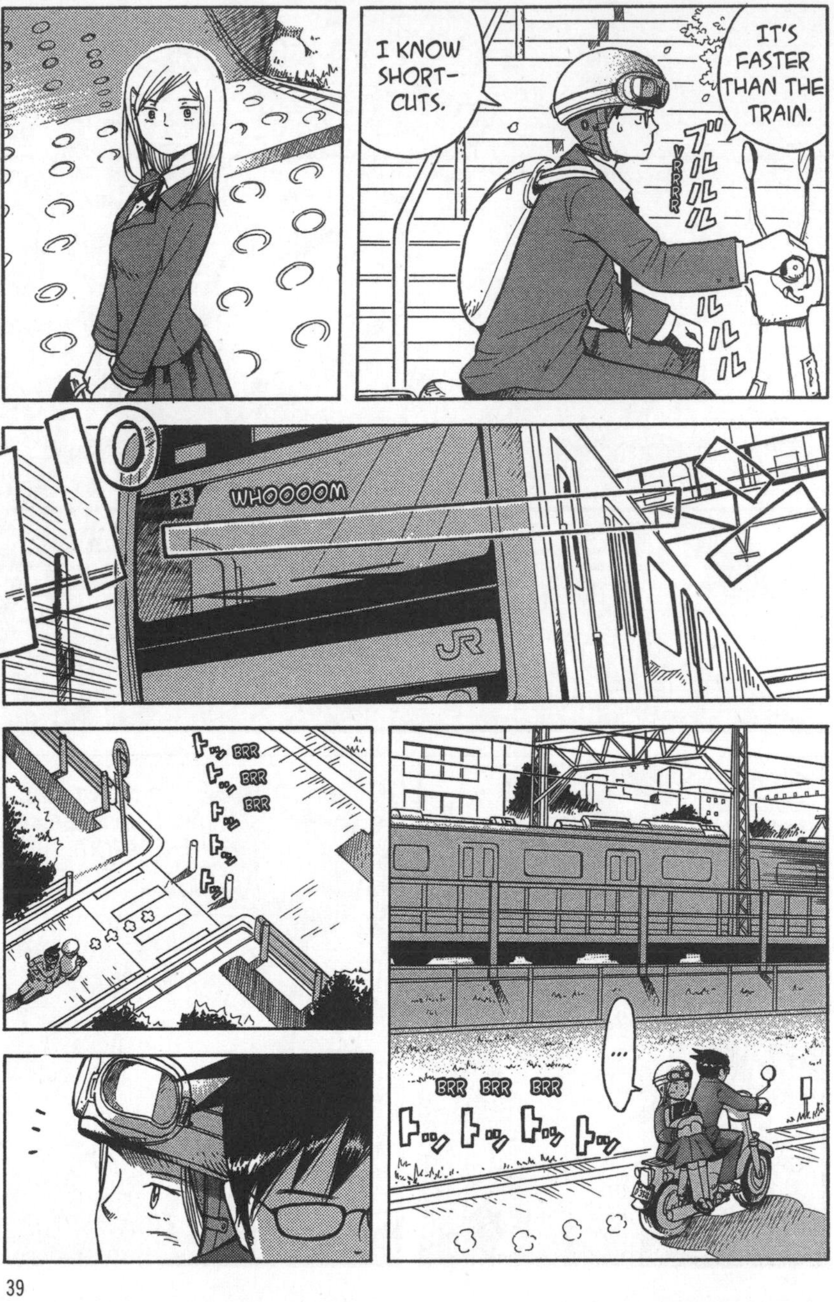
IT'S FASTER THAN THE TRAIN.
I KNOW SHORT-CUTS.
ブルルル
VRRRR
ルルル
WHOOOOM
...
BRR BRR BRR
トッ トッ トッ トッ
トッ BRR
トッ BRR
トッ BRR
トッ
トッ
トッ

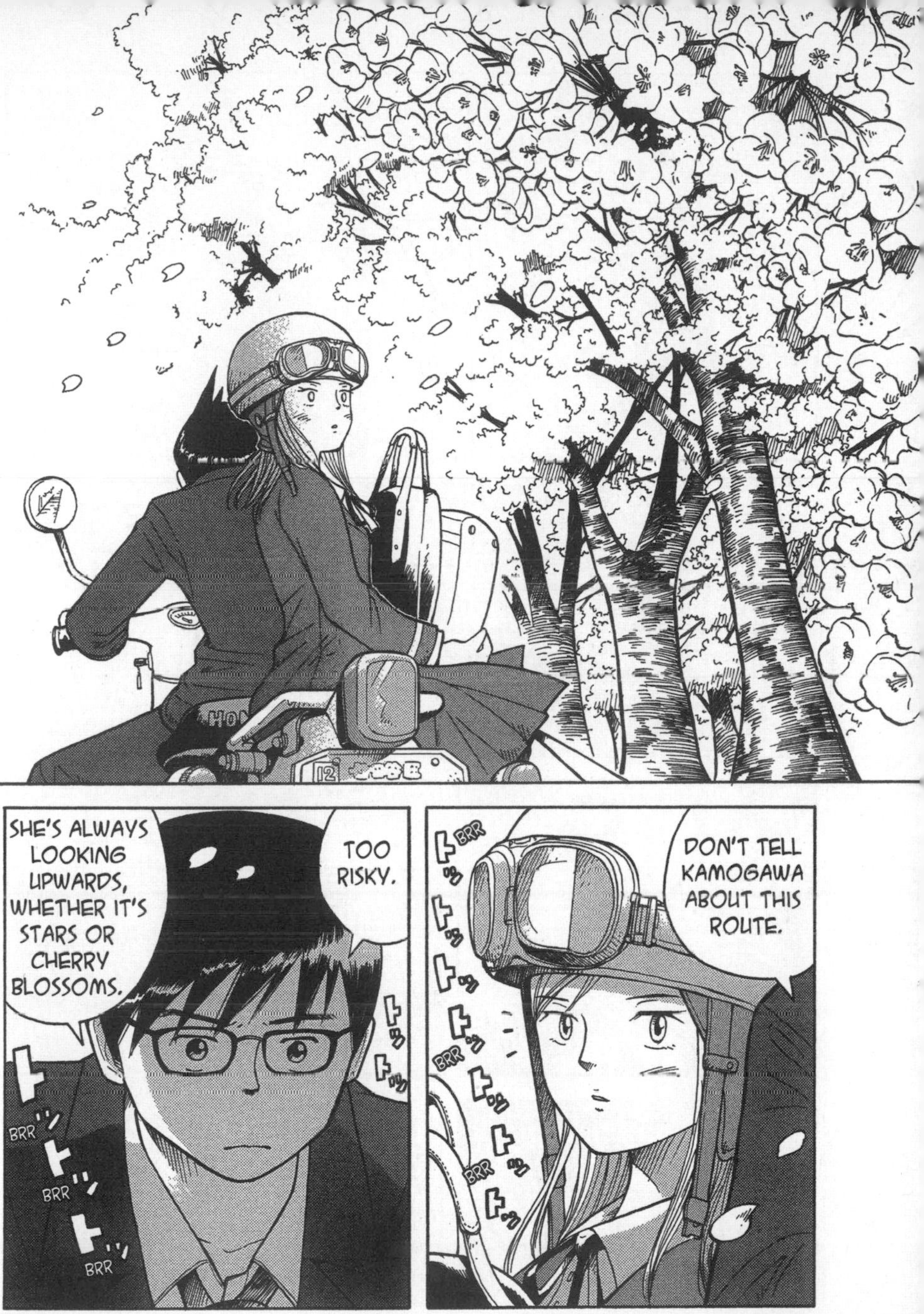
DON'T TELL KAMOGAWA ABOUT THIS ROUTE.
BRR
BRR
BRR
TOO RISKY.
SHE'S ALWAYS LOOKING UPWARDS, WHETHER IT'S STARS OR CHERRY BLOSSOMS.
BRR
BRR
BRR

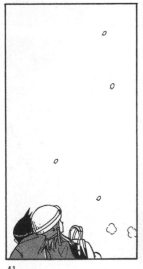

トッ BRR
トッ BRR
トッ BRR
トッ

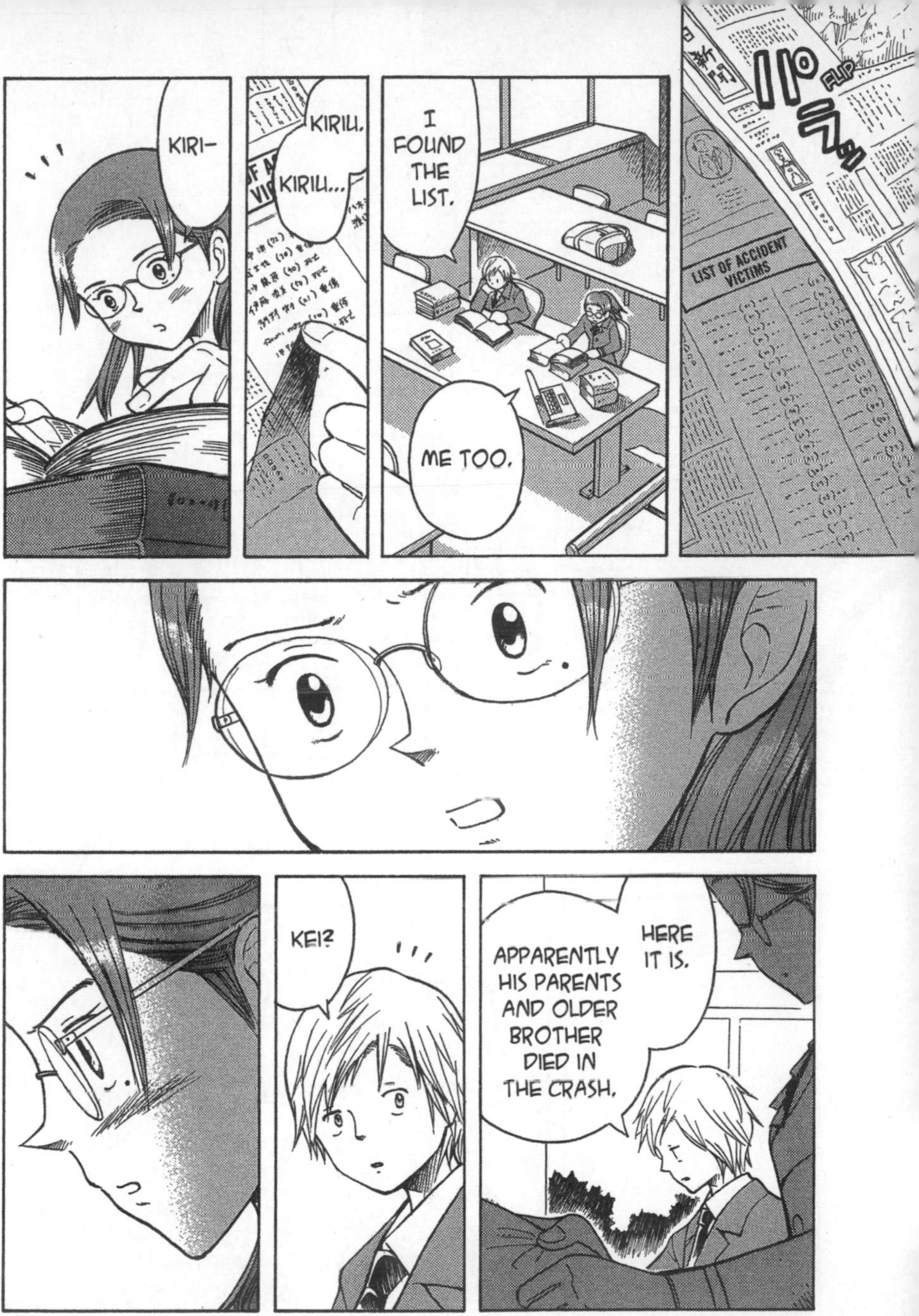
FLIP
LIST OF ACCIDENT VICTIMS
I FOUND THE LIST.
ME TOO.
KIRIU.
KIRIU...
KIRI-
HERE IT IS.
APPARENTLY HIS PARENTS AND OLDER BROTHER DIED IN THE CRASH.
KEI?

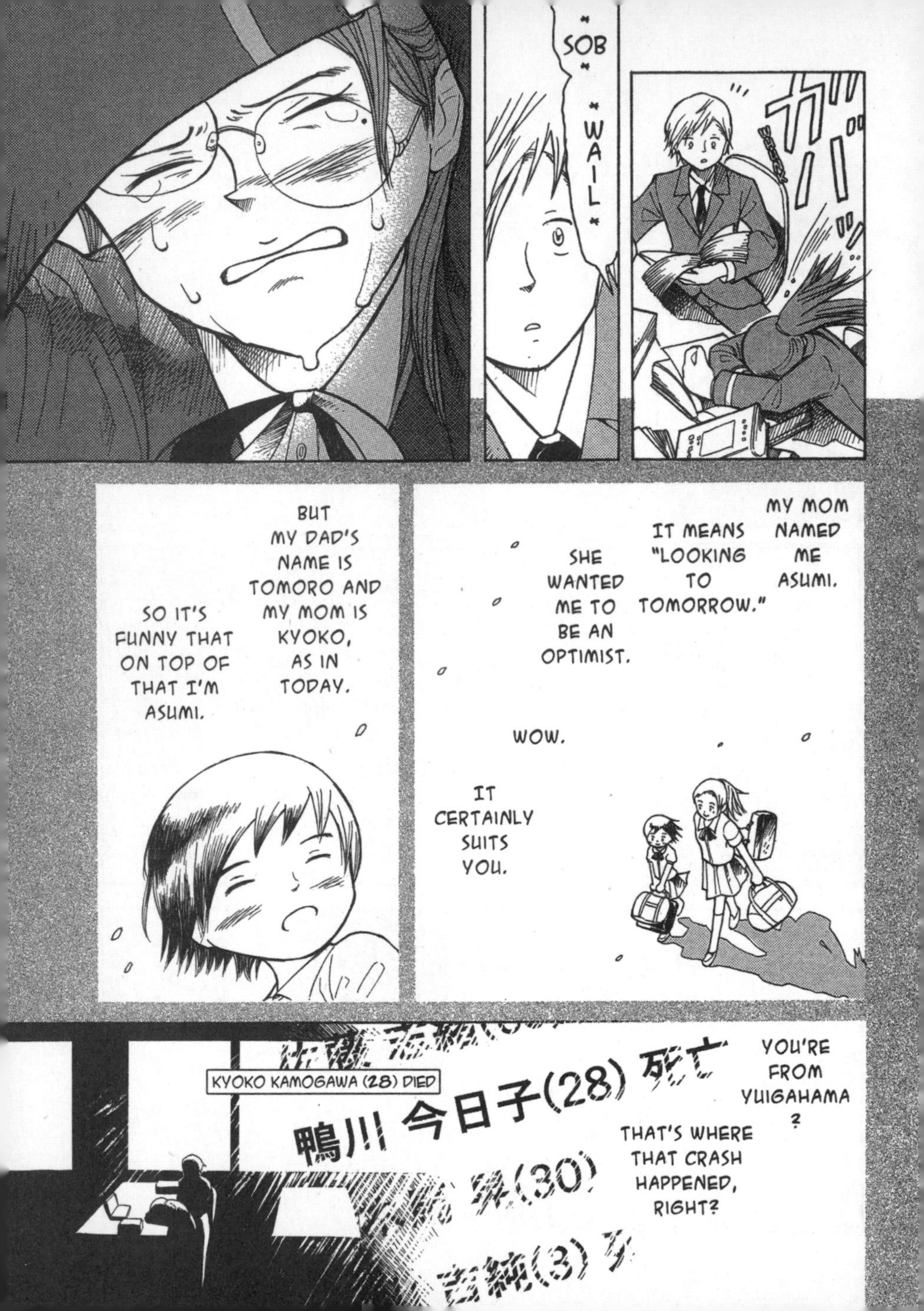
SOB
WAIL
MY MOM NAMED ME ASUMI.
IT MEANS "LOOKING TO TOMORROW."
SHE WANTED ME TO BE AN OPTIMIST.
WOW.
IT CERTAINLY SUITS YOU.
BUT MY DAD'S NAME IS TOMORO AND MY MOM IS KYOKO, AS IN TODAY.
SO IT'S FUNNY THAT ON TOP OF THAT I'M ASUMI.
YOU'RE FROM YUIGAHAMA?
THAT'S WHERE THAT CRASH HAPPENED, RIGHT?
鴨川 今日子(28) 死亡
KYOKO KAMOGAWA (28) DIED

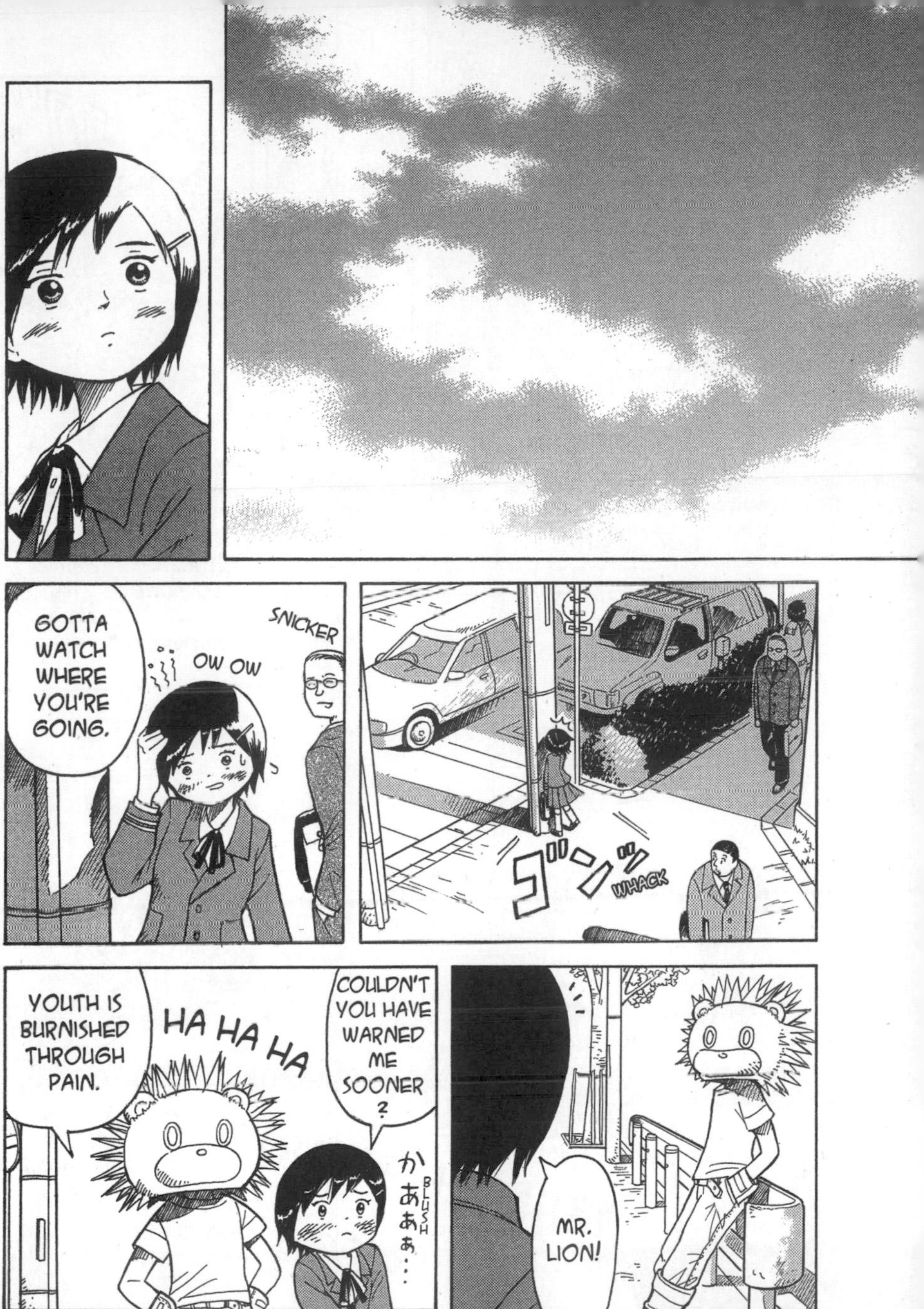
ゴツン
WHACK
SNICKER
OW OW
GOTTA WATCH WHERE YOU'RE GOING.
MR. LION!
COULDN'T YOU HAVE WARNED ME SOONER?
HA HA HA
YOUTH IS BURNISHED THROUGH PAIN.
かあぁ…
BLUSH

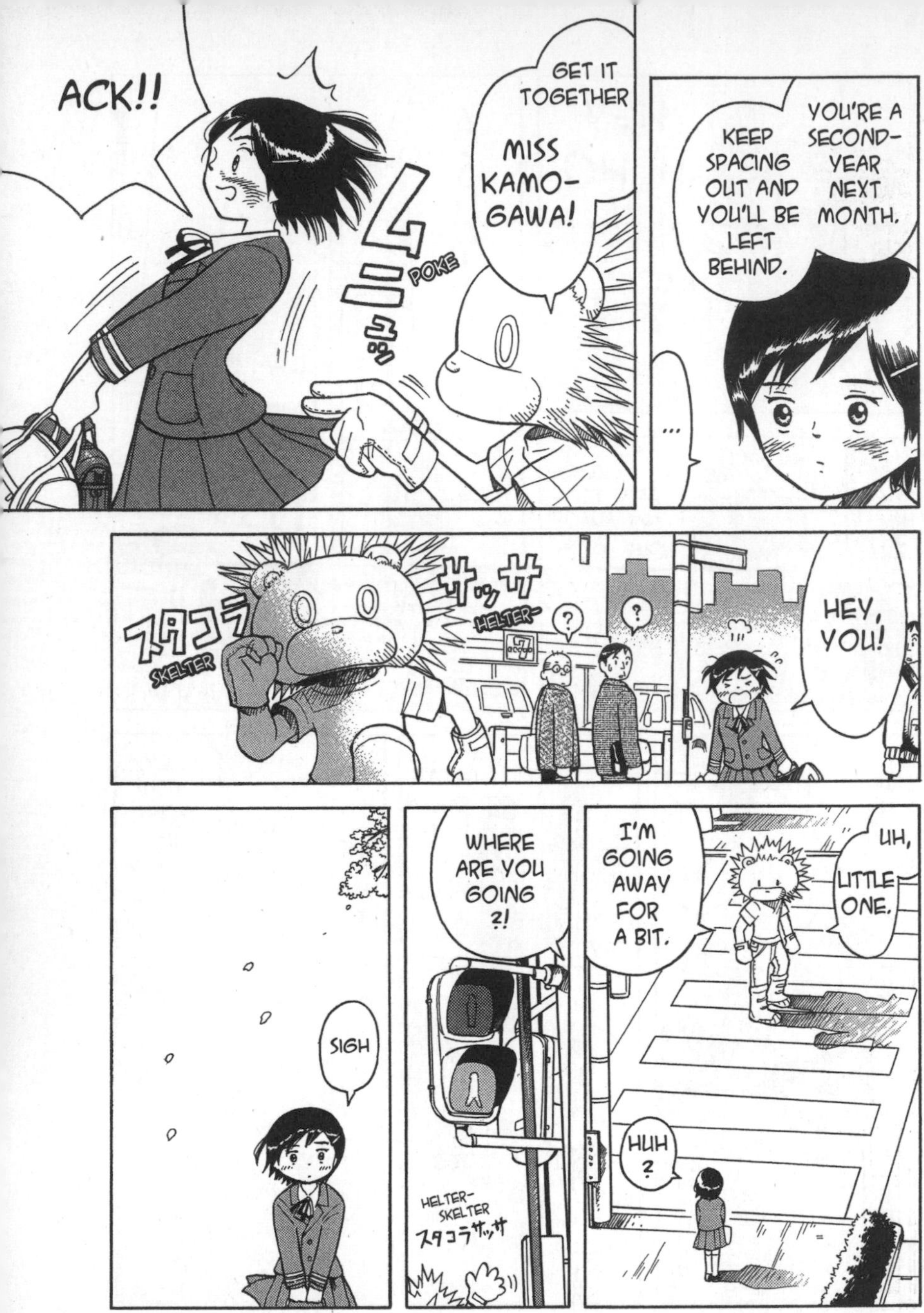
YOU'RE A SECOND-YEAR NEXT MONTH.
KEEP SPACING OUT AND YOU'LL BE LEFT BEHIND.
...
GET IT TOGETHER
MISS KAMO-GAWA!
ムニュッ
POKE
ACK!!
HEY, YOU!
?
?
サッサ
HELTER-
スタコラ
SKELTER
UH, LITTLE ONE.
I'M GOING AWAY FOR A BIT.
HUH ?
WHERE ARE YOU GOING ?!
HELTER-SKELTER
スタコラサッサ
SIGH

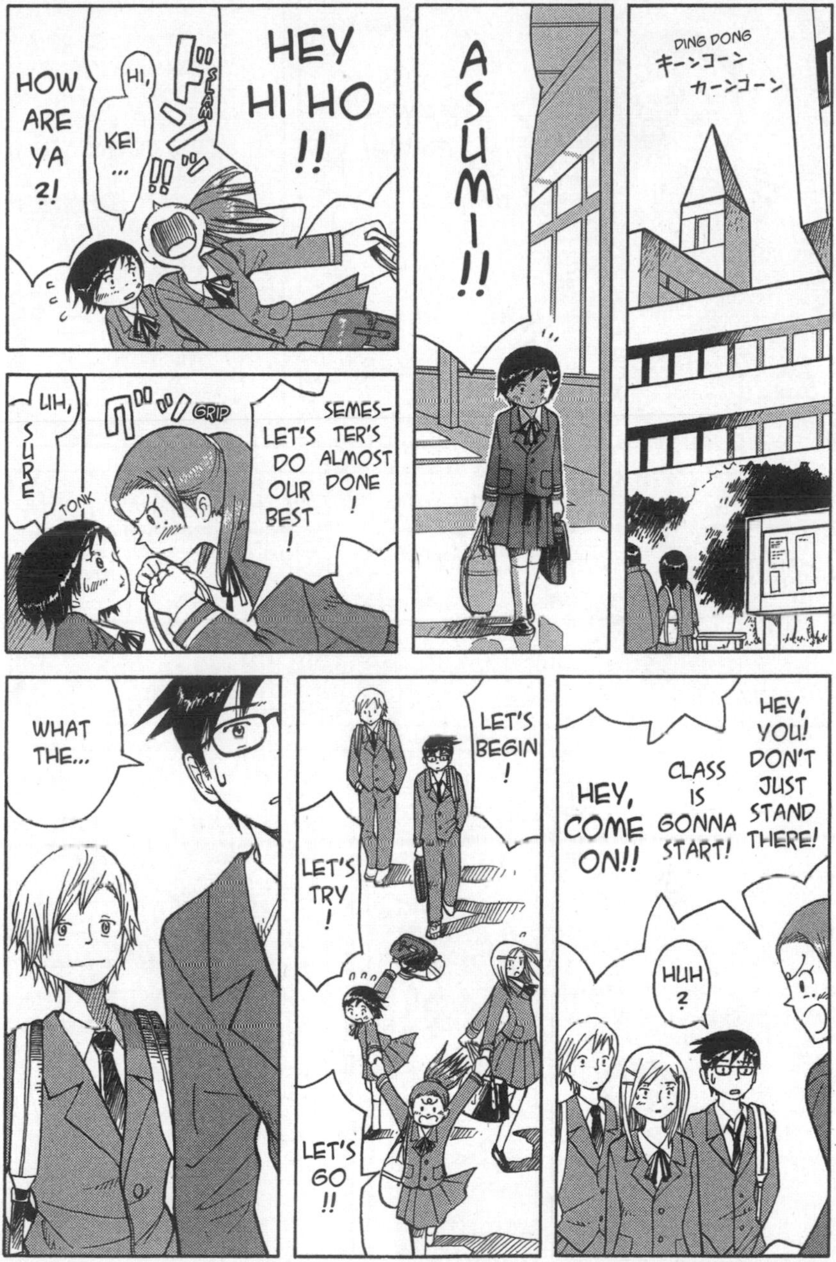
DING DONG
キーンコーン
カーンコーン
ASUMI!!
HEY HI HO!!
SLAM
HI, KEI...
HOW ARE YA?!
SEMESTER'S ALMOST DONE!
LET'S DO OUR BEST!
GRIP
TONK
UH, SURE
HEY, YOU! DON'T JUST STAND THERE!
CLASS IS GONNA START!
HEY, COME ON!!
HUH?
LET'S BEGIN!
LET'S TRY!
LET'S GO!!
WHAT THE...

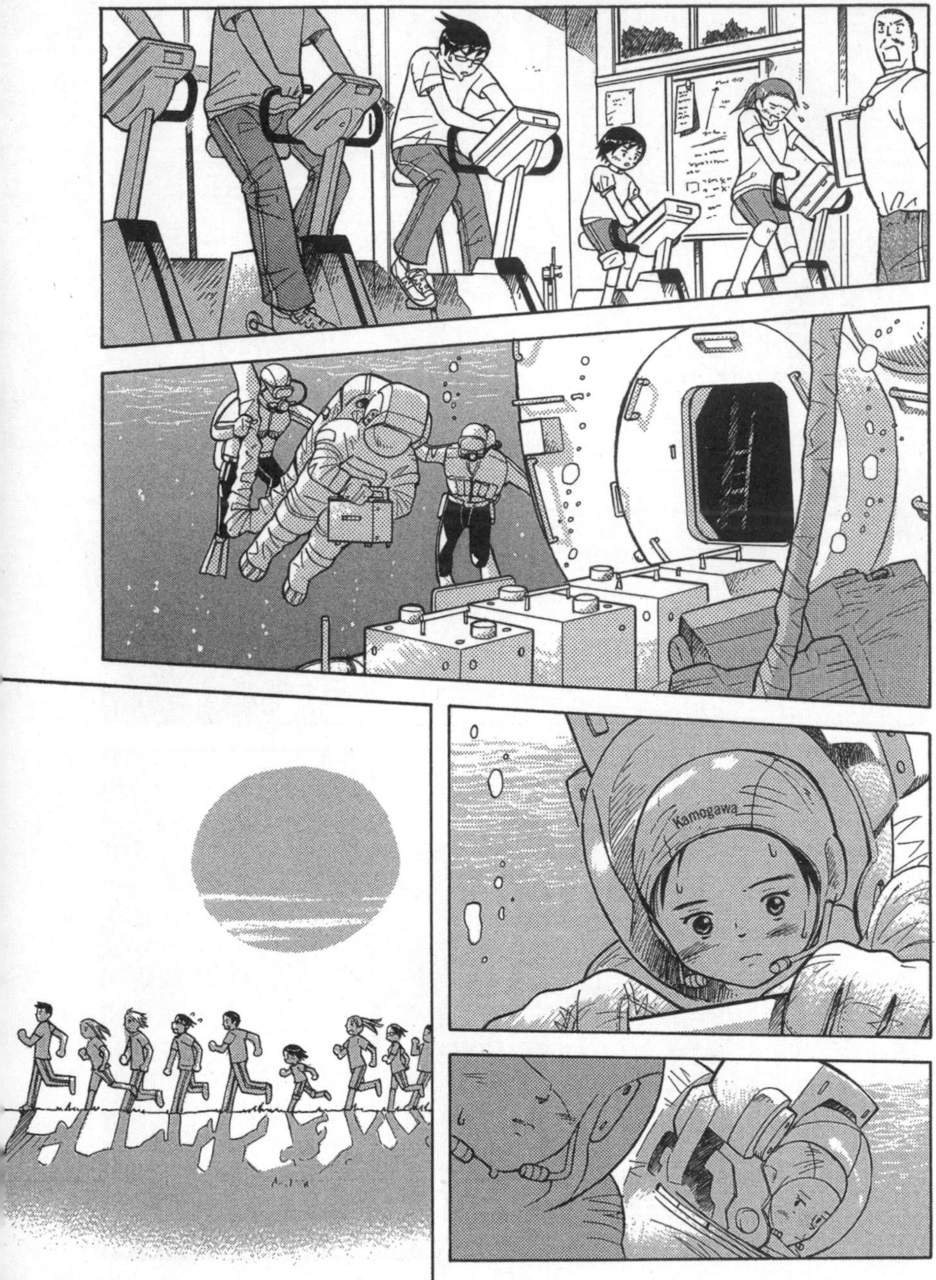
Kamogawa

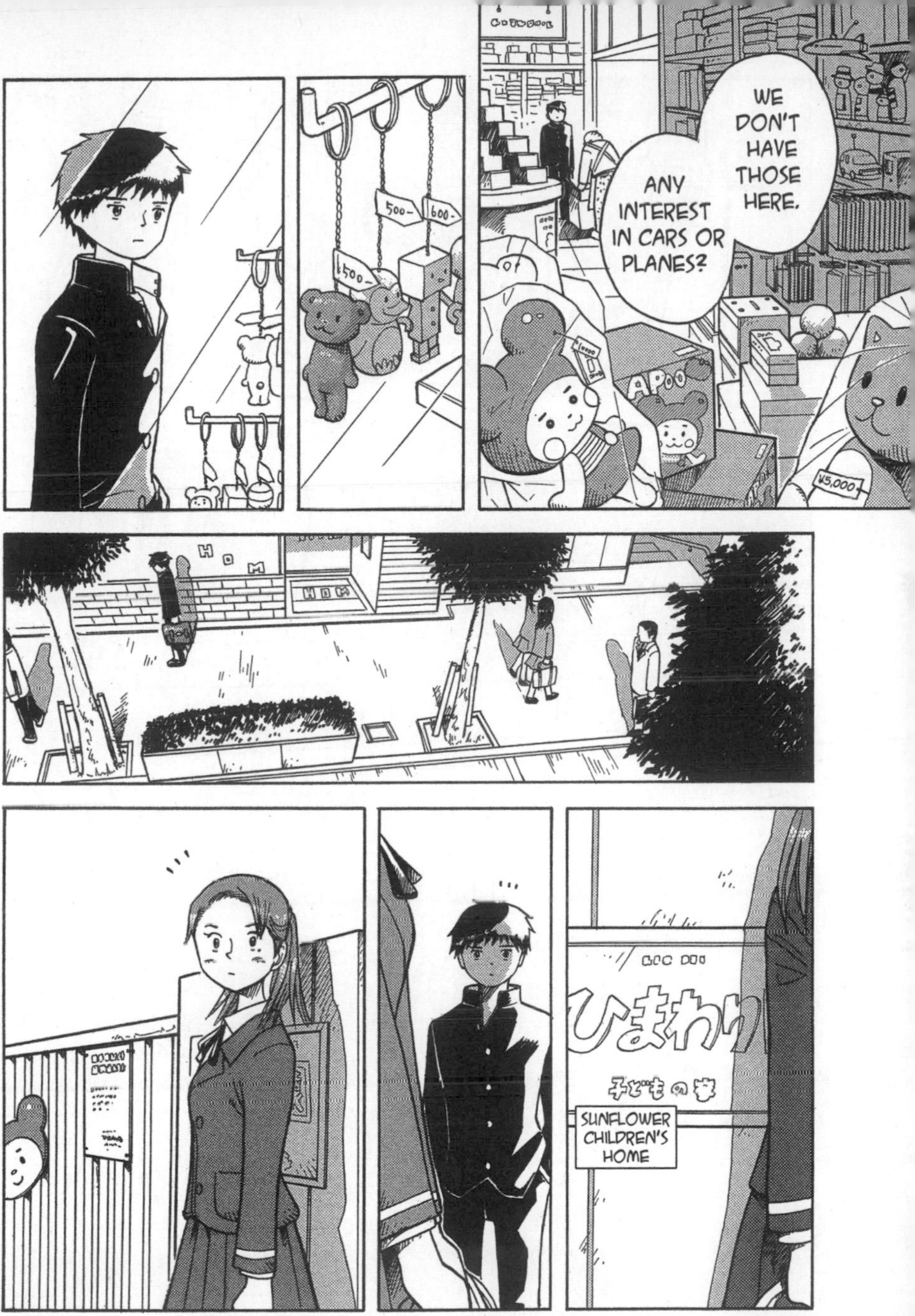
WE DON'T HAVE THOSE HERE.
ANY INTEREST IN CARS OR PLANES?
ひまわり
子どもの家
SUNFLOWER CHILDREN'S HOME

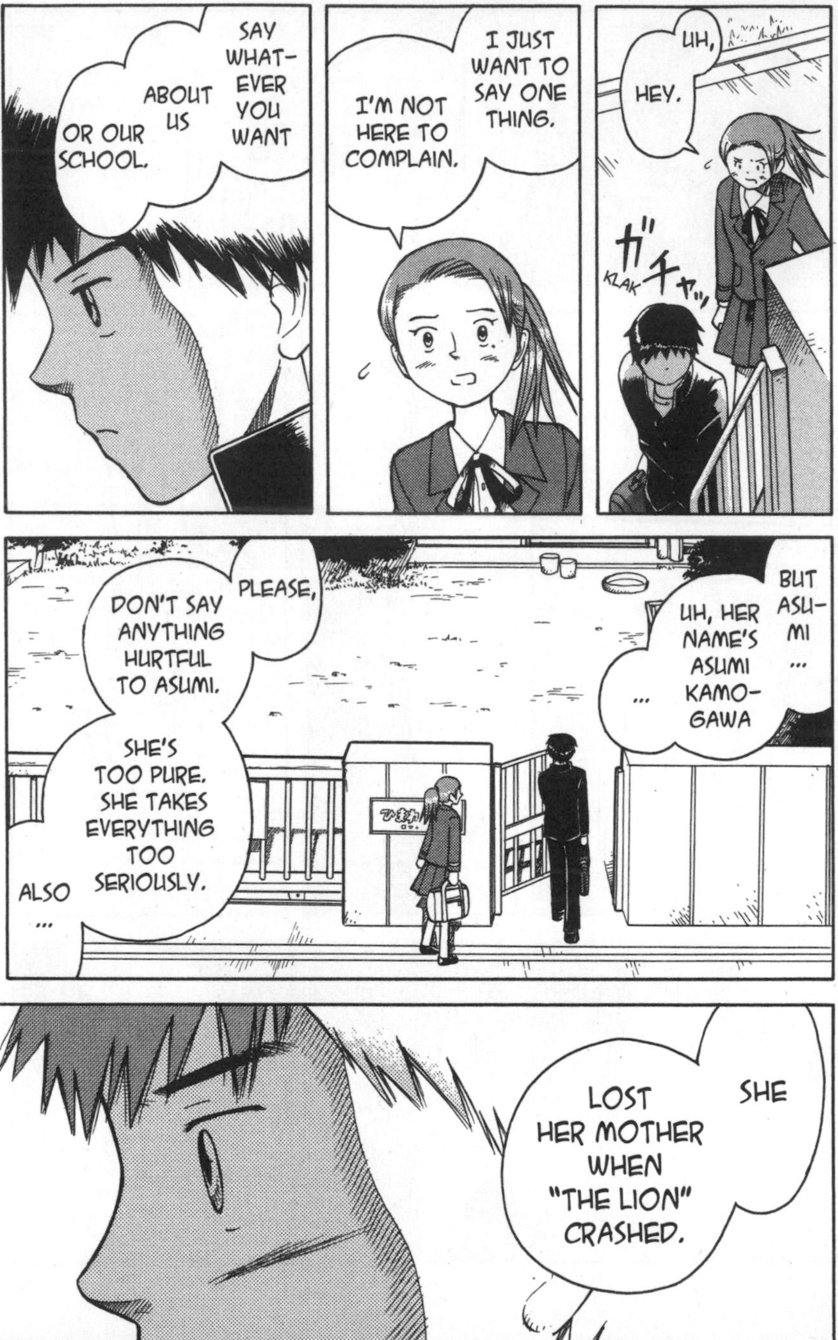
UH,
HEY.
ガチャッ
KLAK
I JUST WANT TO SAY ONE THING.
I'M NOT HERE TO COMPLAIN.
SAY WHAT-EVER YOU WANT
ABOUT US
OR OUR SCHOOL.
BUT ASUMI ...
UH, HER NAME'S ASUMI KAMOGAWA
...
PLEASE,
DON'T SAY ANYTHING HURTFUL TO ASUMI.
SHE'S TOO PURE. SHE TAKES EVERYTHING TOO SERIOUSLY.
ALSO ...
SHE
LOST HER MOTHER WHEN "THE LION" CRASHED.

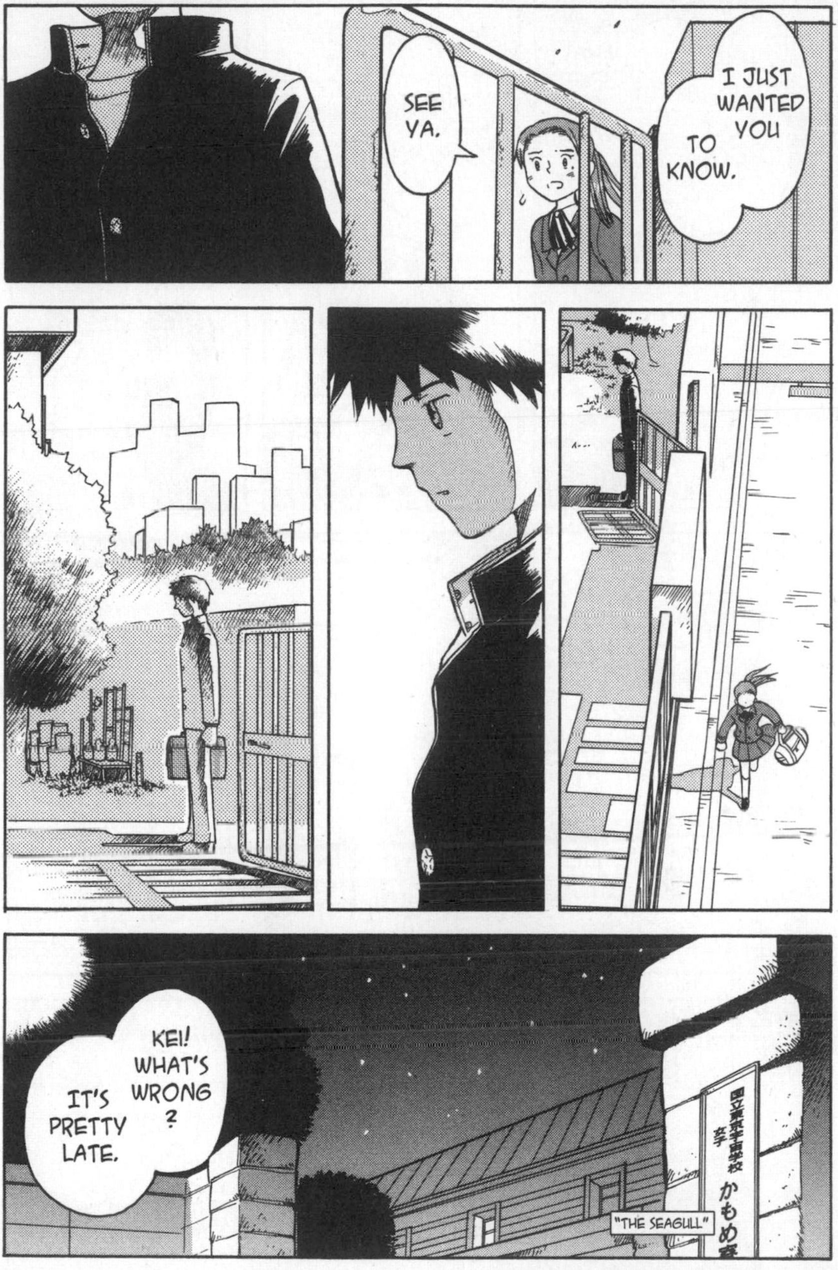
I JUST WANTED YOU TO KNOW.
SEE YA.
KEI! WHAT'S WRONG?
IT'S PRETTY LATE.
国立東京宇宙学校
"THE SEAGULL"

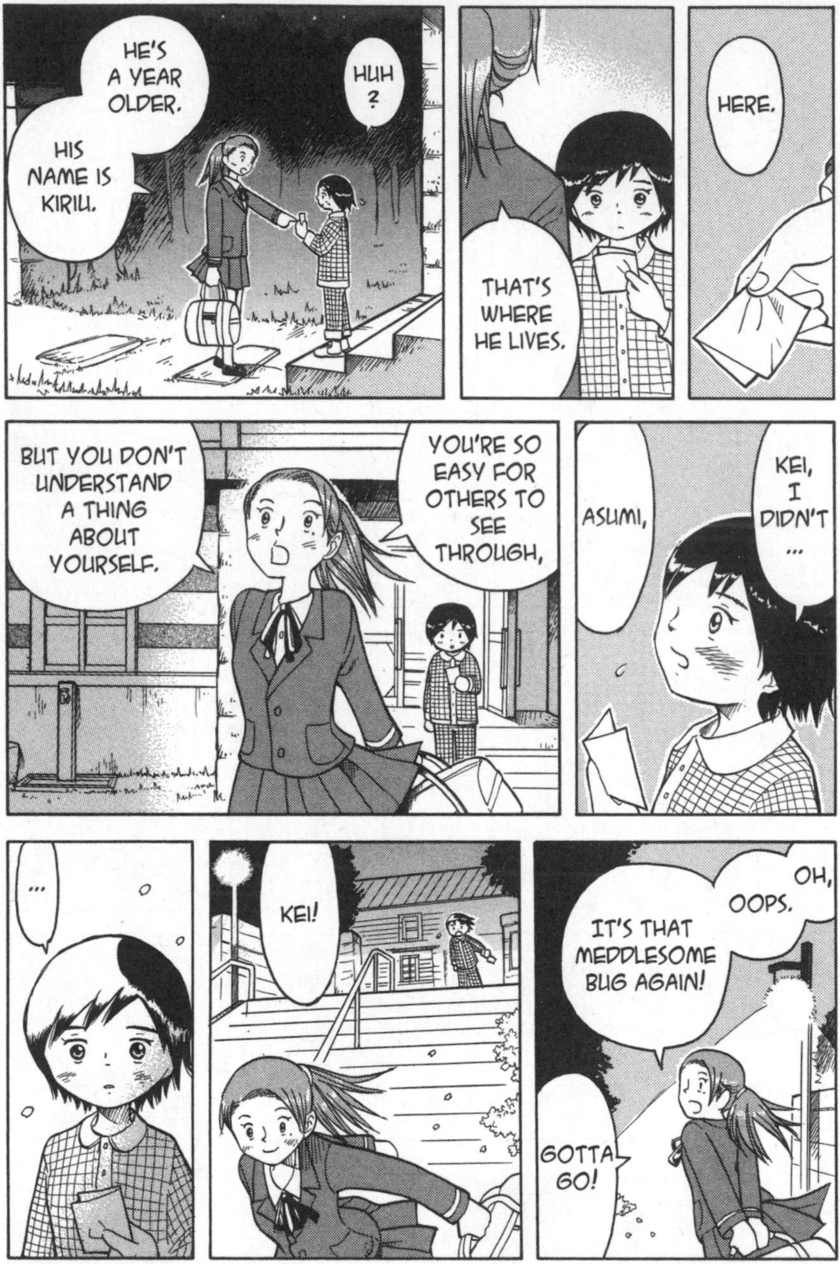
HERE.
THAT'S WHERE HE LIVES.
HUH ?
HE'S A YEAR OLDER.
HIS NAME IS KIRIU.
KEI, I DIDN'T ...
ASUMI,
YOU'RE SO EASY FOR OTHERS TO SEE THROUGH,
BUT YOU DON'T UNDERSTAND A THING ABOUT YOURSELF.
OH, OOPS.
IT'S THAT MEDDLESOME BUG AGAIN!
GOTTA GO!
KEI!
...

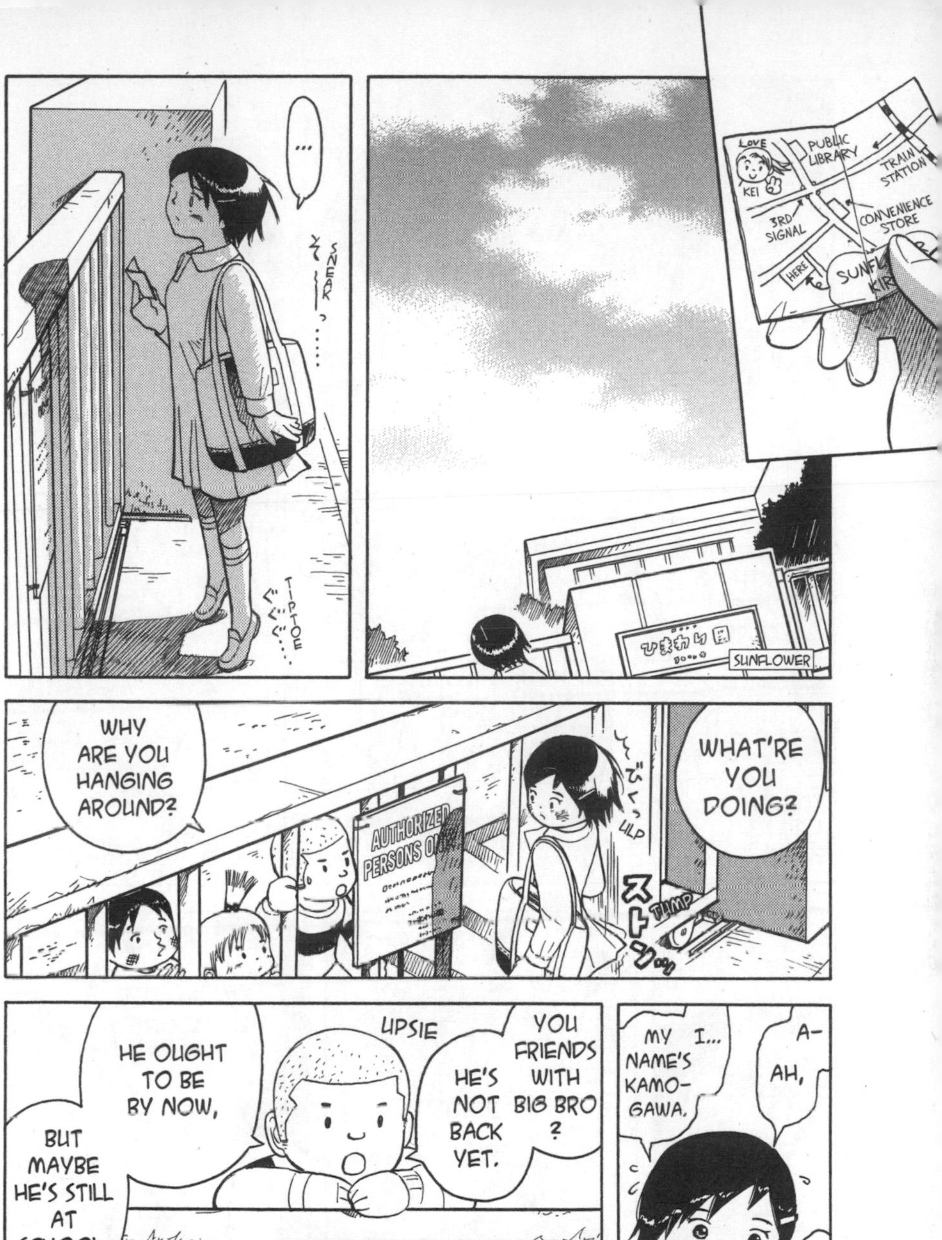
LOVE
KEI
PUBLIC LIBRARY
TRAIN STATION
3RD SIGNAL
CONVENIENCE STORE
HERE
SUNFLOWER
...
SNEAK
TIPTOE
WHAT'RE YOU DOING?
ULP
THMP
WHY ARE YOU HANGING AROUND?
AUTHORIZED PERSONS ONLY
A- AH,
I...
MY NAME'S KAMO-GAWA.
UHM...
YOU FRIENDS WITH BIG BRO?
HE'S NOT BACK YET.
UPSIE
HE OUGHT TO BE BY NOW,
BUT MAYBE HE'S STILL AT SCHOOL.
AUTH

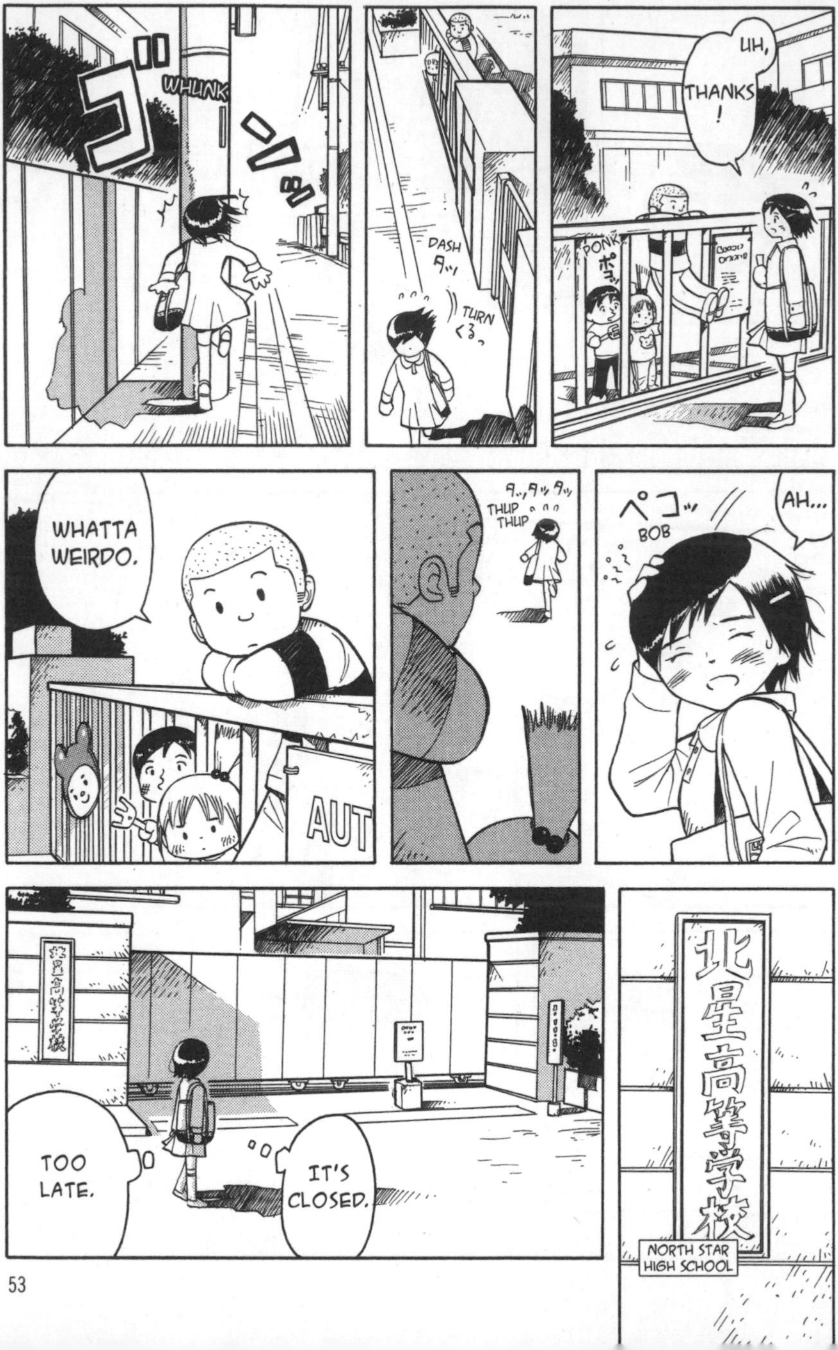
UH, THANKS!
PONK
ポコッ
DASH
タッ
TURN
くるっ
ゴッ
WHUNK
AH...
ペコッ
BOB
タッ,タッタッ
THUP THUP
WHATTA WEIRDO.
AUT
北星高等学校
NORTH STAR HIGH SCHOOL
IT'S CLOSED.
TOO LATE.

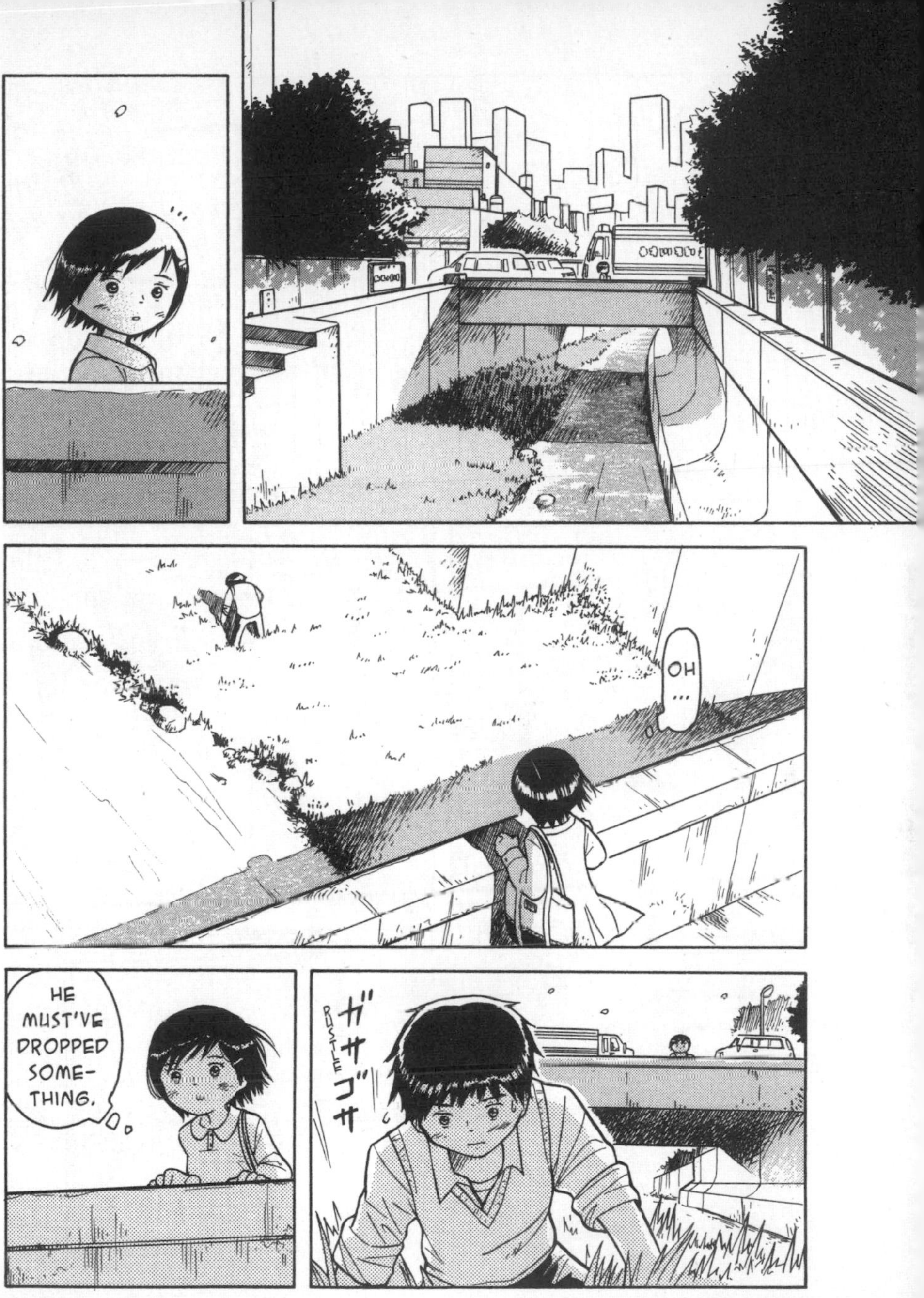
OH ...
ガサゴサ
RUSTLE
HE MUST'VE DROPPED SOMETHING.

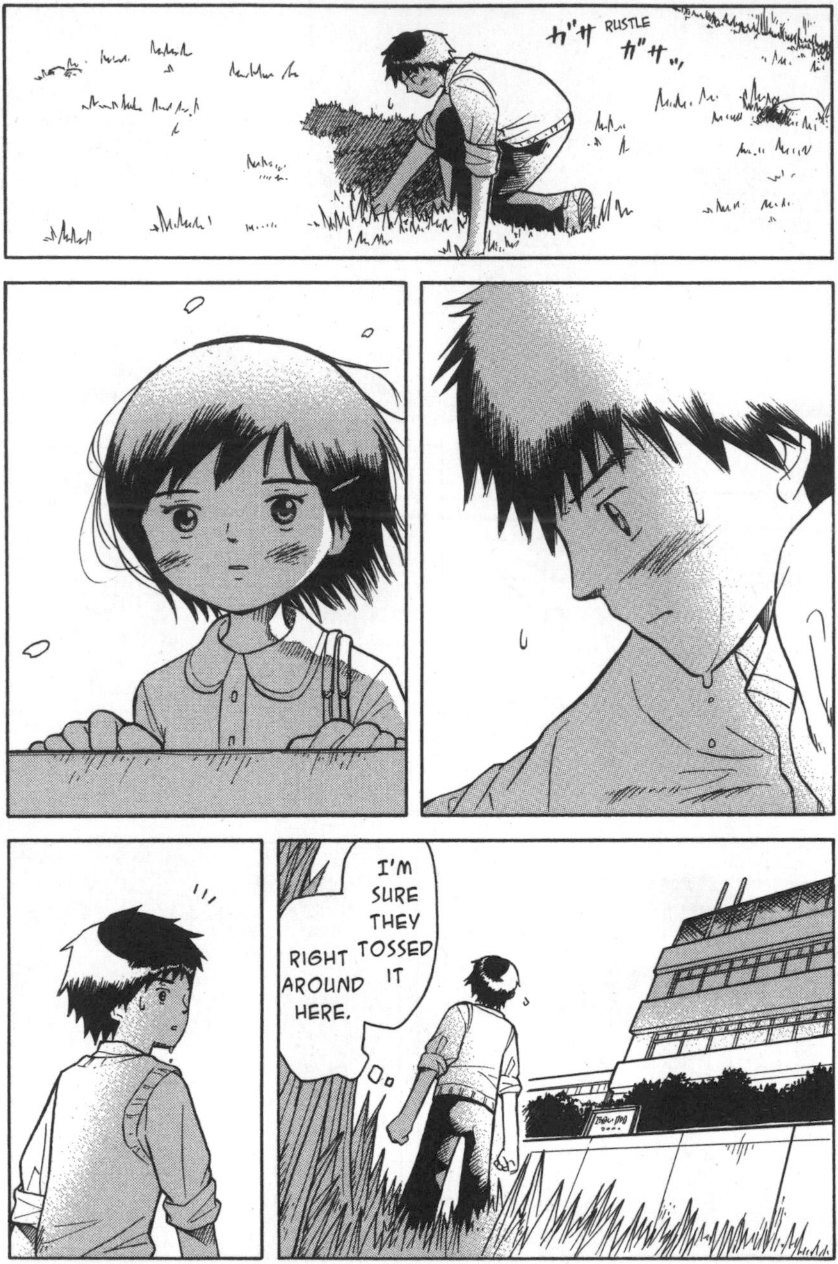
ガサ RUSTLE
ガサッ
I'M SURE THEY TOSSED IT RIGHT AROUND HERE.

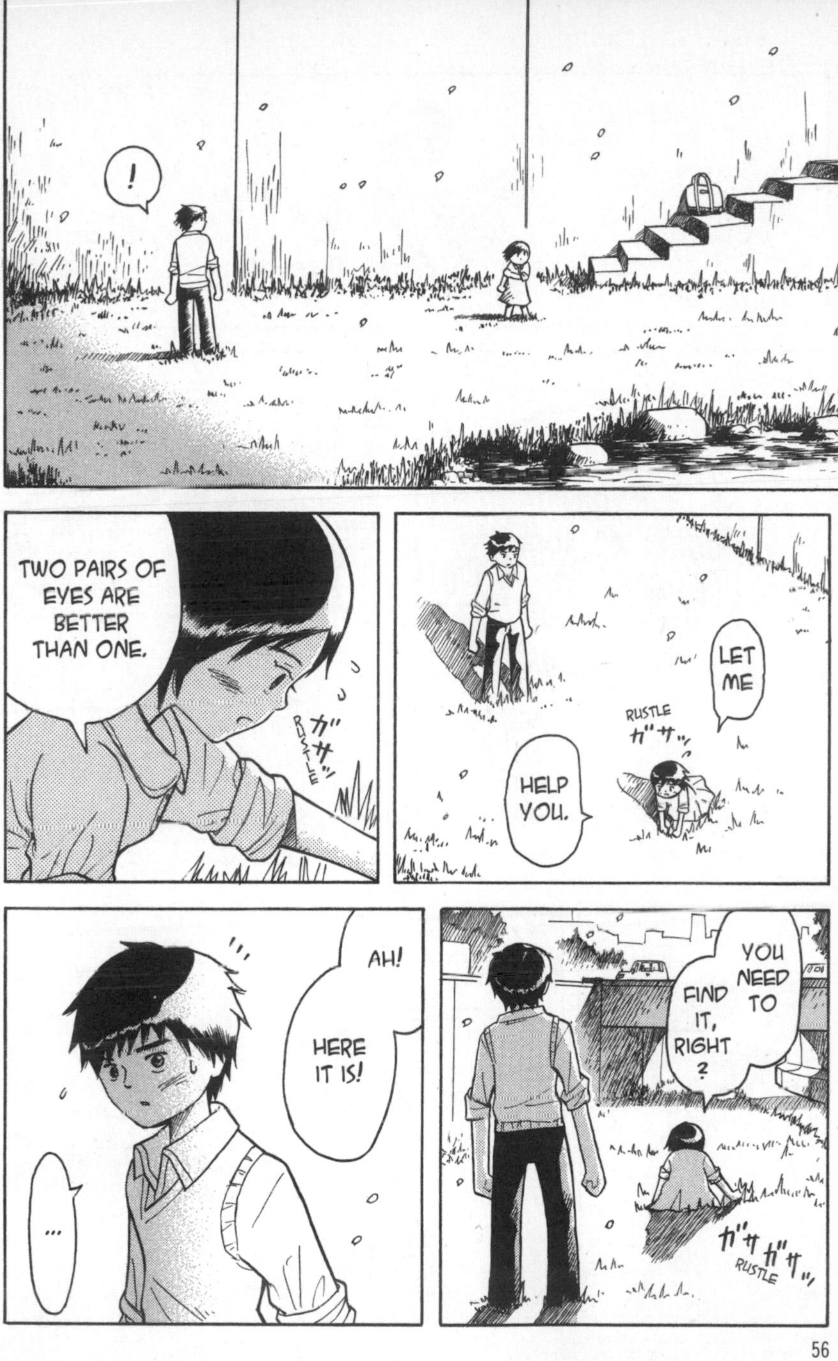
!
LET ME
HELP YOU.
RUSTLE
ガサッ
TWO PAIRS OF EYES ARE BETTER THAN ONE.
ガサッ
RUSTLE
YOU NEED TO FIND IT, RIGHT?
ガサガサ
RUSTLE
AH!
HERE IT IS!
...

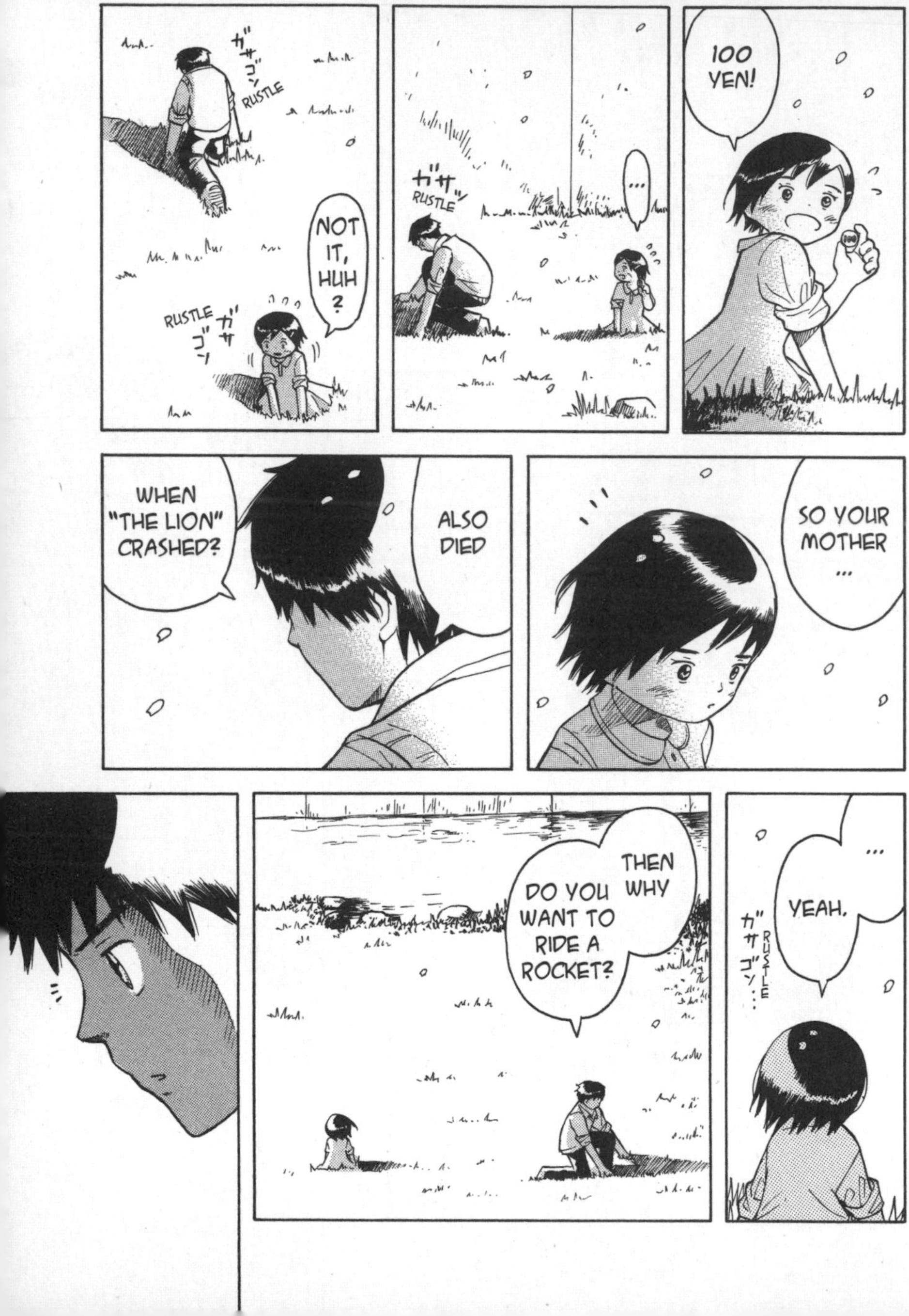
100 YEN!
ガサッ RUSTLE
...
ガサゴソ RUSTLE
NOT IT, HUH?
RUSTLE ガサゴソ
SO YOUR MOTHER ...
ALSO DIED
WHEN "THE LION" CRASHED?
...
YEAH.
ガサゴソ... RUSTLE
THEN WHY DO YOU WANT TO RIDE A ROCKET?

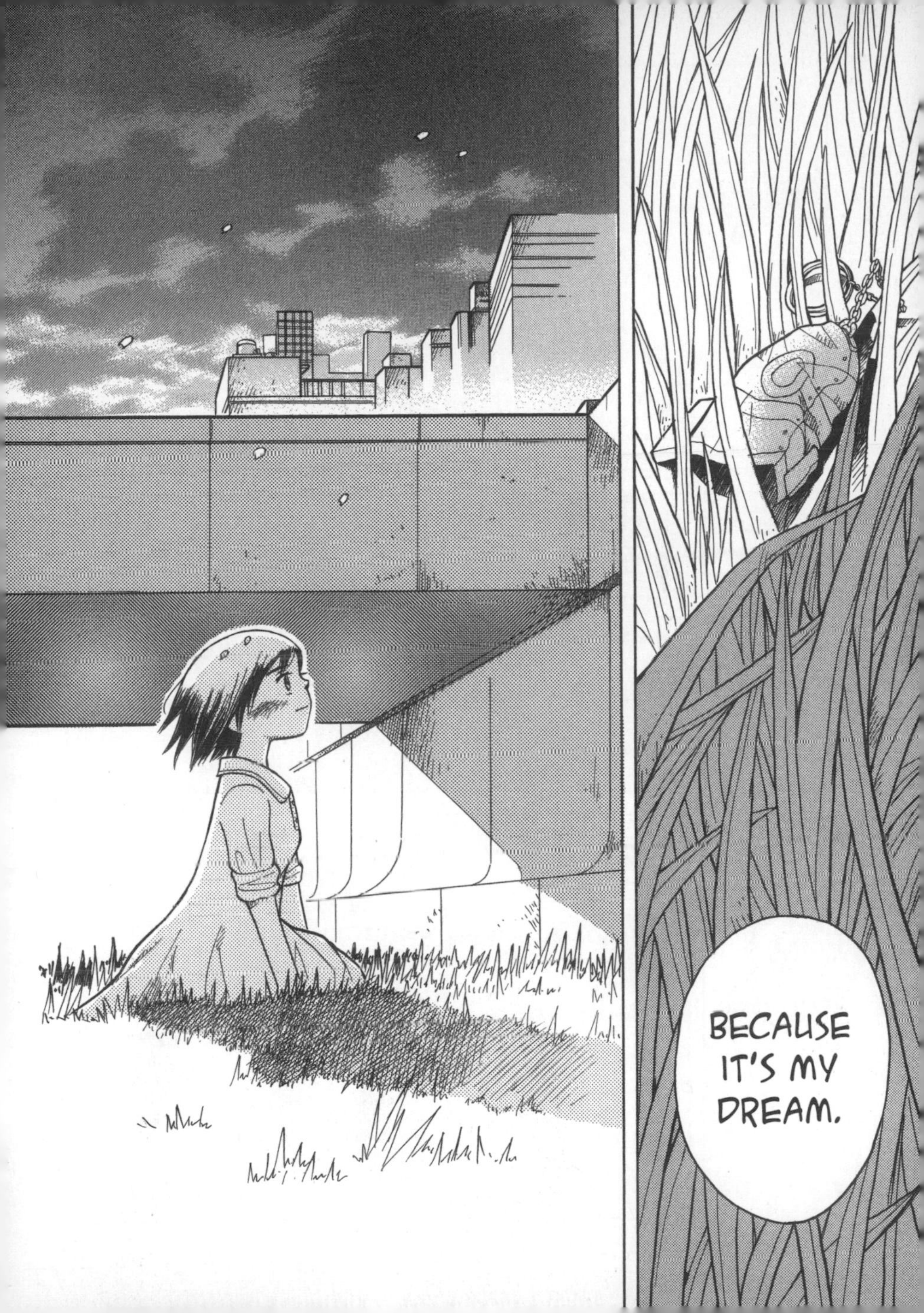
BECAUSE IT'S MY DREAM.

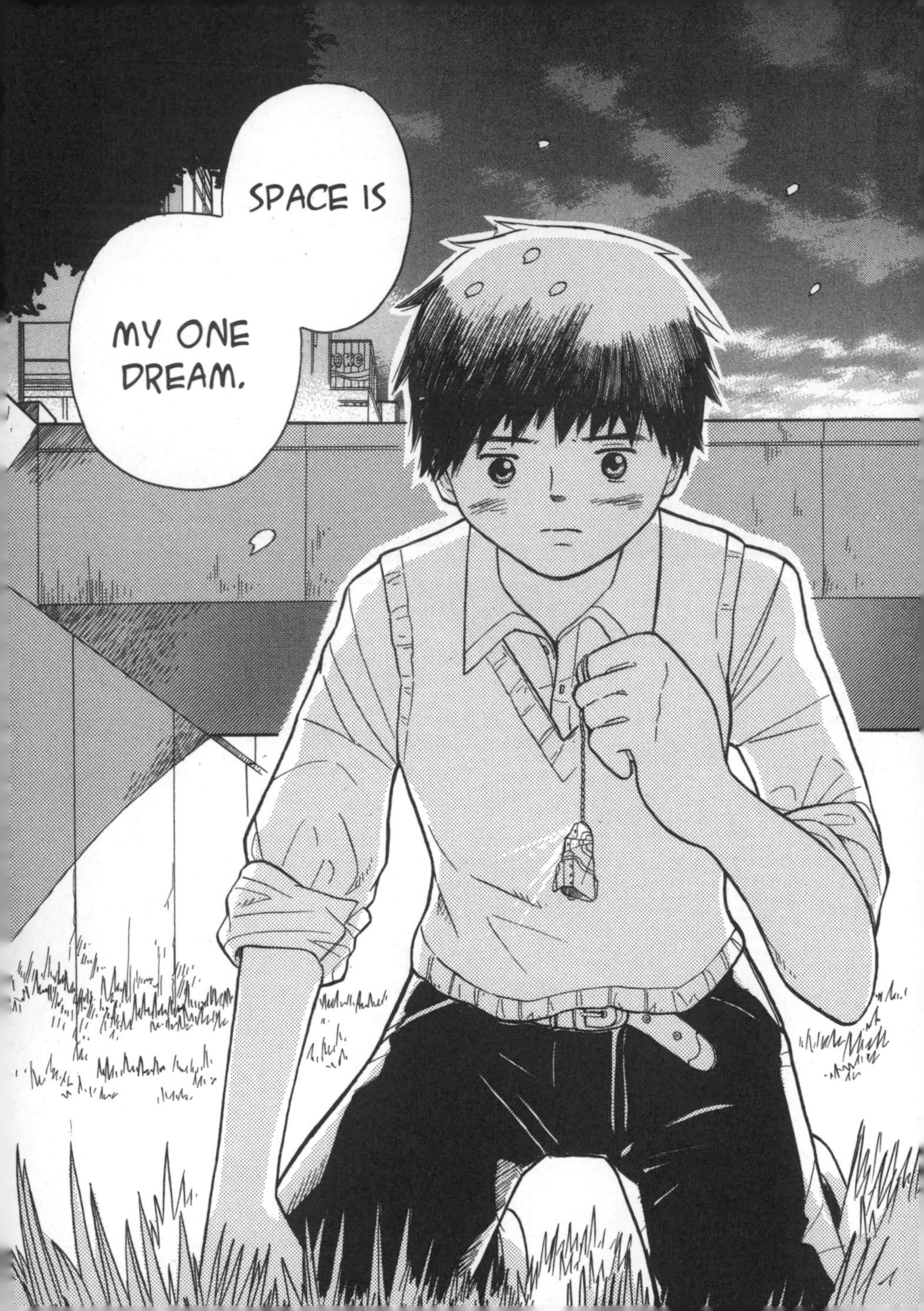
SPACE IS
MY ONE DREAM.

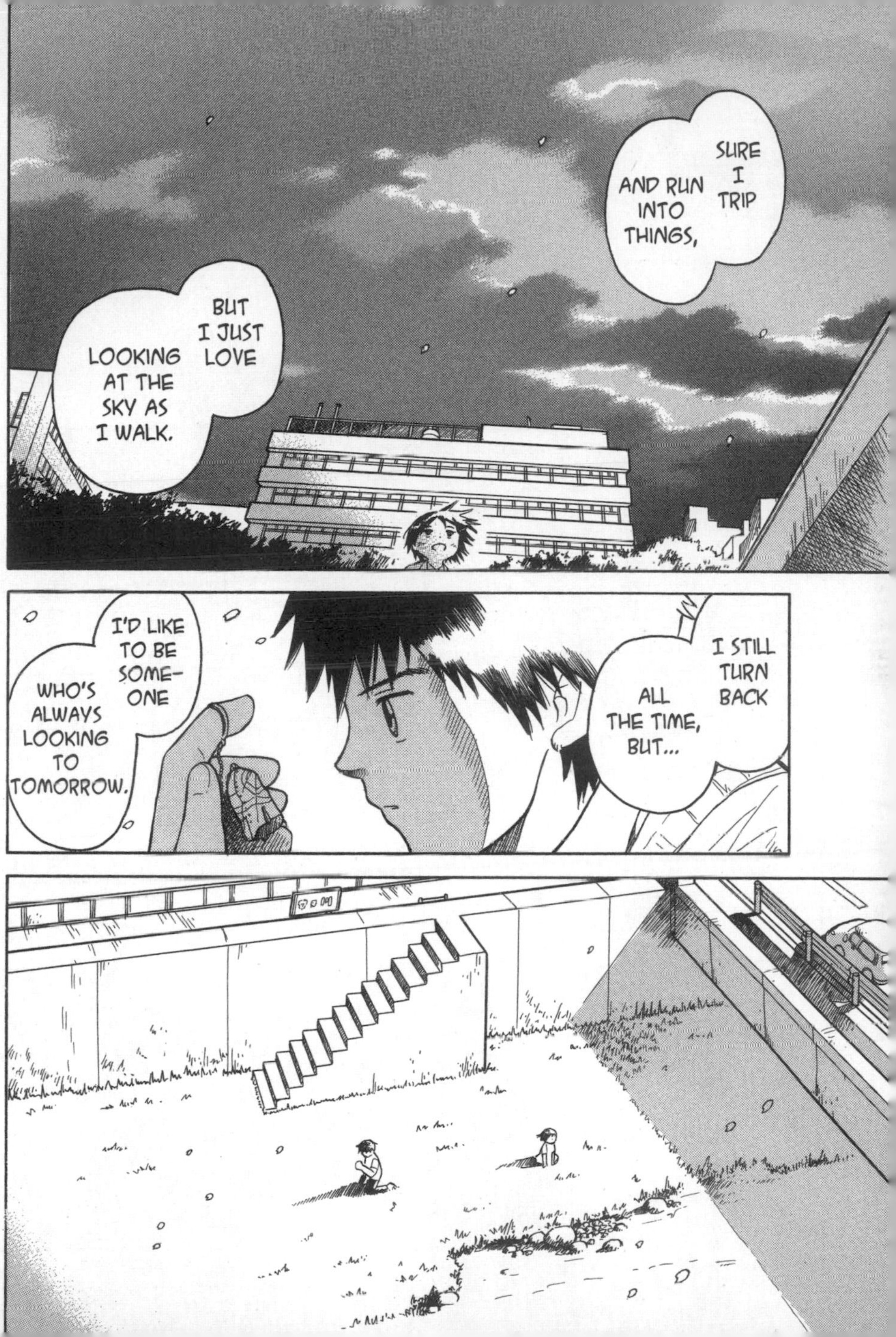
SURE I TRIP AND RUN INTO THINGS,
BUT I JUST LOVE LOOKING AT THE SKY AS I WALK.
I STILL TURN BACK ALL THE TIME, BUT...
I'D LIKE TO BE SOMEONE WHO'S ALWAYS LOOKING TO TOMORROW.

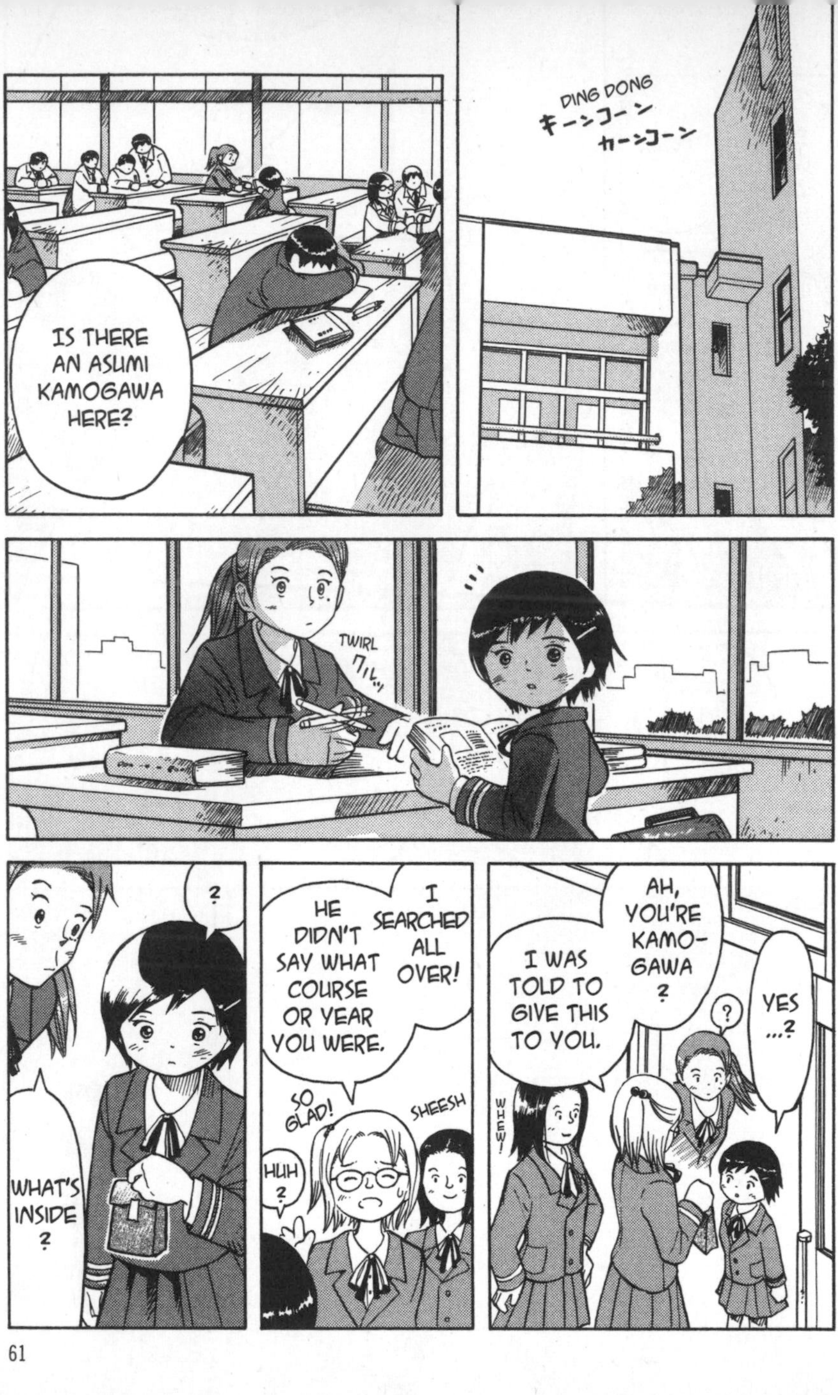
DING DONG
キーンコーン
カーンコーン
IS THERE AN ASUMI KAMOGAWA HERE?
TWIRL
クルッ
AH, YOU'RE KAMOGAWA?
I WAS TOLD TO GIVE THIS TO YOU.
YES ...?
?
WHEW!
I SEARCHED ALL OVER!
HE DIDN'T SAY WHAT COURSE OR YEAR YOU WERE.
SHEESH
SO GLAD!
HUH?
?
WHAT'S INSIDE?

IT GOT QUITE A MAKE-OVER.

WOW.

AH!

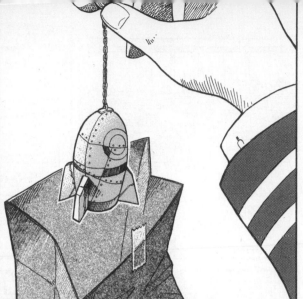

I GUESS SO!

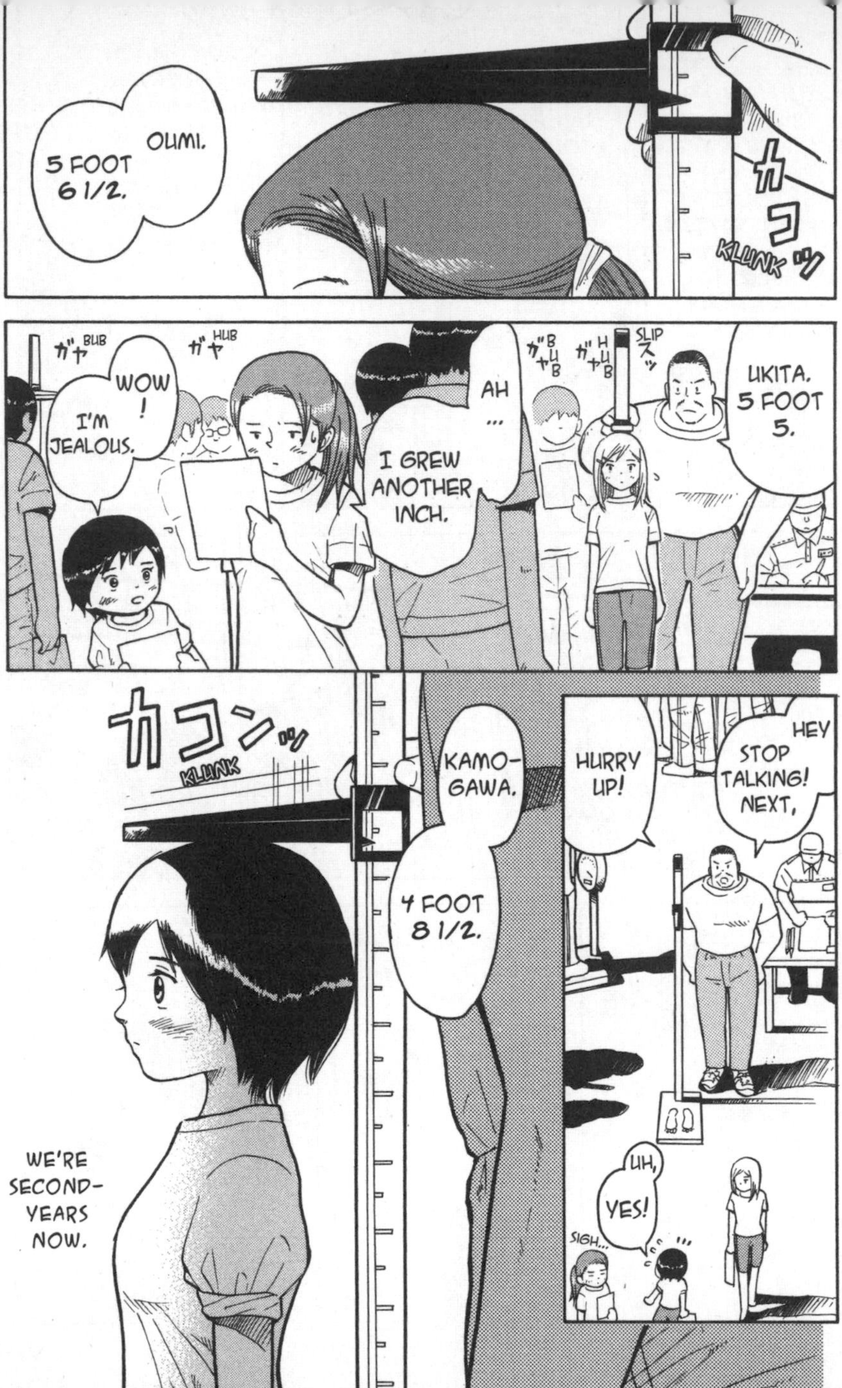
カッ KLUNK ッ
OUMI. 5 FOOT 6 1/2.
UKITA. 5 FOOT 5.
SLIP スッ
ガヤ HUB ガヤ BUB
AH... I GREW ANOTHER INCH.
ガヤ HUB
ガヤ BUB
WOW! I'M JEALOUS.
HEY STOP TALKING! NEXT,
HURRY UP!
UH, YES!
SIGH...
KAMO-GAWA.
4 FOOT 8 1/2.
カコンッ KLUNK
WE'RE SECOND-YEARS NOW.

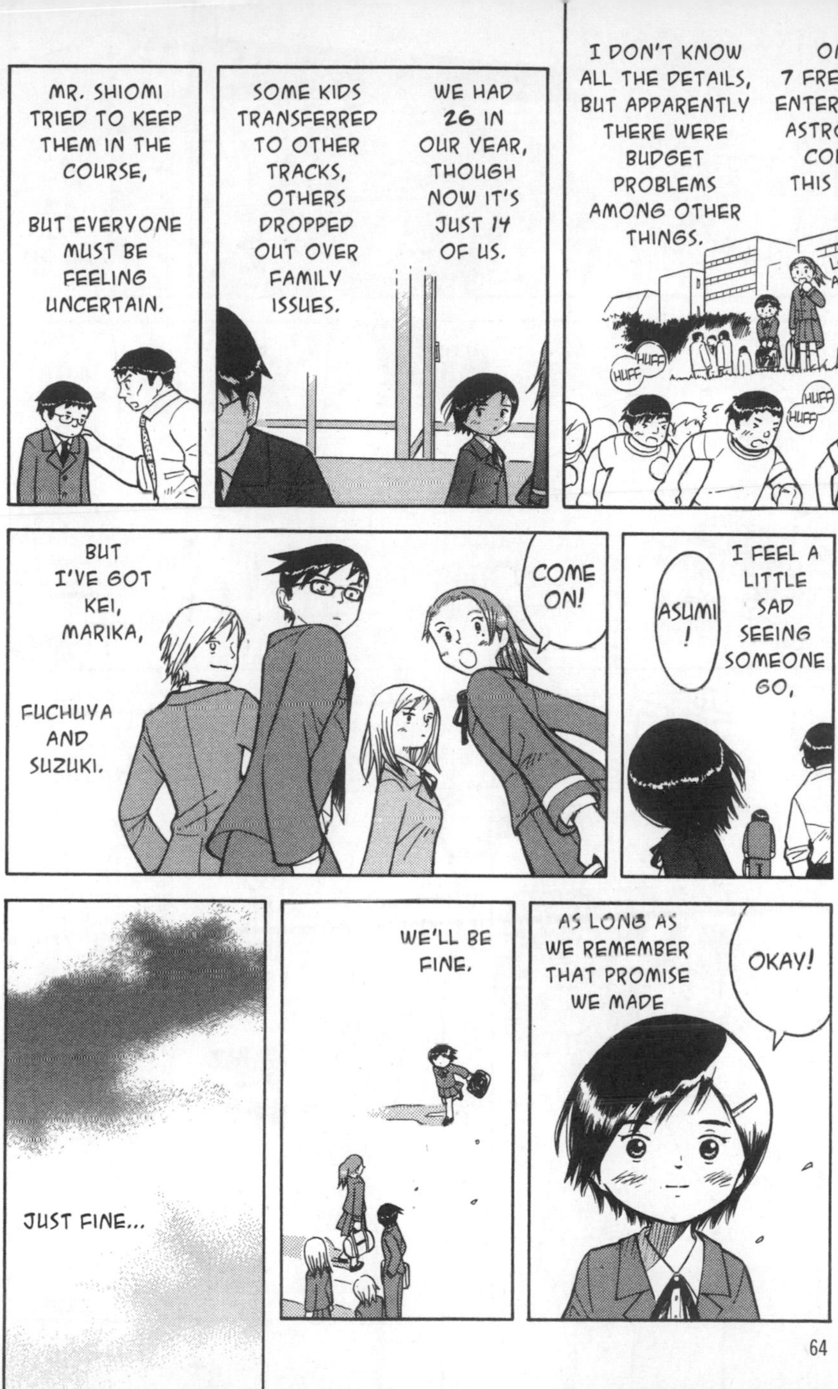
ONLY 7 FRESHMEN ENTERED THE ASTRONAUT COURSE THIS YEAR.
I DON'T KNOW ALL THE DETAILS, BUT APPARENTLY THERE WERE BUDGET PROBLEMS AMONG OTHER THINGS.
LOOK AT 'EM GO!
HUFF
HUFF
HUFF
HUFF
HUFF
WE HAD 26 IN OUR YEAR, THOUGH NOW IT'S JUST 14 OF US.
SOME KIDS TRANSFERRED TO OTHER TRACKS, OTHERS DROPPED OUT OVER FAMILY ISSUES.
MR. SHIOMI TRIED TO KEEP THEM IN THE COURSE,
BUT EVERYONE MUST BE FEELING UNCERTAIN.
I FEEL A LITTLE SAD SEEING SOMEONE GO,
ASUMI!
COME ON!
BUT I'VE GOT KEI, MARIKA,
FUCHUYA AND SUZUKI.
OKAY!
AS LONG AS WE REMEMBER THAT PROMISE WE MADE
WE'LL BE FINE.
JUST FINE...

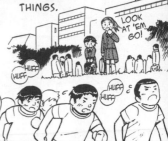

MISSION:21

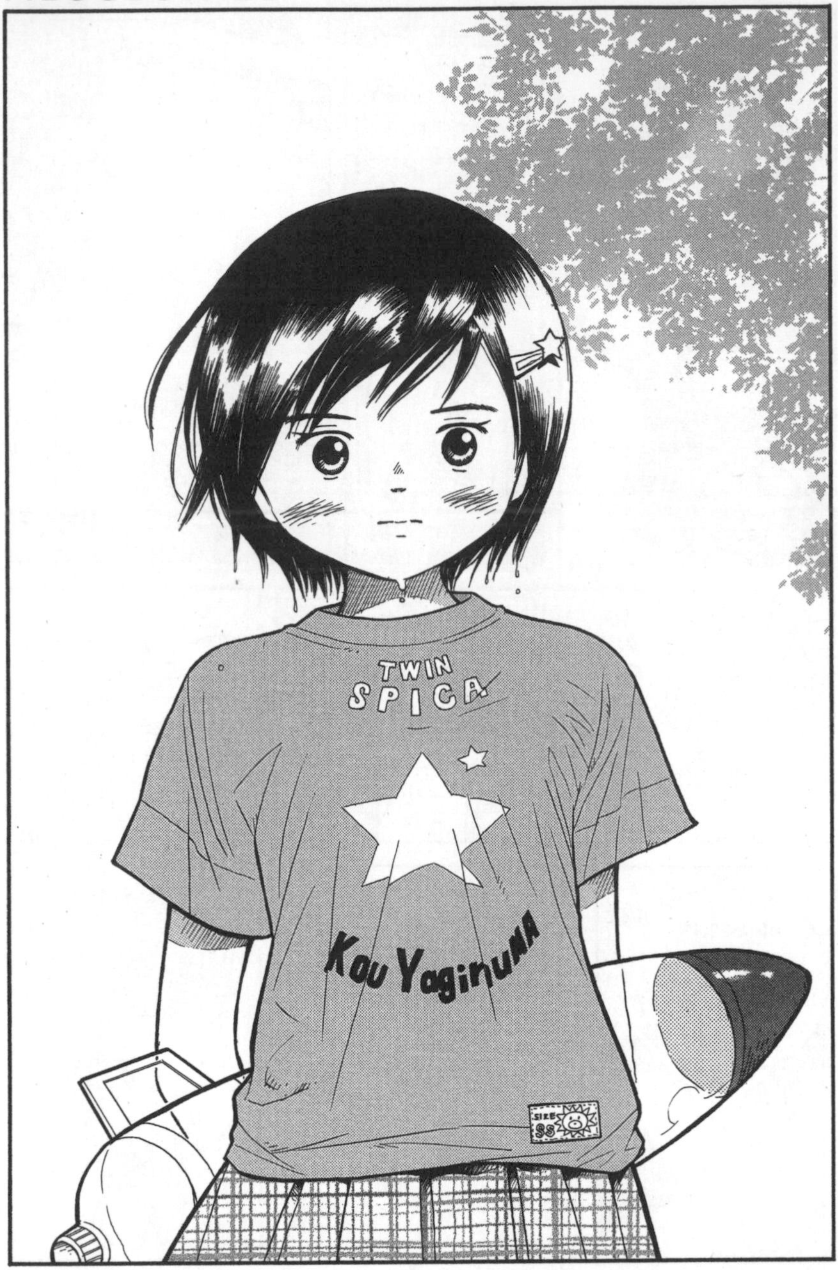
TWIN SPICA
Kou YaginumA
SIZE SS

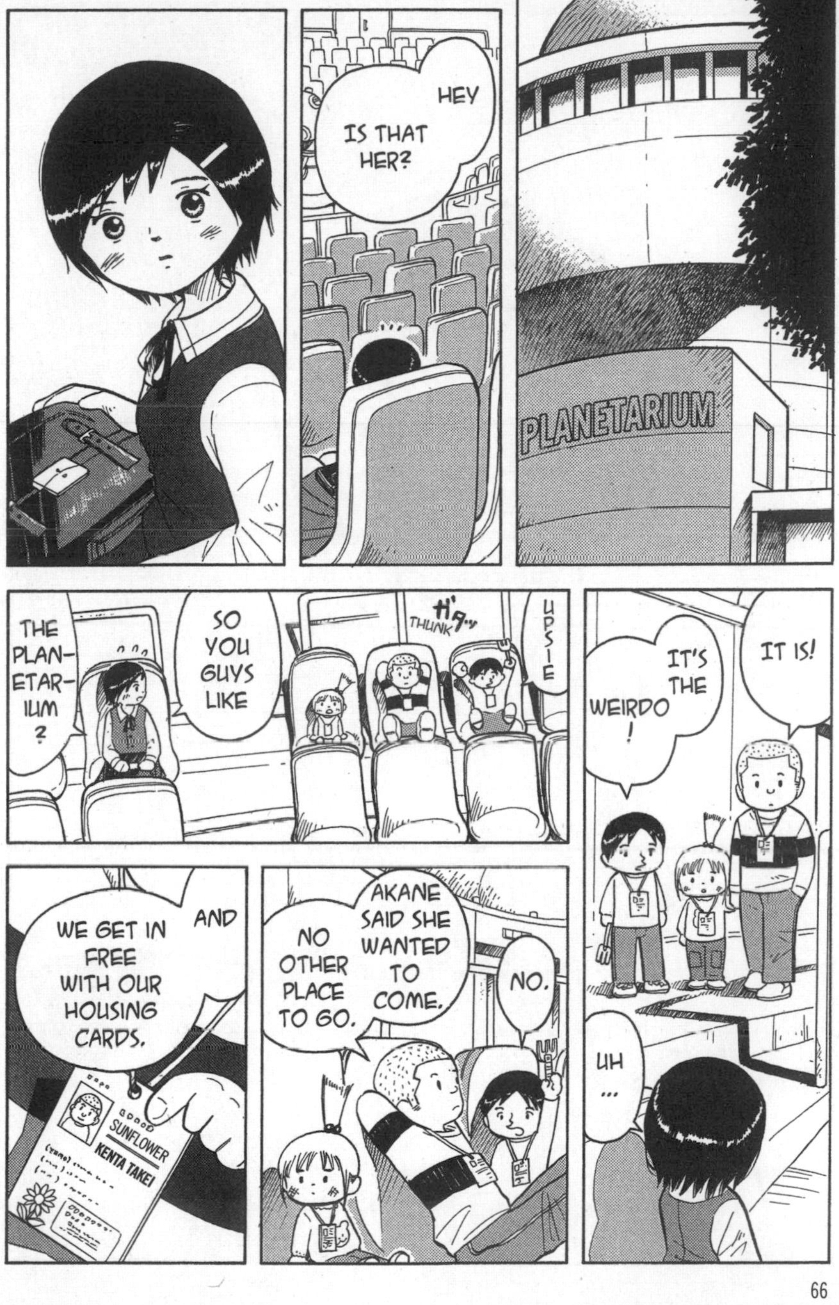
PLANETARIUM
HEY
IS THAT HER?
IT IS!
IT'S THE WEIRDO!
UH ...
UPSIE
THUNK
SO YOU GUYS LIKE
THE PLANETARIUM?
NO.
AKANE SAID SHE WANTED TO COME.
NO OTHER PLACE TO GO.
AND
WE GET IN FREE WITH OUR HOUSING CARDS.
SUNFLOWER
KENTA TAKEI

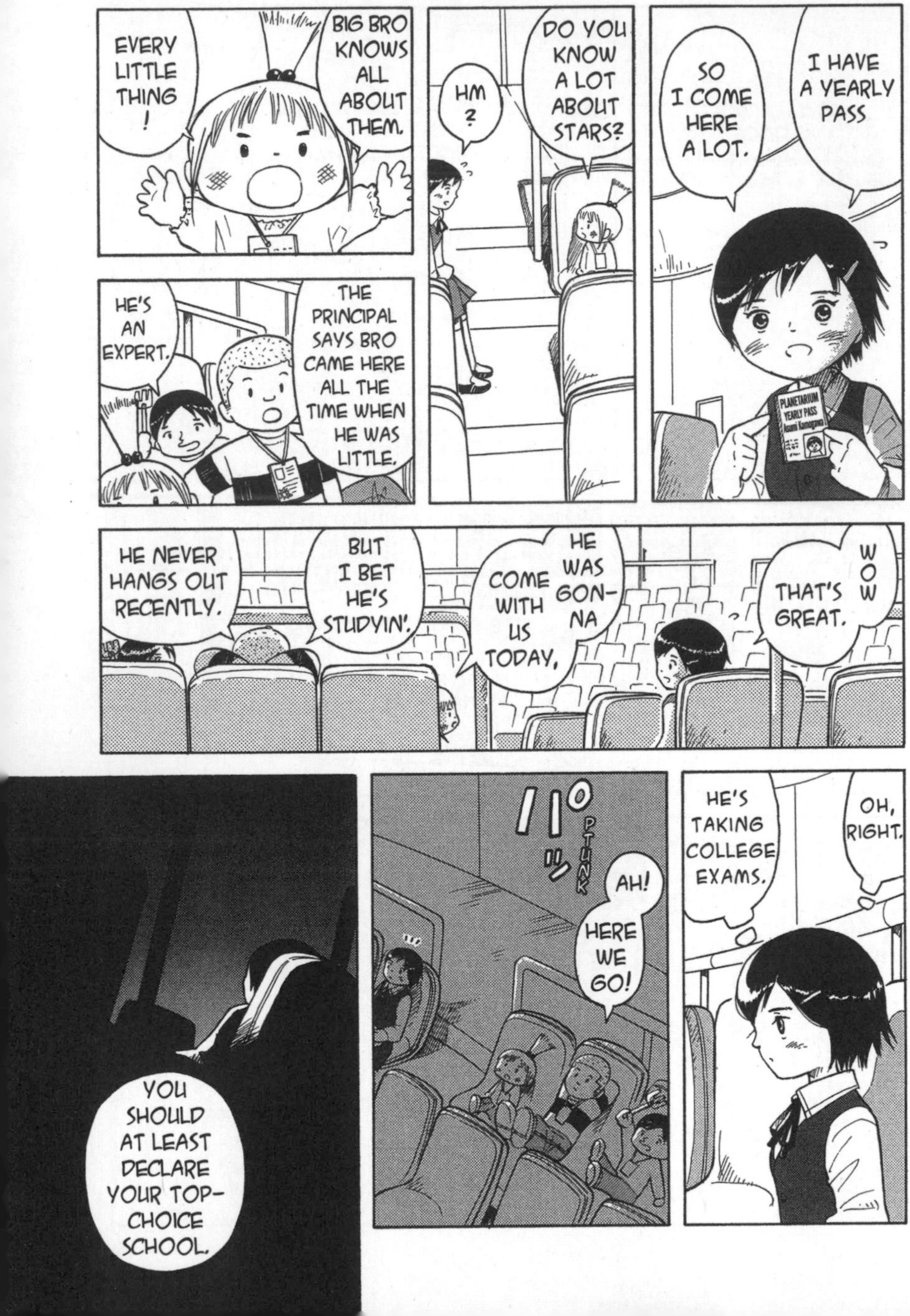
I HAVE A YEARLY PASS
SO I COME HERE A LOT.
PLANETARIUM YEARLY PASS Asumi Kamogawa
DO YOU KNOW A LOT ABOUT STARS?
HM?
BIG BRO KNOWS ALL ABOUT THEM.
EVERY LITTLE THING!
THE PRINCIPAL SAYS BRO CAME HERE ALL THE TIME WHEN HE WAS LITTLE.
HE'S AN EXPERT.
WOW
THAT'S GREAT.
HE WAS GON-NA
COME WITH US TODAY,
BUT I BET HE'S STUDYIN'.
HE NEVER HANGS OUT RECENTLY.
OH, RIGHT.
HE'S TAKING COLLEGE EXAMS.
パッ
PTUNK
AH!
HERE WE GO!
YOU SHOULD AT LEAST DECLARE YOUR TOP-CHOICE SCHOOL.

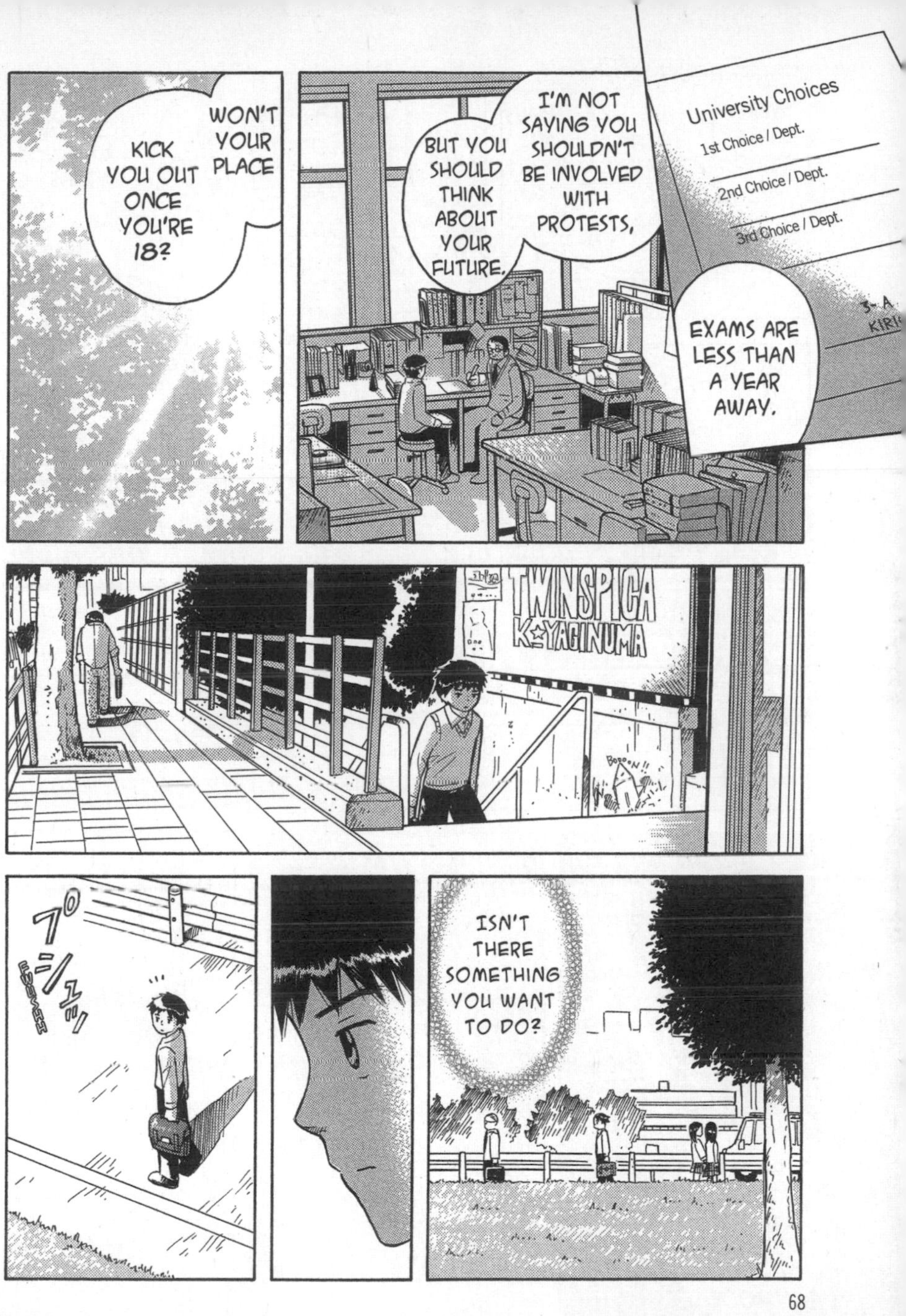
University Choices
1st Choice / Dept.
2nd Choice / Dept.
3rd Choice / Dept.
EXAMS ARE LESS THAN A YEAR AWAY.
I'M NOT SAYING YOU SHOULDN'T BE INVOLVED WITH PROTESTS,
BUT YOU SHOULD THINK ABOUT YOUR FUTURE.
WON'T YOUR PLACE
KICK YOU OUT ONCE YOU'RE 18?
TWINSPICA
K☆YAGINUMA
BOOOON!!
ISN'T THERE SOMETHING YOU WANT TO DO?

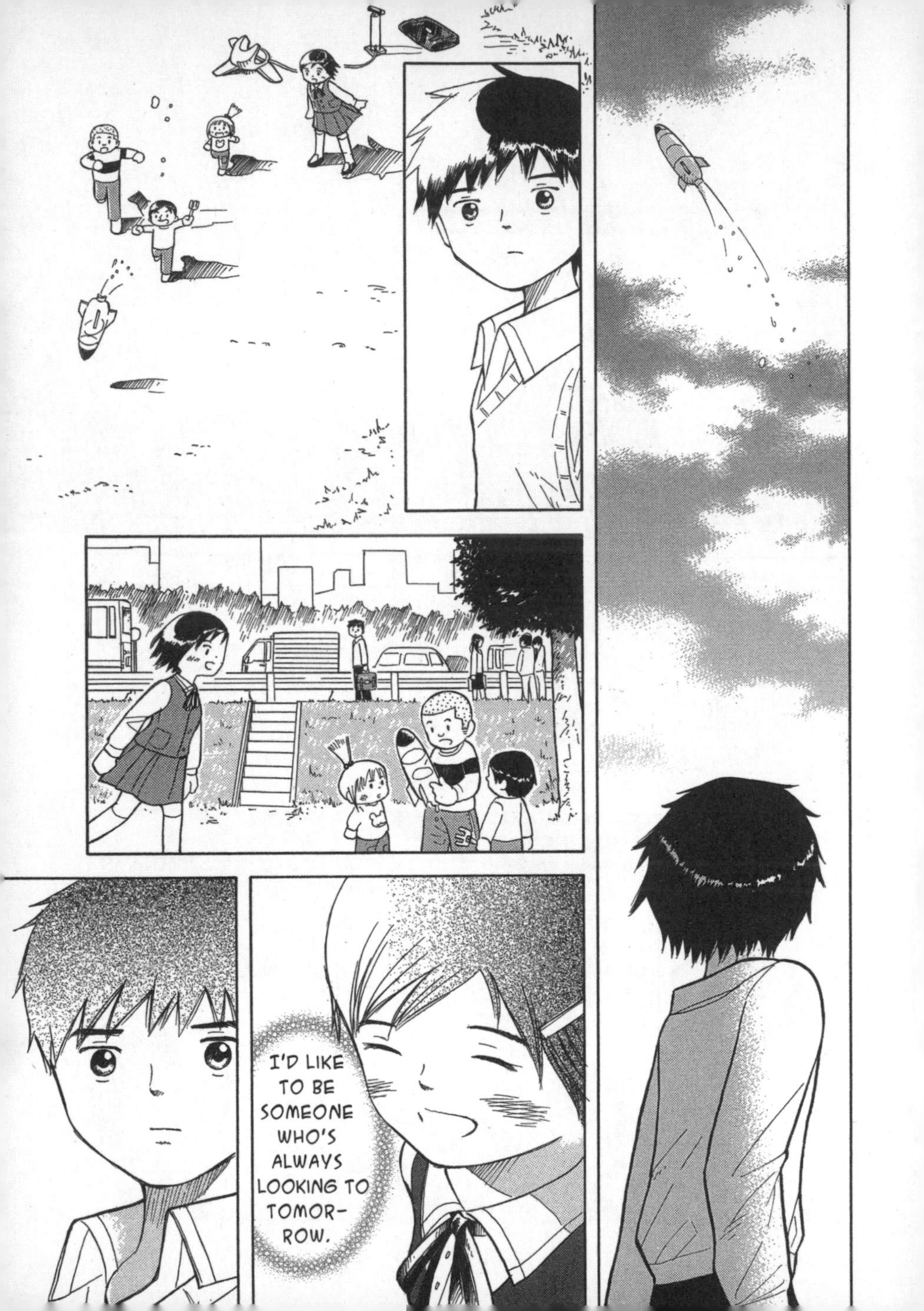
I'D LIKE TO BE SOMEONE WHO'S ALWAYS LOOKING TO TOMOR-ROW.

THE BRIGHT ONE THERE IS VENUS,
THE ONE DIAGONALLY ABOVE IT IS JUPITER.
THEY'RE JUST STARS?
I THOUGHT THEY WERE UFOS.
THEY'RE PLANETS, NOT STARS.
LIKE THE EARTH, THEY DON'T SHINE ON THEIR OWN.
JUPITER IS A GAS GIANT.
ISN'T THAT NEAT?
SO THAT ONE IS LIKE A BIG FART?
EWW, GROSS!
UH, NO,
THAT'S NOT WHAT I MEANT...
LONG BEFORE YOU, KENTA, SATOSHI, AND AKANE, WERE EVEN BORN,

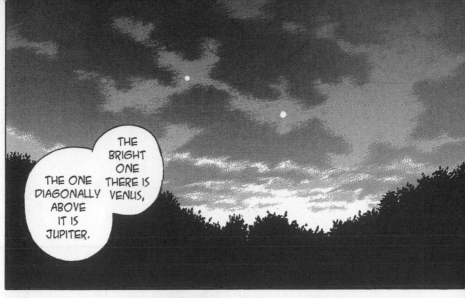

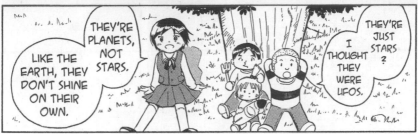

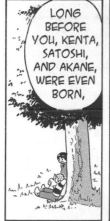

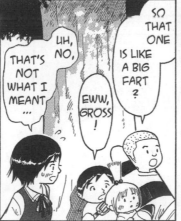

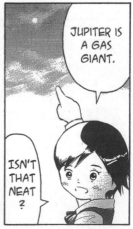

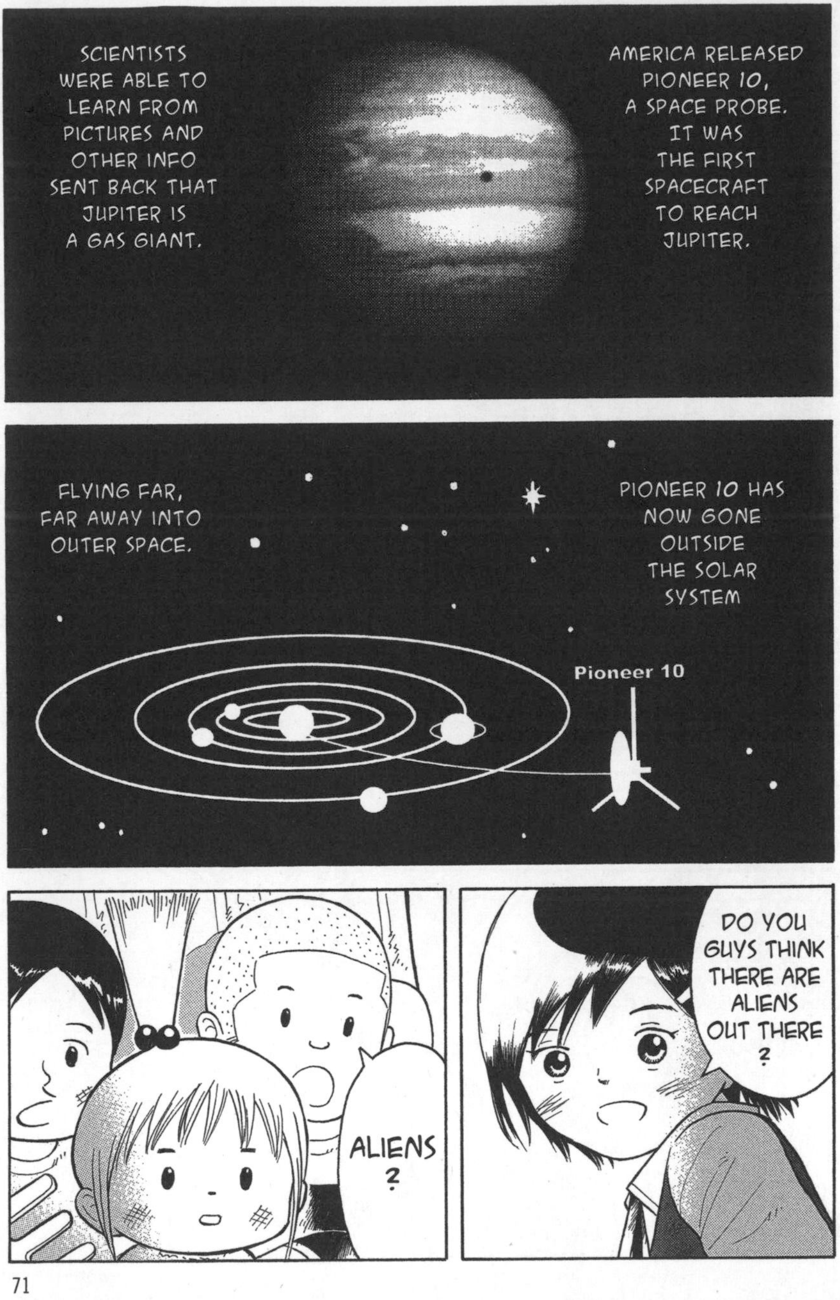
AMERICA RELEASED PIONEER 10, A SPACE PROBE. IT WAS THE FIRST SPACECRAFT TO REACH JUPITER.
SCIENTISTS WERE ABLE TO LEARN FROM PICTURES AND OTHER INFO SENT BACK THAT JUPITER IS A GAS GIANT.
PIONEER 10 HAS NOW GONE OUTSIDE THE SOLAR SYSTEM
FLYING FAR, FAR AWAY INTO OUTER SPACE.
Pioneer 10
DO YOU GUYS THINK THERE ARE ALIENS OUT THERE ?
ALIENS ?

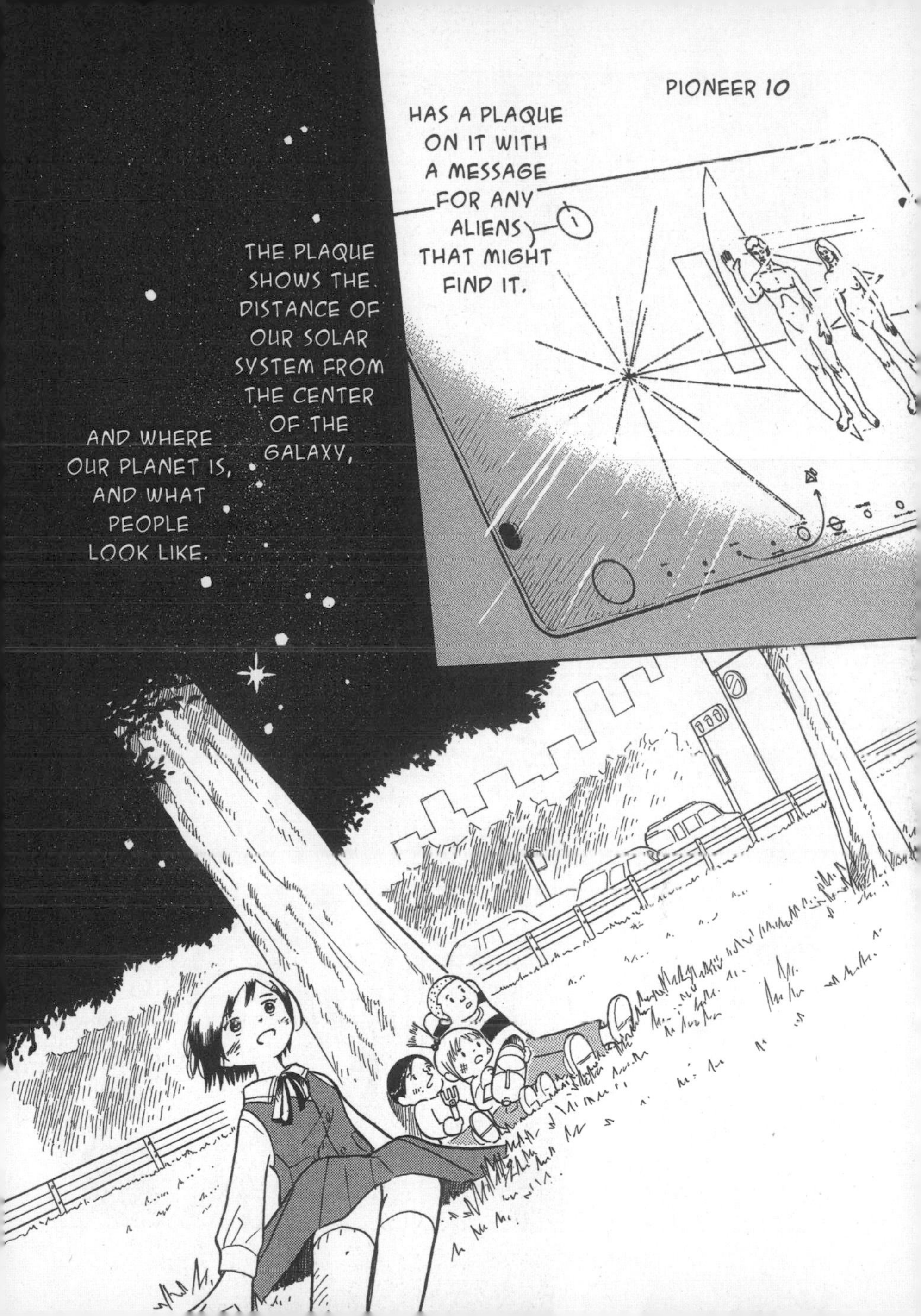
PIONEER 10
HAS A PLAQUE ON IT WITH A MESSAGE FOR ANY ALIENS THAT MIGHT FIND IT.
THE PLAQUE SHOWS THE DISTANCE OF OUR SOLAR SYSTEM FROM THE CENTER OF THE GALAXY,
AND WHERE OUR PLANET IS, AND WHAT PEOPLE LOOK LIKE.

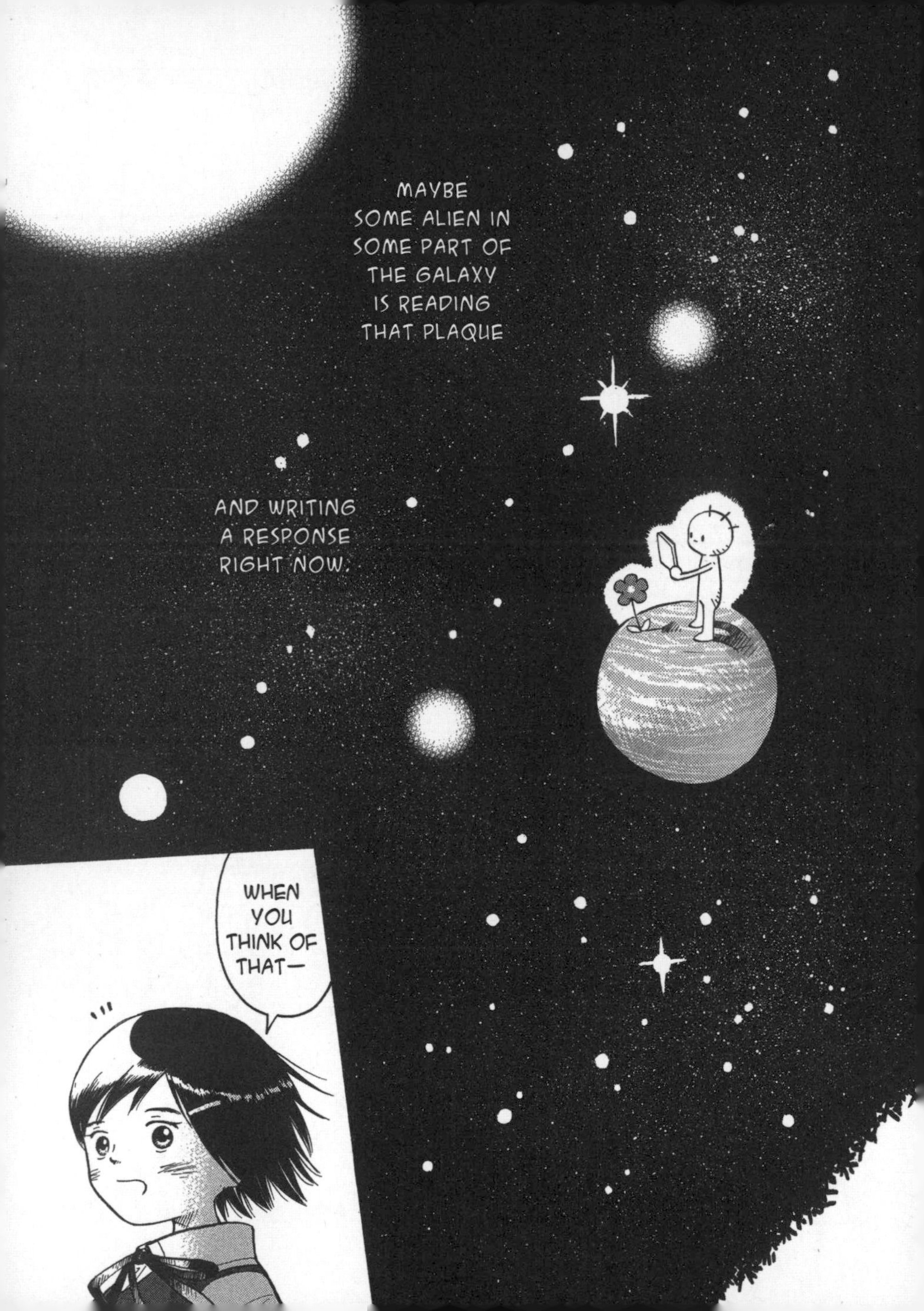
MAYBE SOME ALIEN IN SOME PART OF THE GALAXY IS READING THAT PLAQUE
AND WRITING A RESPONSE RIGHT NOW.
WHEN YOU THINK OF THAT—

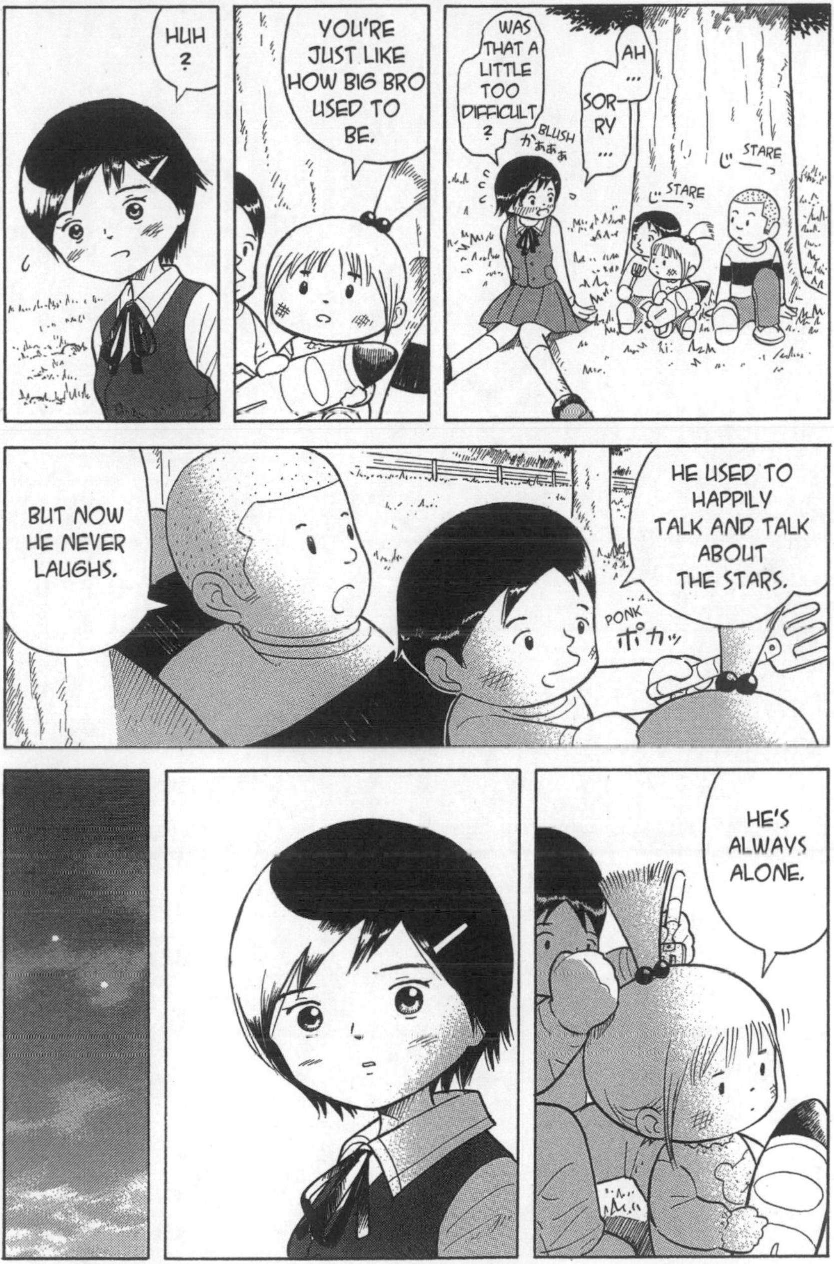

AH ... SORRY ...
WAS THAT A LITTLE TOO DIFFICULT?
BLUSH かあぁぁ
STARE じーっ
STARE じーっ
YOU'RE JUST LIKE HOW BIG BRO USED TO BE.
HUH?
HE USED TO HAPPILY TALK AND TALK ABOUT THE STARS.
PONK ポカッ
BUT NOW HE NEVER LAUGHS.
HE'S ALWAYS ALONE.

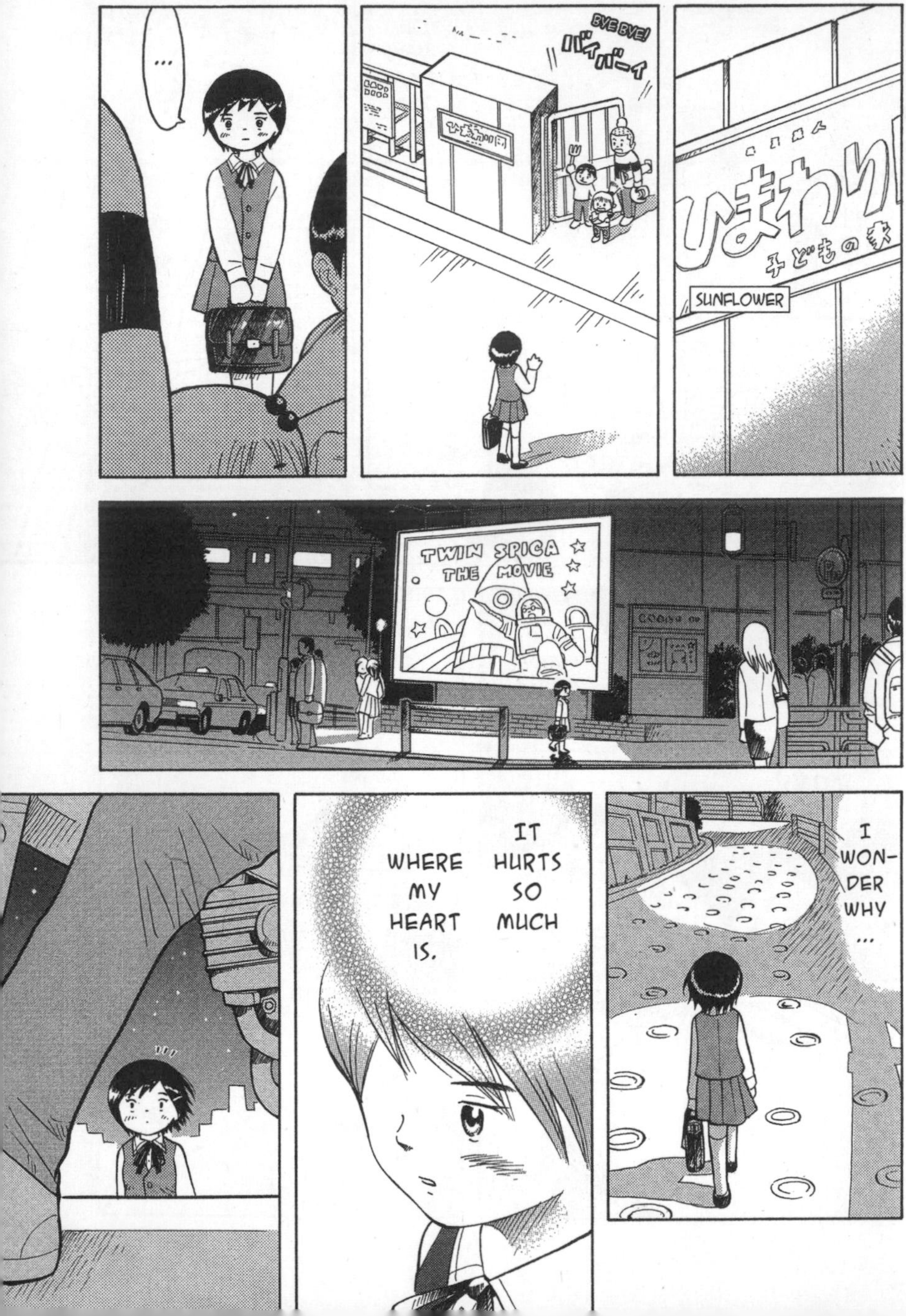
ひまわり
子どもの
SUNFLOWER
BYE BYE!
バイバーイ
...
TWIN SPICA THE MOVIE
I WONDER WHY...
IT HURTS SO MUCH
WHERE MY HEART IS.

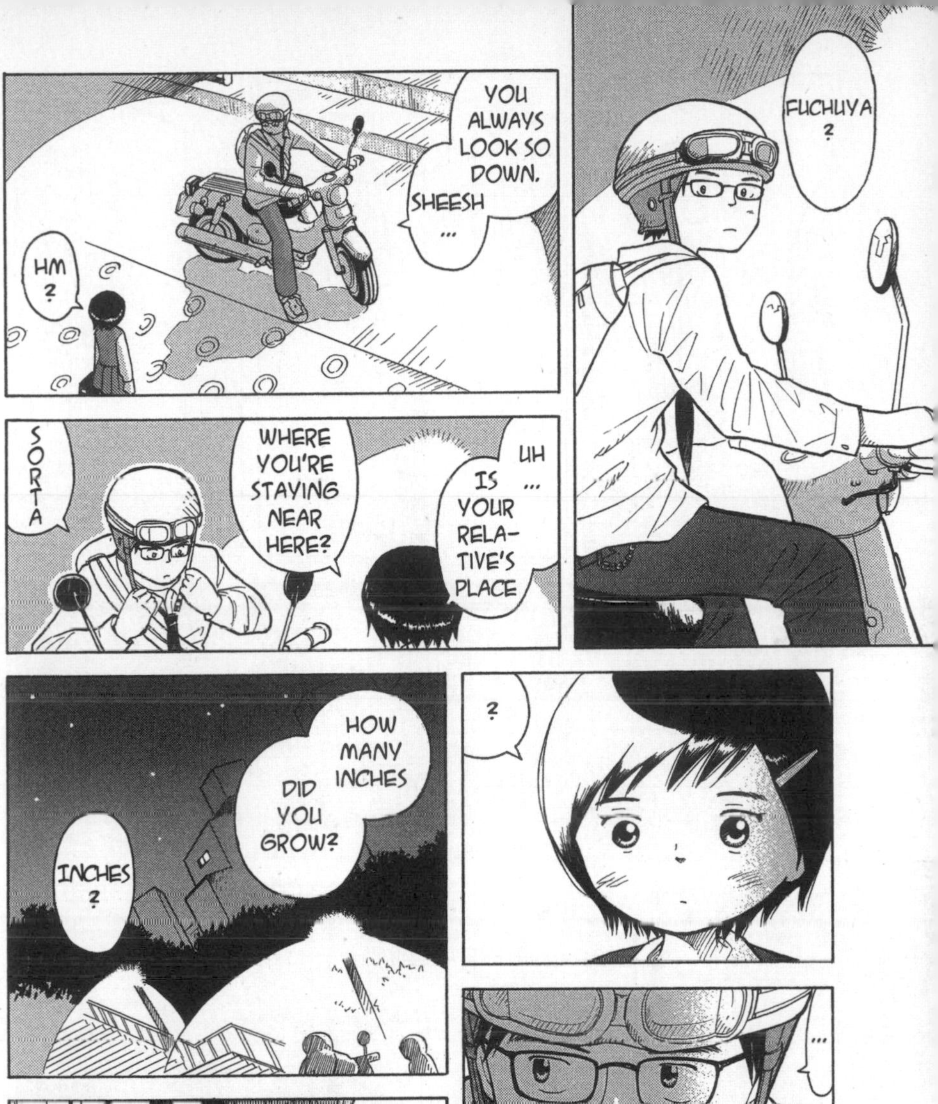
FUCHUYA ?
YOU ALWAYS LOOK SO DOWN.
SHEESH ...
HM ?
UH ... IS YOUR RELATIVE'S PLACE
WHERE YOU'RE STAYING NEAR HERE?
SORTA
?
HOW MANY INCHES DID YOU GROW?
INCHES ?
...
カチッ
KLIK
YOUR HEIGHT.

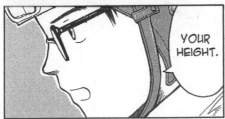

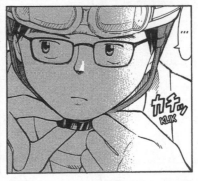

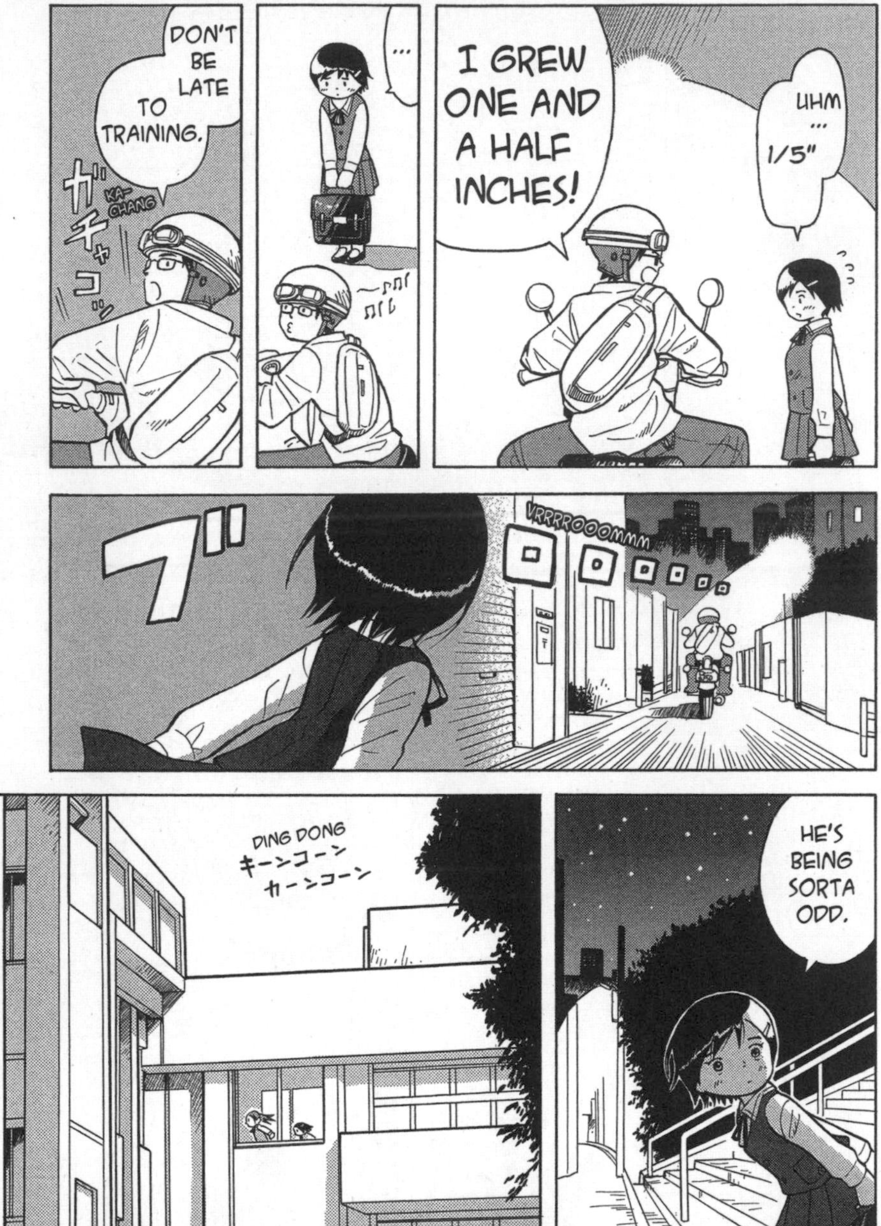
UHM ... 1/5"
I GREW ONE AND A HALF INCHES!
...
DON'T BE LATE TO TRAINING.
KA-CHANG
VRRRROOOOMMM
HE'S BEING SORTA ODD.
DING DONG
キーンコーン
カーンコーン

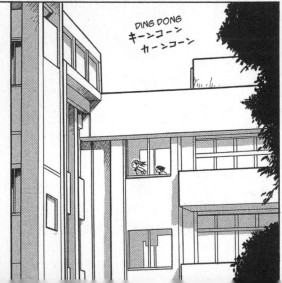

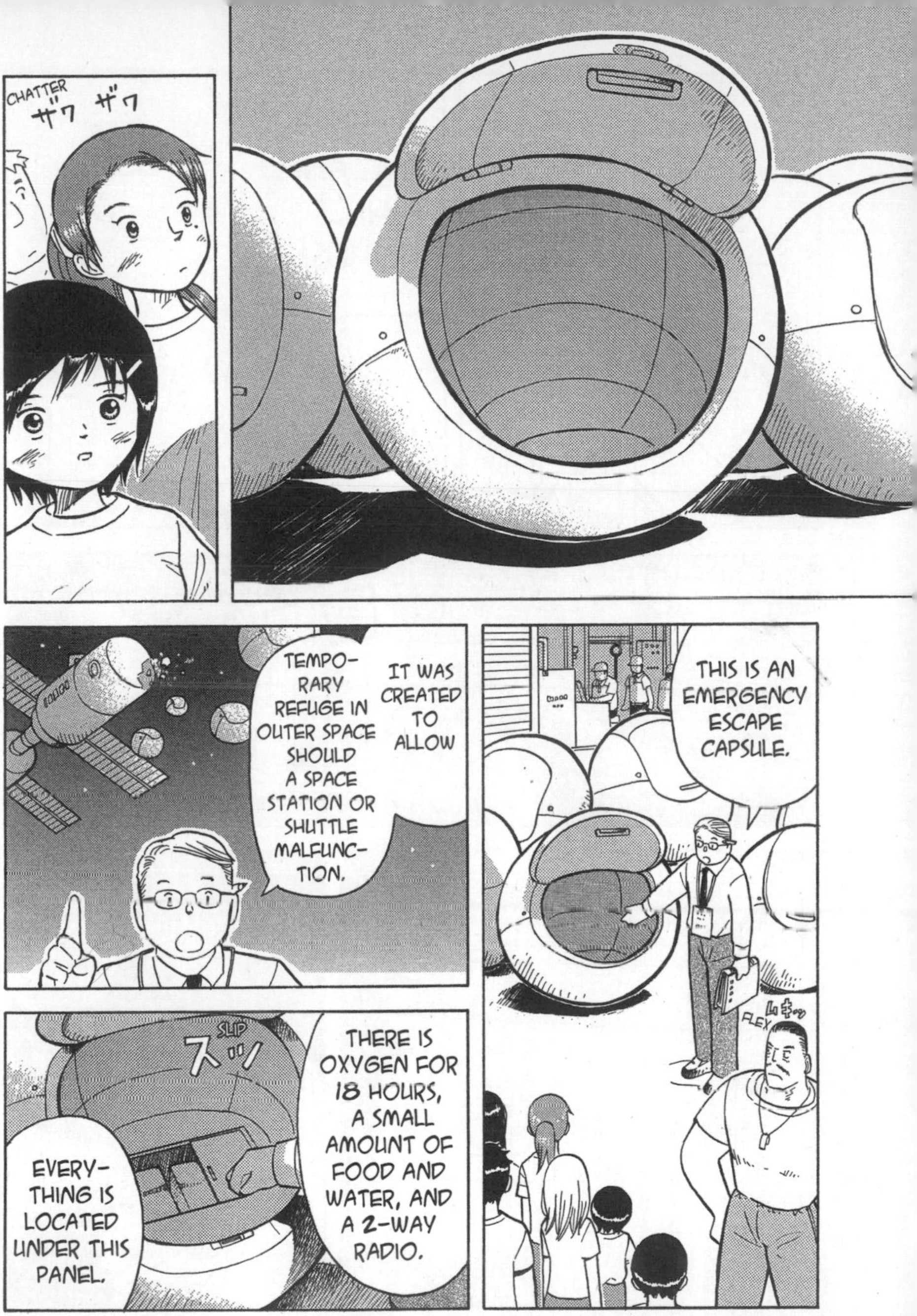
CHATTER
ザワ ザワ
THIS IS AN EMERGENCY ESCAPE CAPSULE.
FLEX
ムキッ
IT WAS CREATED TO ALLOW
TEMPORARY REFUGE IN OUTER SPACE SHOULD A SPACE STATION OR SHUTTLE MALFUNCTION.
SLIP
スッ
THERE IS OXYGEN FOR 18 HOURS, A SMALL AMOUNT OF FOOD AND WATER, AND A 2-WAY RADIO.
EVERYTHING IS LOCATED UNDER THIS PANEL.

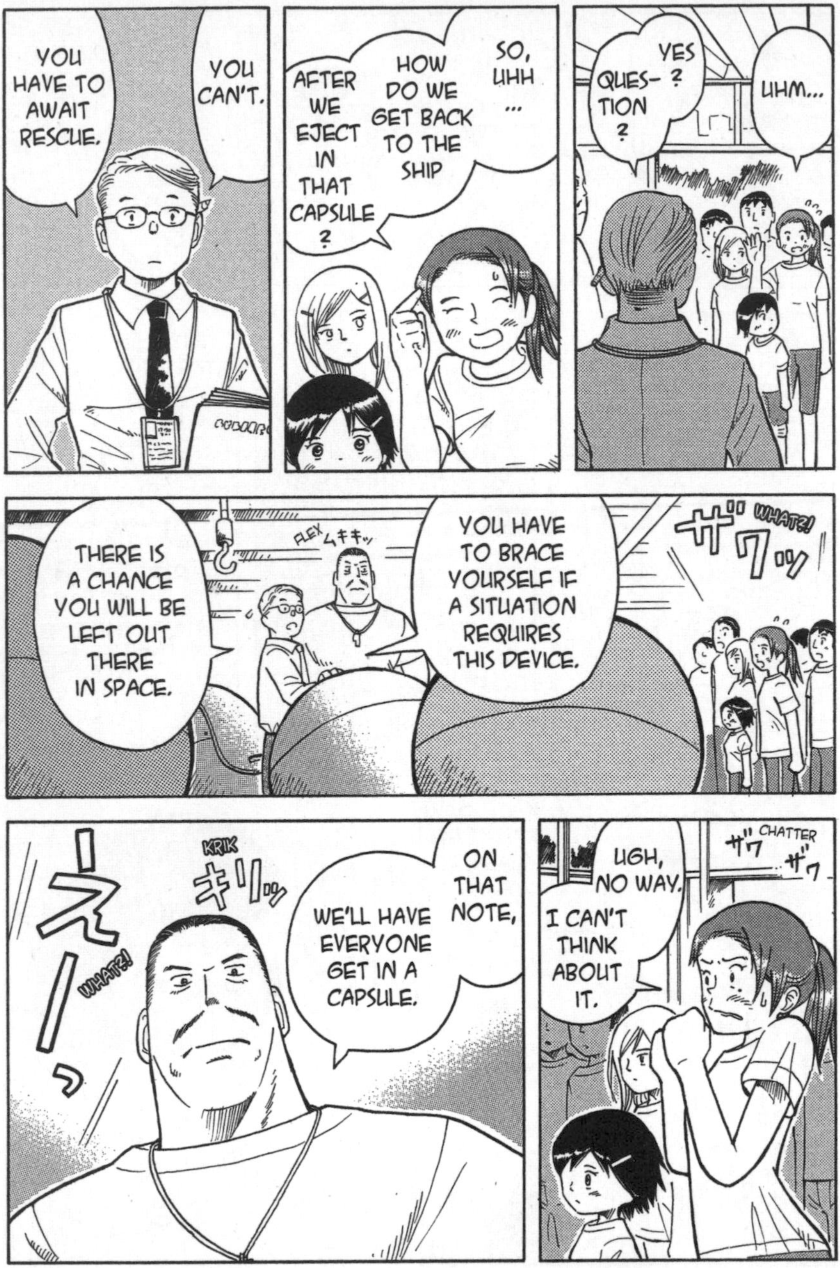
UHM...
YES? QUESTION?
SO, UHH ...
HOW DO WE GET BACK TO THE SHIP AFTER WE EJECT IN THAT CAPSULE?
YOU CAN'T.
YOU HAVE TO AWAIT RESCUE.
ザワッ WHAT?!
YOU HAVE TO BRACE YOURSELF IF A SITUATION REQUIRES THIS DEVICE.
FLEX ムキキッ
THERE IS A CHANCE YOU WILL BE LEFT OUT THERE IN SPACE.
ザワ ザワ CHATTER
UGH, NO WAY.
I CAN'T THINK ABOUT IT.
ON THAT NOTE,
WE'LL HAVE EVERYONE GET IN A CAPSULE.
KRIK キリッ
えーっ WHAT?!

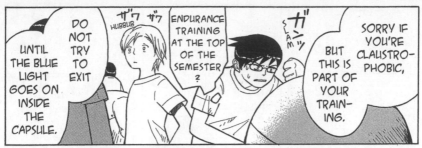

SORRY IF YOU'RE CLAUSTRO-PHOBIC,
BUT THIS IS PART OF YOUR TRAIN-ING.
ガン SLAM ッ
ENDURANCE TRAINING AT THE TOP OF THE SEMESTER?
ザワ ザワ HUBBUB
DO NOT TRY TO EXIT
UNTIL THE BLUE LIGHT GOES ON INSIDE THE CAPSULE.
HEY, WAIT.
PUT THESE ON BEFORE YOU GO INSIDE.
DO NOT DROP OR LOSE THIS
UNTIL THE END OF THE EXERCISE.
BUT
IT'S SO TINY.
WHAT'S THIS?
I WON-DER IF IT'S ...
KAMOGAWA WON'T FEEL CLAUSTRO-PHOBIC AT ALL.
HUH?
HAH HAH!

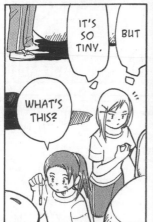

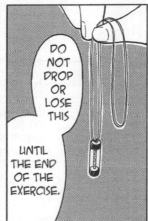

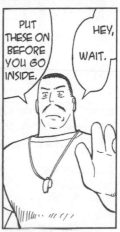

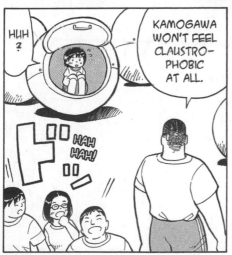

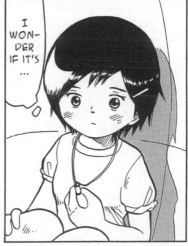

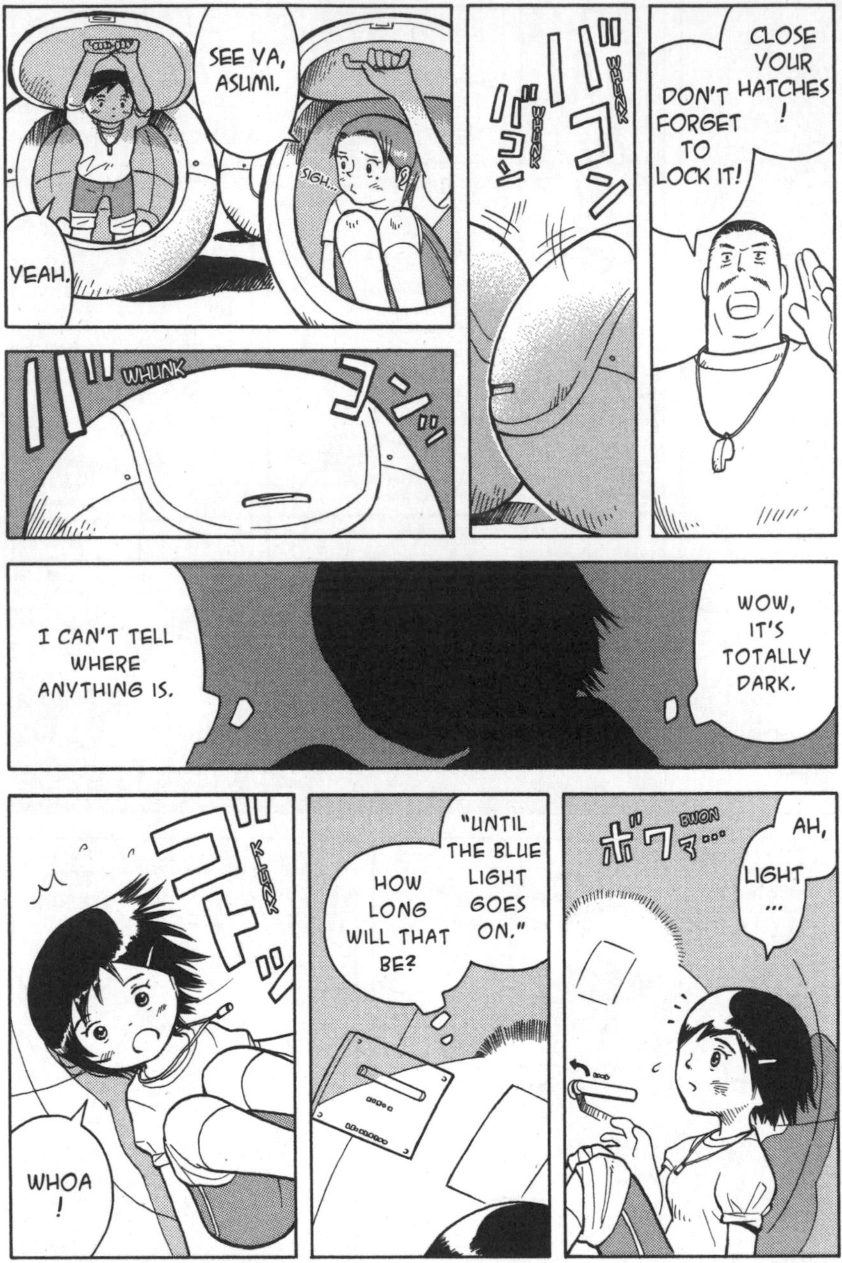
CLOSE YOUR HATCHES!
DON'T FORGET TO LOCK IT!
WHUNK
WHUNK
SEE YA, ASUMI.
SIGH...
YEAH.
WHUNK
WOW, IT'S TOTALLY DARK.
I CAN'T TELL WHERE ANYTHING IS.
BWON
AH, LIGHT...
"UNTIL THE BLUE LIGHT GOES ON."
HOW LONG WILL THAT BE?
KLUNK
WHOA!

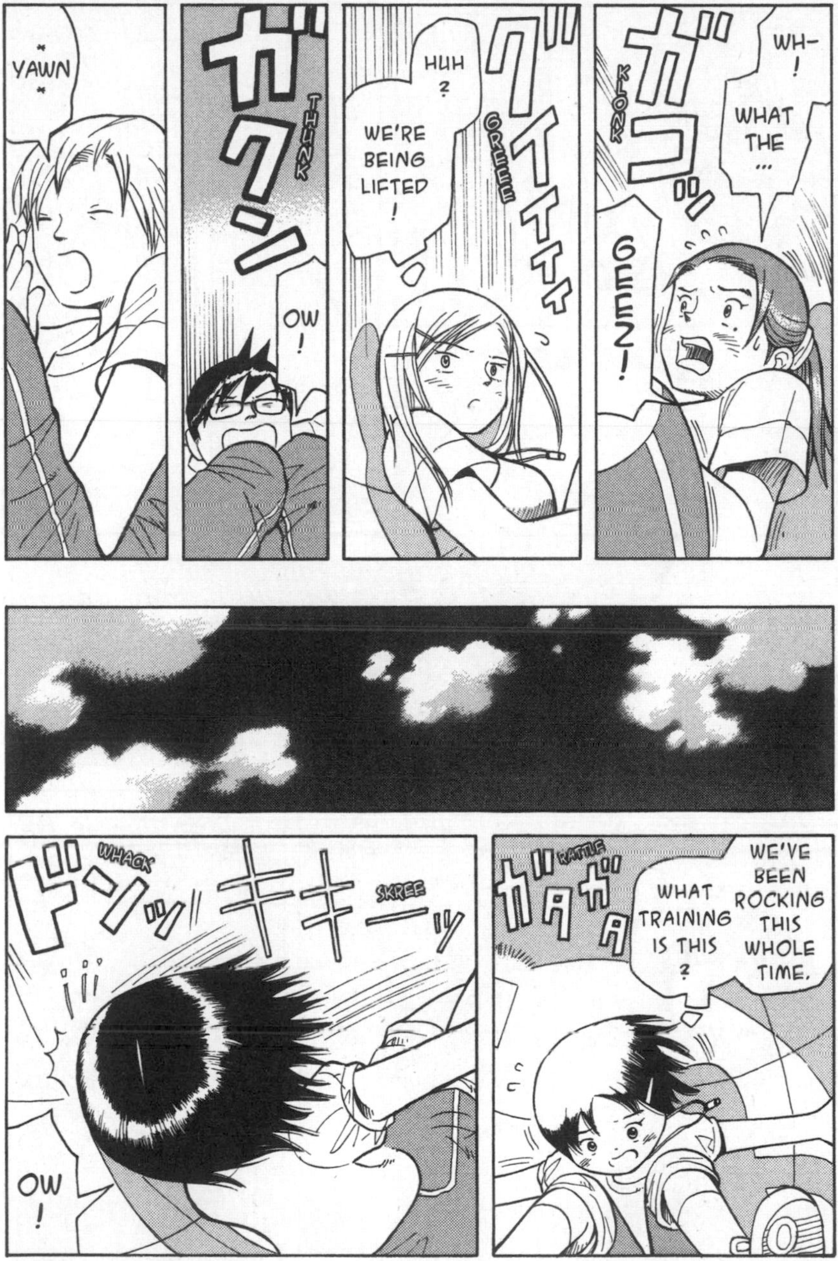
WH-! WHAT THE ....
KLONK
GEEZ!
GREEE
HUH? WE'RE BEING LIFTED!
THUNK
OW!
* YAWN *
RATTLE
WE'VE BEEN ROCKING THIS WHOLE TIME.
WHAT TRAINING IS THIS?
SKREE
WHACK
OW!

...

I FEEL SICK.

IT'S STOPPED.

ZZZ

ガクーン!!

THUNK

!!

HOW MUCH LONGER?

THE BLUE LIGHT'S STILL NOT ON.

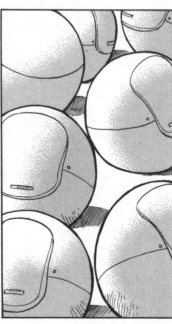

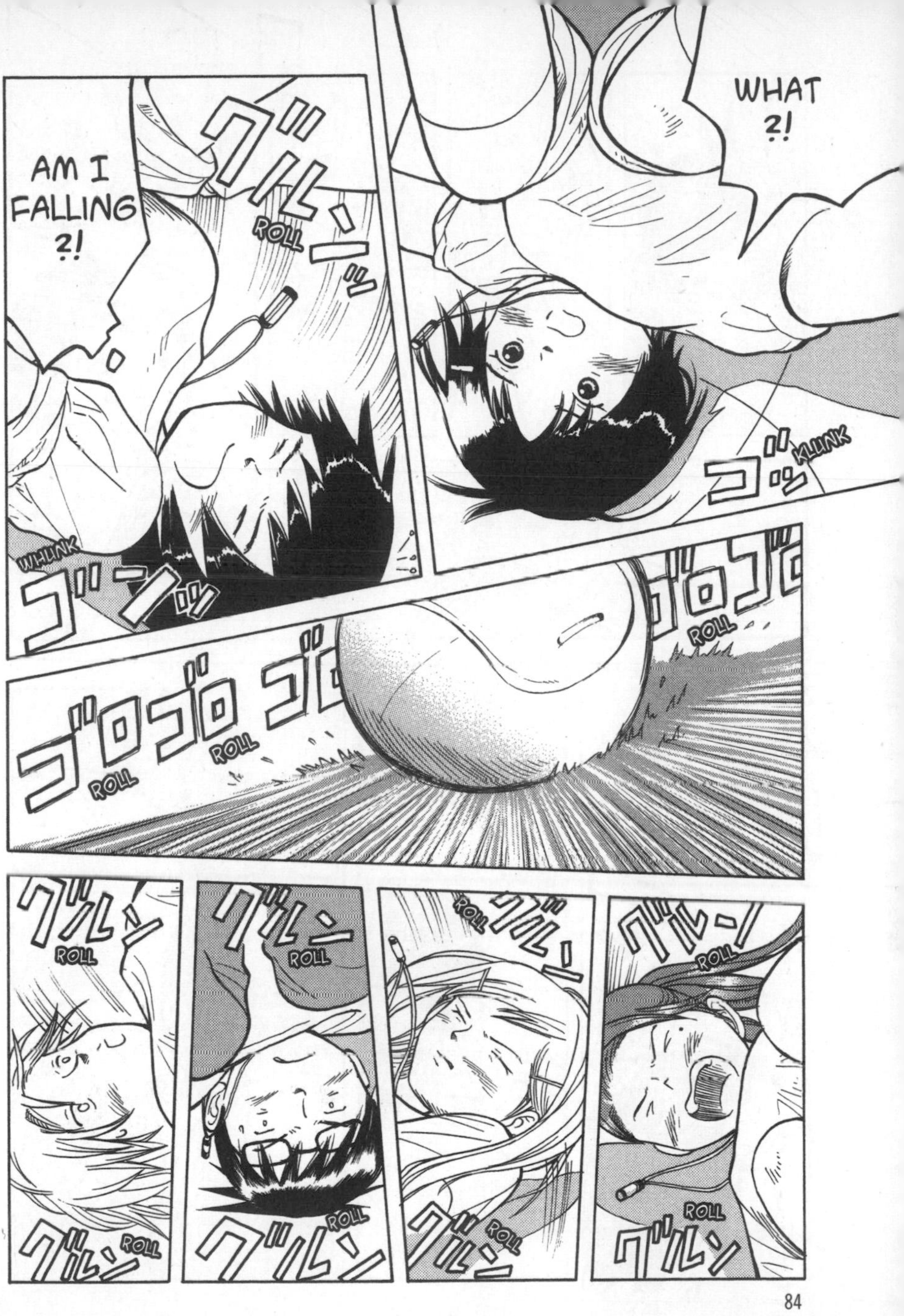
WHAT ?!
KLUNK
AM I FALLING ?!
ROLL
WHUNK
ROLL
ROLL
ROLL
ROLL
ROLL
ROLL
ROLL
ROLL
ROLL
ROLL
ROLL
ROLL

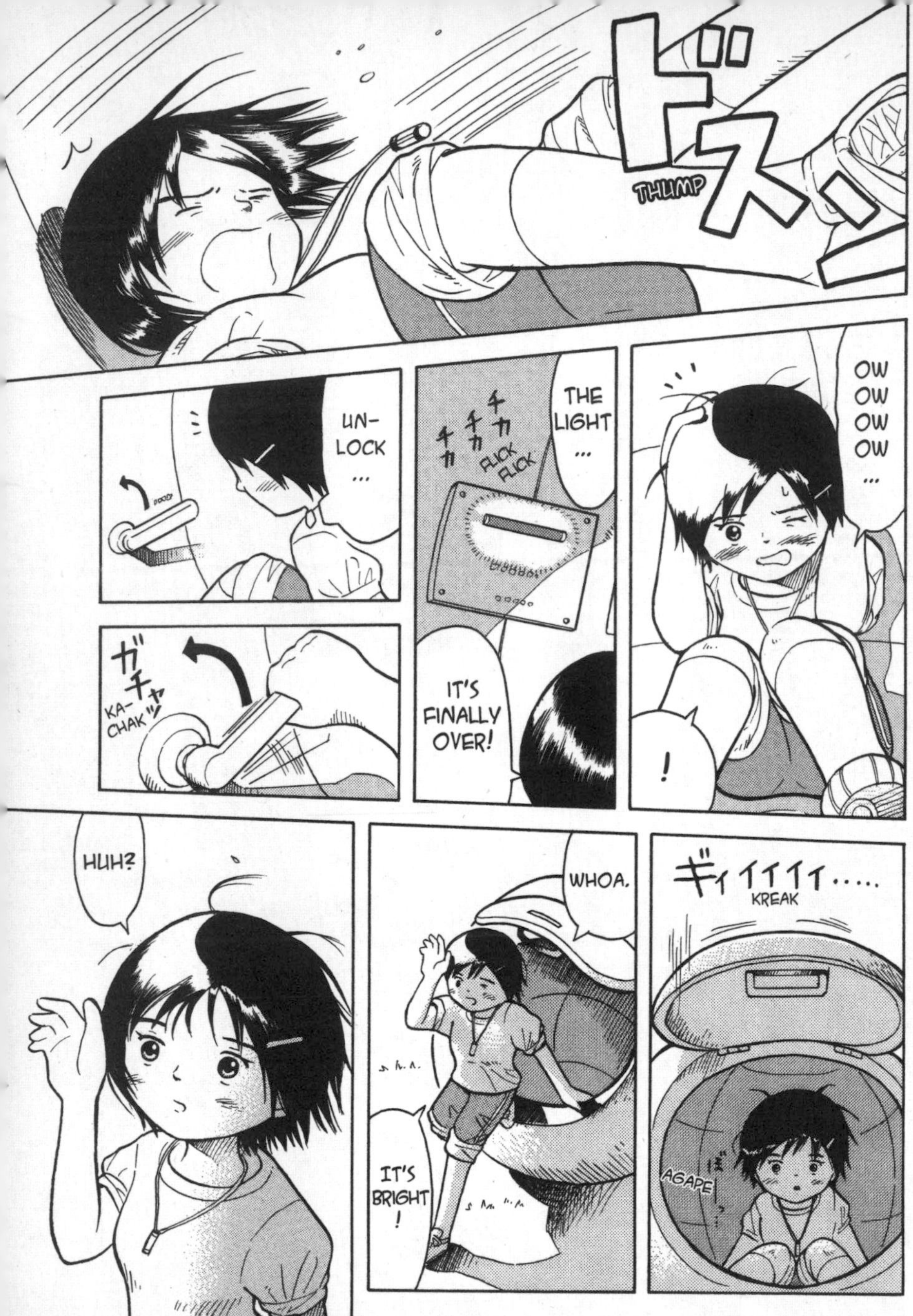

ドスン
THUMP
OW OW OW OW ...
!
チカチカ
FLICK FLICK
THE LIGHT ...
IT'S FINALLY OVER!
UN-LOCK ...
ガチャッ
KA-CHAK
ギィイイイイ.....
KREAK
AGAPE
WHOA.
IT'S BRIGHT!
HUH?

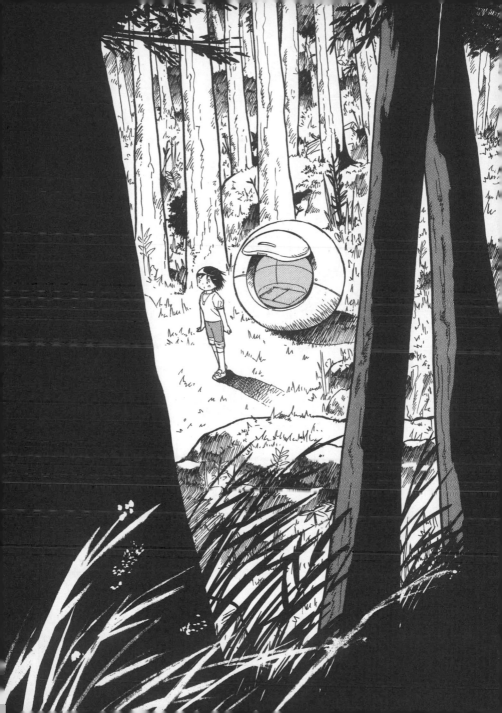

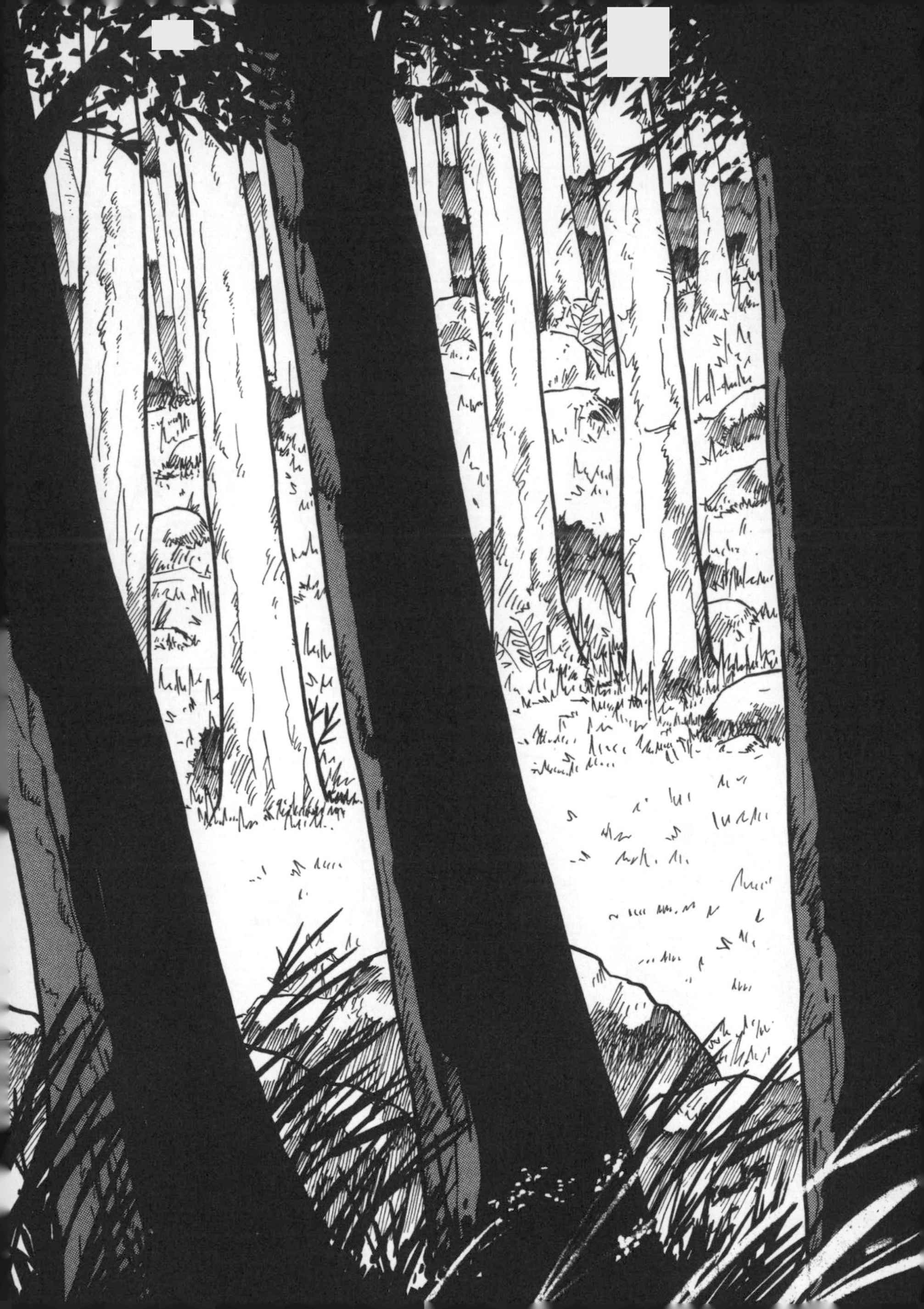

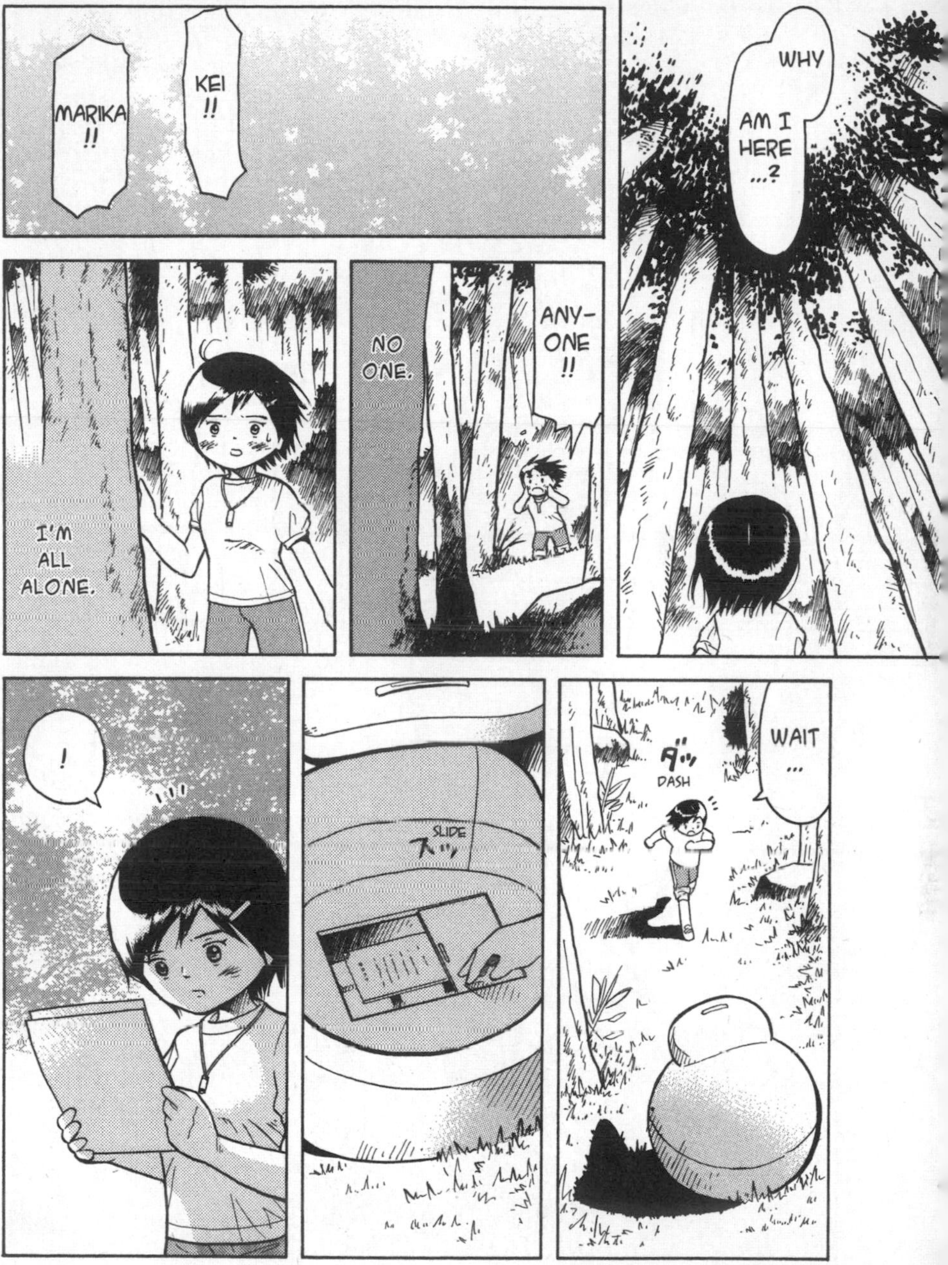

WHY AM I HERE ...?
KEI !!
MARIKA !!
ANY-ONE !!
NO ONE.
I'M ALL ALONE.
WAIT ...
ダッ
DASH
スッ
SLIDE
!

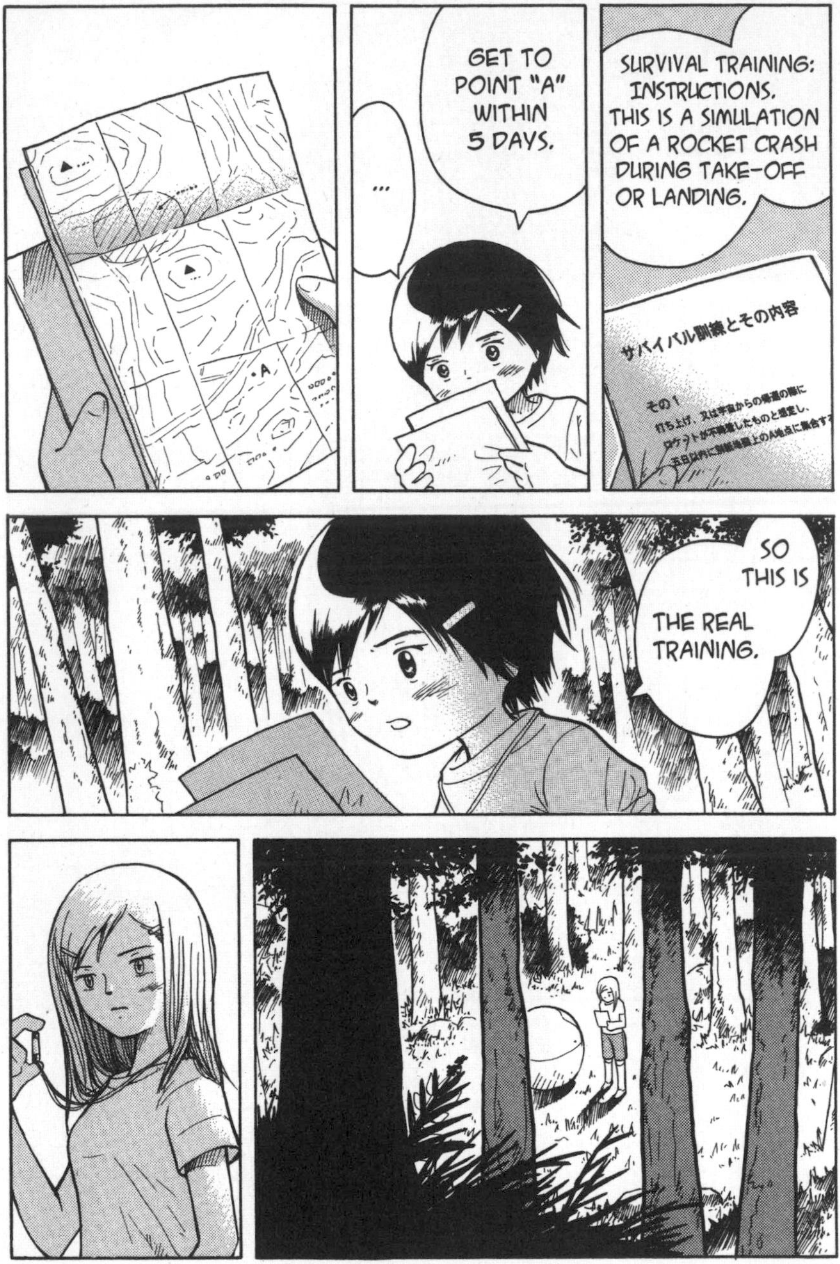
SURVIVAL TRAINING: INSTRUCTIONS. THIS IS A SIMULATION OF A ROCKET CRASH DURING TAKE-OFF OR LANDING.
サバイバル訓練とその内容
その1
打ち上げ、又は宇宙からの帰還の際に
ロケットが不時着したものと想定し、
五日以内に訓練地図上のA地点に集合す
GET TO POINT "A" WITHIN 5 DAYS.
...
SO THIS IS THE REAL TRAINING.

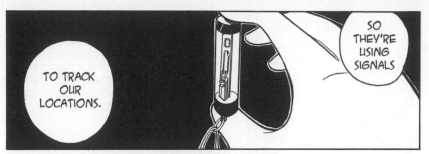

SO THEY'RE USING SIGNALS

TO TRACK OUR LOCATIONS.

THIS ISN'T JUST AN EXERCISE.

FROM HERE ON

THEY'RE LOOKING TO WEED PEOPLE OUT.

I HAVE TO GET TO THE GOAL FIRST.

ゴホッ
ゴホッ KOFF
ゴホッ KOFF

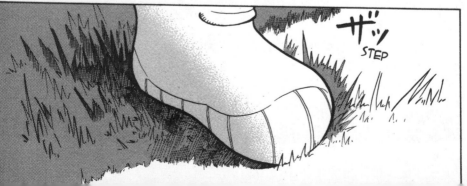

ザッ
STEP

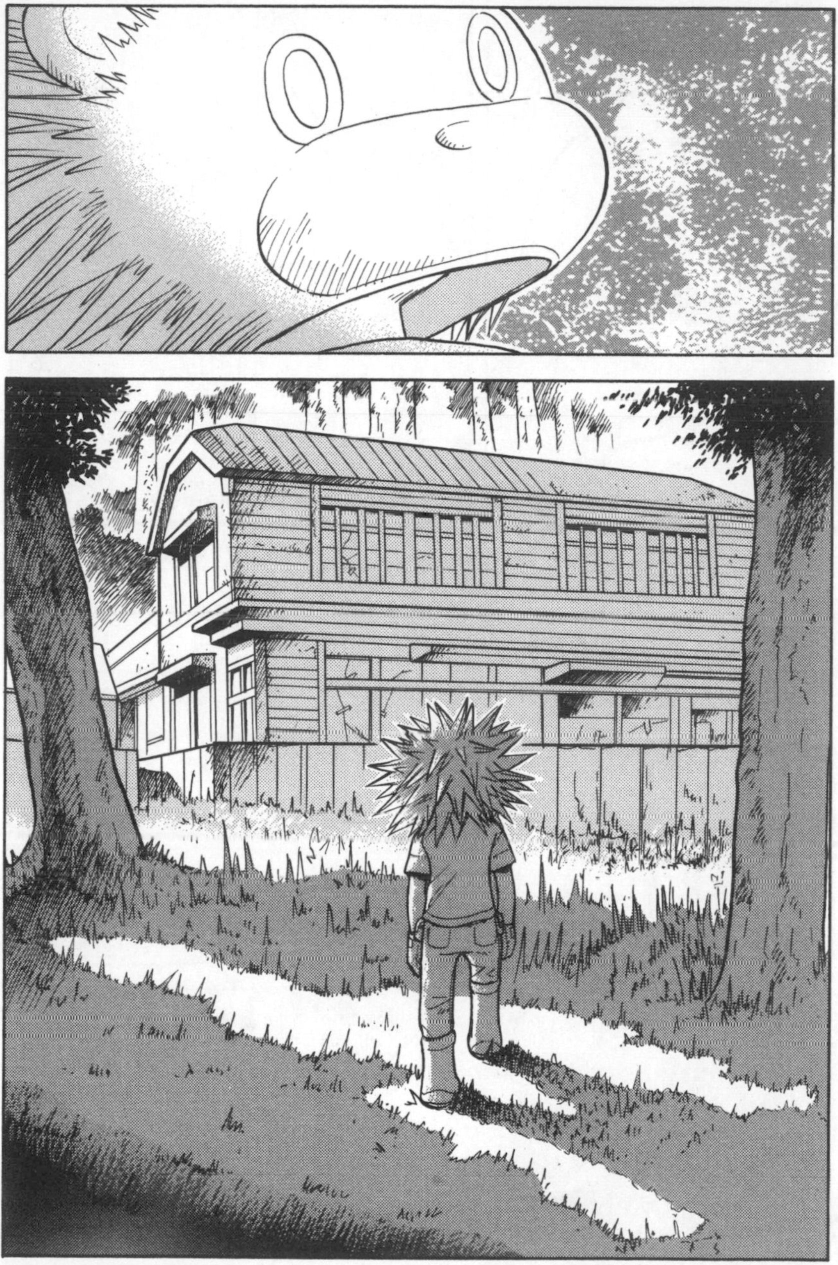

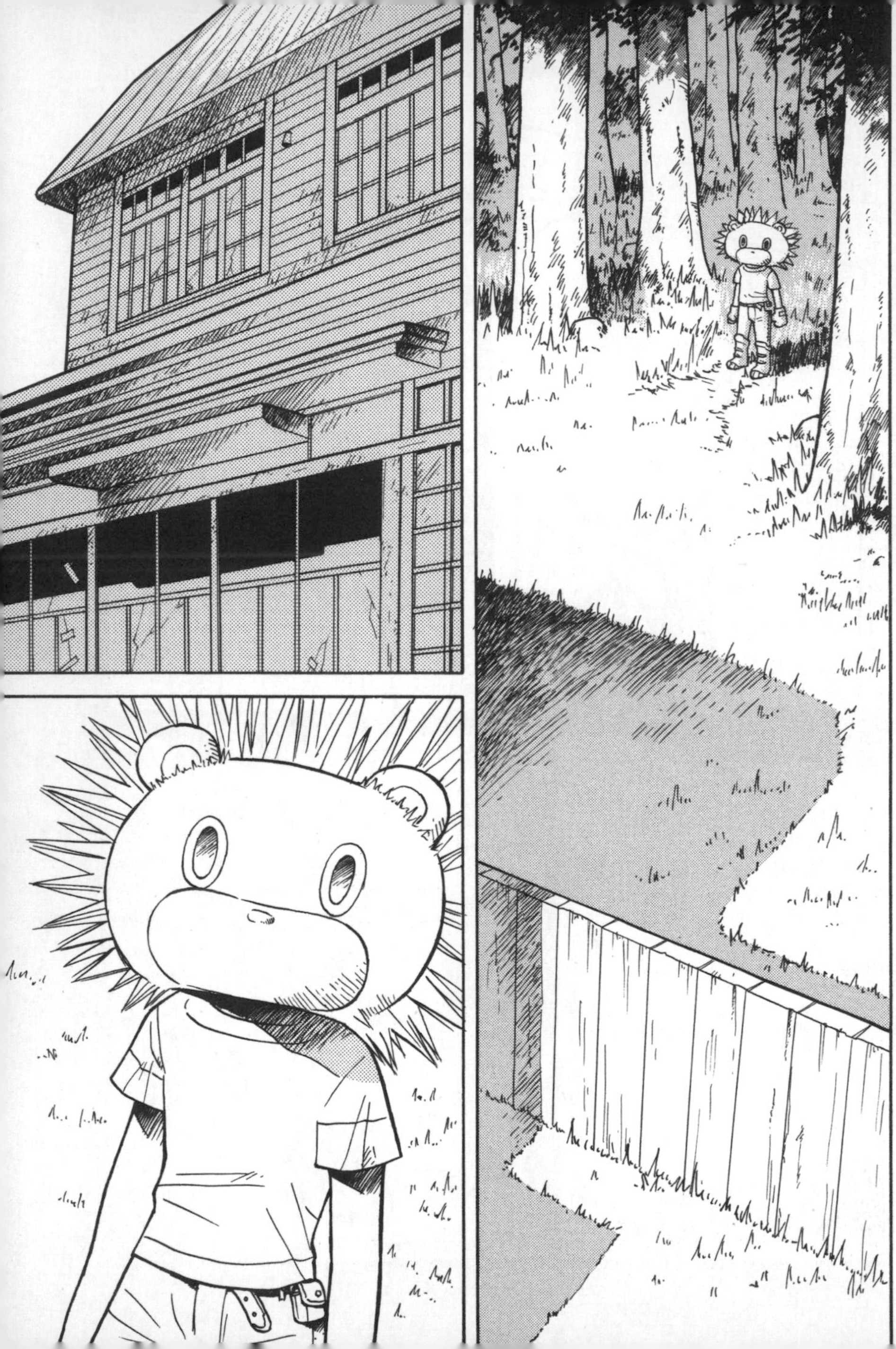

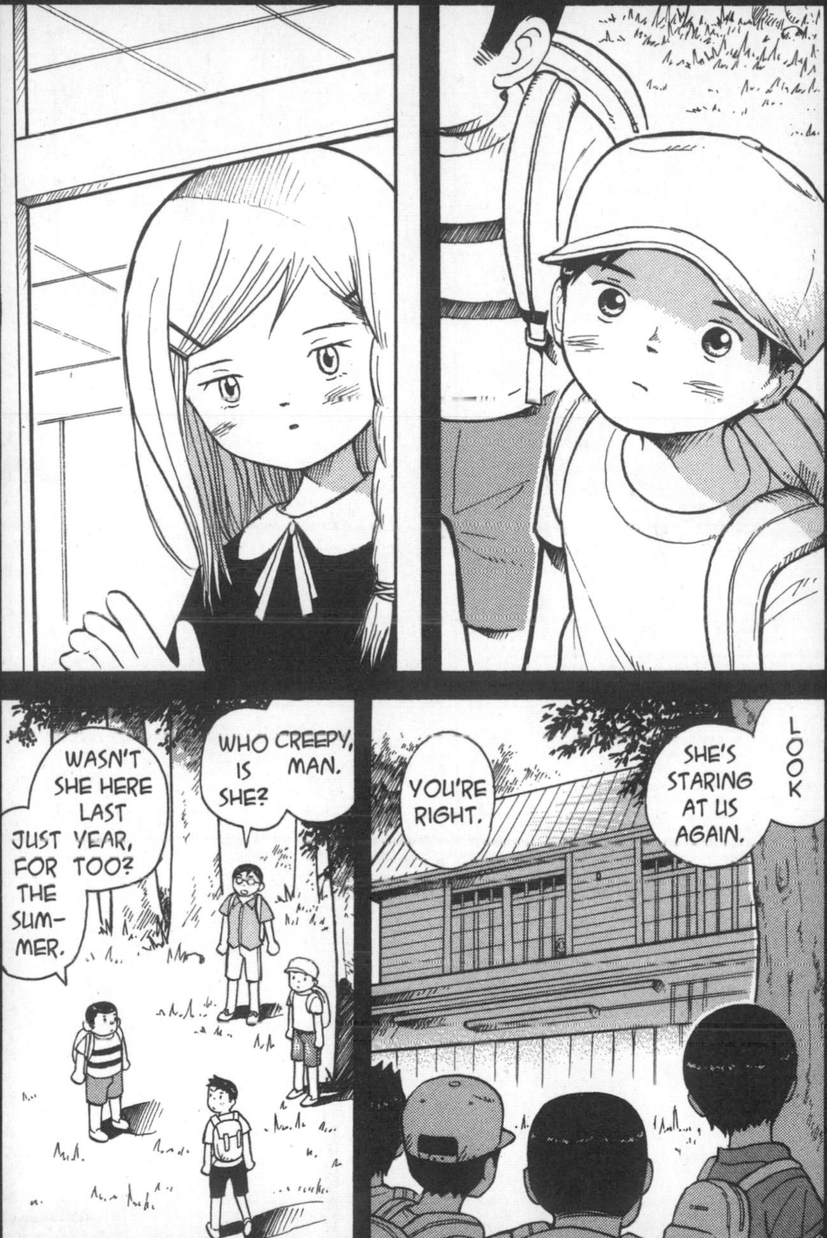
LOOK
SHE'S STARING AT US AGAIN.
YOU'RE RIGHT.
CREEPY, MAN.
WHO IS SHE?
WASN'T SHE HERE LAST YEAR, TOO?
JUST FOR THE SUMMER.

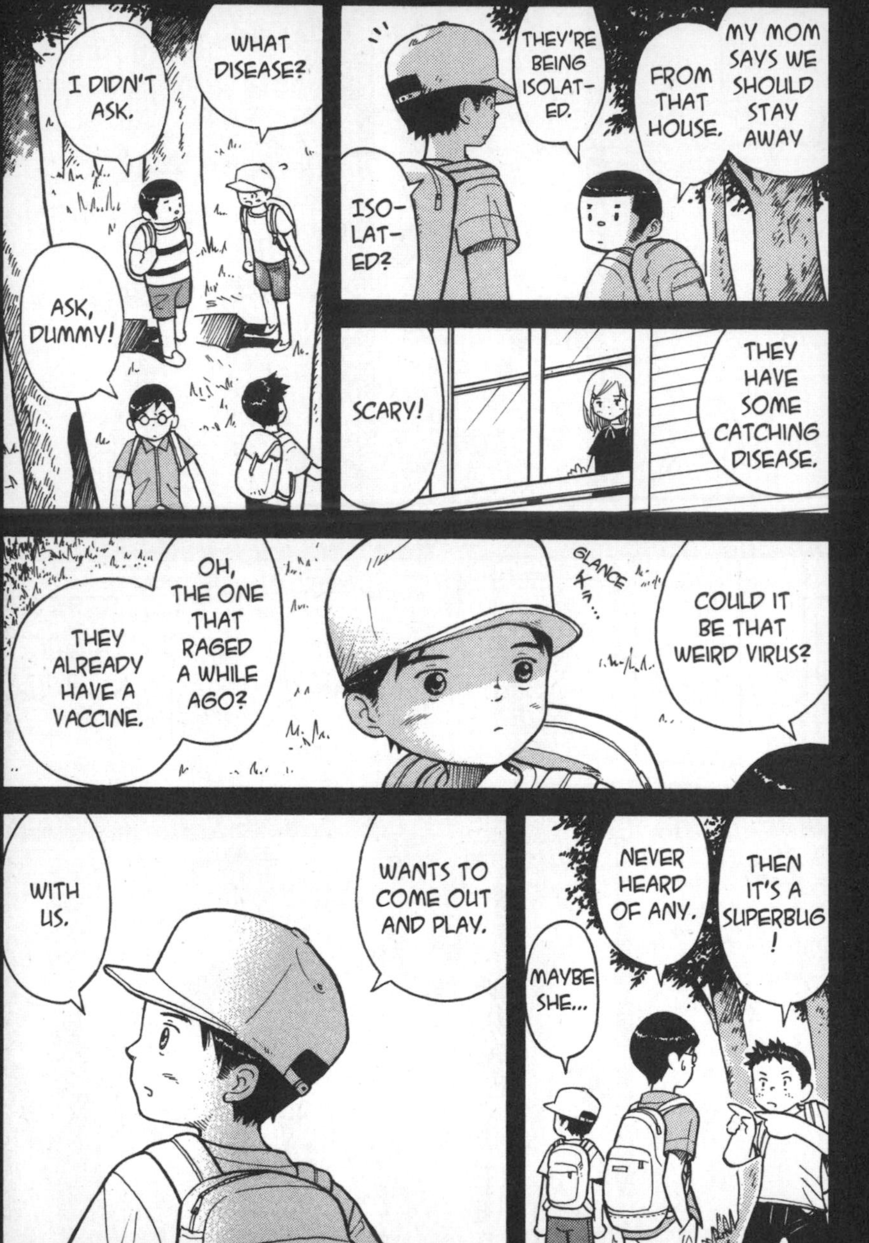
MY MOM SAYS WE SHOULD STAY AWAY
FROM THAT HOUSE.
THEY'RE BEING ISOLAT-ED.
ISO-LAT-ED?
THEY HAVE SOME CATCHING DISEASE.
SCARY!
WHAT DISEASE?
I DIDN'T ASK.
ASK, DUMMY!
COULD IT BE THAT WEIRD VIRUS?
GLANCE
OH, THE ONE THAT RAGED A WHILE AGO?
THEY ALREADY HAVE A VACCINE.
THEN IT'S A SUPERBUG!
NEVER HEARD OF ANY.
MAYBE SHE...
WANTS TO COME OUT AND PLAY.
WITH US.

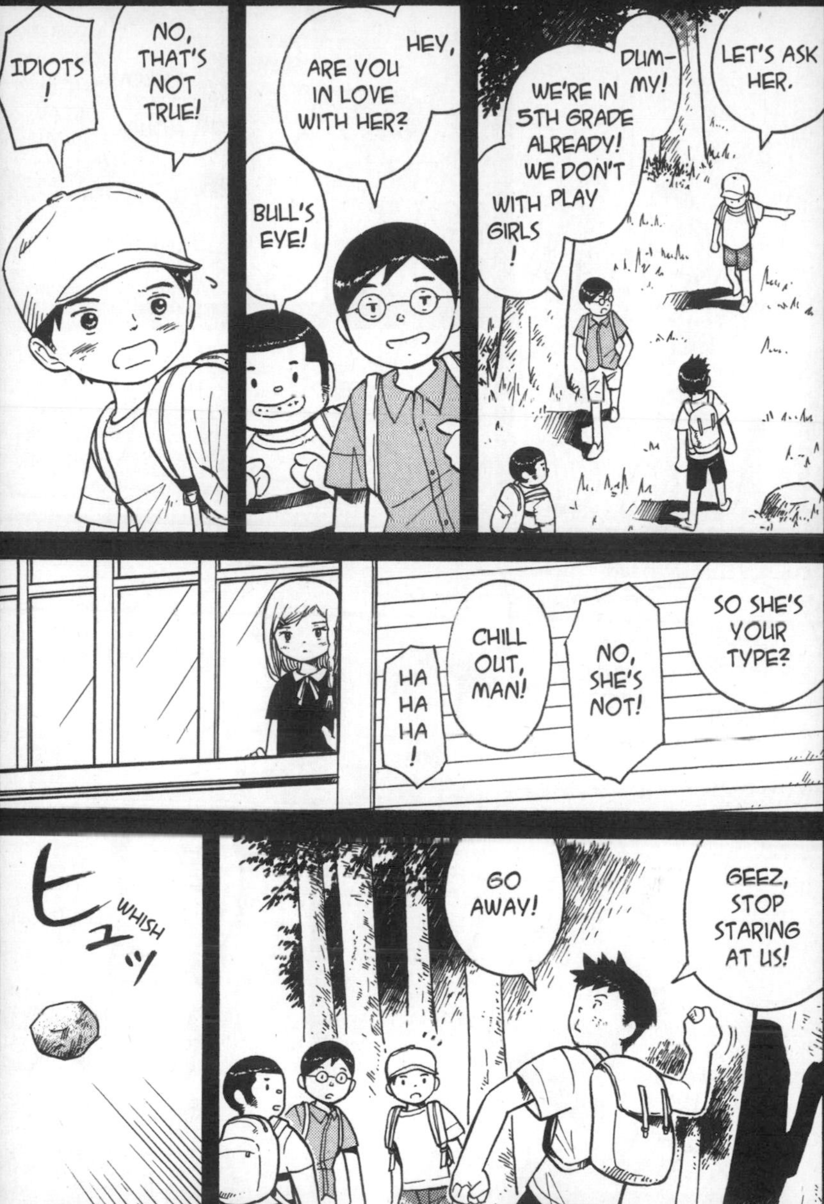
LET'S ASK HER.
DUM-MY!
WE'RE IN 5TH GRADE ALREADY! WE DON'T PLAY WITH GIRLS!
HEY, ARE YOU IN LOVE WITH HER?
BULL'S EYE!
NO, THAT'S NOT TRUE!
IDIOTS!
SO SHE'S YOUR TYPE?
NO, SHE'S NOT!
CHILL OUT, MAN!
HA HA HA!
GEEZ, STOP STARING AT US!
GO AWAY!
ヒュッ
WHISH

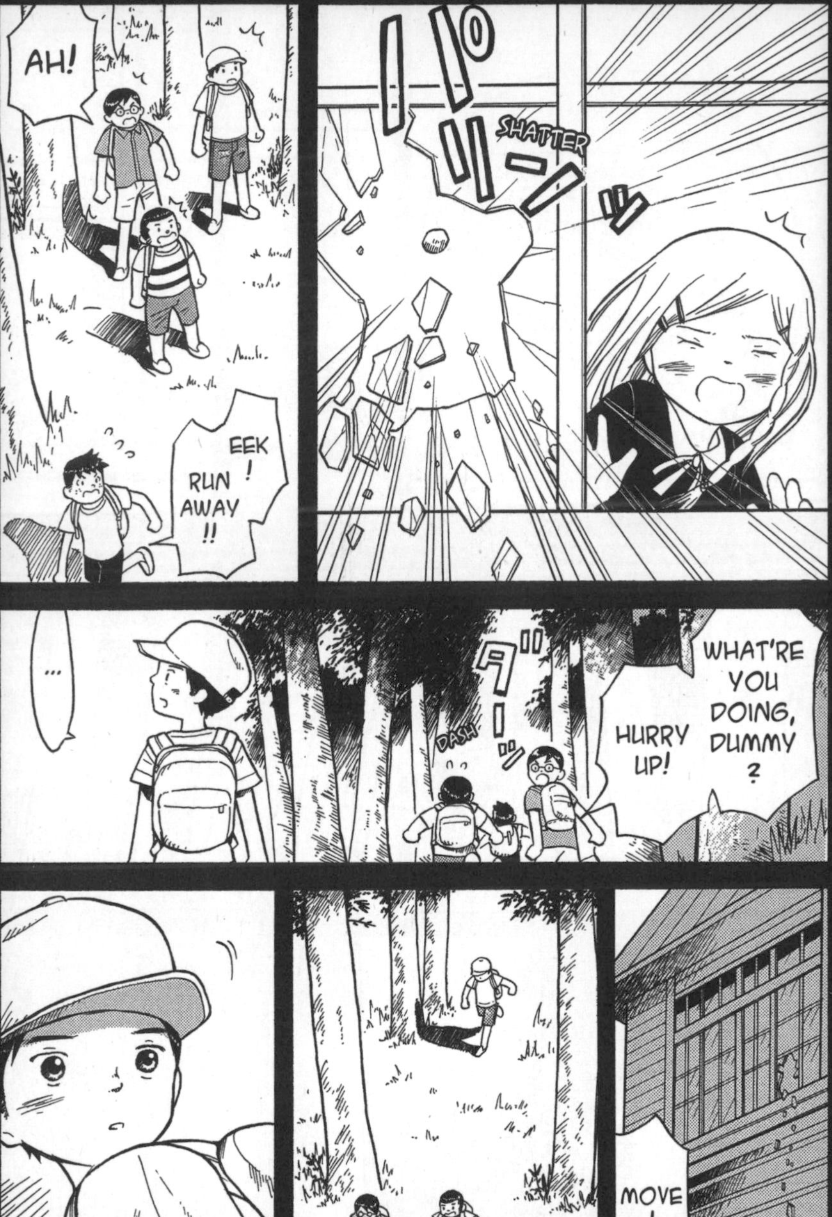
SHATTER
AH!
EEK! RUN AWAY!!
WHAT'RE YOU DOING, DUMMY?
HURRY UP!
DASH
...
MOVE!

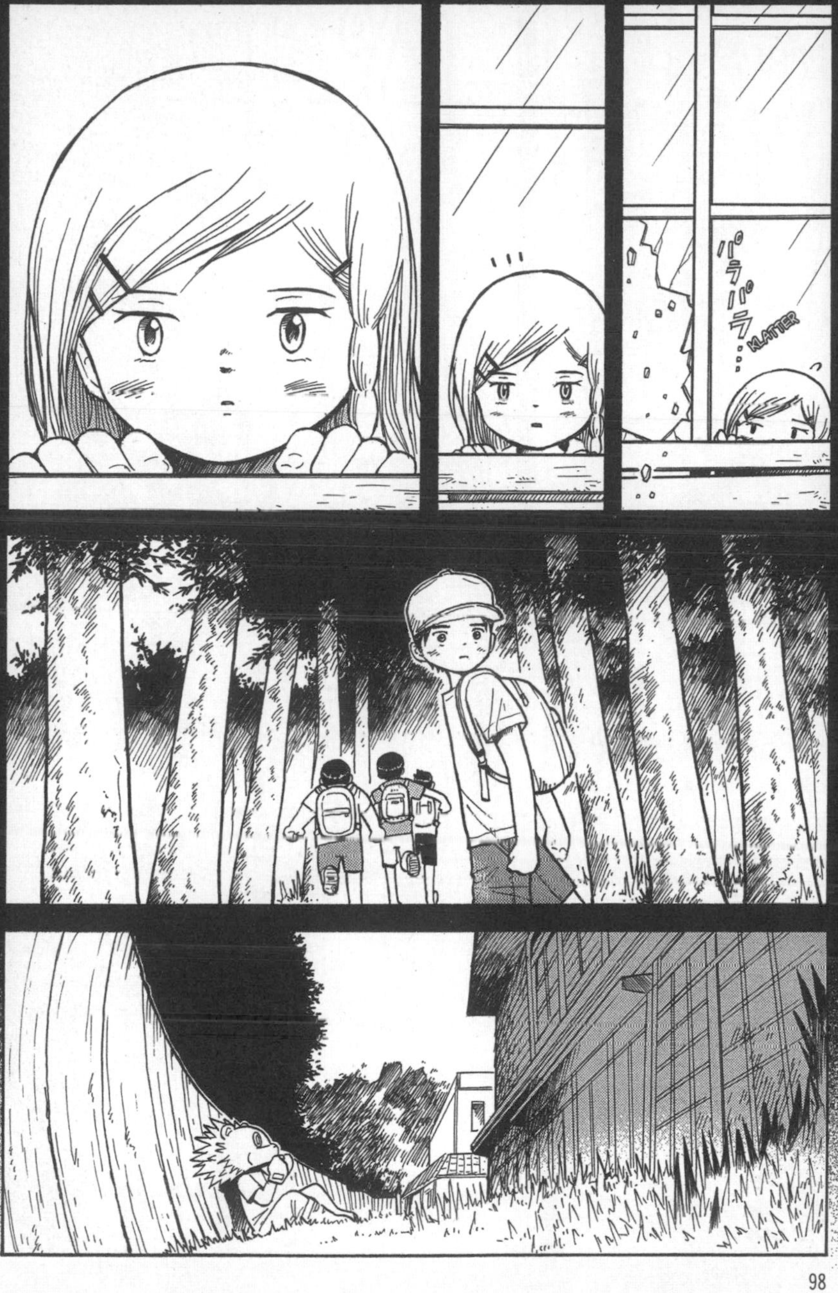
パラパラ…
KLATTER

MISSION:22

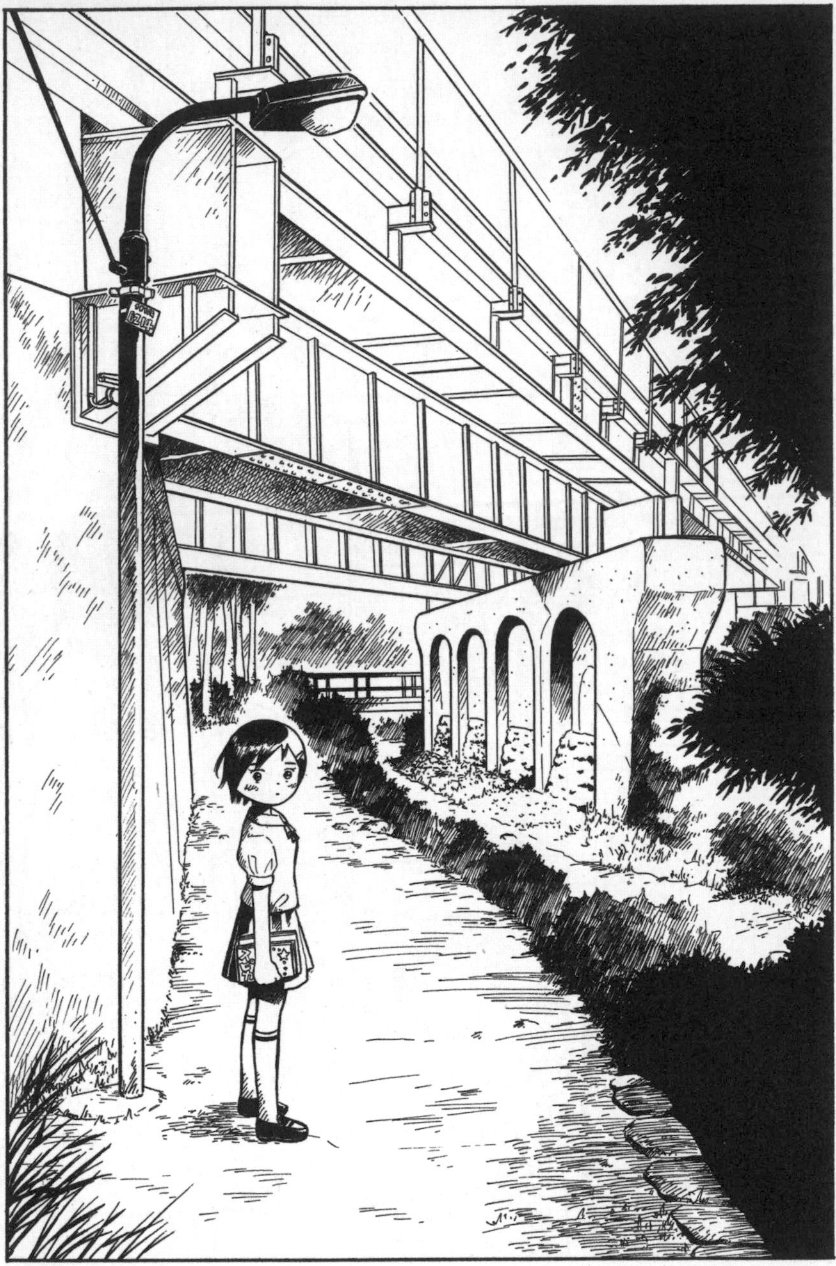

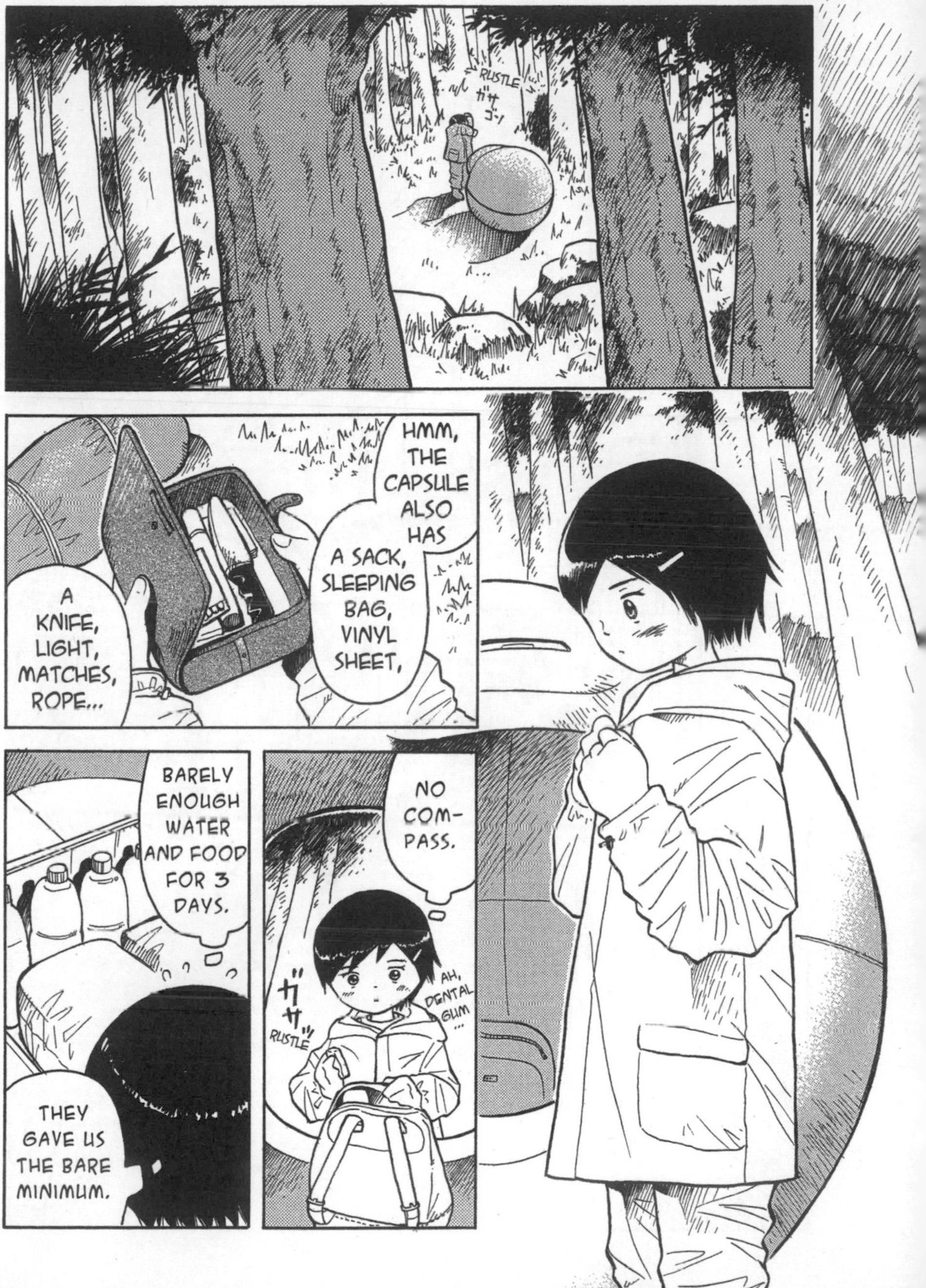
RUSTLE
ガサゴソ
HMM, THE CAPSULE ALSO HAS
A SACK, SLEEPING BAG, VINYL SHEET,
A KNIFE, LIGHT, MATCHES, ROPE...
NO COM-PASS.
AH, DENTAL GUM...
ガサッ
RUSTLE
BARELY ENOUGH WATER AND FOOD FOR 3 DAYS.
THEY GAVE US THE BARE MINIMUM.

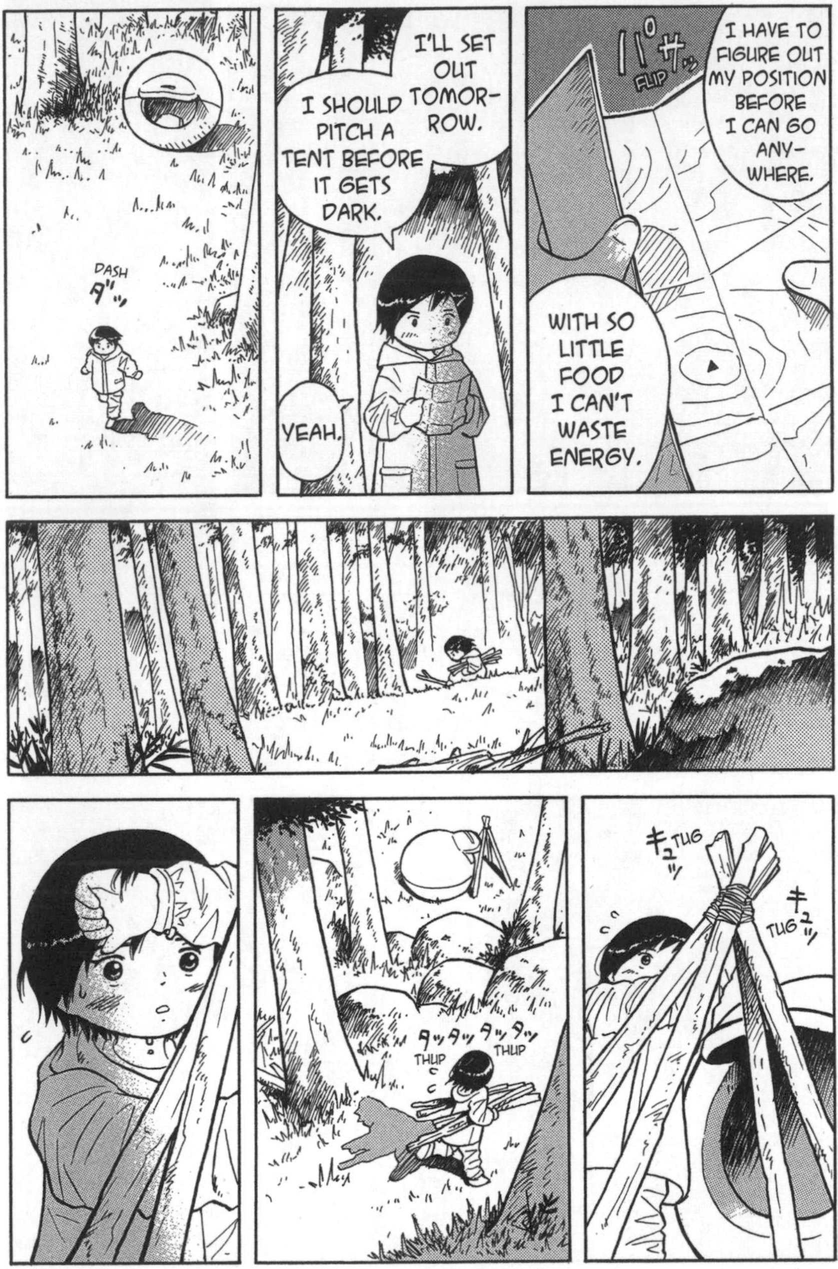
パサッ
FLIP
I HAVE TO FIGURE OUT MY POSITION BEFORE I CAN GO ANYWHERE.
WITH SO LITTLE FOOD I CAN'T WASTE ENERGY.
I'LL SET OUT TOMORROW.
I SHOULD PITCH A TENT BEFORE IT GETS DARK.
YEAH.
DASH
ダッ
キュッ
TUG
キュッ
TUG
タッタッ タッタッ
THUP
THUP

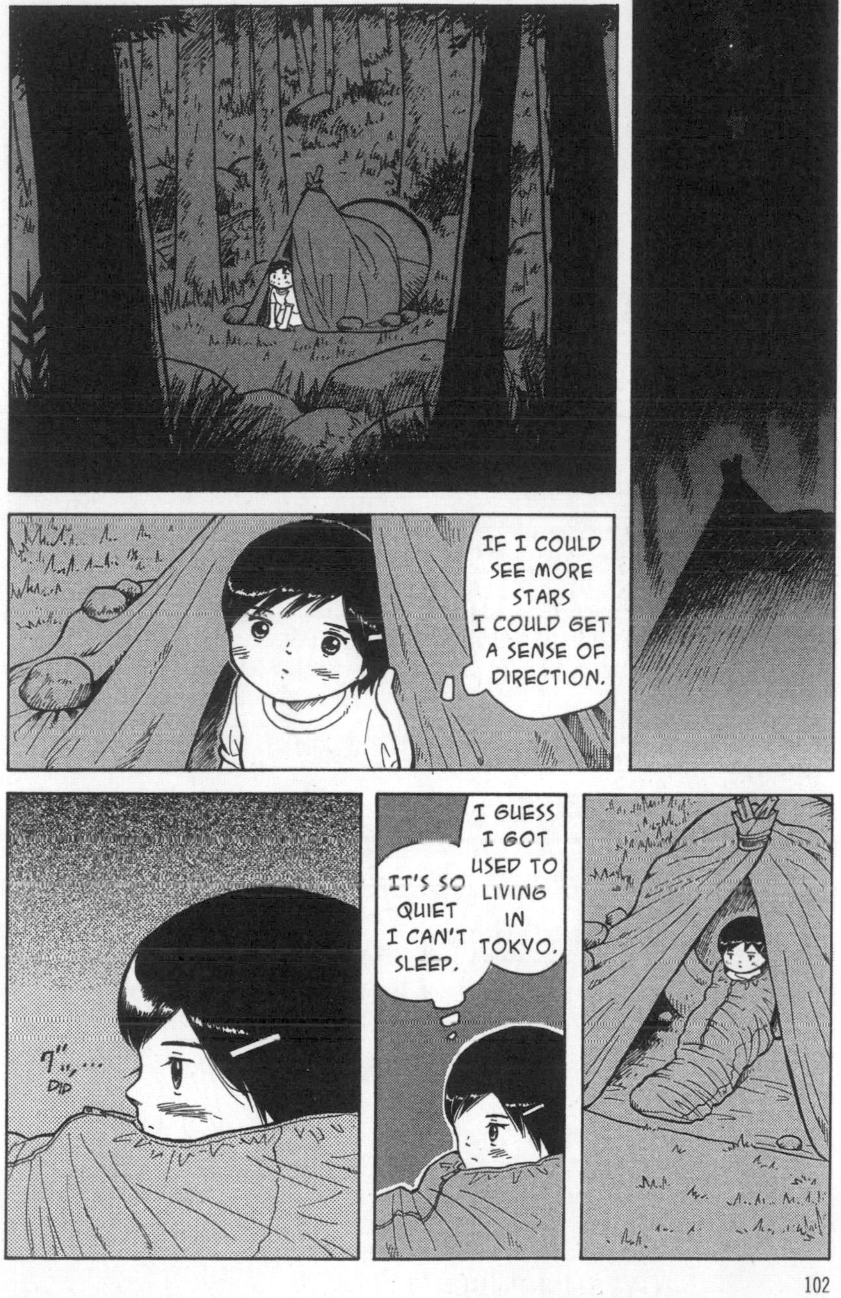
IF I COULD SEE MORE STARS I COULD GET A SENSE OF DIRECTION.
I GUESS I GOT USED TO LIVING IN TOKYO.
IT'S SO QUIET I CAN'T SLEEP.
DIP

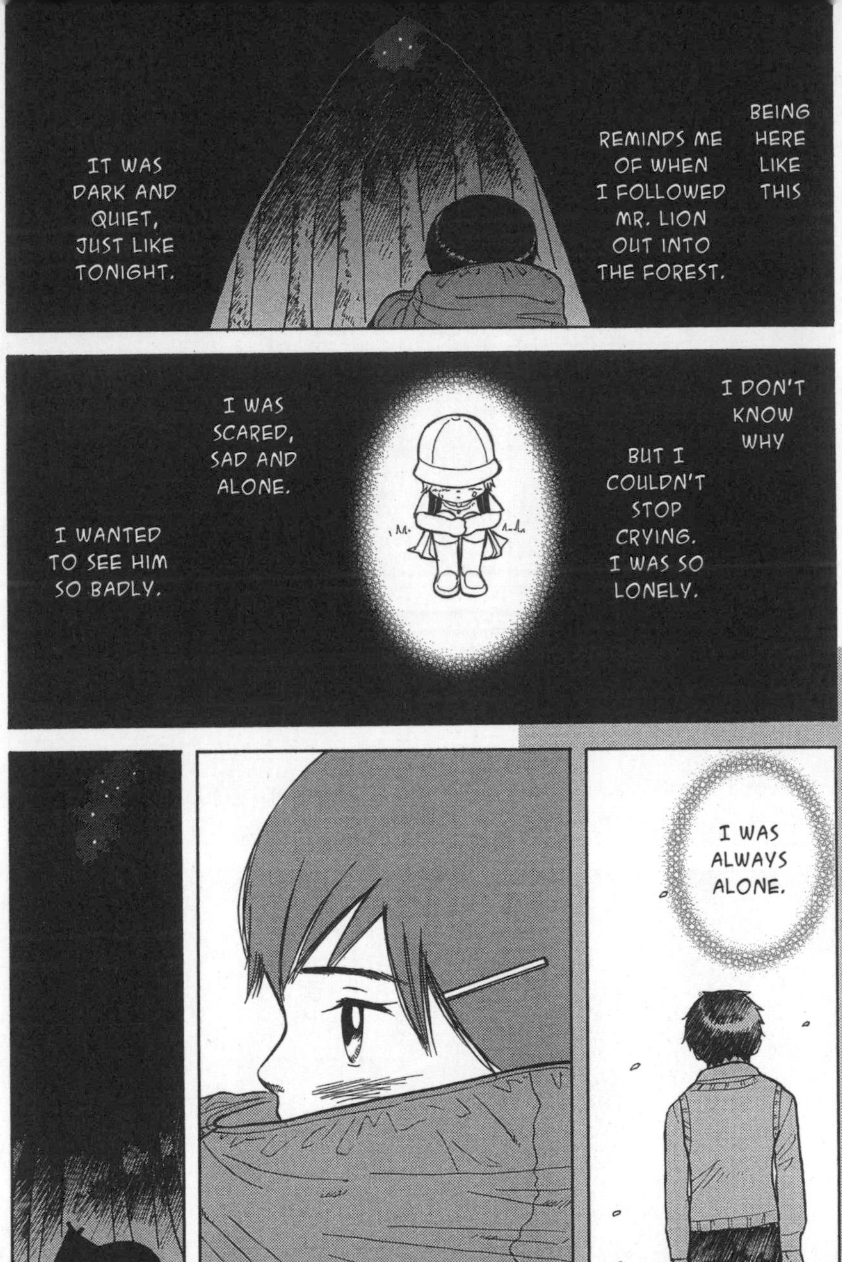
BEING HERE LIKE THIS
REMINDS ME OF WHEN I FOLLOWED MR. LION OUT INTO THE FOREST.
IT WAS DARK AND QUIET, JUST LIKE TONIGHT.
I DON'T KNOW WHY
BUT I COULDN'T STOP CRYING. I WAS SO LONELY.
I WAS SCARED, SAD AND ALONE.
I WANTED TO SEE HIM SO BADLY.
I WAS ALWAYS ALONE.

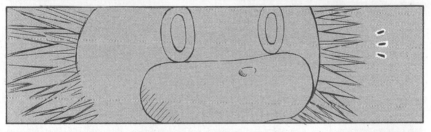

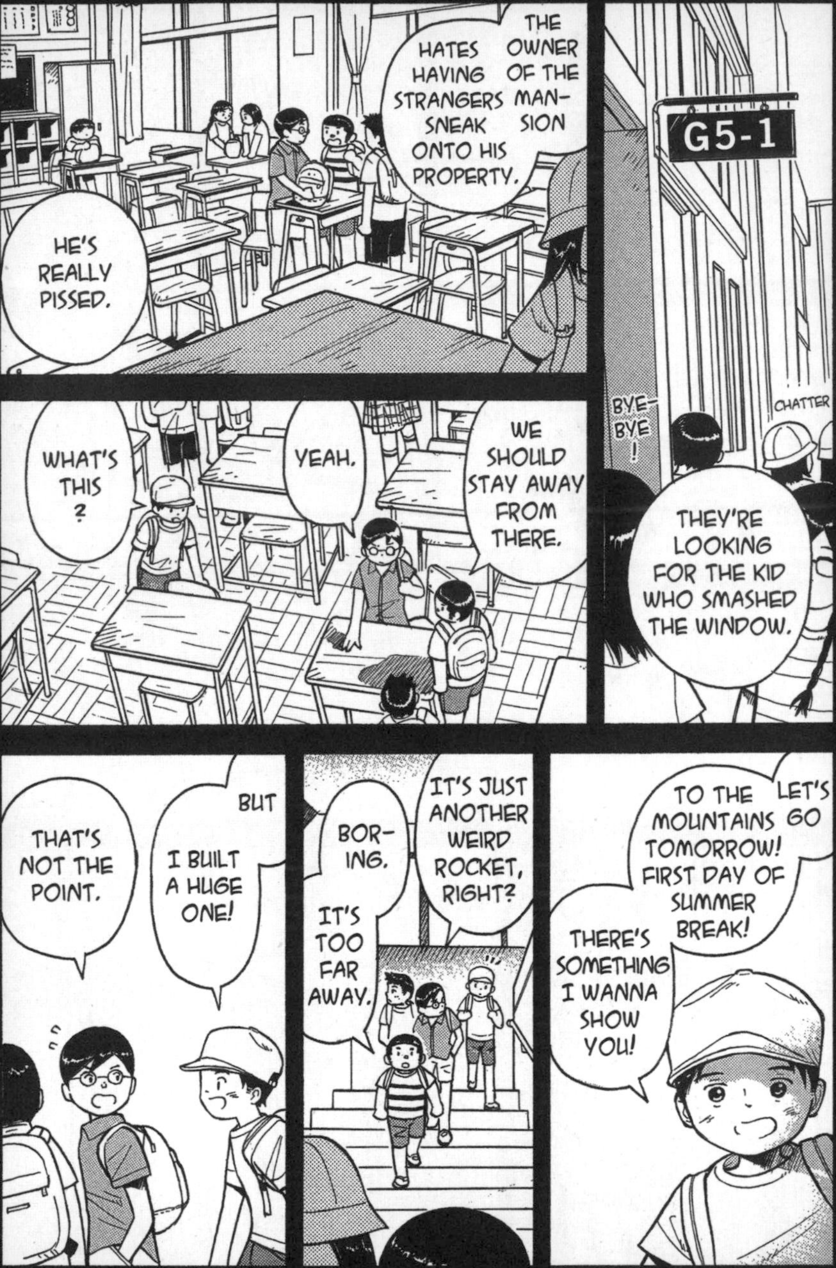
G5-1
BYE-BYE!
CHATTER
THEY'RE LOOKING FOR THE KID WHO SMASHED THE WINDOW.
THE OWNER OF THE MAN-SION HATES HAVING STRANGERS SNEAK ONTO HIS PROPERTY.
HE'S REALLY PISSED.
WE SHOULD STAY AWAY FROM THERE.
YEAH.
WHAT'S THIS ?
LET'S GO TO THE MOUNTAINS TOMORROW! FIRST DAY OF SUMMER BREAK!
THERE'S SOMETHING I WANNA SHOW YOU!
IT'S JUST ANOTHER WEIRD ROCKET, RIGHT?
BOR-ING.
IT'S TOO FAR AWAY.
BUT I BUILT A HUGE ONE!
THAT'S NOT THE POINT.

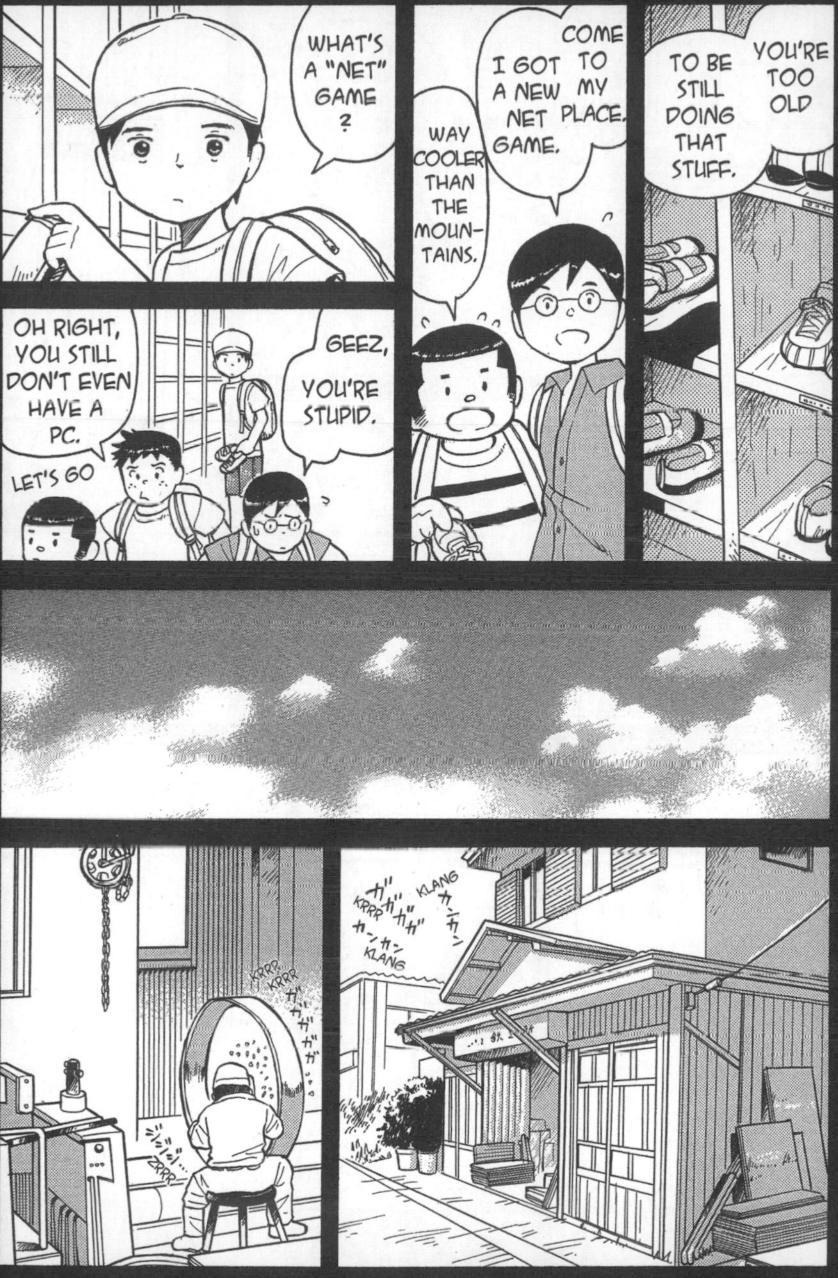
YOU'RE TOO OLD
TO BE STILL DOING THAT STUFF.
COME TO MY PLACE.
I GOT A NEW NET GAME.
WAY COOLER THAN THE MOUN-TAINS.
WHAT'S A "NET" GAME?
GEEZ, YOU'RE STUPID.
OH RIGHT, YOU STILL DON'T EVEN HAVE A PC.
LET'S GO
KLANG
KRRR
KLANG
KRRR. KRRR
ZRRR

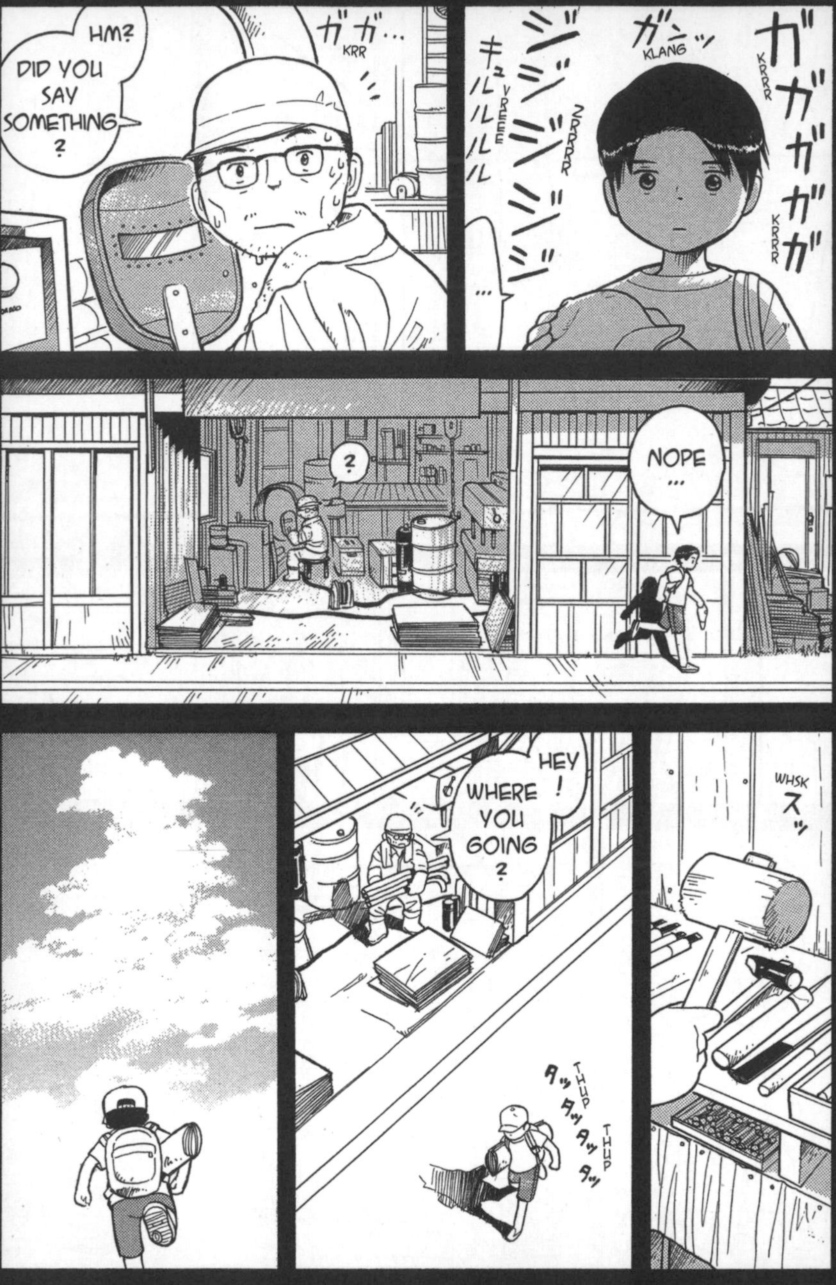

ガガガガ
KRRRR
KRRRR
ガンッ
KLANG
ジジジジ
ZRRRRR
キュルルルル
VREEE
...
ガガ…
KRR
HM?
DID YOU SAY SOMETHING?
?
NOPE ...
スッ
WHSK
HEY!
WHERE YOU GOING?
タッタッタッタッ
THUP
THUP

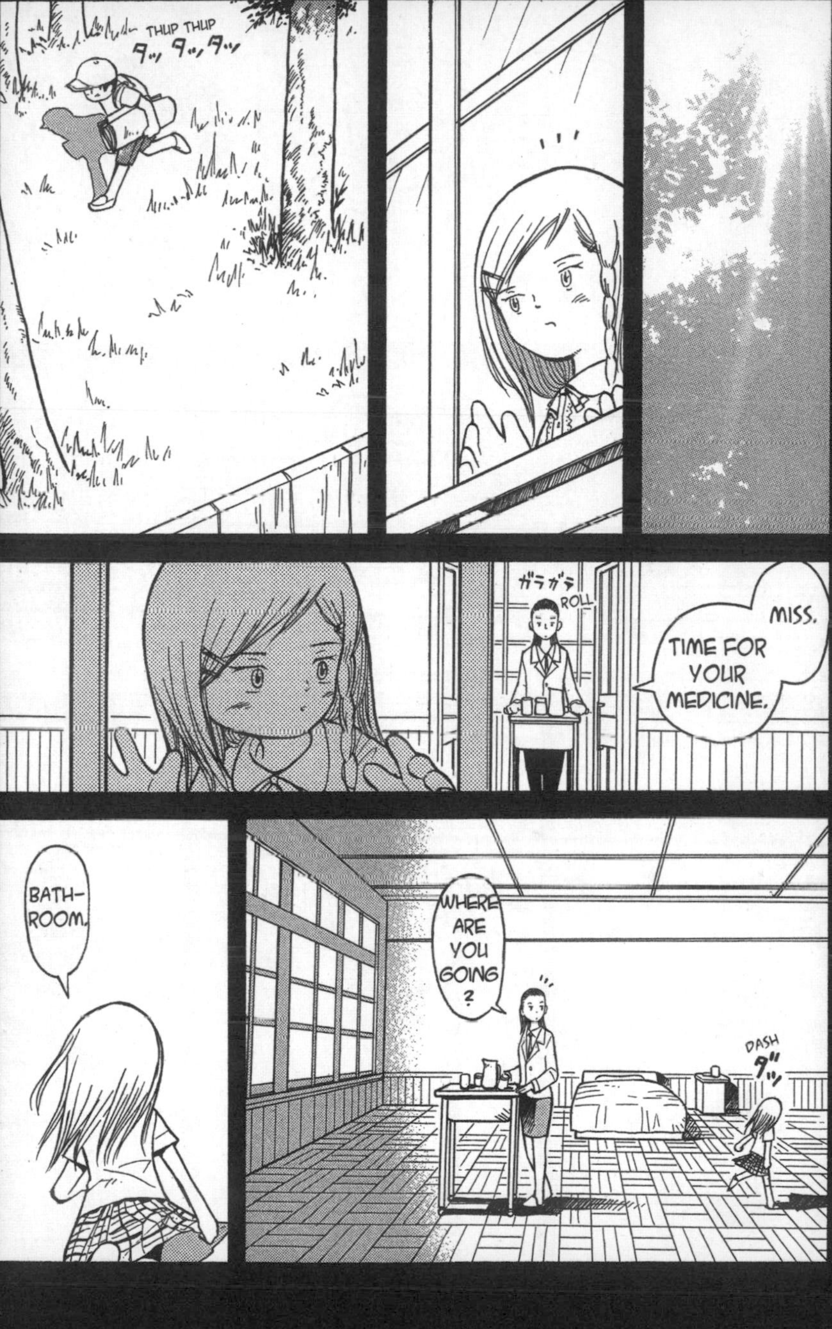
THUP THUP
タッ、タッ、タッ
ガラガラ
ROLL
MISS.
TIME FOR YOUR MEDICINE.
WHERE ARE YOU GOING?
DASH
ダッ
BATH-ROOM.

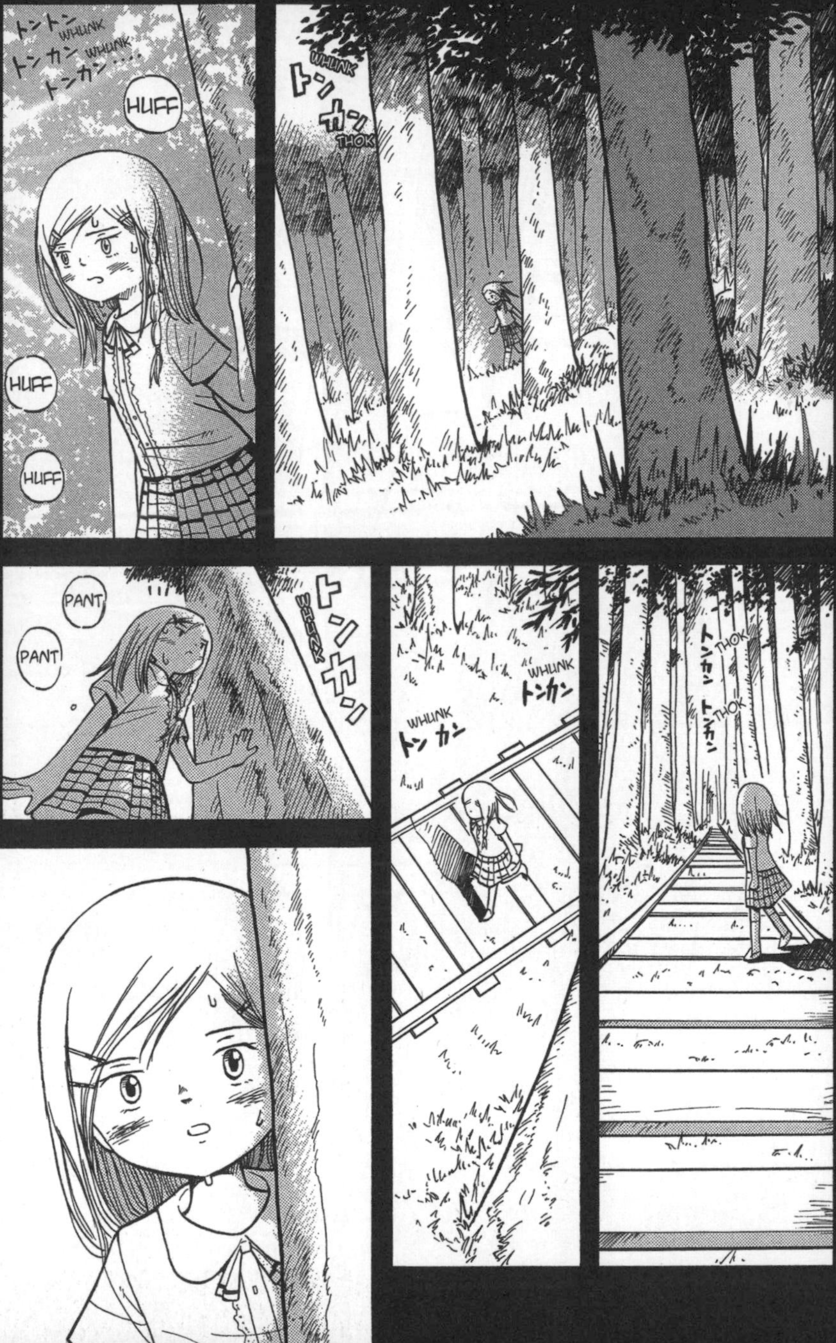
WHUNK
トン
カン
THOK
トントン
WHUNK
トンカン
WHUNK
トンカン……
HUFF
HUFF
HUFF
トンカン
THOK
トンカン
THOK
WHUNK
トンカン
WHUNK
トン カン
トン
カン
WHUNK
PANT
PANT

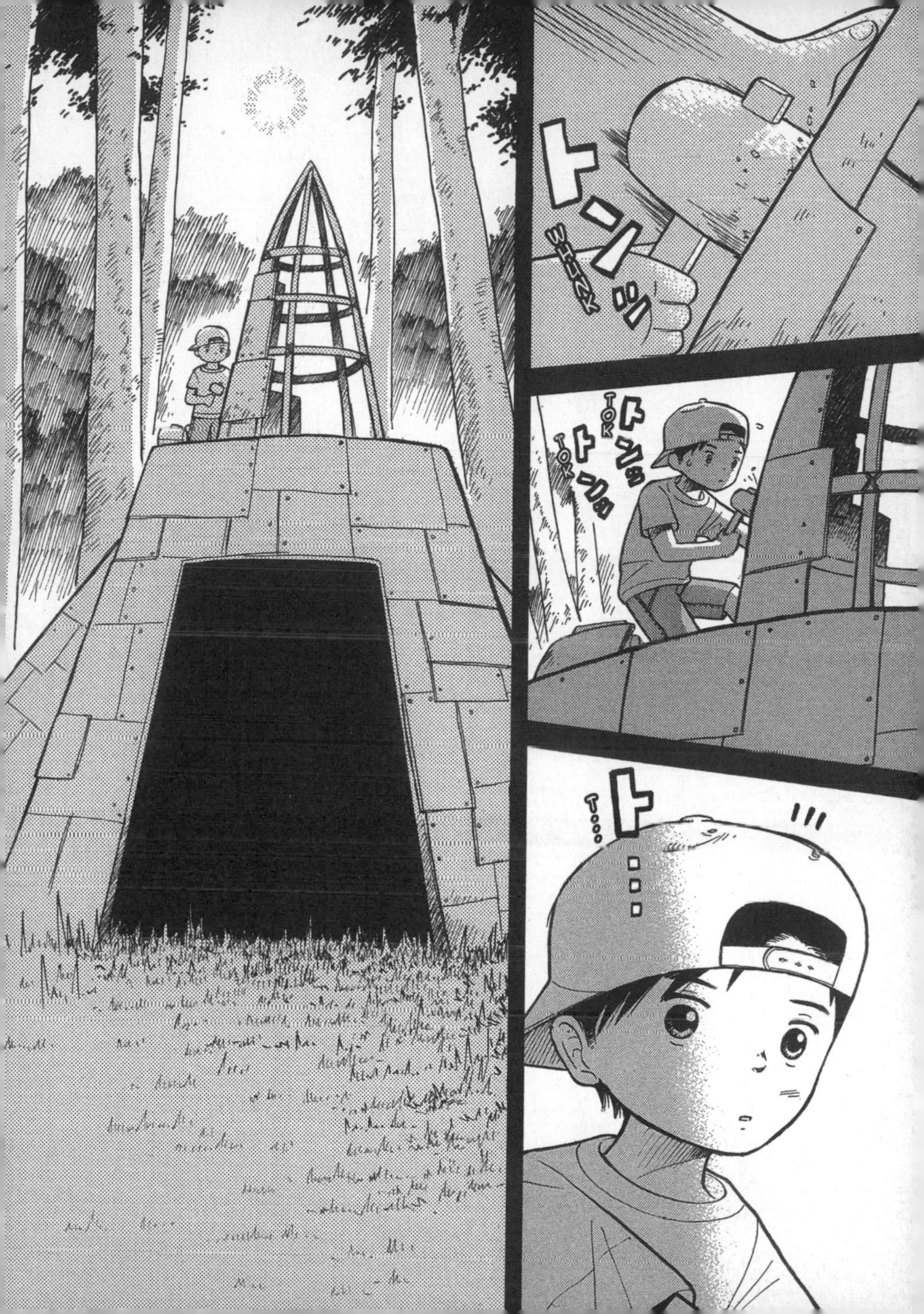
トンッ
WHACK
トンッ
TOK
トンッ
TOK
ト・・・
T...

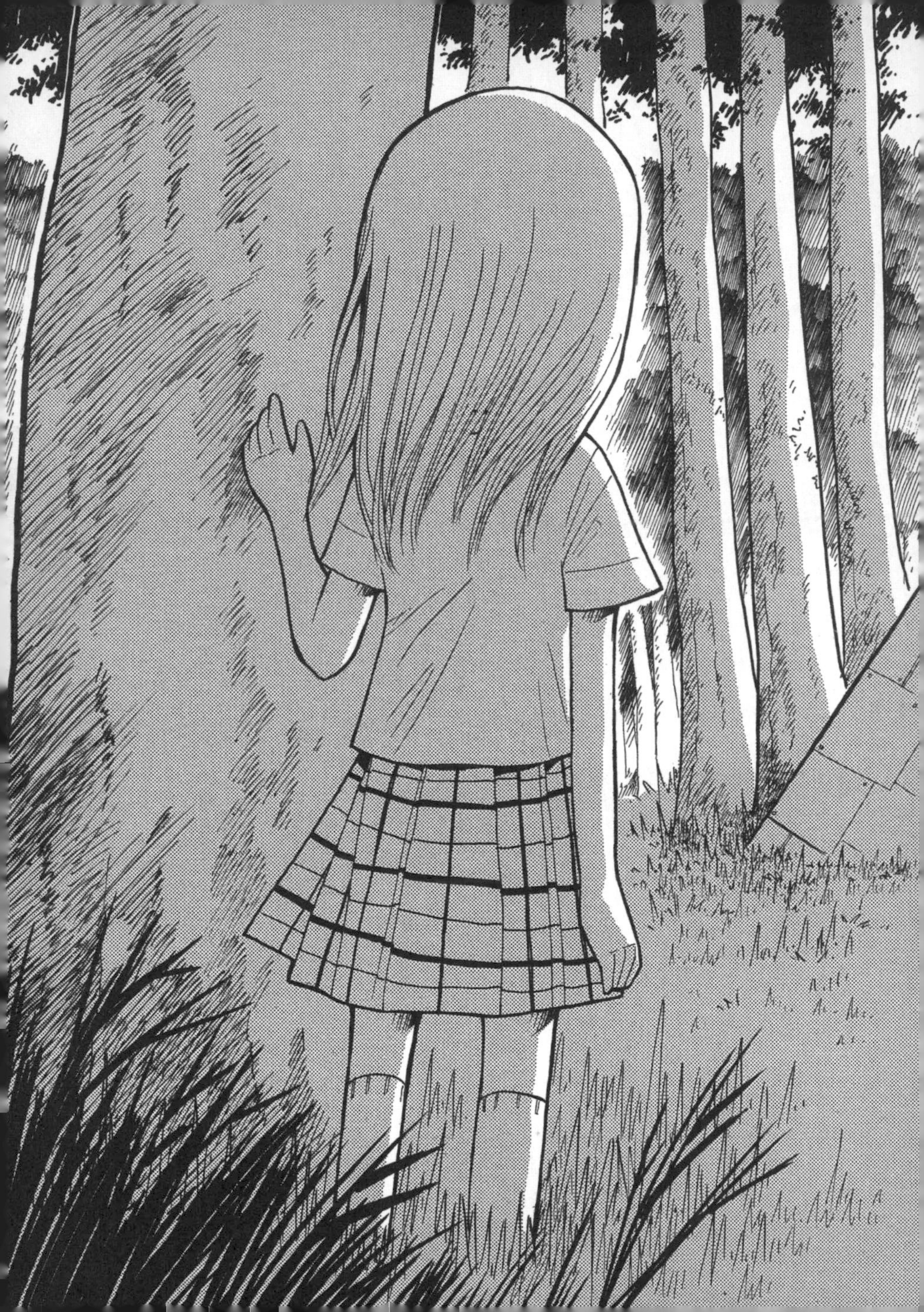

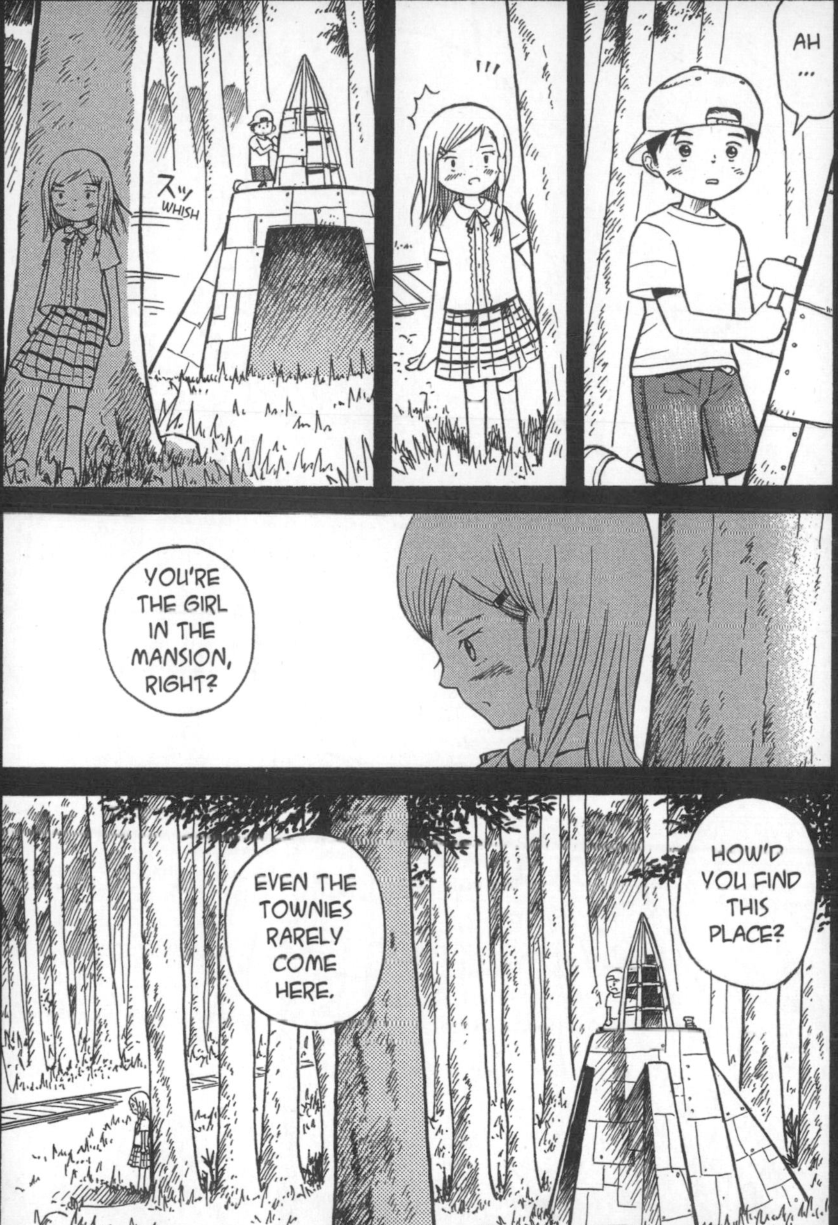
AH ...
スッ
WHISH
YOU'RE THE GIRL IN THE MANSION, RIGHT?
HOW'D YOU FIND THIS PLACE?
EVEN THE TOWNIES RARELY COME HERE.

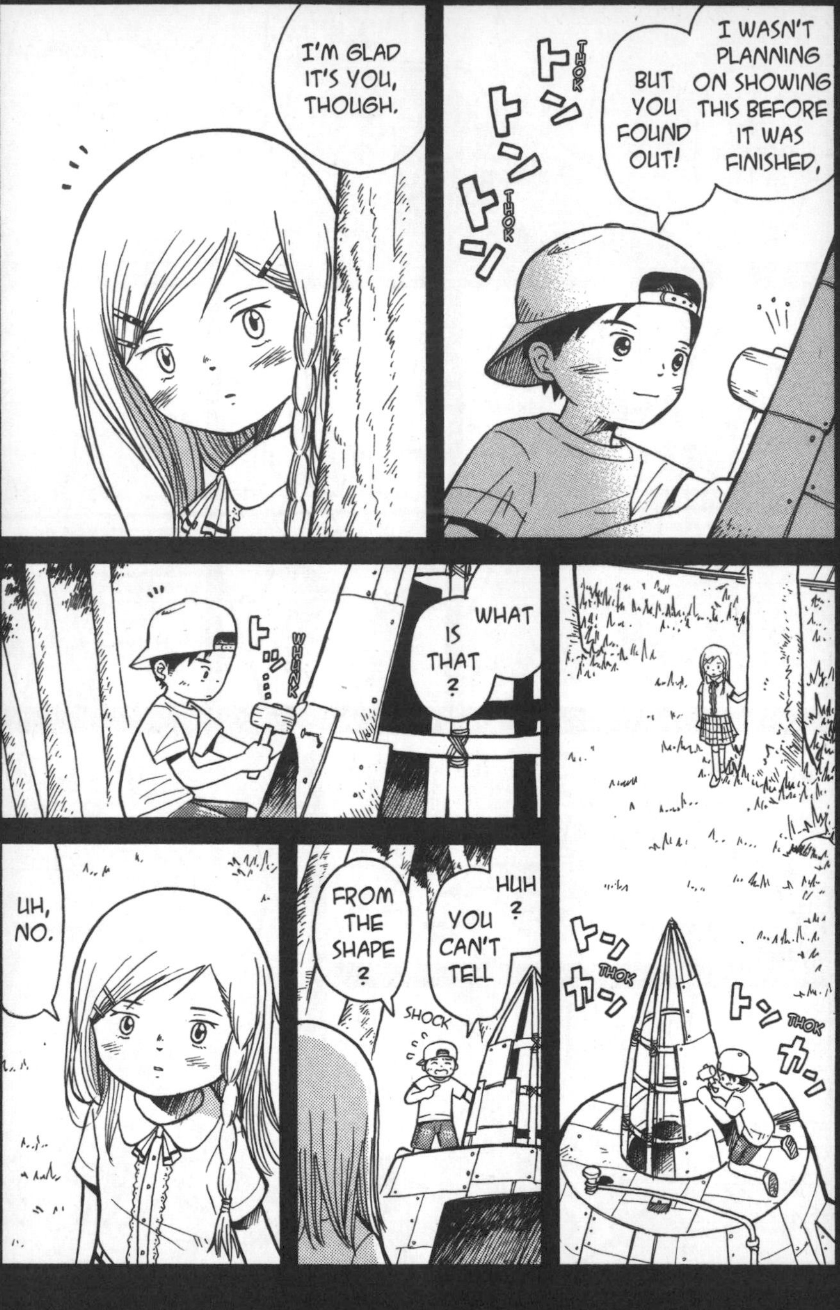
THOK
THOK
I WASN'T PLANNING ON SHOWING THIS BEFORE IT WAS FINISHED,
BUT YOU FOUND OUT!
I'M GLAD IT'S YOU, THOUGH.
THOK
THOK
WHUNK
WHAT IS THAT?
HUH? YOU CAN'T TELL
SHOCK
FROM THE SHAPE?
UH, NO.

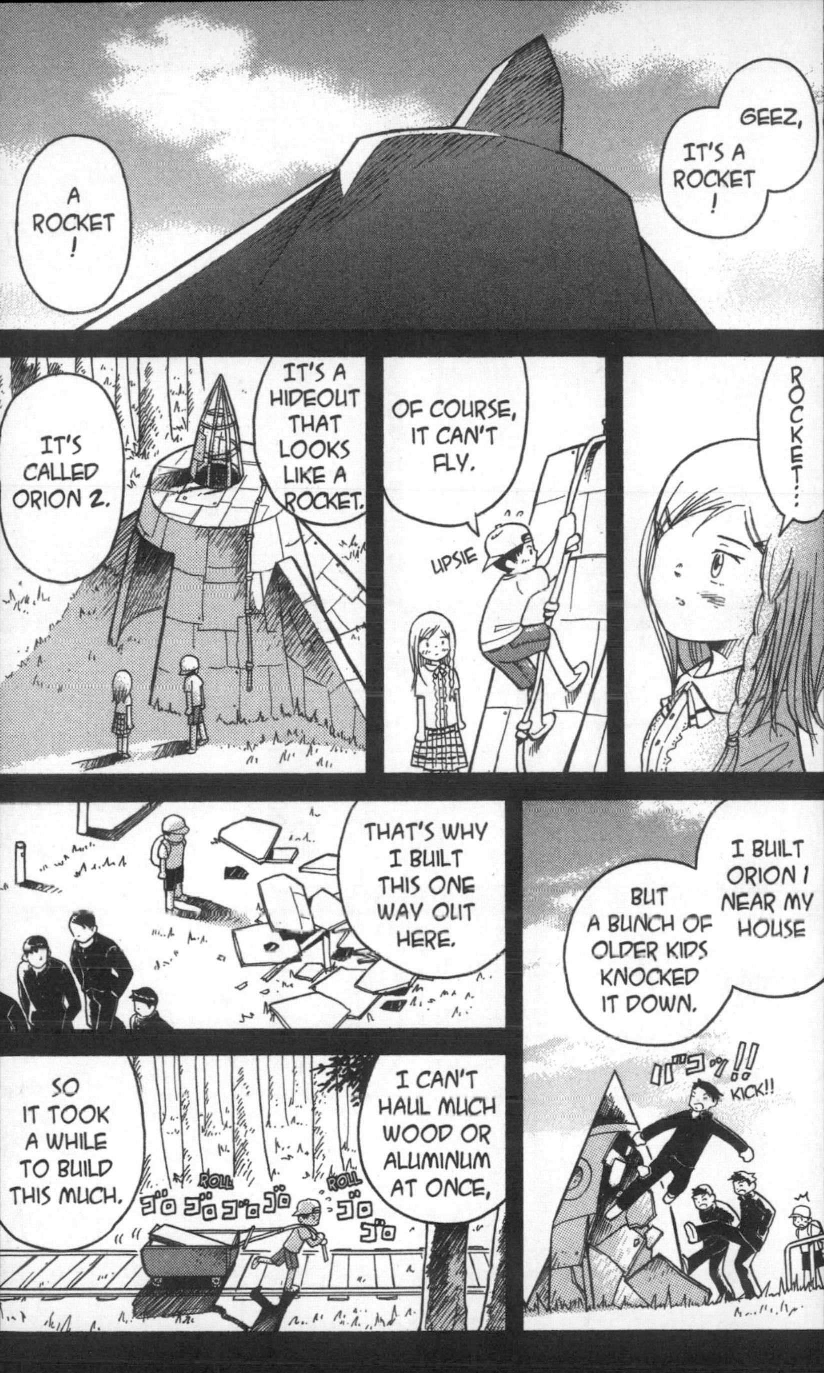
GEEZ, IT'S A ROCKET!
A ROCKET!
ROCKET...
OF COURSE, IT CAN'T FLY.
UPSIE
IT'S A HIDEOUT THAT LOOKS LIKE A ROCKET.
IT'S CALLED ORION 2.
I BUILT ORION 1 NEAR MY HOUSE
BUT A BUNCH OF OLDER KIDS KNOCKED IT DOWN.
バコッ!!
KICK!!
THAT'S WHY I BUILT THIS ONE WAY OUT HERE.
I CAN'T HAUL MUCH WOOD OR ALUMINUM AT ONCE,
ROLL
ROLL
SO IT TOOK A WHILE TO BUILD THIS MUCH.

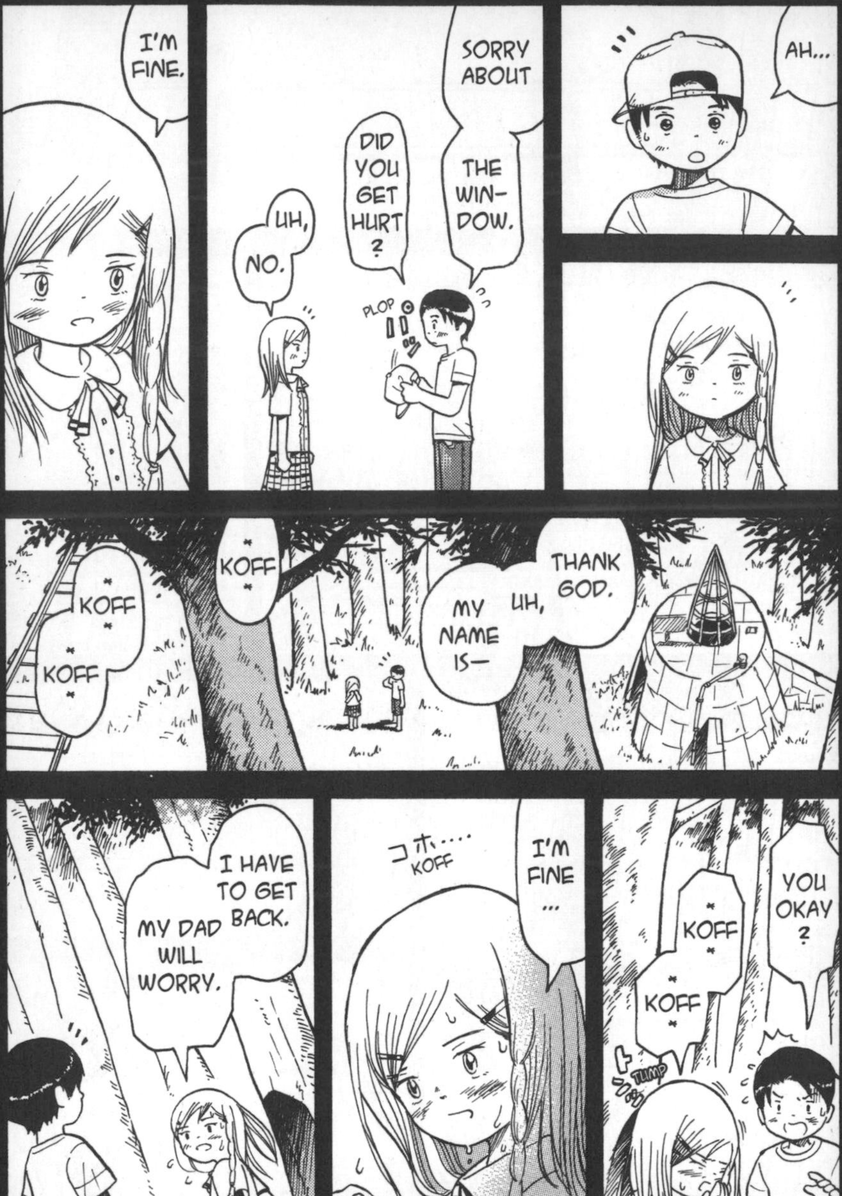
AH...
SORRY ABOUT THE WINDOW.
DID YOU GET HURT?
UH, NO.
PLOP
I'M FINE.
THANK GOD.
UH, MY NAME IS—
* KOFF *
* KOFF *
* KOFF *
YOU OKAY?
* KOFF *
* KOFF *
TUMP
I'M FINE...
コホ.... KOFF
I HAVE TO GET BACK.
MY DAD WILL WORRY.

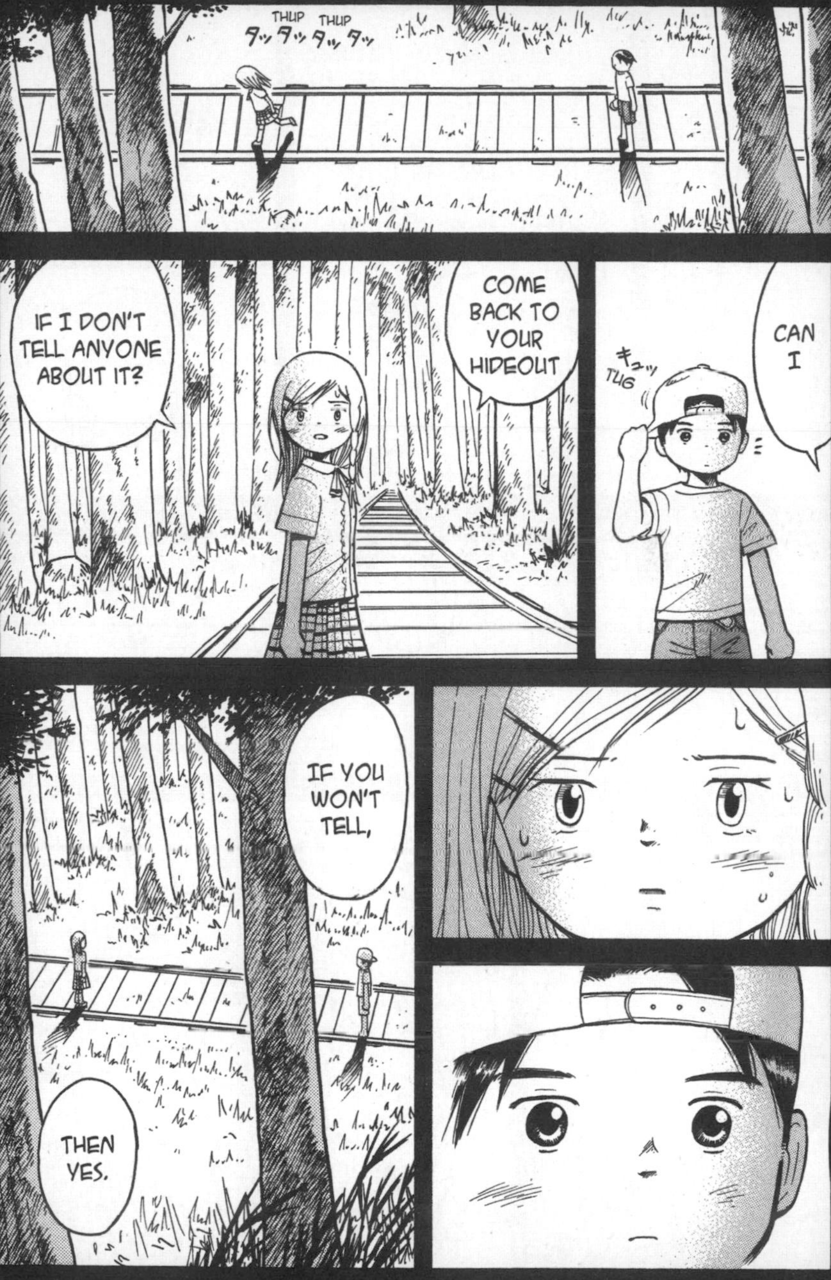

タッタッタッタッ
THUP THUP
キュッ
TUG
CAN I
COME BACK TO YOUR HIDEOUT
IF I DON'T TELL ANYONE ABOUT IT?
IF YOU WON'T TELL,
THEN YES.

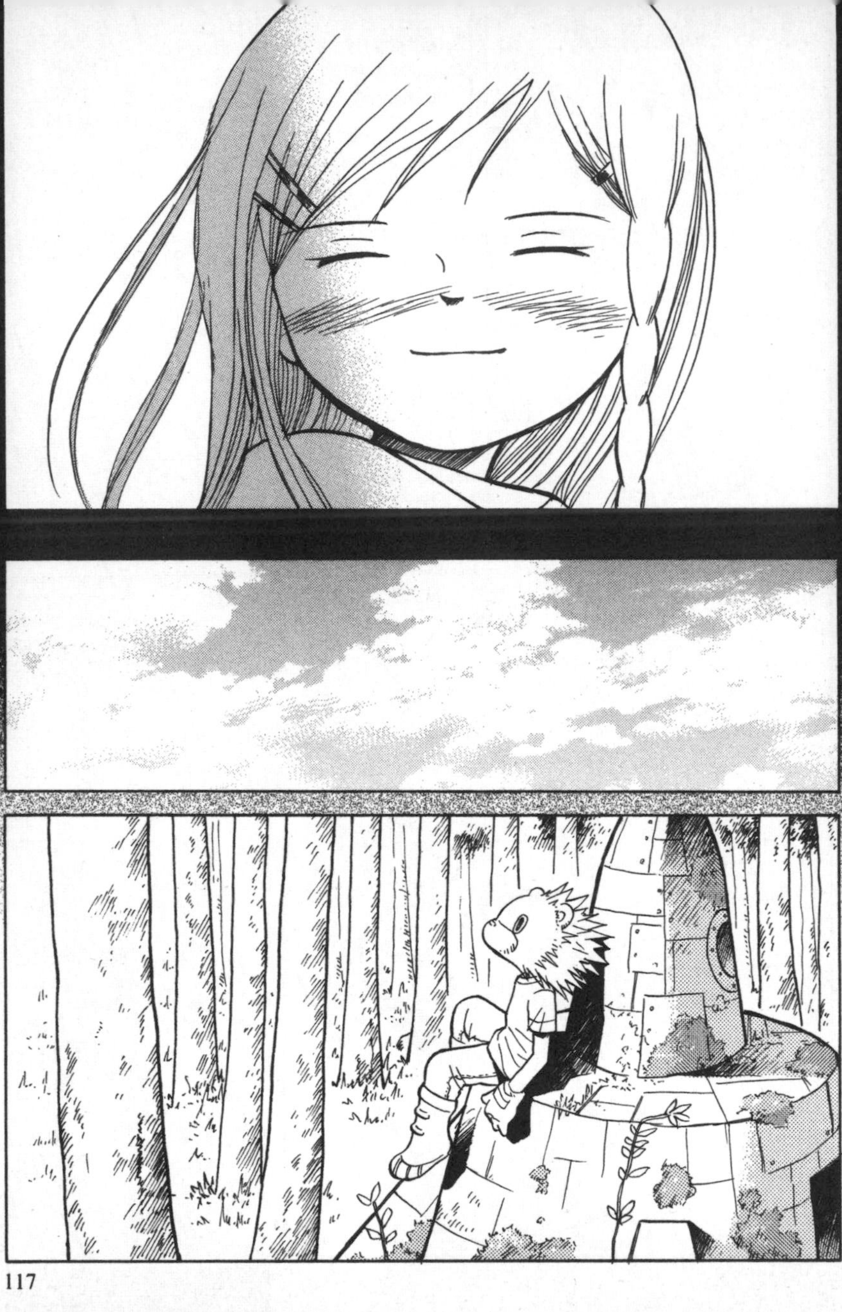

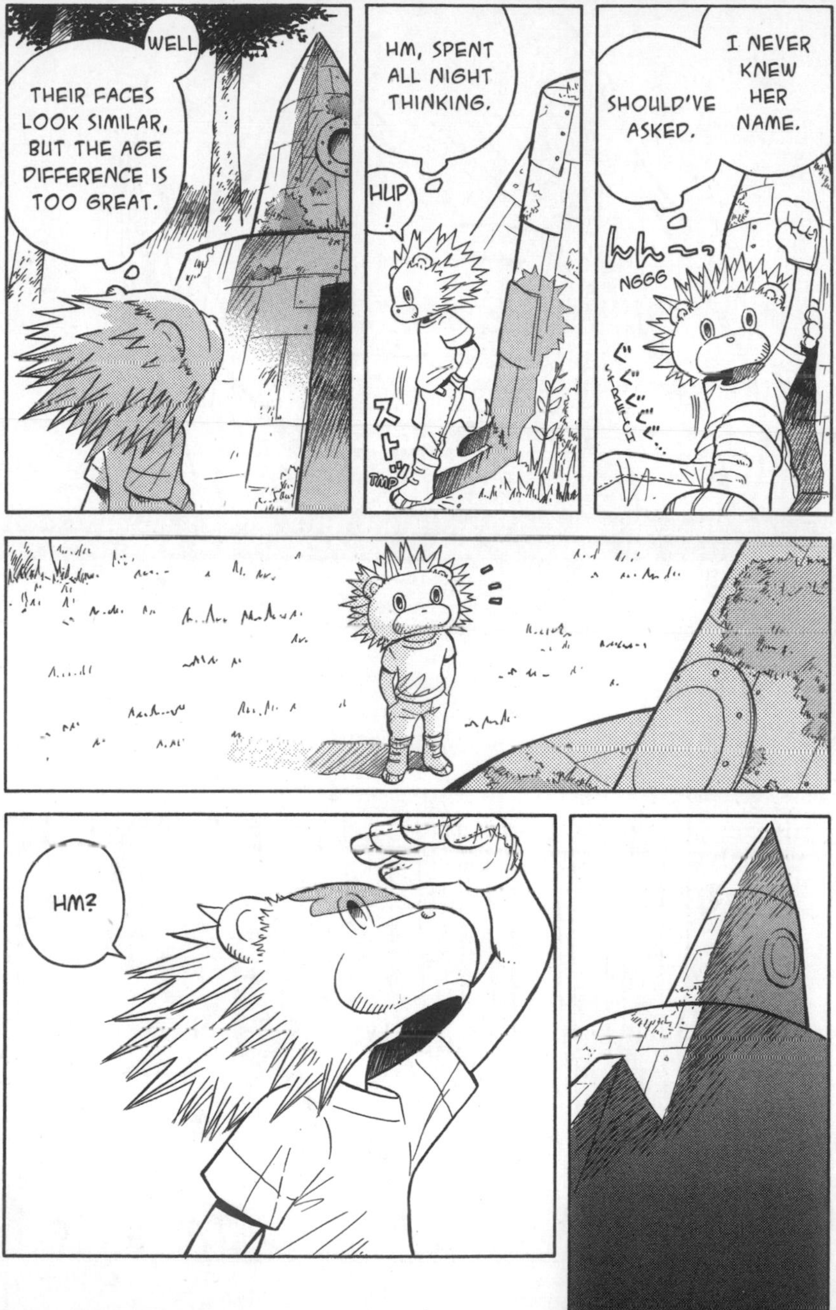
I NEVER KNEW HER NAME.
SHOULD'VE ASKED.
んん〜っ
NGGG
ぐぐぐぐぐ…
STRETCH
HM, SPENT ALL NIGHT THINKING.
HUP!
ストッ
TMP
WELL
THEIR FACES LOOK SIMILAR, BUT THE AGE DIFFERENCE IS TOO GREAT.
HM?

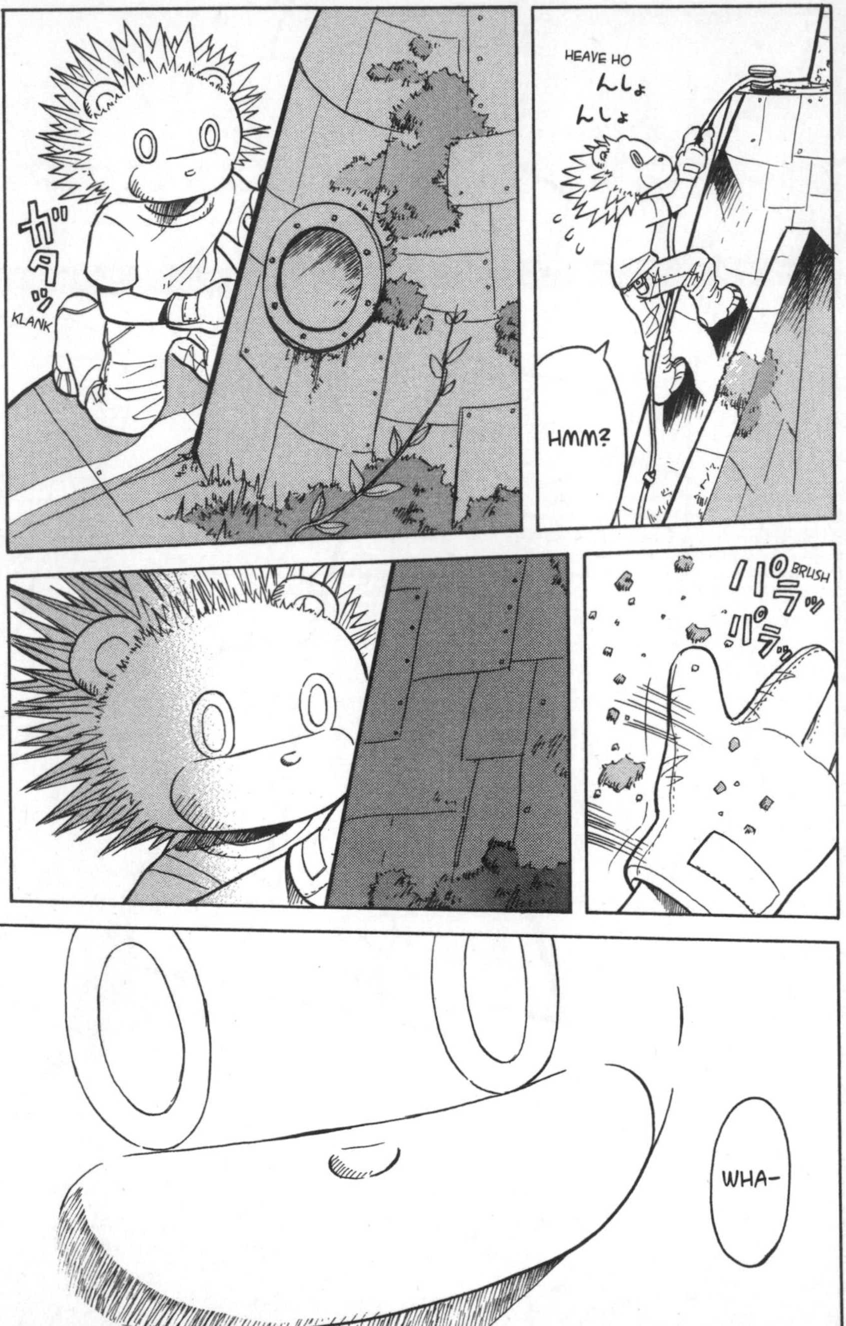
HEAVE HO
んしょ
んしょ
HMM?
カタッ
KLANK
BRUSH
パラッ
パラッ
WHA-

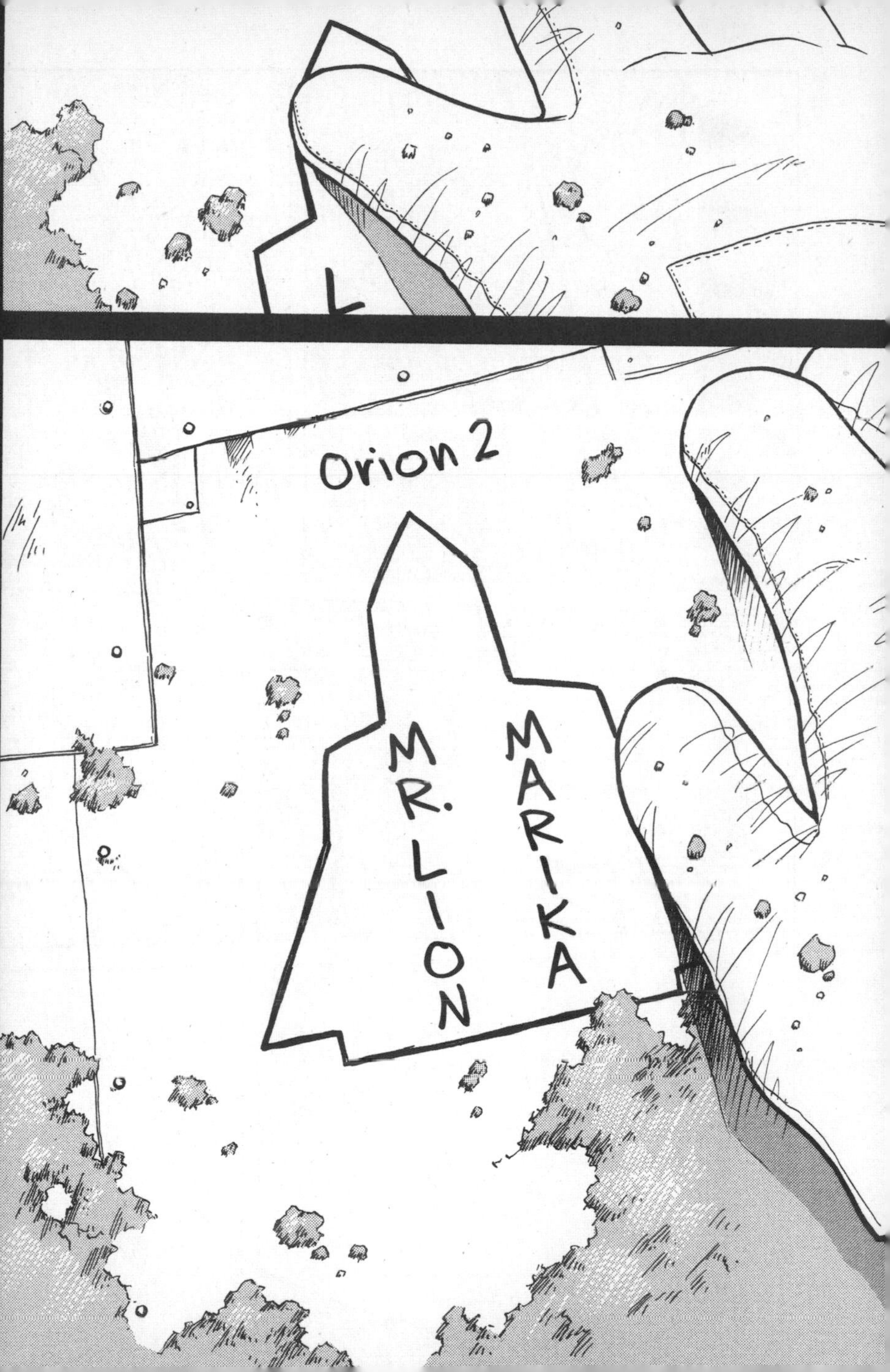
Orion 2
MARIKA
MR. LION

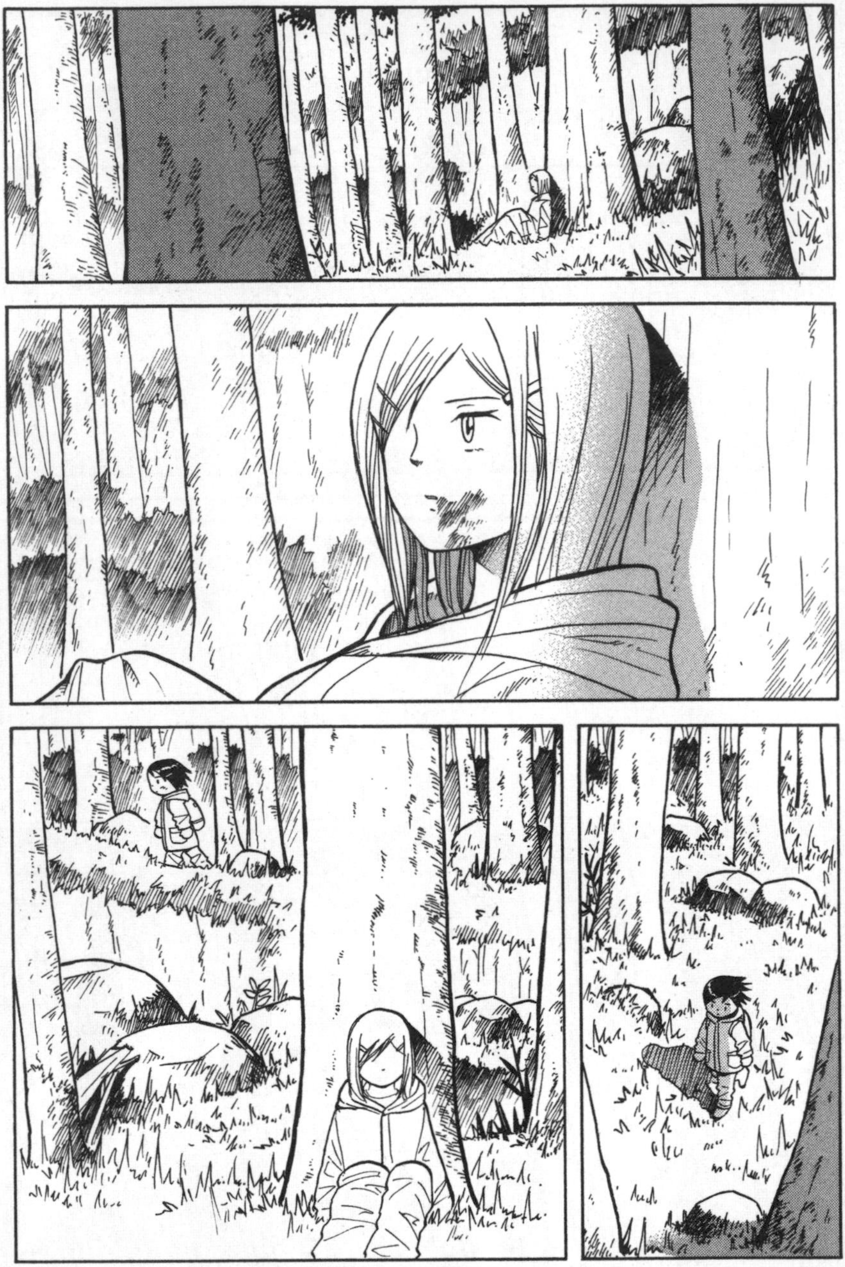

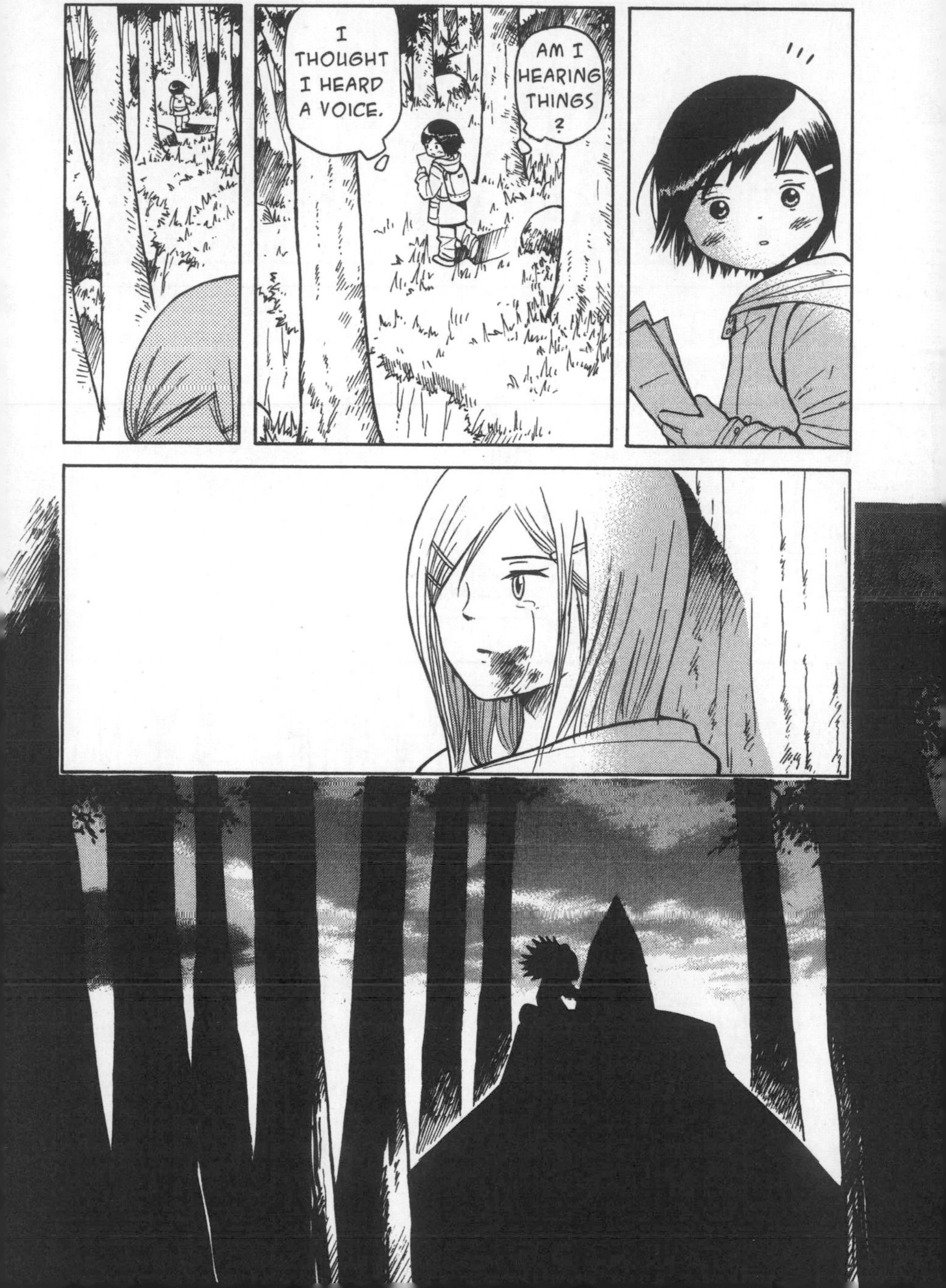
AM I HEARING THINGS?
I THOUGHT I HEARD A VOICE.

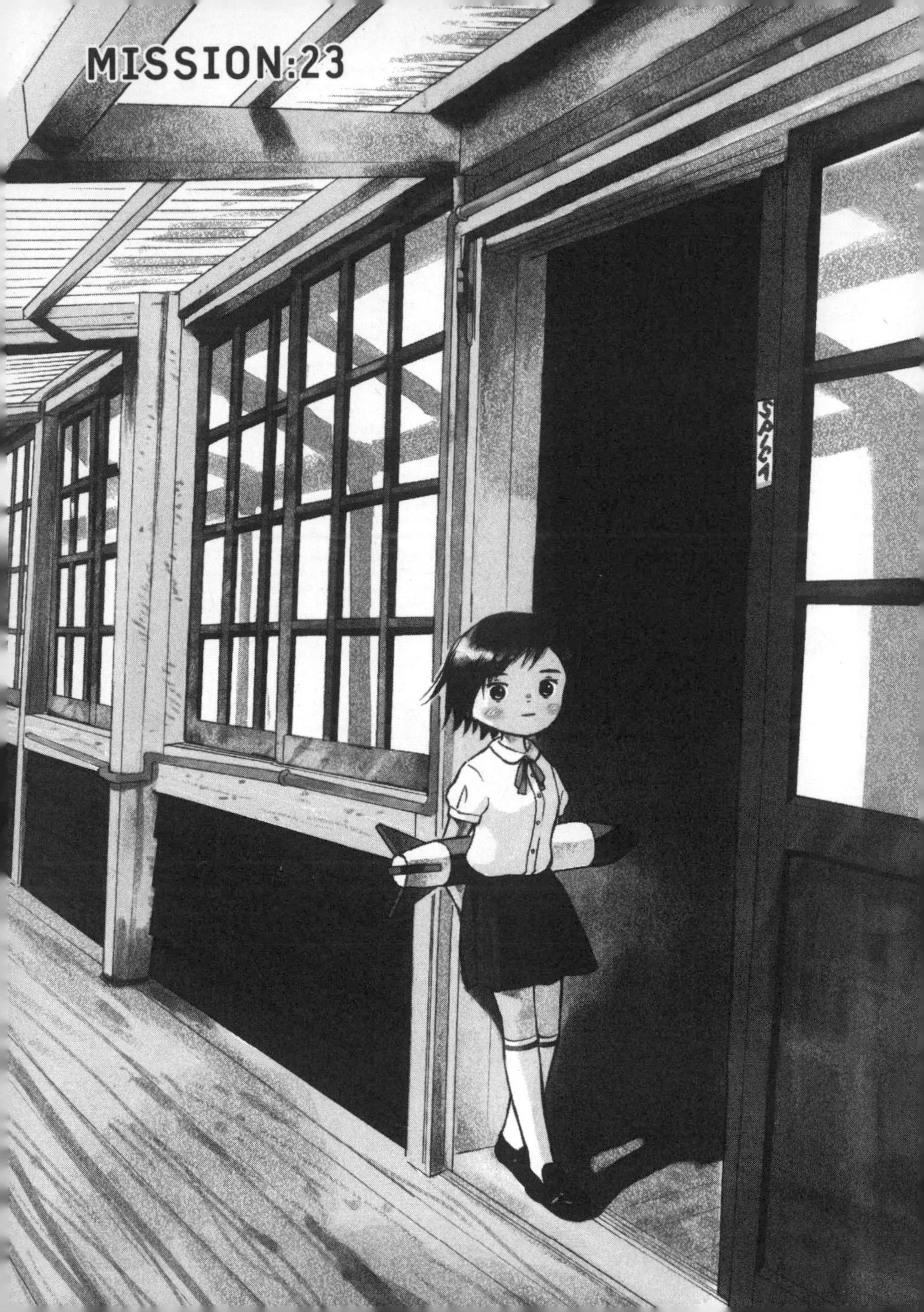
MISSION:23

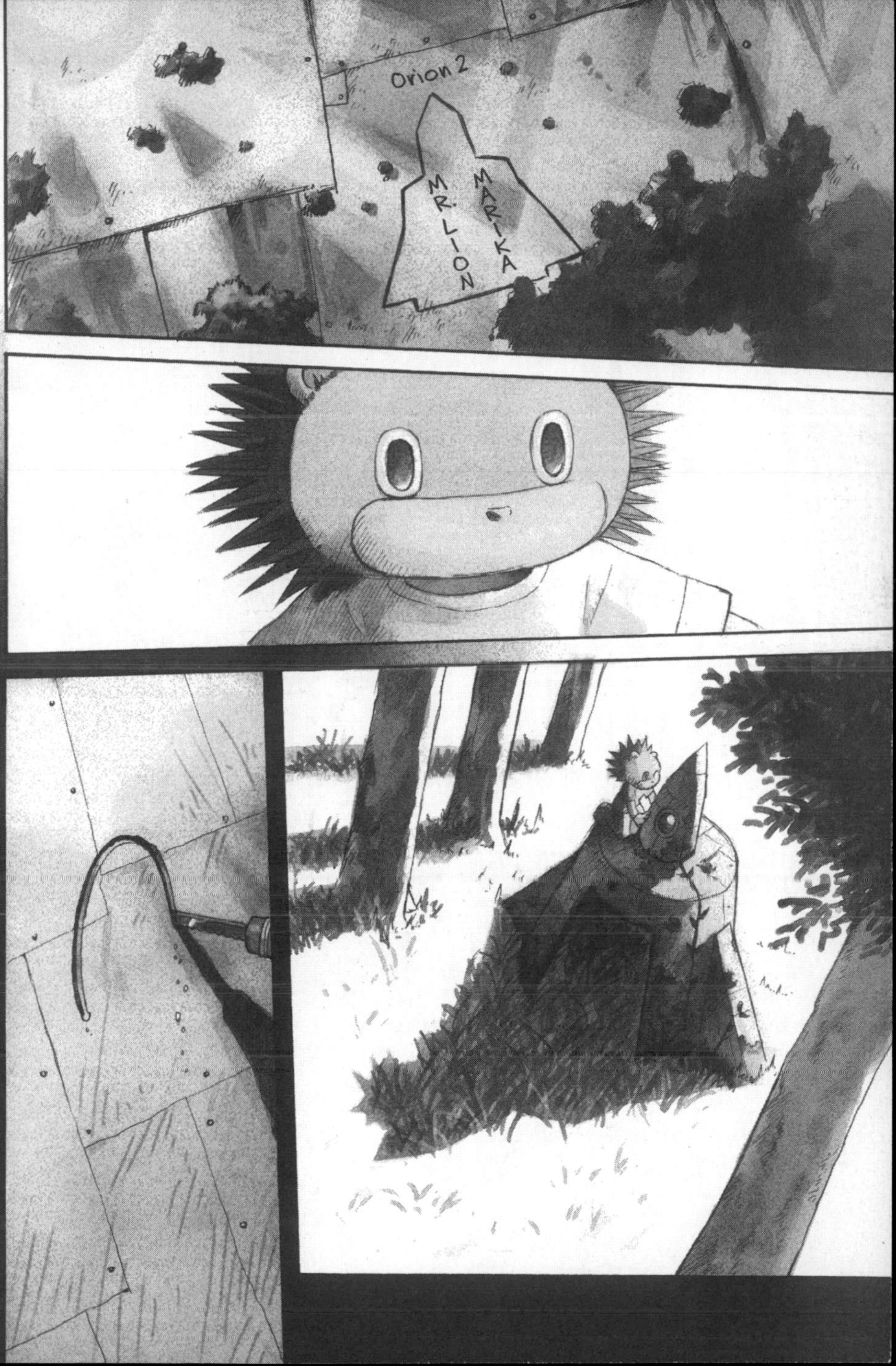
Orion 2
MARIKA
MR. LION

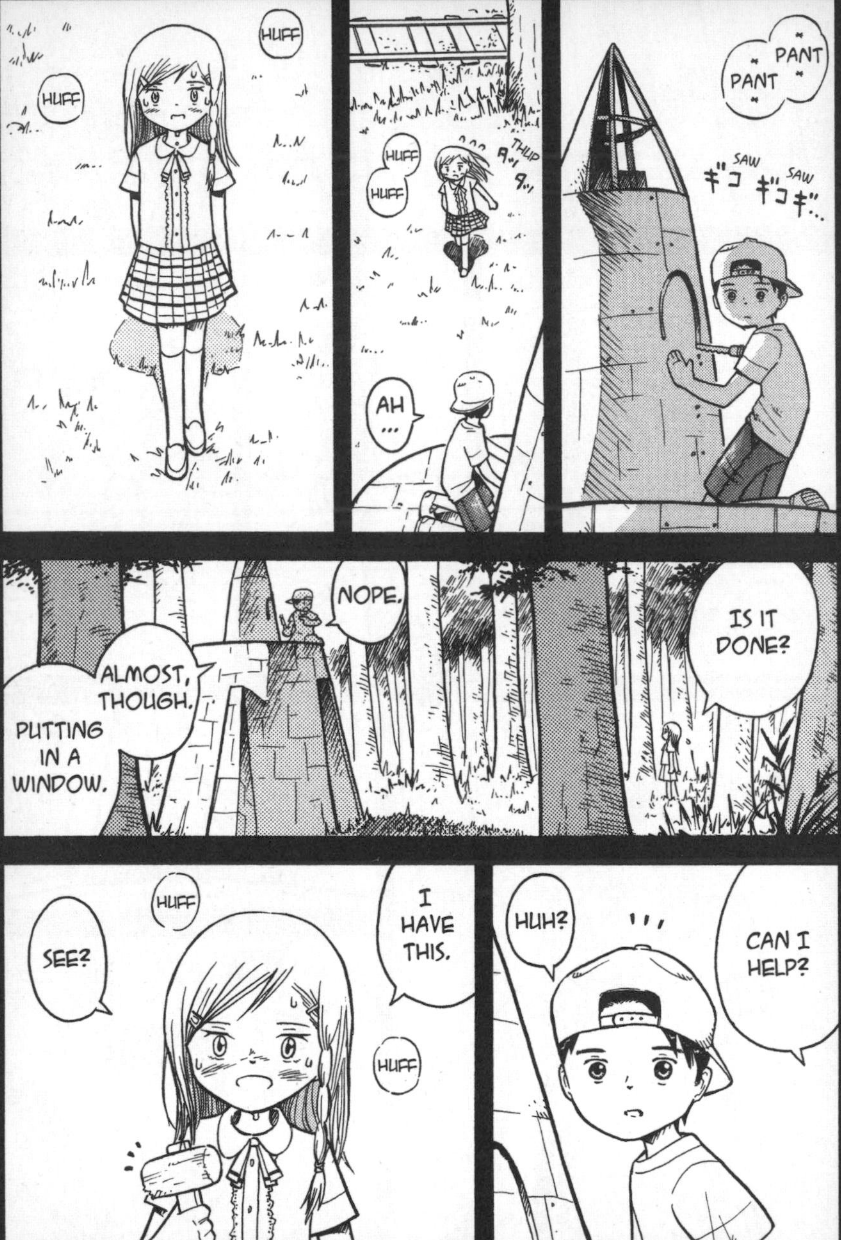
PANT
PANT
SAW
ギコ
SAW
ギコギ…
HUFF
HUFF
THUD
タッ タッ
AH ...
HUFF
HUFF
IS IT DONE?
NOPE.
ALMOST, THOUGH.
PUTTING IN A WINDOW.
CAN I HELP?
HUH?
I HAVE THIS.
HUFF
SEE?
HUFF

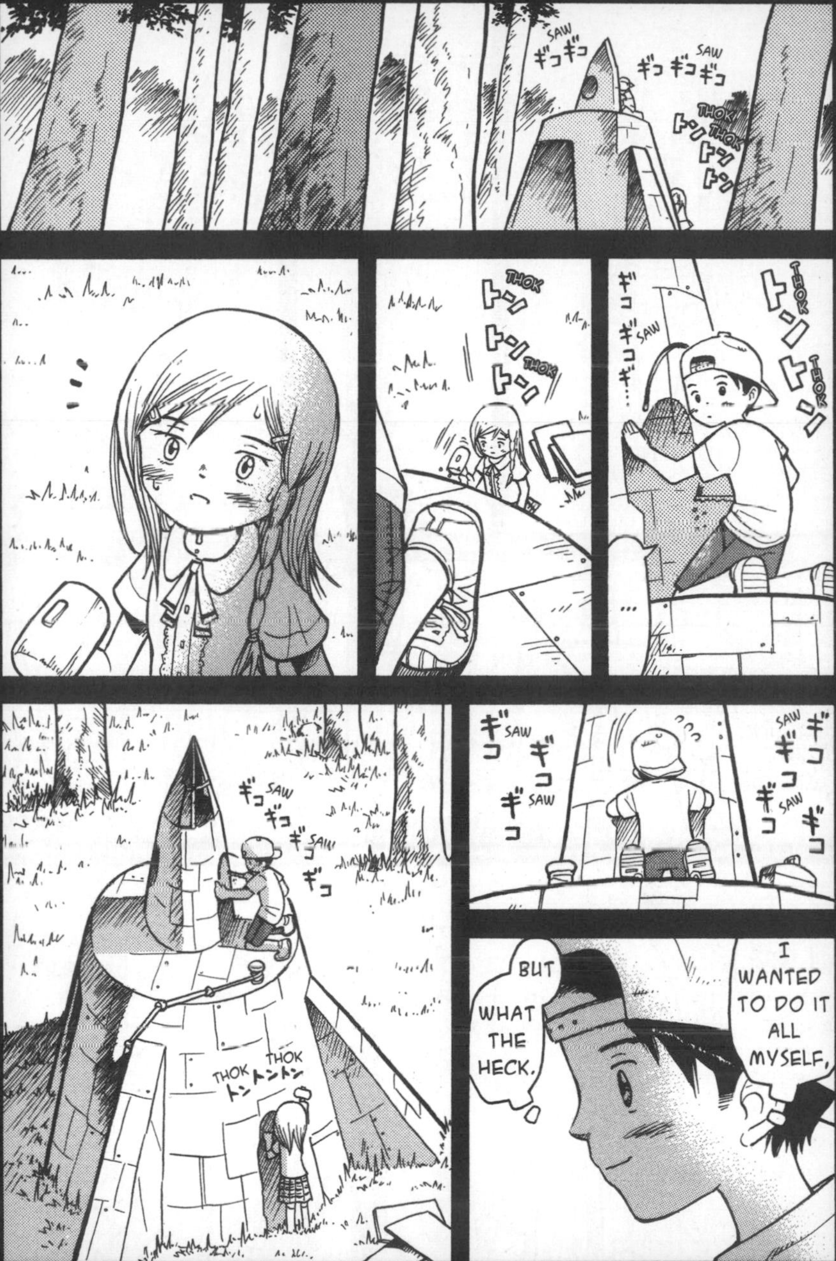
SAW
ギコギコ
SAW
ギコギコギコ
THOK
THOK
トンットントン
THOK
トンッ
トンッ
THOK
ギコ
SAW
ギコギ…
…
THOK
トンッ
トンッ
THOK
トンッ
トンッ
…
SAW
ギコ
ギコ
ギコ
SAW
ギコ
ギコ
SAW
ギコ
SAW
ギコ
I WANTED TO DO IT ALL MYSELF,
BUT WHAT THE HECK.
ギコ
SAW
ギコ
ギコ
SAW
ギコ
THOK
トン
THOK
トントン

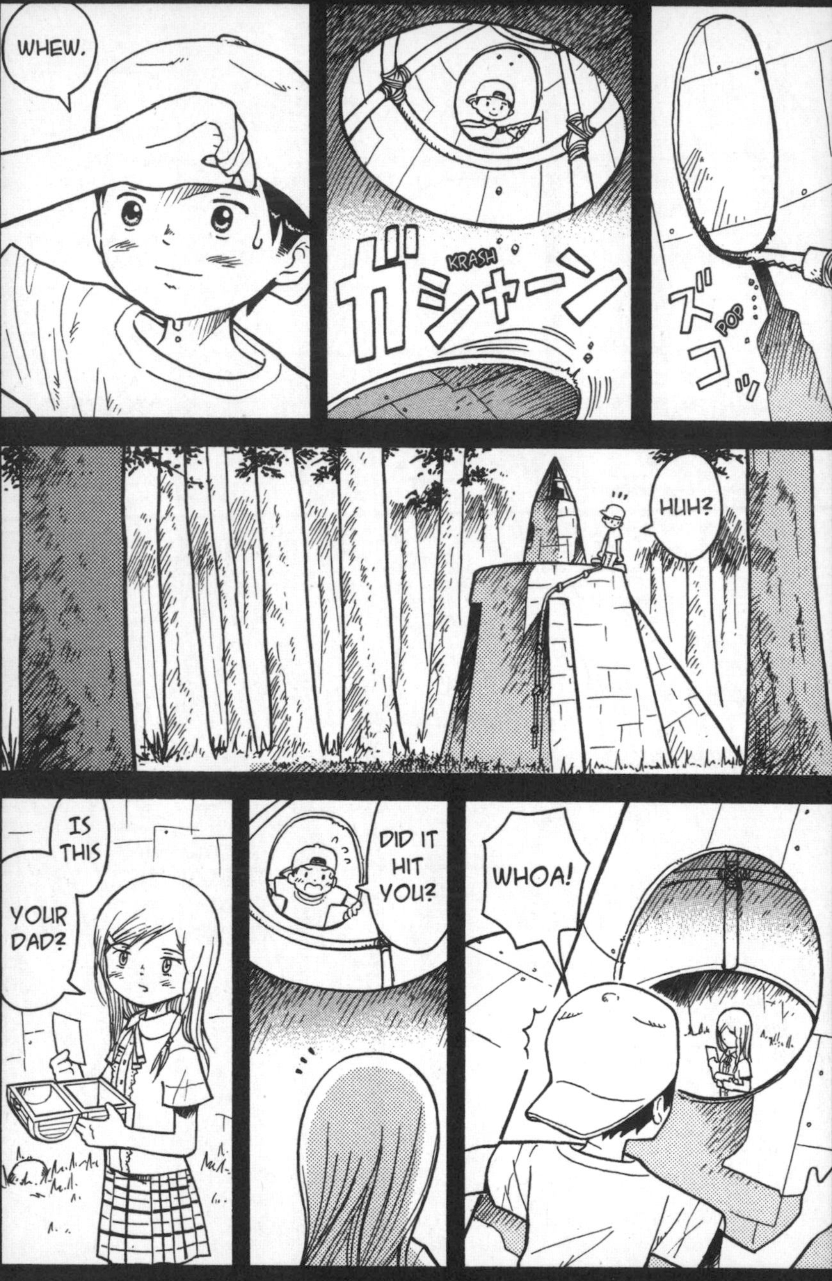
ズコッ
POP
ガシャーン
KRASH
WHEW.
HUH?
WHOA!
DID IT HIT YOU?
IS THIS YOUR DAD?

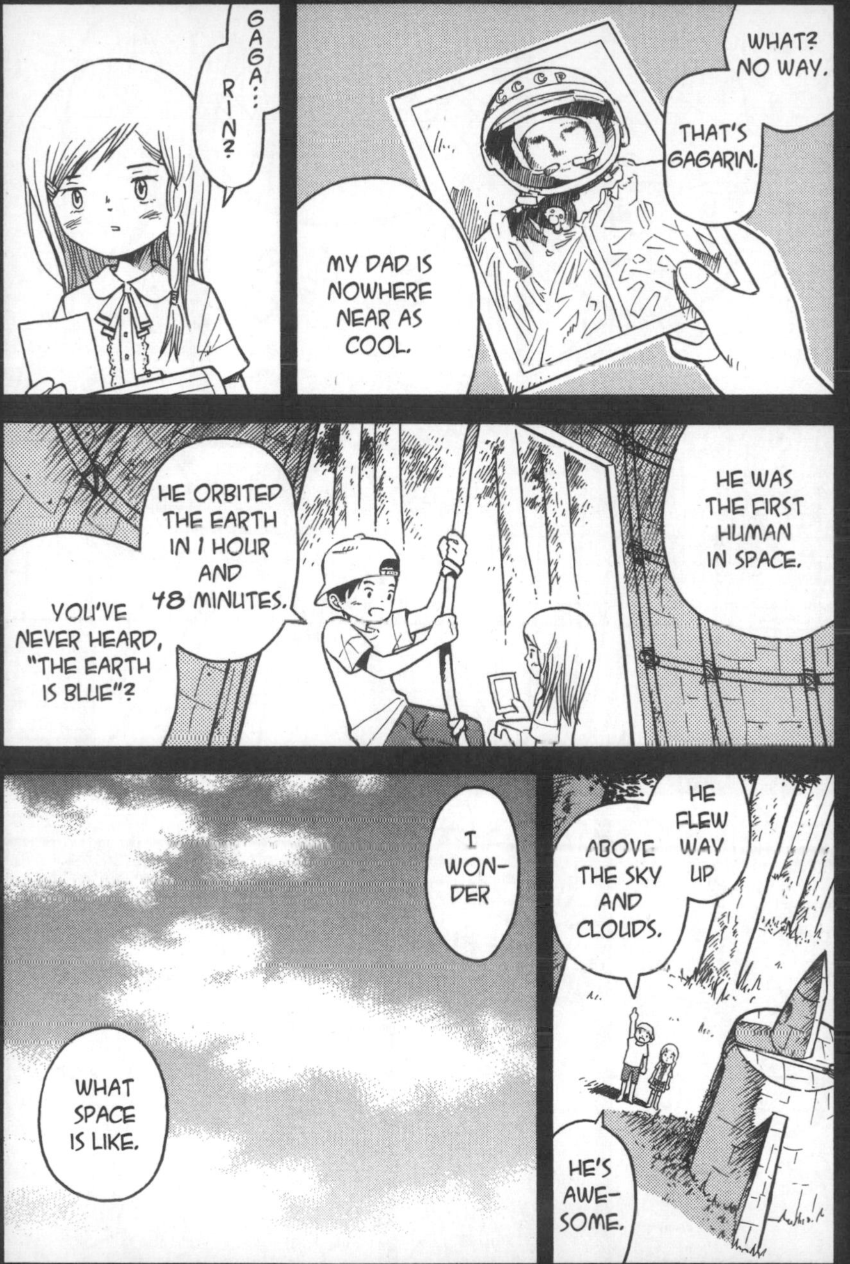
WHAT? NO WAY.
THAT'S GAGARIN.
MY DAD IS NOWHERE NEAR AS COOL.
GAGA... RIN?
HE WAS THE FIRST HUMAN IN SPACE.
HE ORBITED THE EARTH IN 1 HOUR AND 48 MINUTES.
YOU'VE NEVER HEARD, "THE EARTH IS BLUE"?
HE FLEW WAY UP
ABOVE THE SKY AND CLOUDS.
HE'S AWE-SOME.
I WON-DER
WHAT SPACE IS LIKE.

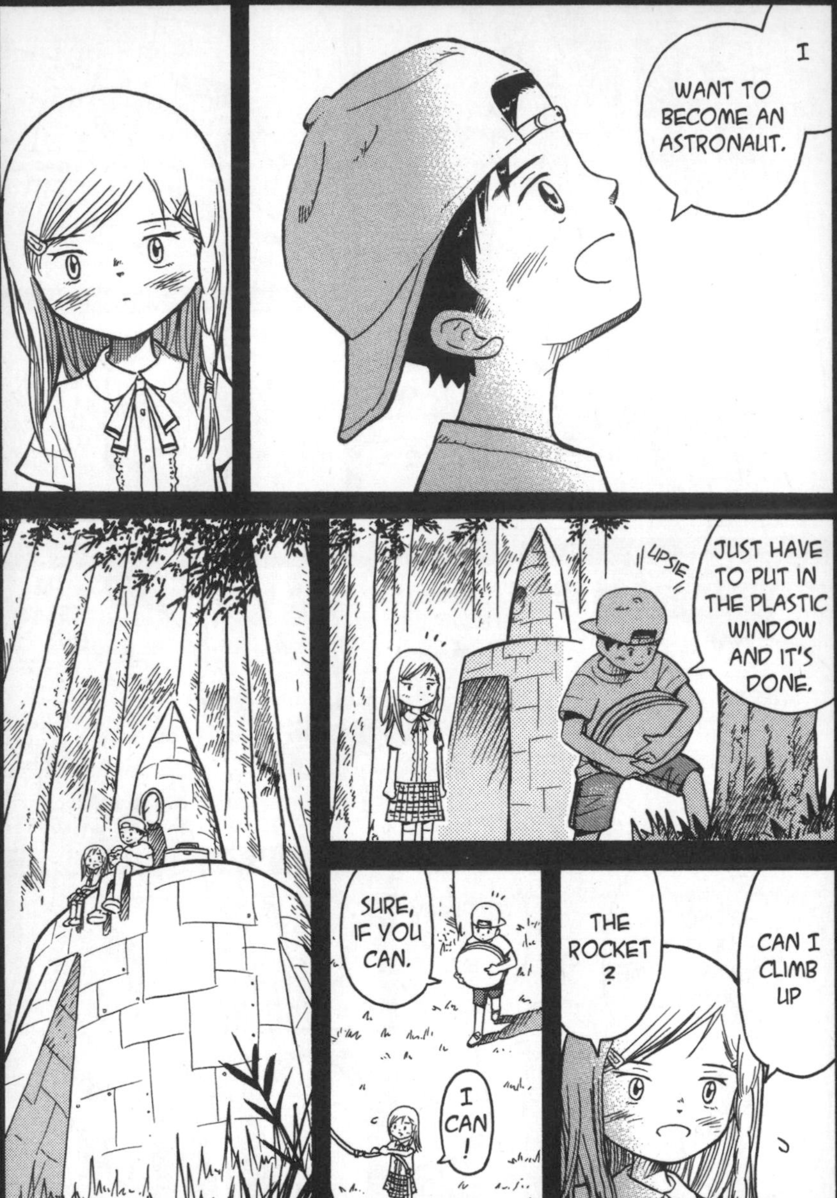
I
WANT TO BECOME AN ASTRONAUT.
UPSIE
JUST HAVE TO PUT IN THE PLASTIC WINDOW AND IT'S DONE.
CAN I CLIMB UP
THE ROCKET?
SURE, IF YOU CAN.
I CAN!

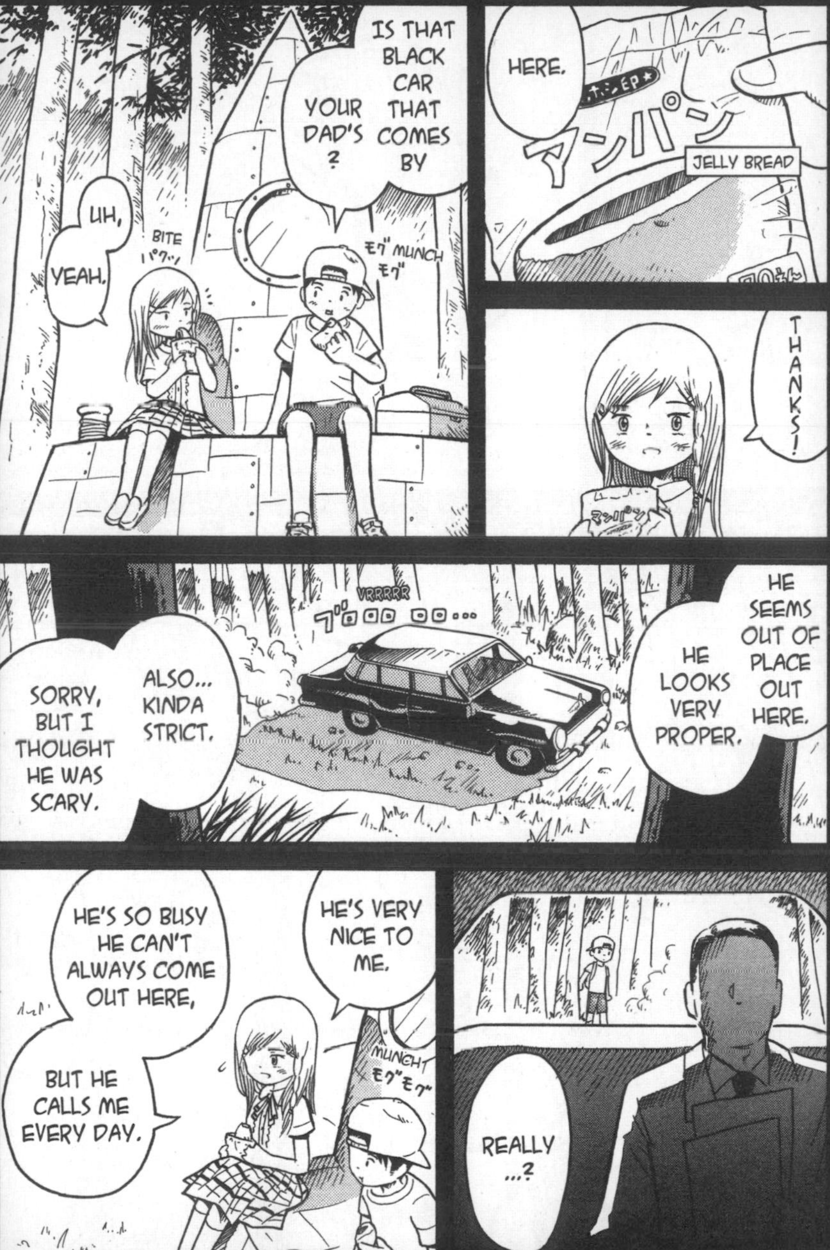
HERE.
JELLY BREAD
THANKS!
IS THAT BLACK CAR THAT COMES BY YOUR DAD'S?
UH, YEAH.
BITE
MUNCH
HE SEEMS OUT OF PLACE OUT HERE.
HE LOOKS VERY PROPER.
VRRRRR
ALSO... KINDA STRICT.
SORRY, BUT I THOUGHT HE WAS SCARY.
REALLY ...?
HE'S VERY NICE TO ME.
HE'S SO BUSY HE CAN'T ALWAYS COME OUT HERE,
BUT HE CALLS ME EVERY DAY.
MUNCH

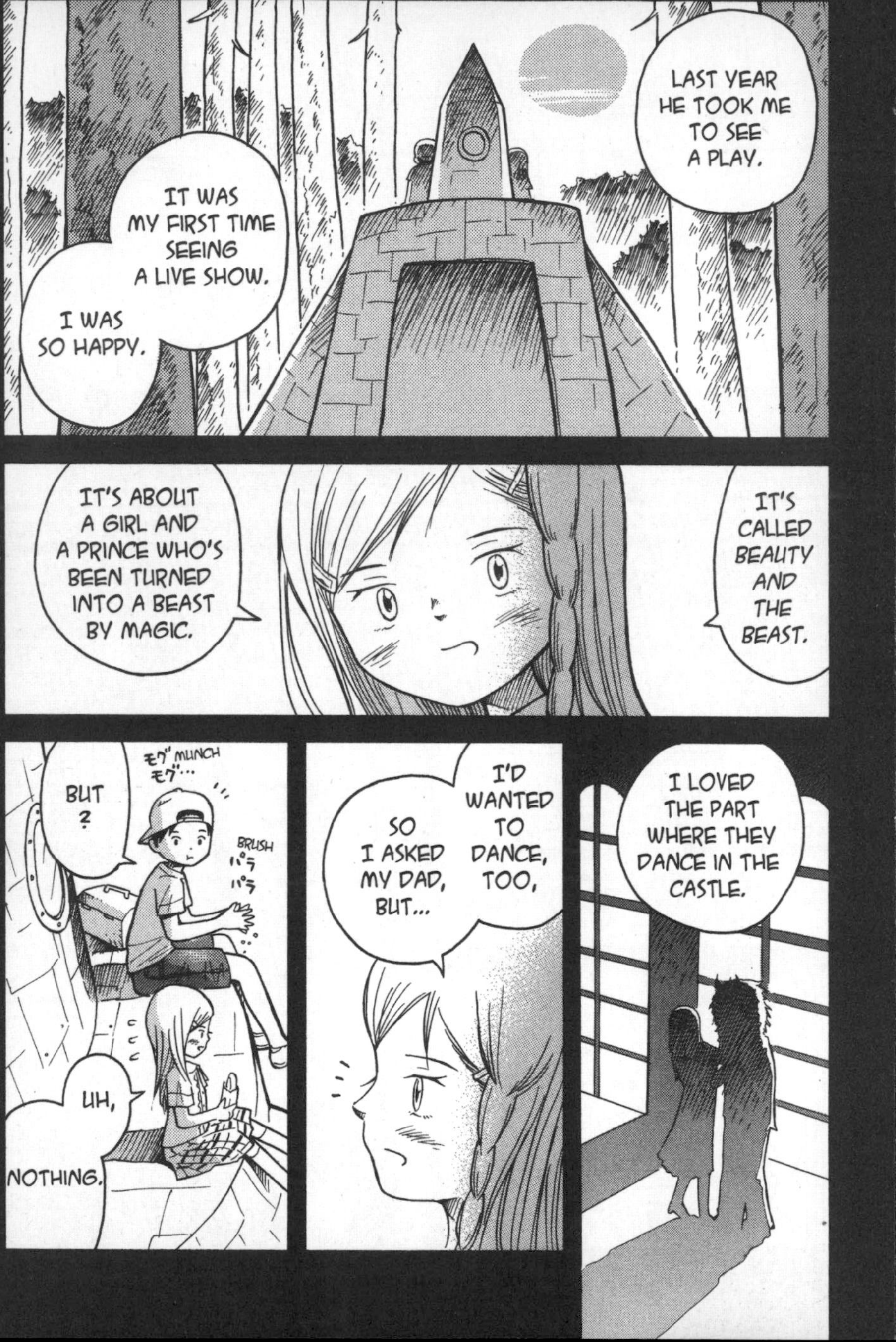
LAST YEAR HE TOOK ME TO SEE A PLAY.
IT WAS MY FIRST TIME SEEING A LIVE SHOW.
I WAS SO HAPPY.
IT'S CALLED BEAUTY AND THE BEAST.
IT'S ABOUT A GIRL AND A PRINCE WHO'S BEEN TURNED INTO A BEAST BY MAGIC.
I LOVED THE PART WHERE THEY DANCE IN THE CASTLE.
I'D WANTED TO DANCE, TOO,
SO I ASKED MY DAD, BUT...
BUT ?
モグ MUNCH モグ...
BRUSH パラ パラ
UH,
NOTHING.

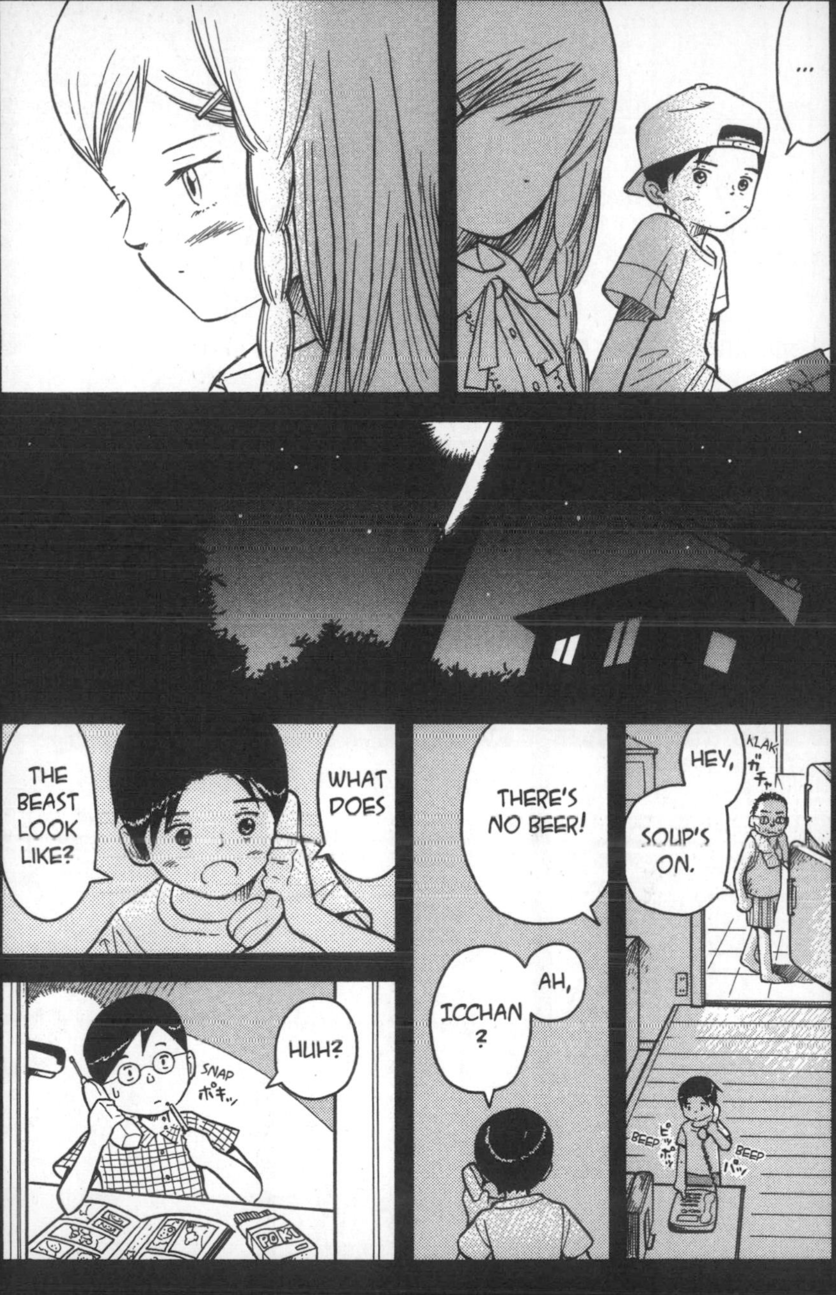
...
HEY,
KLAK
ガチャ
SOUP'S ON.
BEEP
ピッポッ
BEEP
パッ
THERE'S NO BEER!
AH, ICCHAN?
WHAT DOES
THE BEAST LOOK LIKE?
HUH?
SNAP
ポキッ

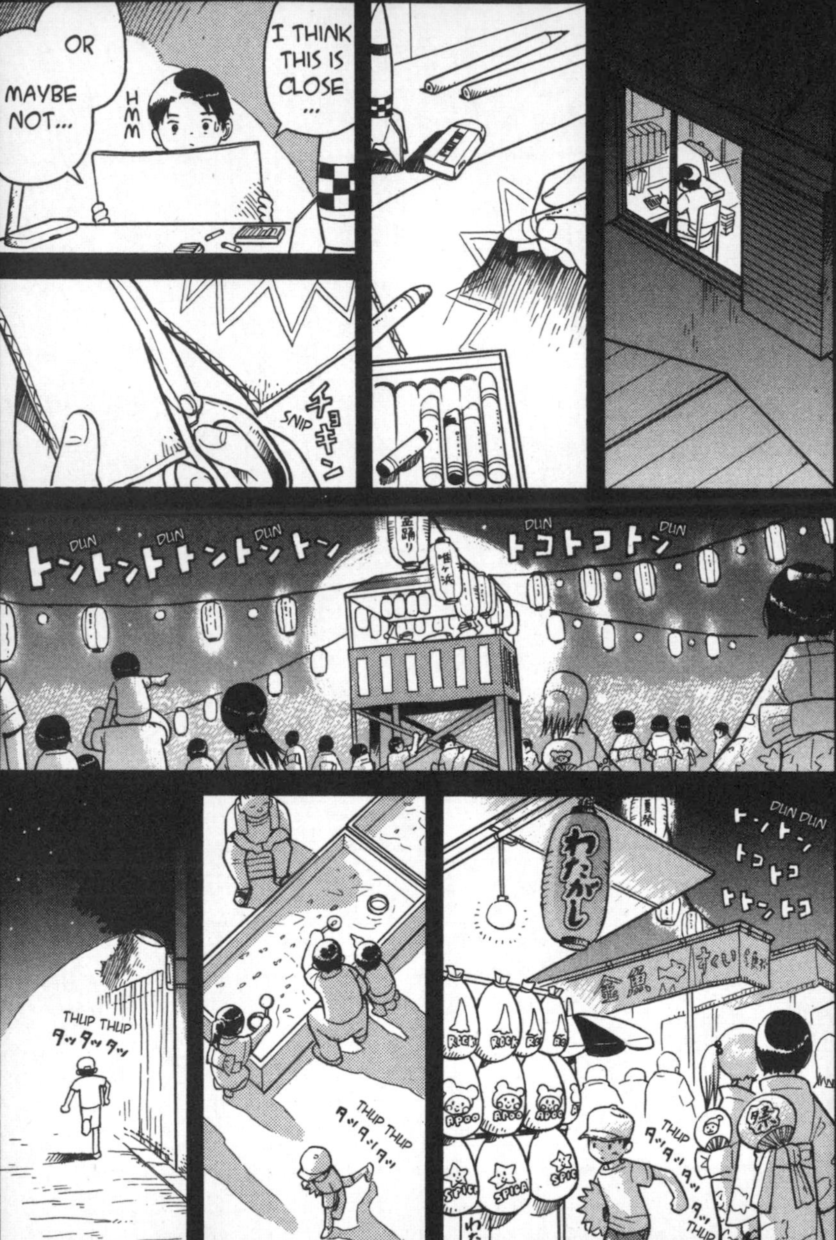
I THINK THIS IS CLOSE...
HMM
OR
MAYBE NOT...
チョキン
SNIP
トコトコトン
DUN
盆踊り
唯ケ浜
トントントントントントーン
DUN DUN DUN
DUN DUN
トーントーン
トコトコ
トトーントコ
わたがし
金魚すくい
THUP
タッタッタッ
THUP
わたがー
THUP THUP
タッタッタッ
THUP THUP
タッタッタッ

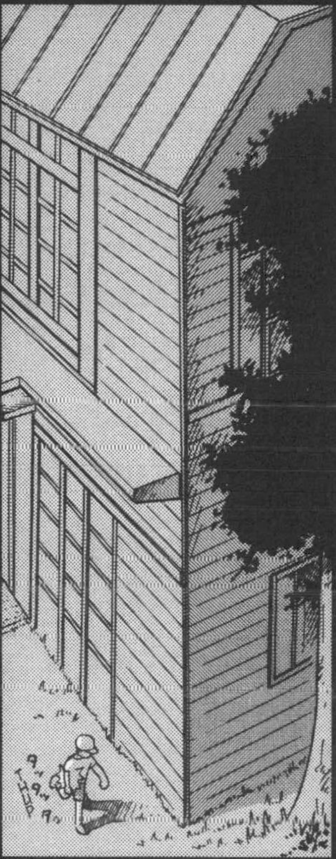
THUD
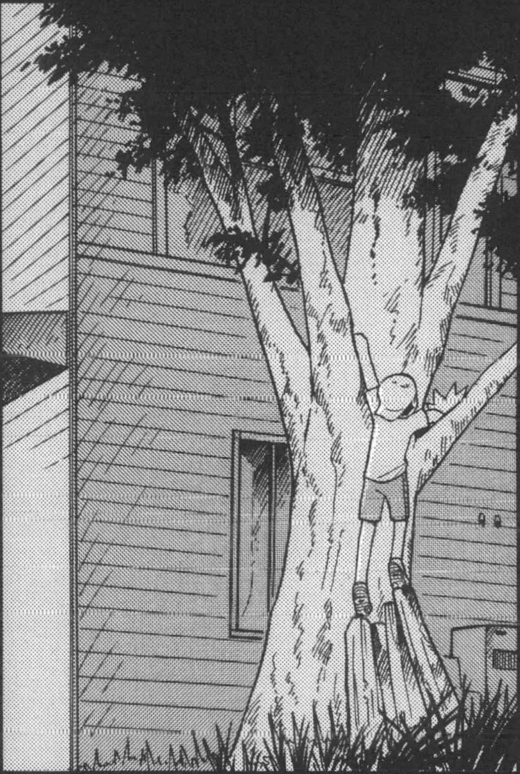
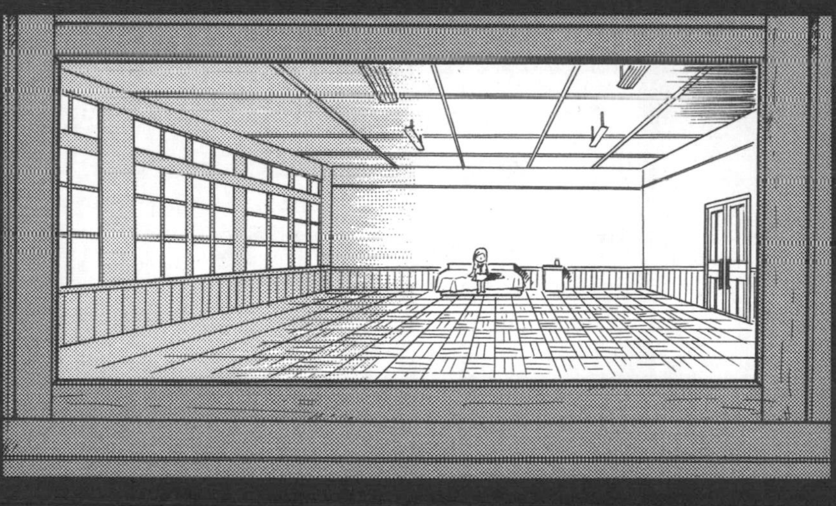

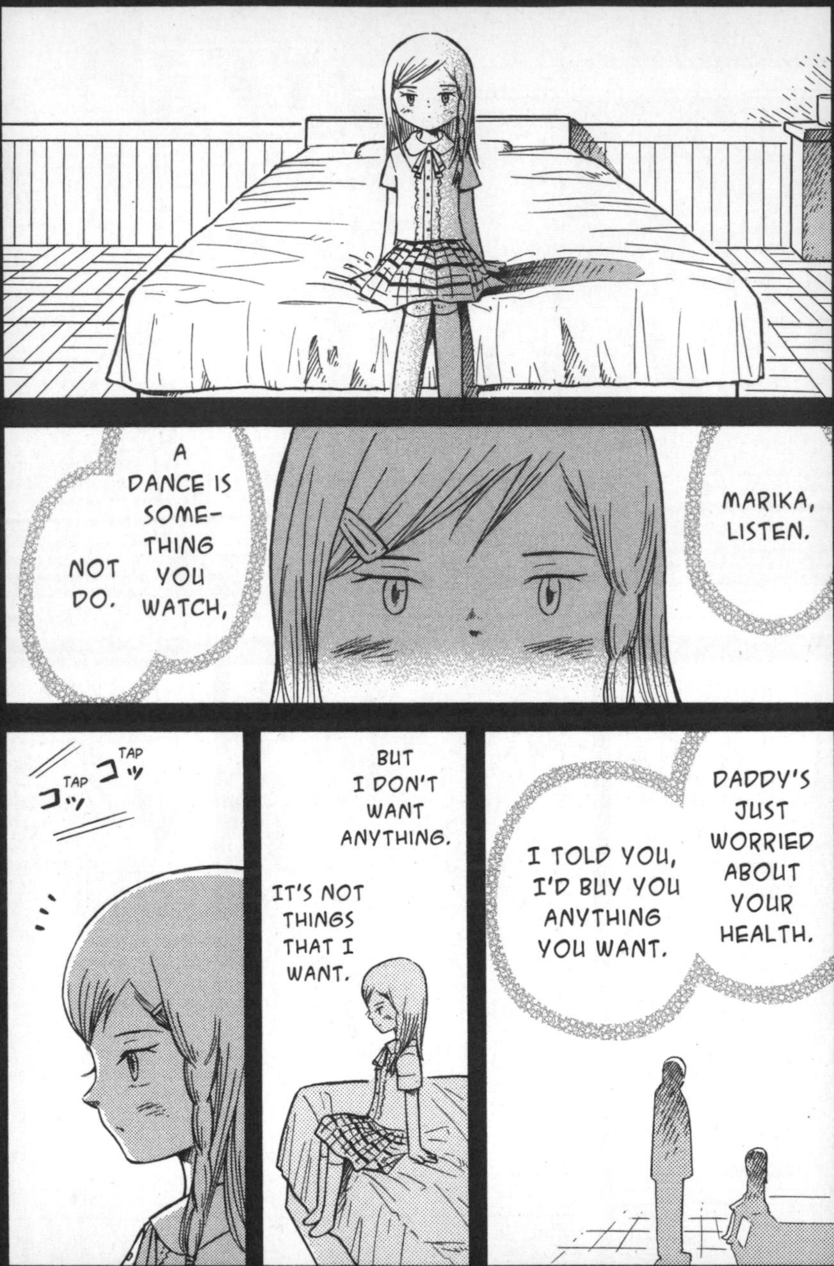
MARIKA, LISTEN.
A DANCE IS SOME-THING YOU WATCH, NOT DO.
DADDY'S JUST WORRIED ABOUT YOUR HEALTH.
I TOLD YOU, I'D BUY YOU ANYTHING YOU WANT.
BUT I DON'T WANT ANYTHING.
IT'S NOT THINGS THAT I WANT.
コッ TAP
コッ TAP
...

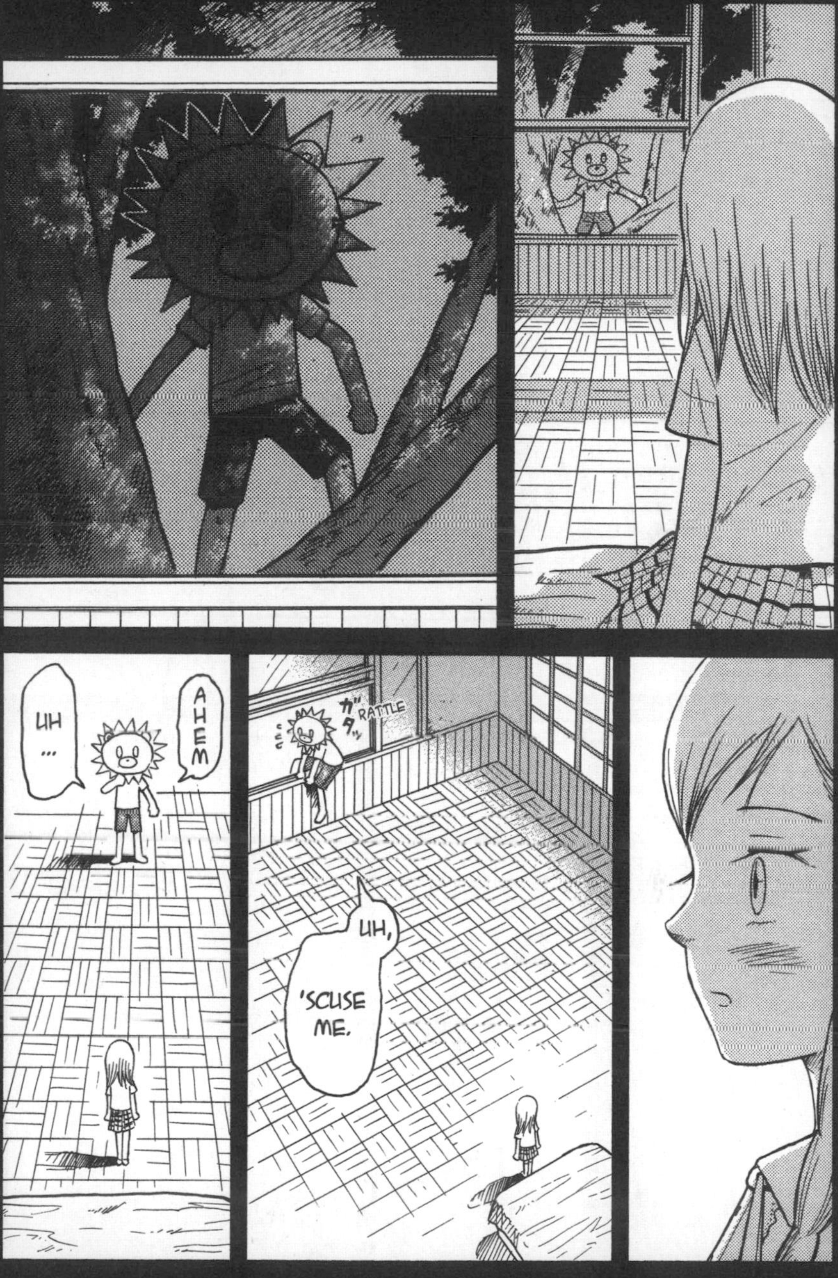
ガタッ
RATTLE
UH, 'SCUSE ME.
AHEM
UH ...

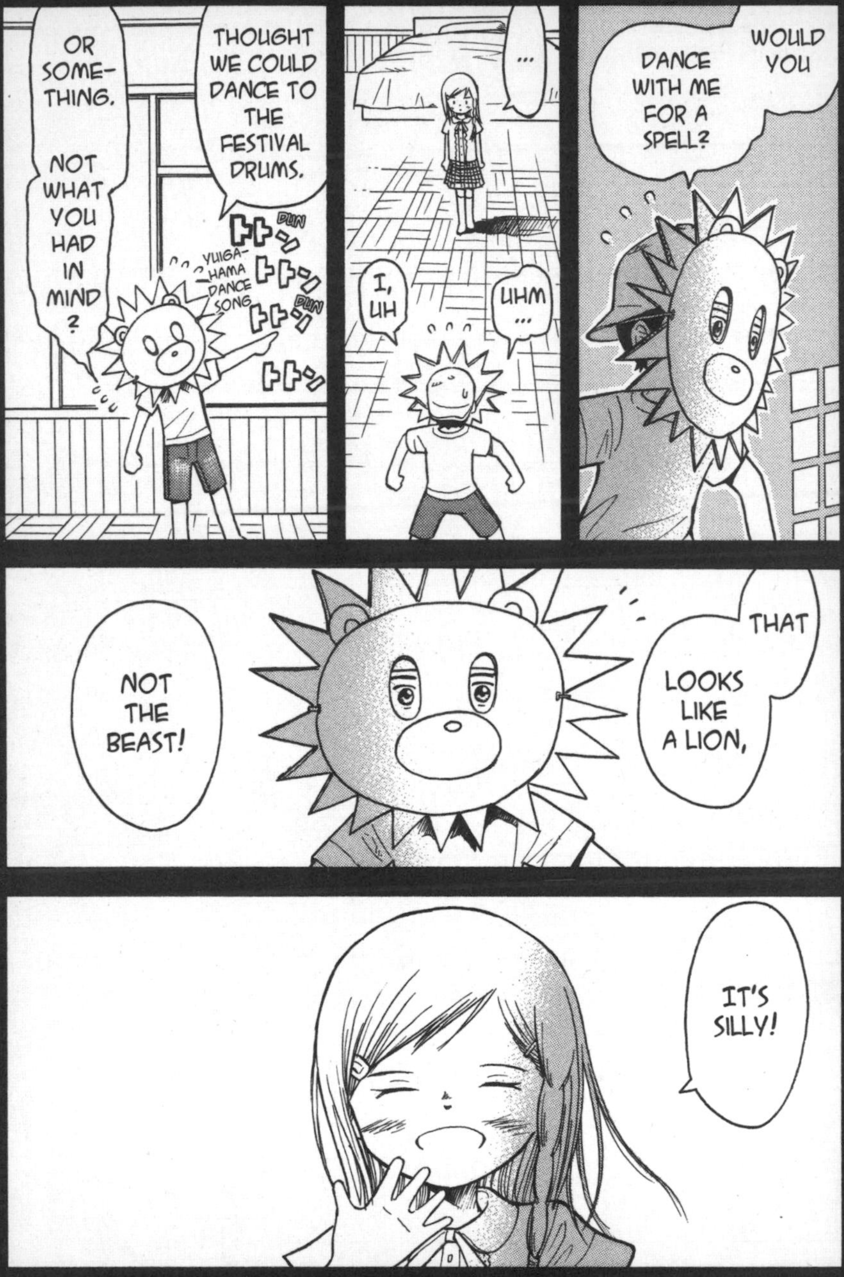
WOULD YOU DANCE WITH ME FOR A SPELL?
...
UHM ...
I, UH
THOUGHT WE COULD DANCE TO THE FESTIVAL DRUMS.
トトッ DUN
YUIGA-HAMA DANCE SONG
トトッ
トトッ DUN
トトッ
OR SOME-THING.
NOT WHAT YOU HAD IN MIND?
THAT LOOKS LIKE A LION,
NOT THE BEAST!
IT'S SILLY!

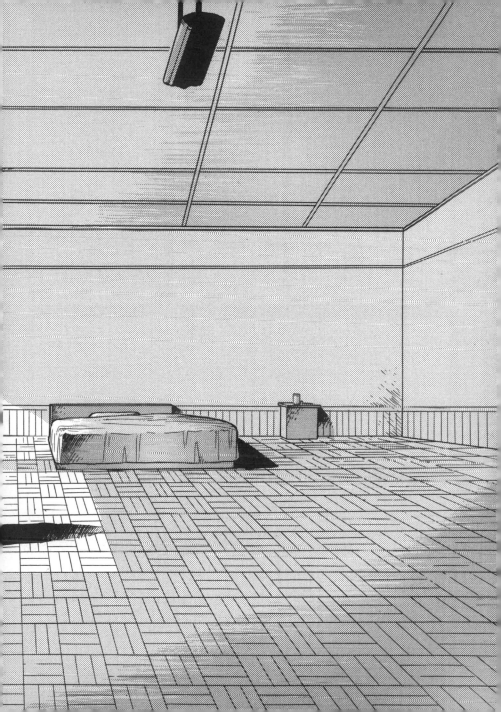

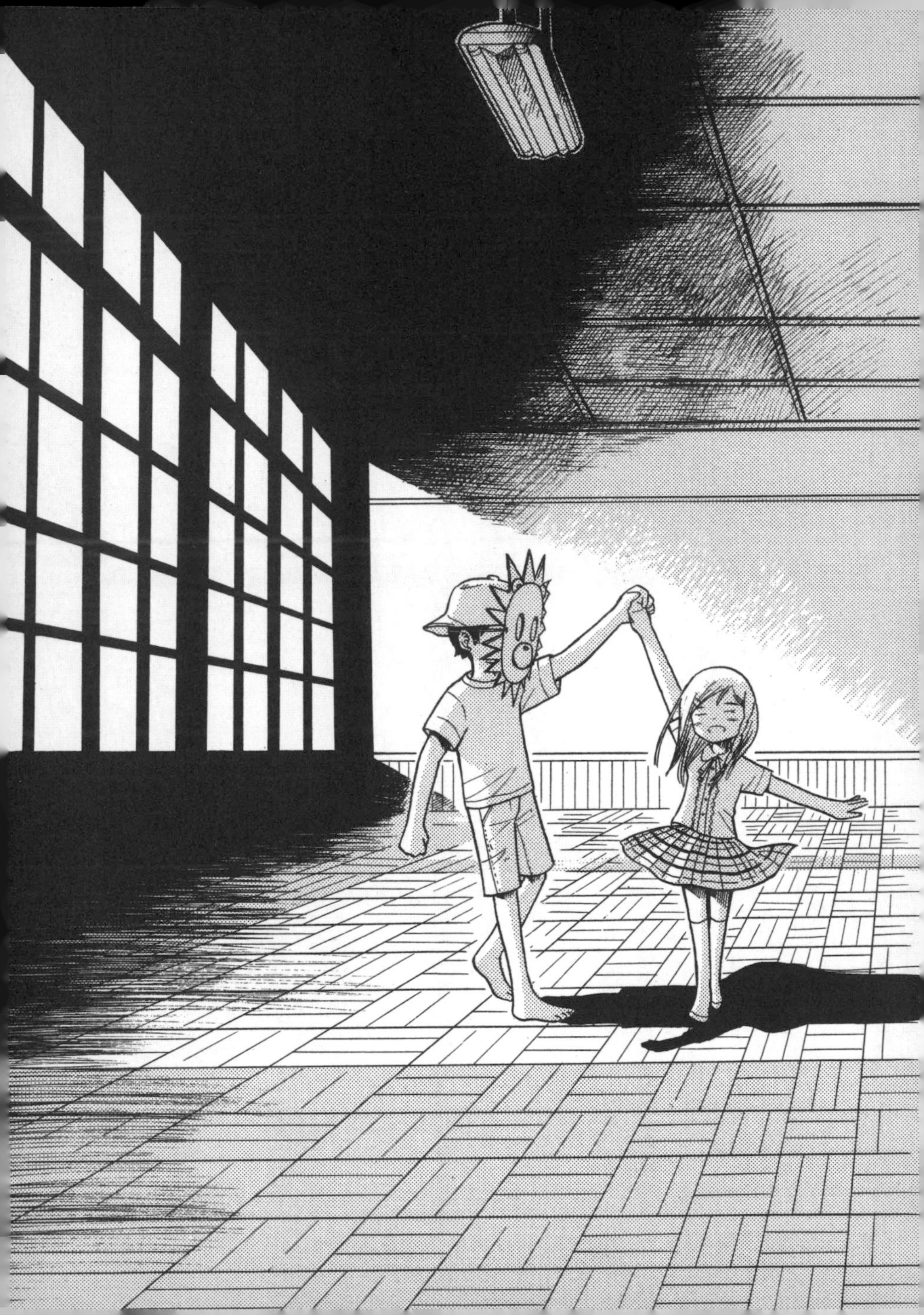

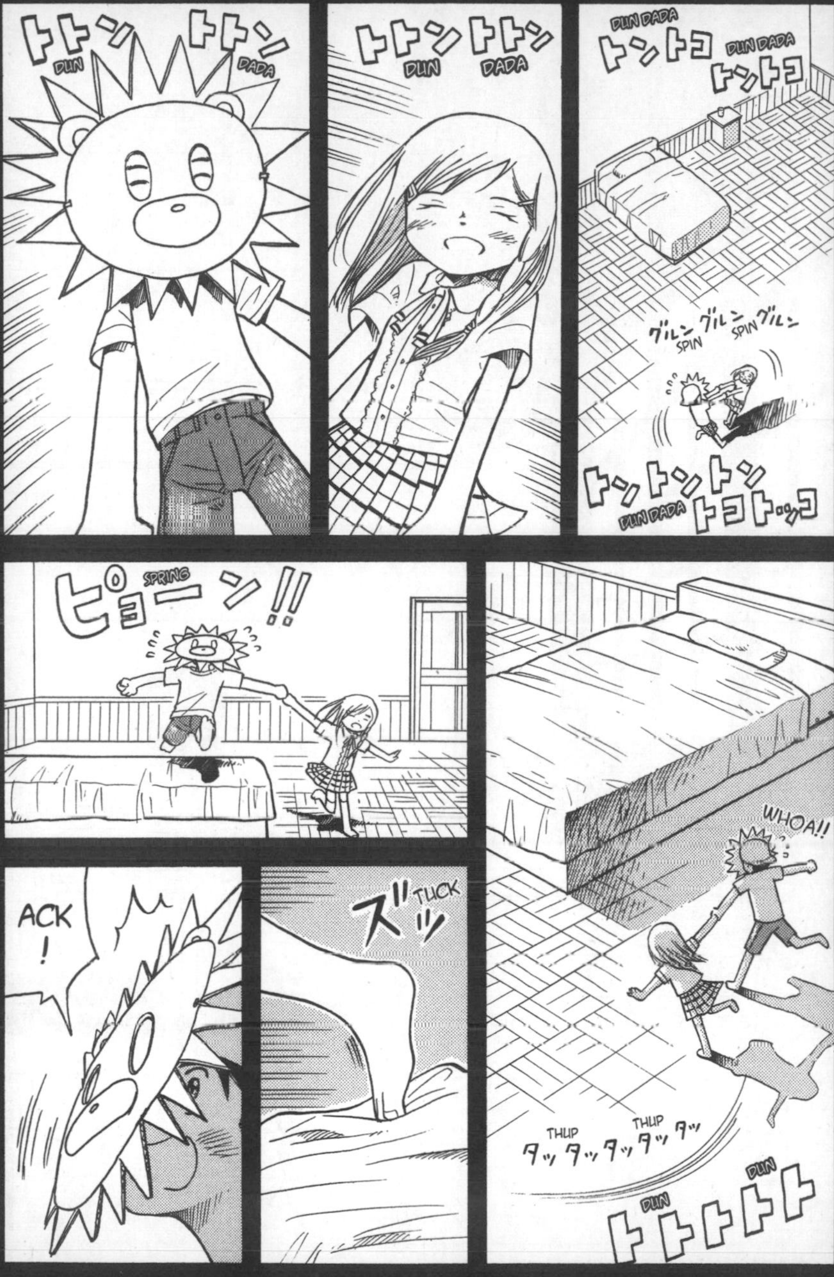

DUN DADA
トントコ
DUN DADA
トントコ
グルン SPIN グルン SPIN グルン
トントントン
DUN DADA
トコトッコ
トトントトン
DUN DADA
トトン
DUN
トトン
DADA
WHOA!!
THUP THUP
タッタッタッタッタッ
DUN DUN
トトトトト
SPRING
ピョーン!!
TUCK
ズッ
ACK!

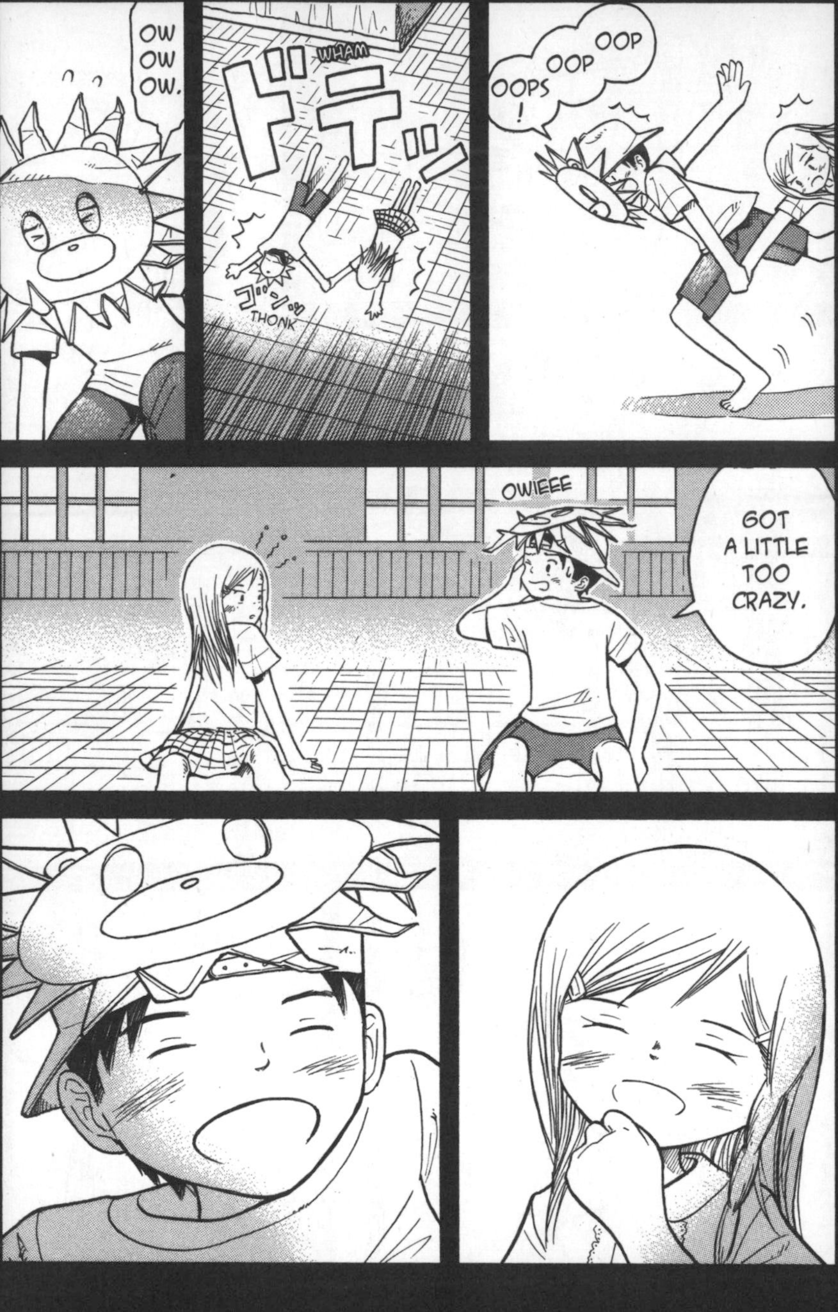
OOPS! OOP OOP
ドテッー
WHAM
ゴンッ
THONK
OW OW OW.
GOT A LITTLE TOO CRAZY.
OWIEEE

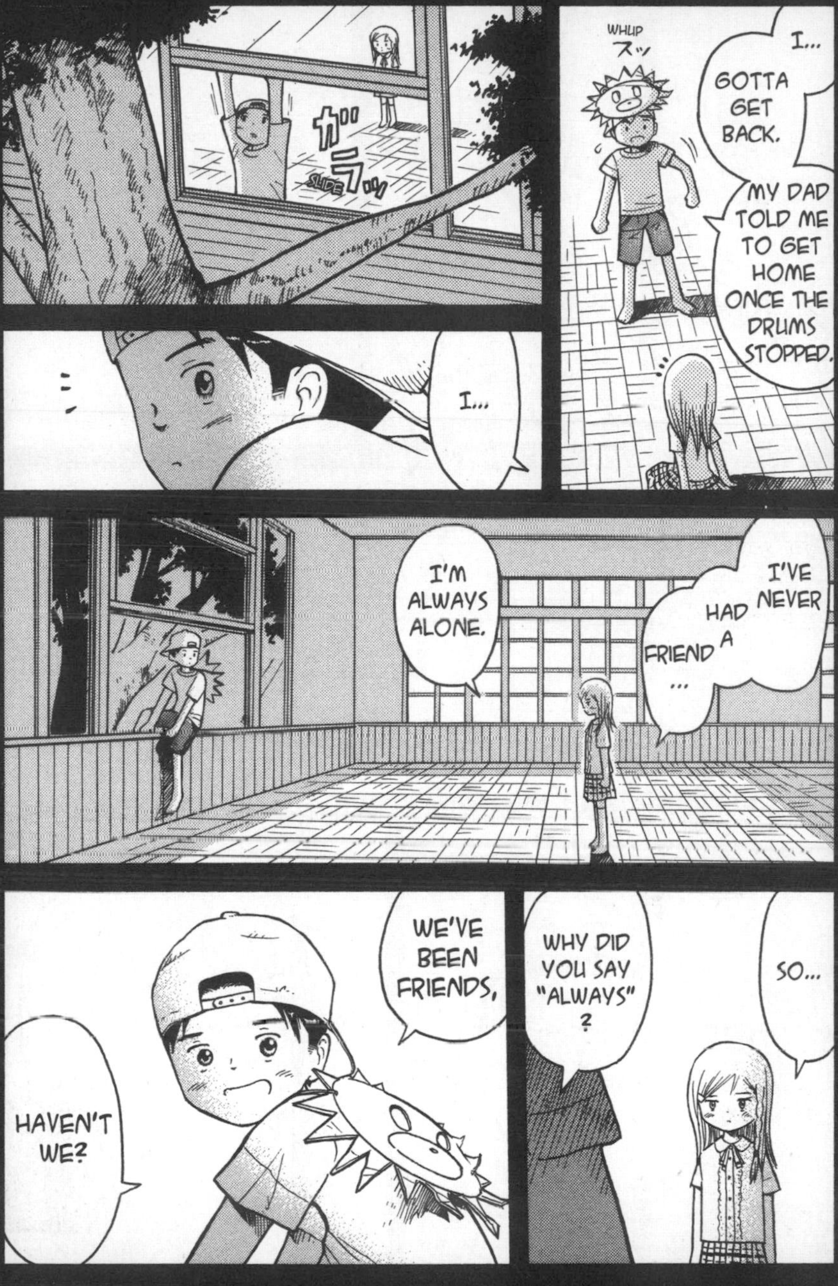
WHUP
スッ
I...
GOTTA GET BACK.
MY DAD TOLD ME TO GET HOME ONCE THE DRUMS STOPPED.
ガラッ
SLIDE
I...
I'VE NEVER HAD A FRIEND...
I'M ALWAYS ALONE.
SO...
WHY DID YOU SAY "ALWAYS"?
WE'VE BEEN FRIENDS,
HAVEN'T WE?

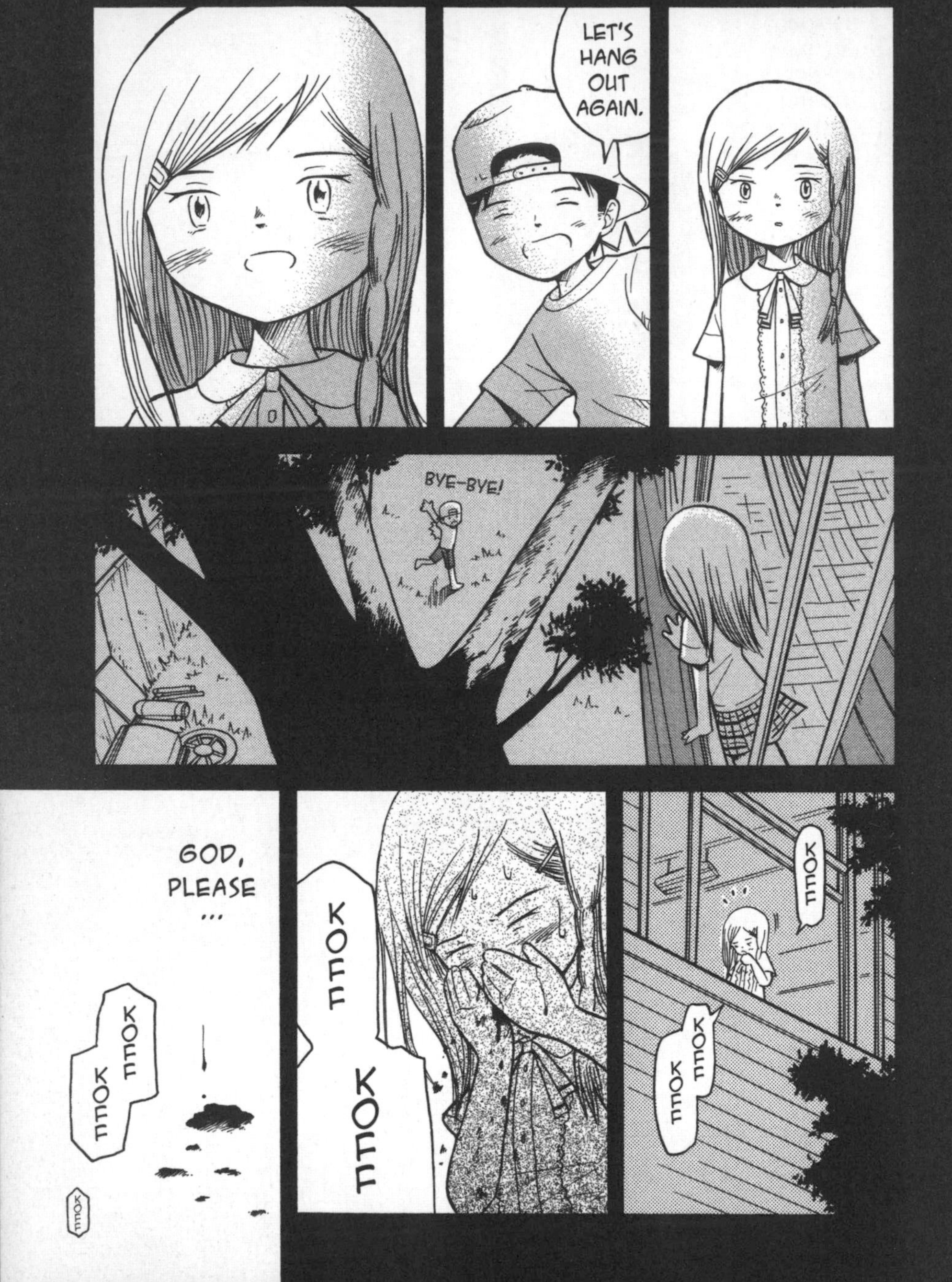
LET'S HANG OUT AGAIN.
BYE-BYE!
KOFF
KOFF KOFF
KOFF KOFF
GOD, PLEASE ...
KOFF KOFF
KOFF

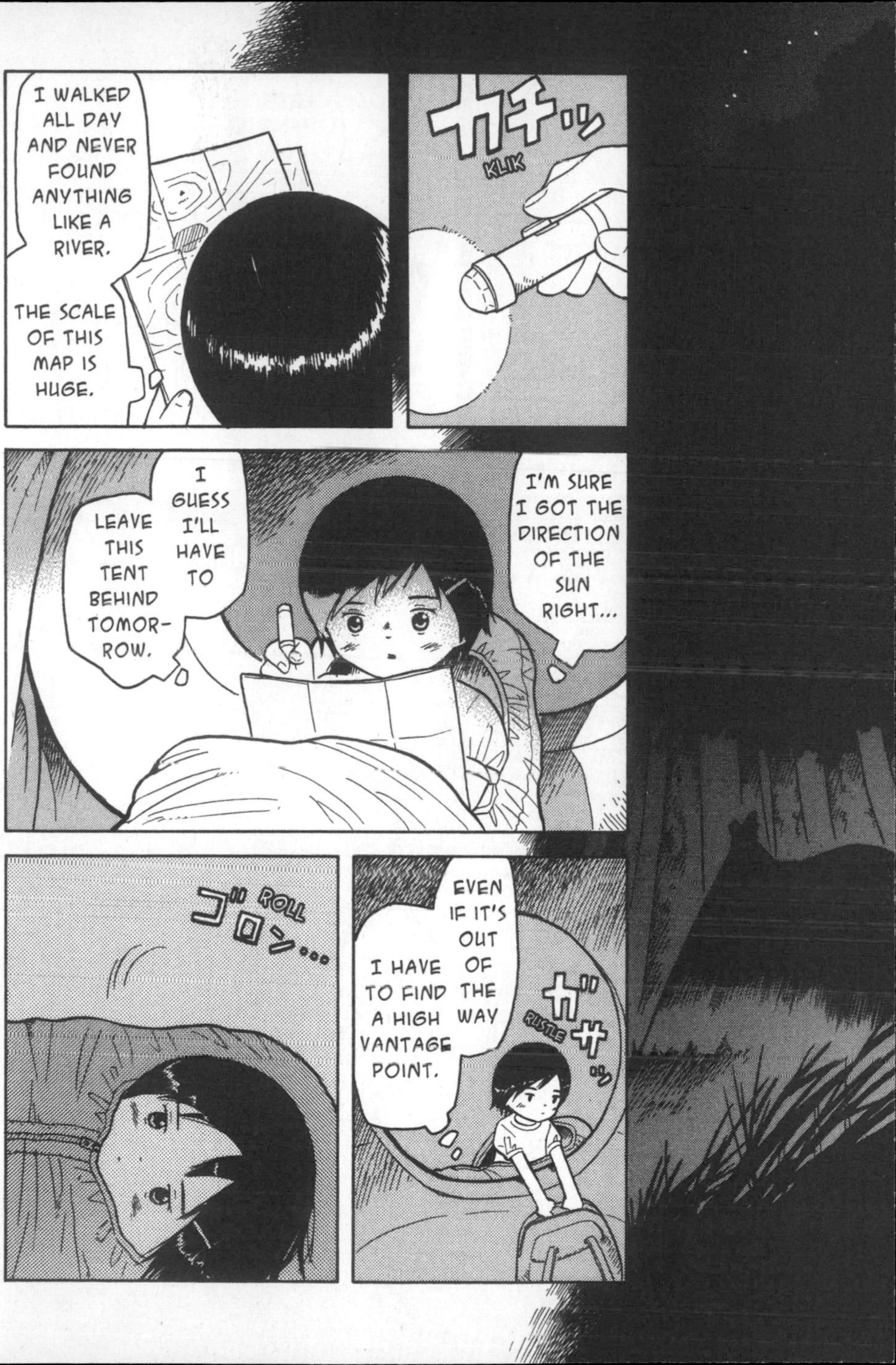
カチッ
KLIK
I WALKED ALL DAY AND NEVER FOUND ANYTHING LIKE A RIVER.
THE SCALE OF THIS MAP IS HUGE.
I'M SURE I GOT THE DIRECTION OF THE SUN RIGHT...
I GUESS I'LL HAVE TO LEAVE THIS TENT BEHIND TOMORROW.
EVEN IF IT'S OUT OF THE WAY I HAVE TO FIND A HIGH VANTAGE POINT.
ガサッ
RUSTLE
ゴロン...
ROLL

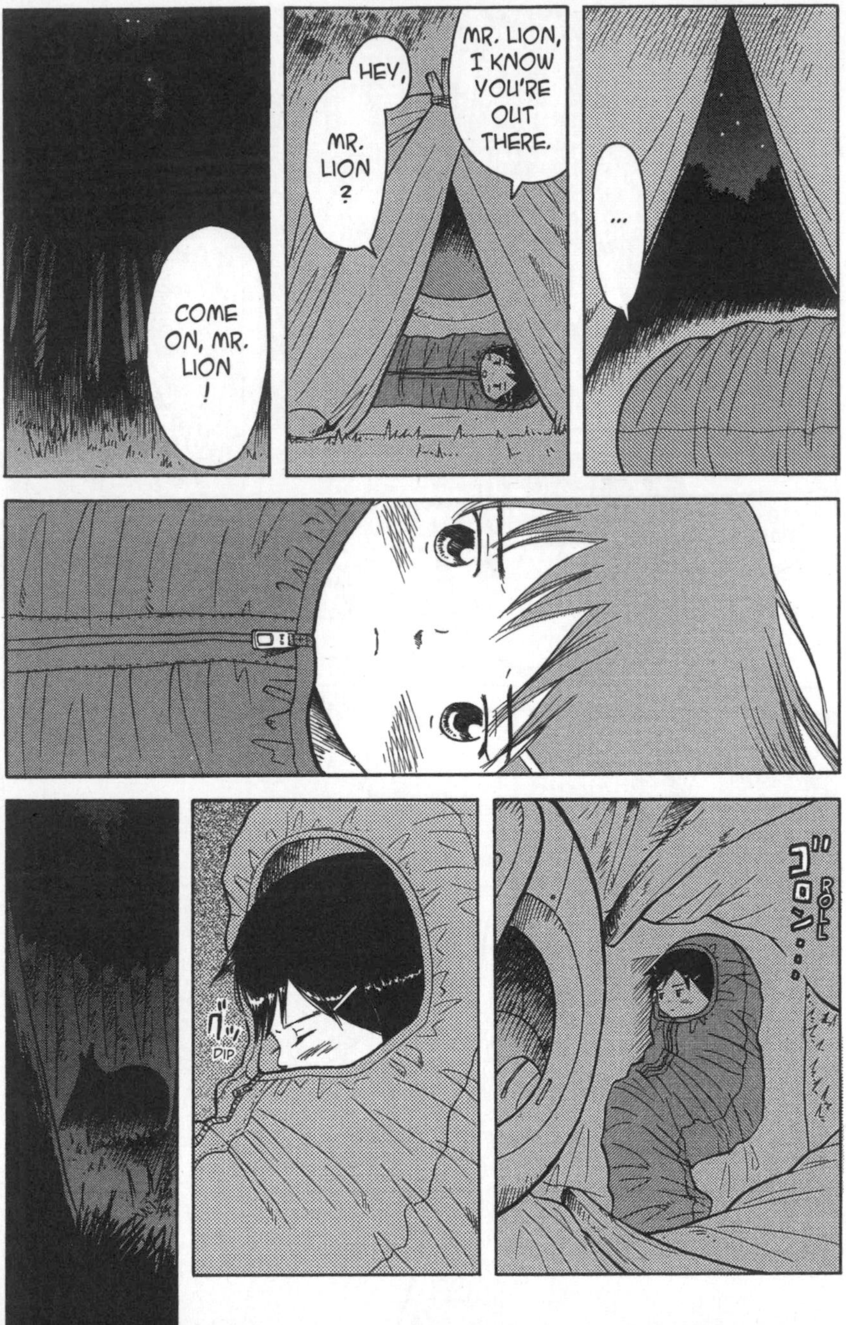
...
MR. LION, I KNOW YOU'RE OUT THERE.
HEY, MR. LION?
COME ON, MR. LION!
ゴロン…
ROLL
グッ
DIP

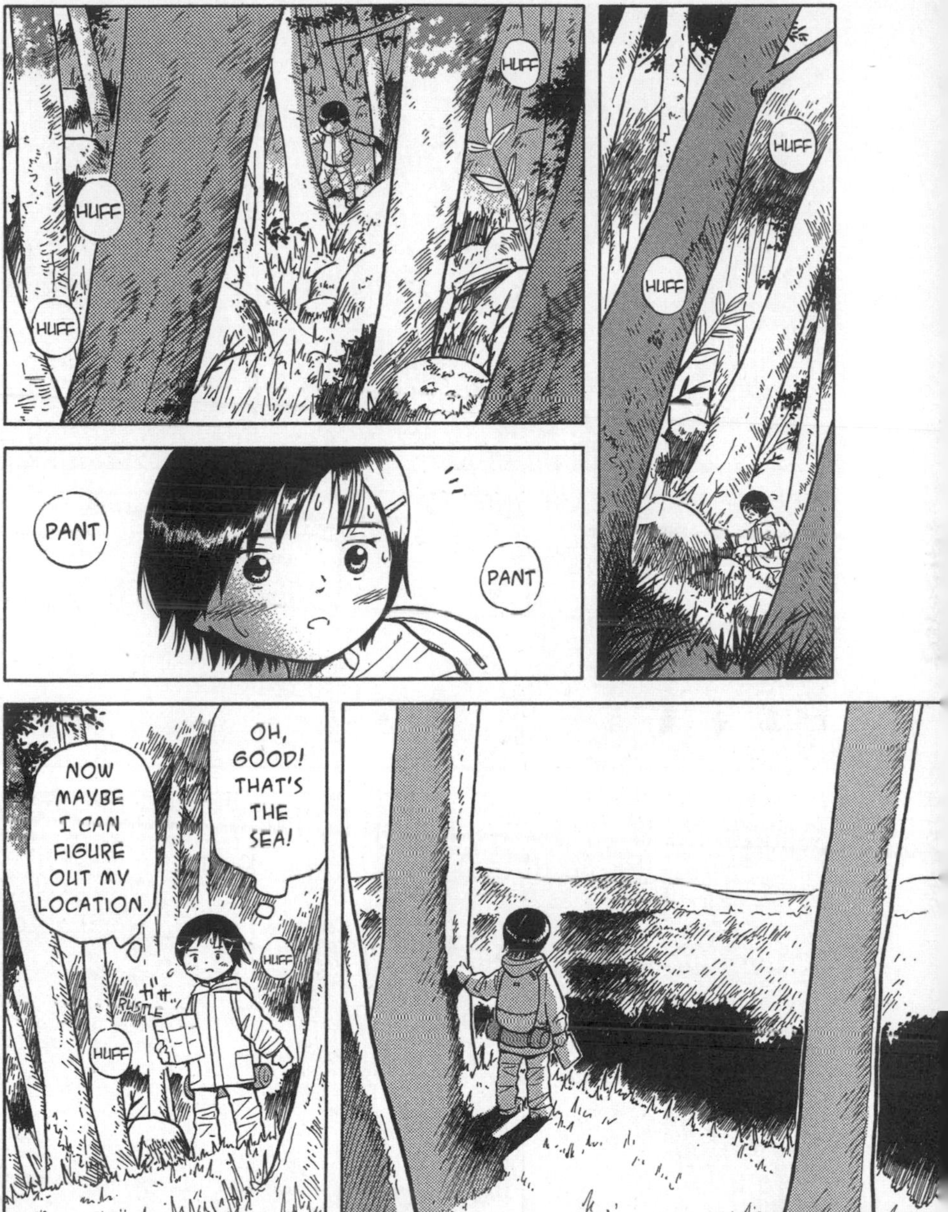
HUFF
HUFF
HUFF
HUFF
HUFF
PANT
PANT
OH, GOOD! THAT'S THE SEA!
NOW MAYBE I CAN FIGURE OUT MY LOCATION.
HUFF
RUSTLE
HUFF

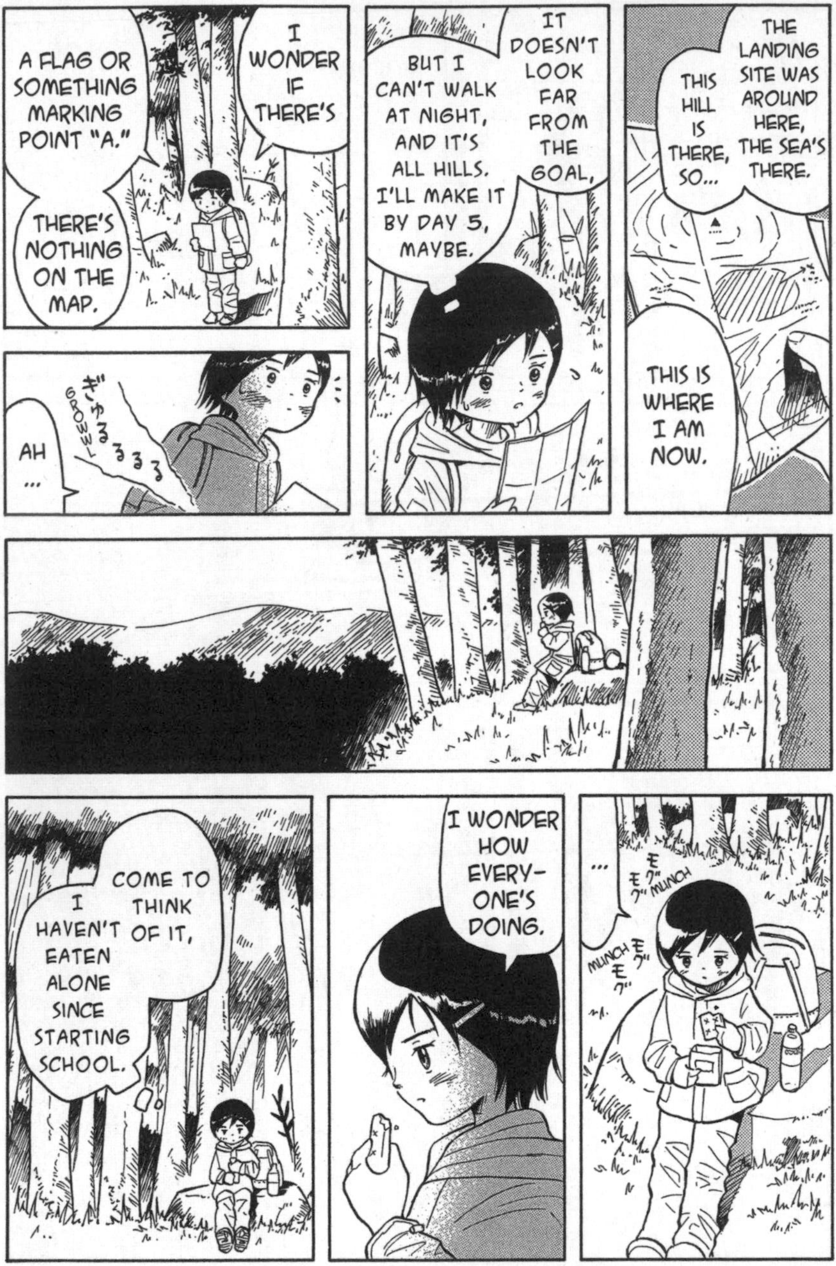
THE LANDING SITE WAS AROUND HERE, THE SEA'S THERE.
THIS HILL IS THERE, SO...
THIS IS WHERE I AM NOW.
IT DOESN'T LOOK FAR FROM THE GOAL,
BUT I CAN'T WALK AT NIGHT, AND IT'S ALL HILLS. I'LL MAKE IT BY DAY 5, MAYBE.
I WONDER IF THERE'S
A FLAG OR SOMETHING MARKING POINT "A."
THERE'S NOTHING ON THE MAP.
ぎゅるるるる
GROWL
AH ...
...
モグモグ
MUNCH
MUNCH
モグモグ
I WONDER HOW EVERY-ONE'S DOING.
COME TO THINK OF IT,
I HAVEN'T EATEN ALONE SINCE STARTING SCHOOL.

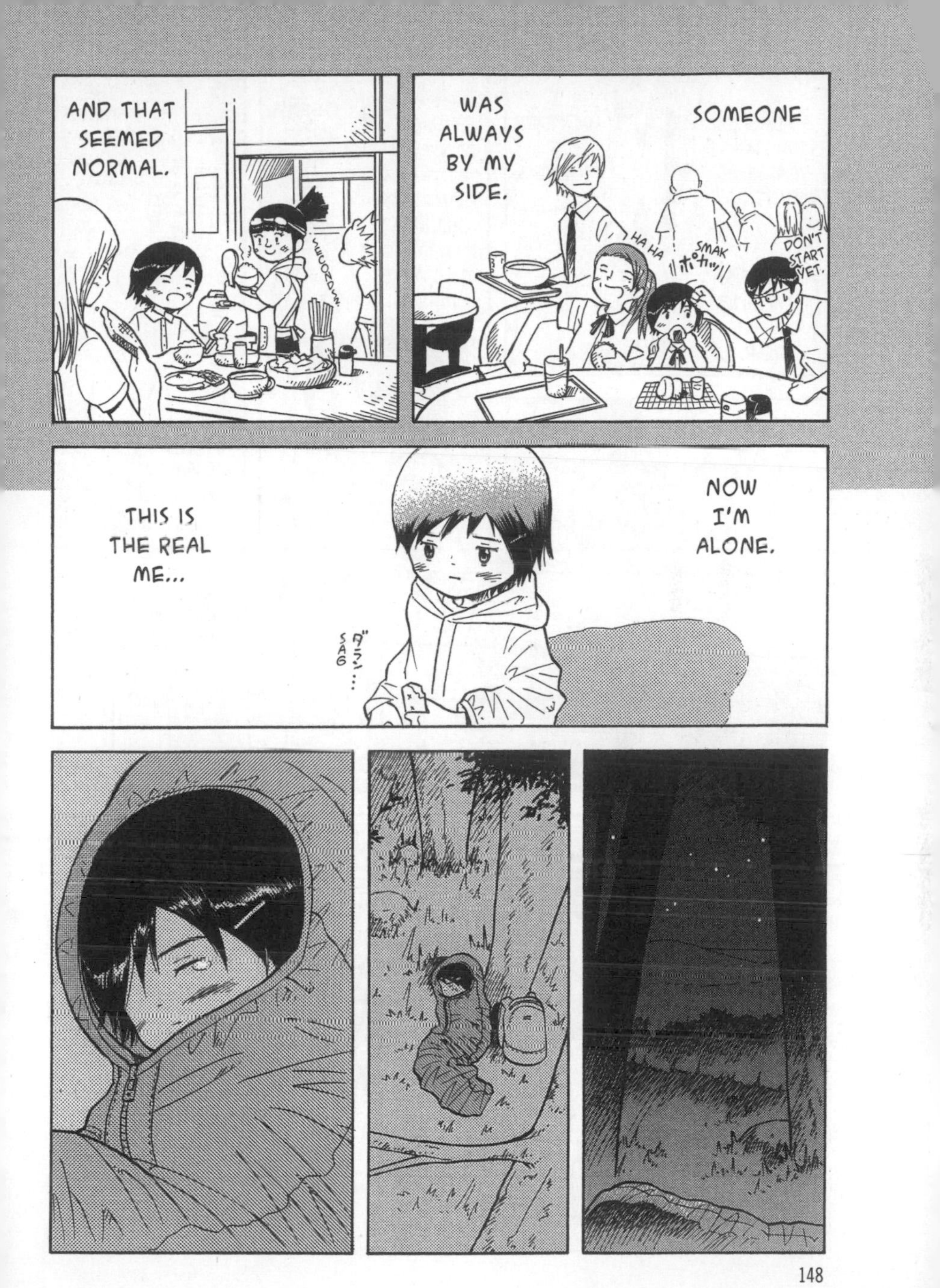
SOMEONE
WAS ALWAYS BY MY SIDE.
HA HA
SMAK
DON'T START YET.
AND THAT SEEMED NORMAL.
SECONDS.
NOW I'M ALONE.
THIS IS THE REAL ME...
SAG

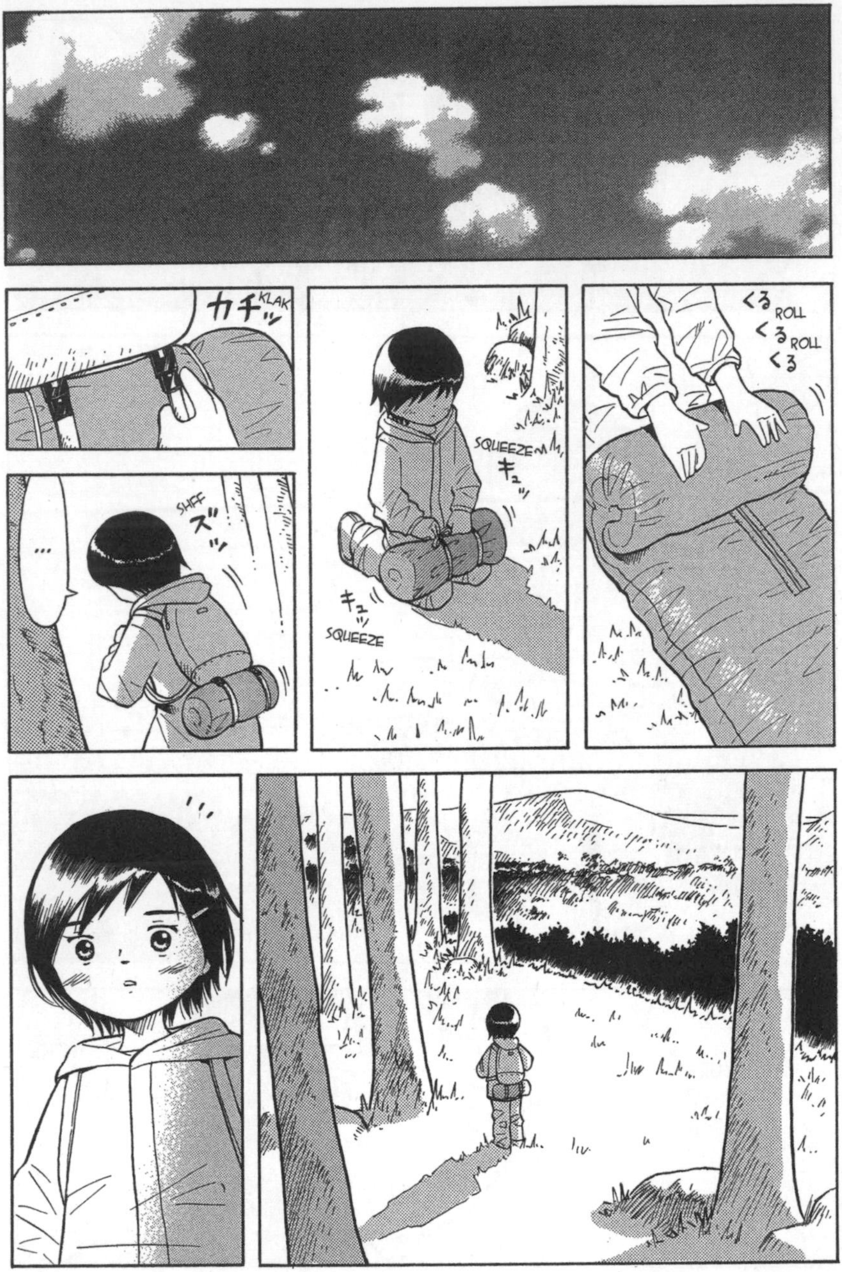
くる ROLL
くる ROLL
くる
SQUEEZE キュッ
キュッ SQUEEZE
カチッ KLAK
SHFF ズッ
...

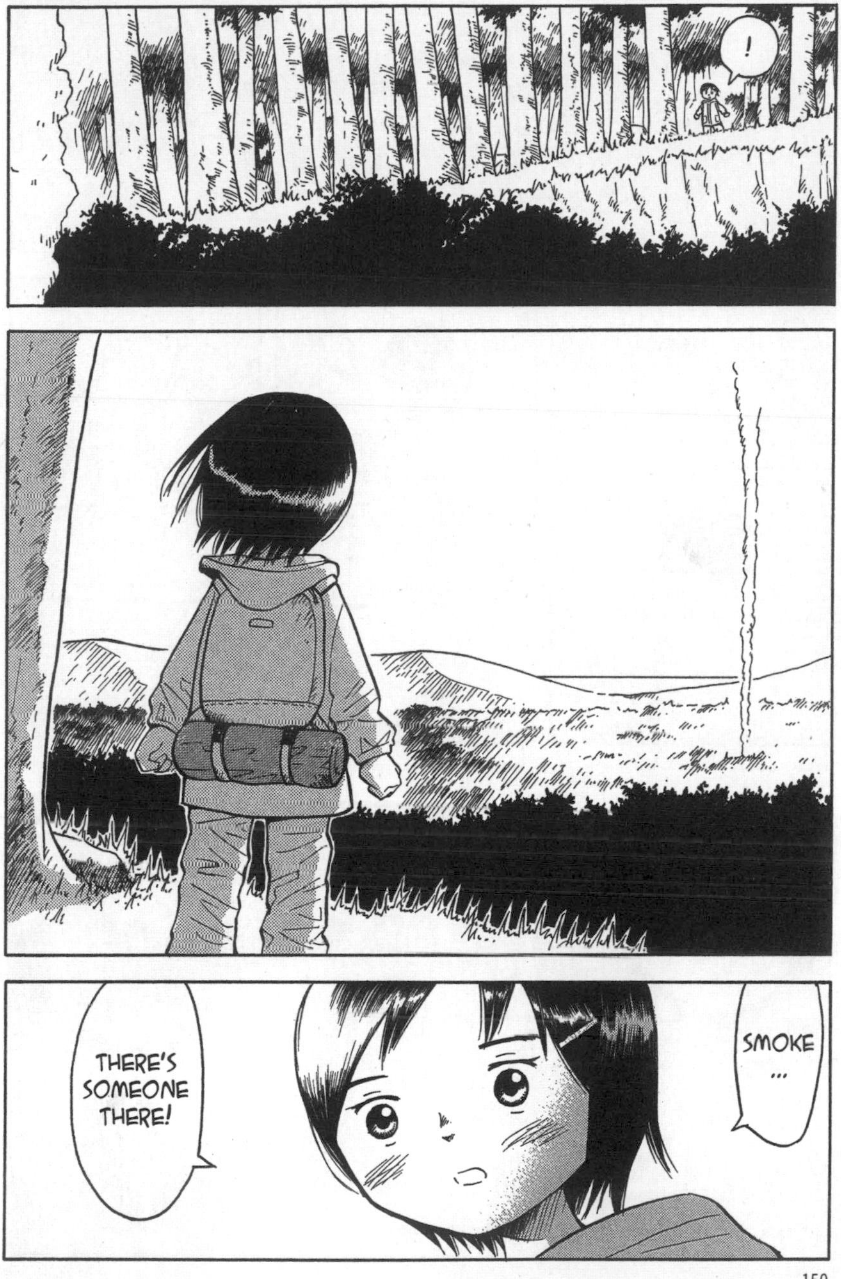
!
SMOKE ...
THERE'S SOMEONE THERE!

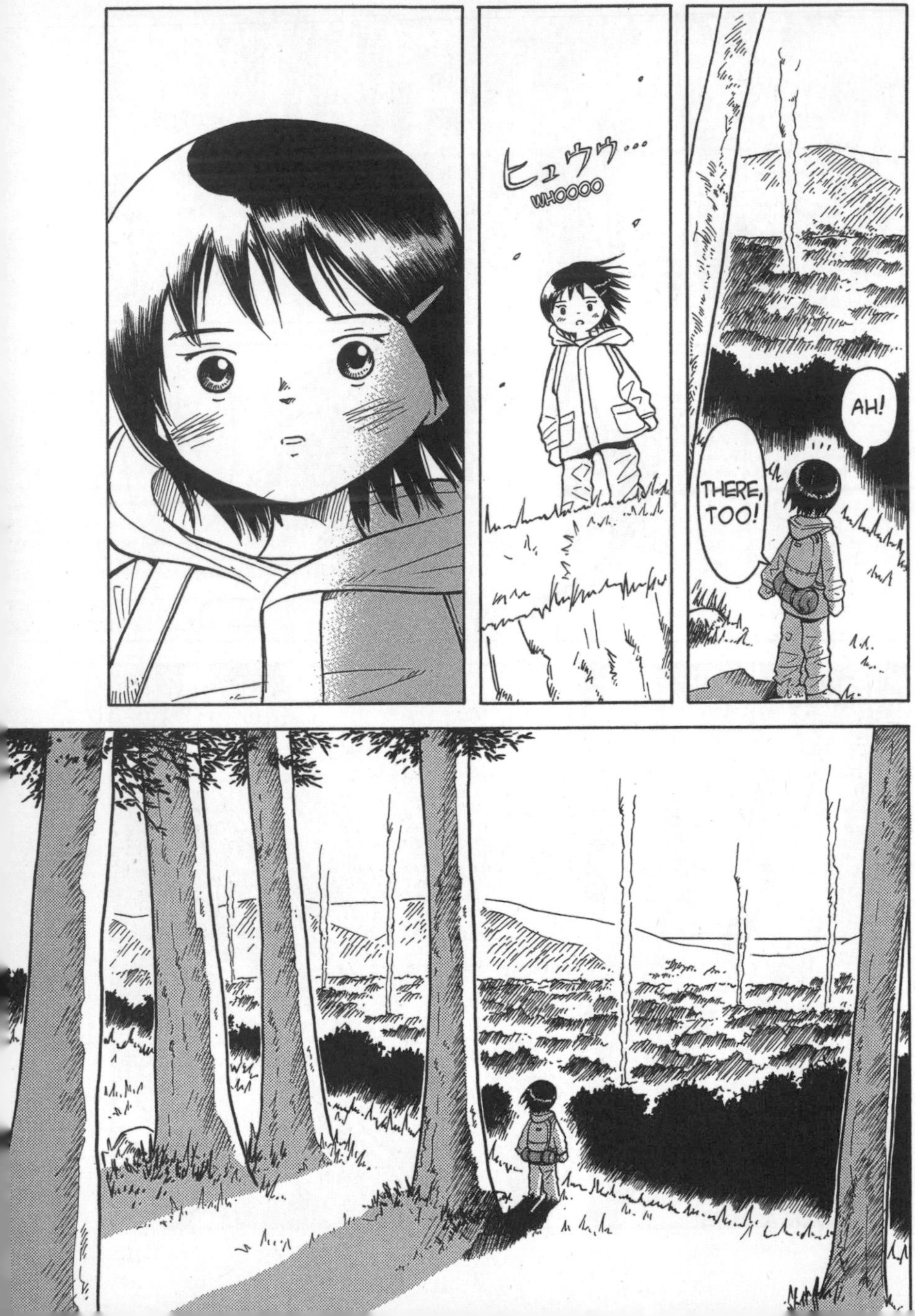
AH!
THERE, TOO!
ヒュウウ…
WHOOOO

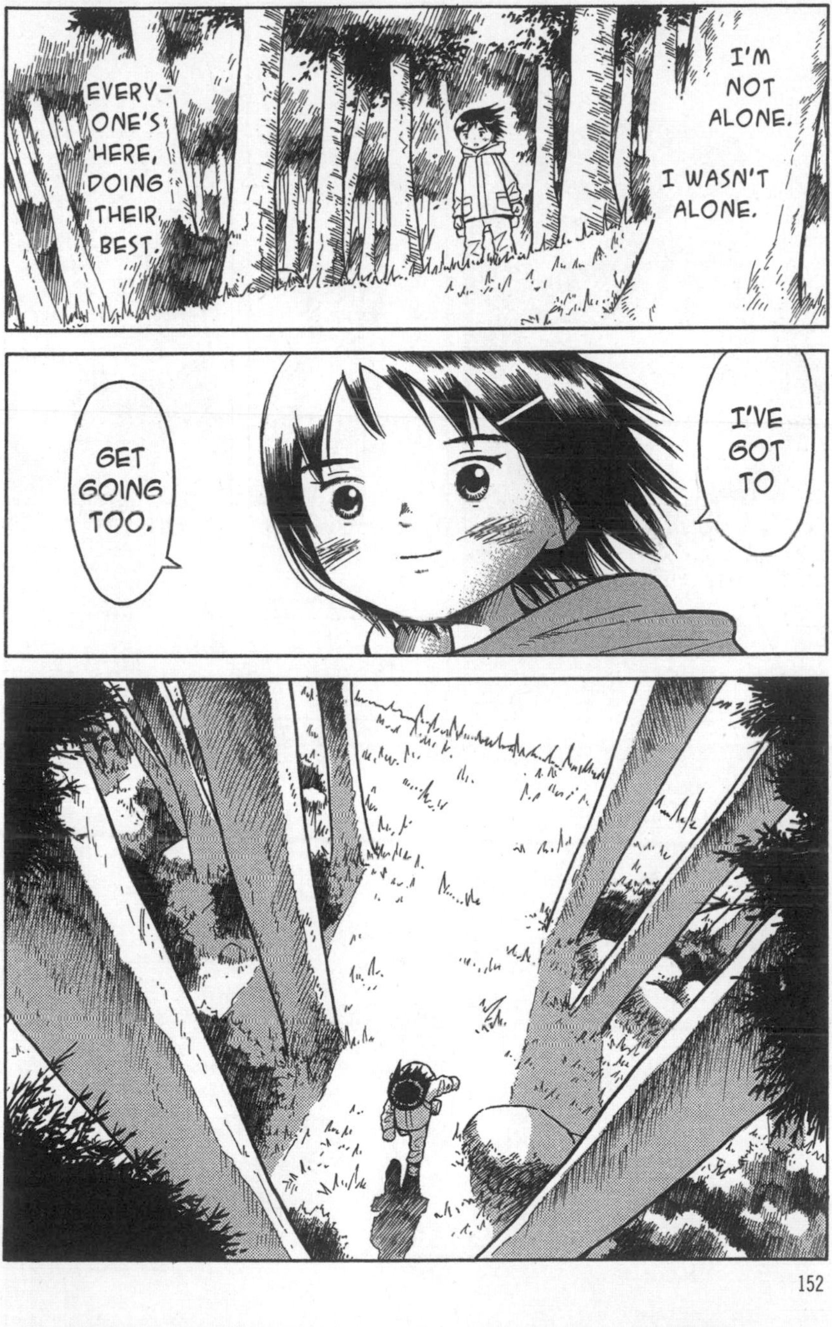
I'M NOT ALONE.
I WASN'T ALONE.
EVERY-ONE'S HERE, DOING THEIR BEST.
I'VE GOT TO
GET GOING TOO.

MISSION:24

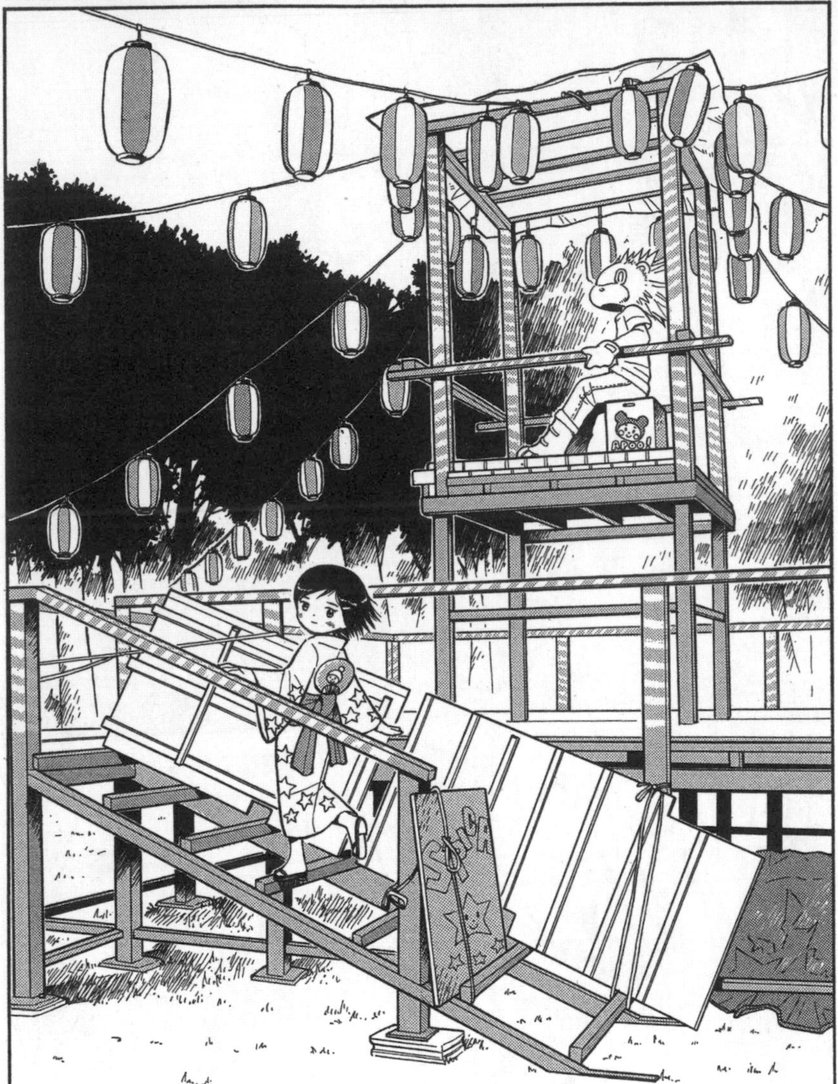
APOO!

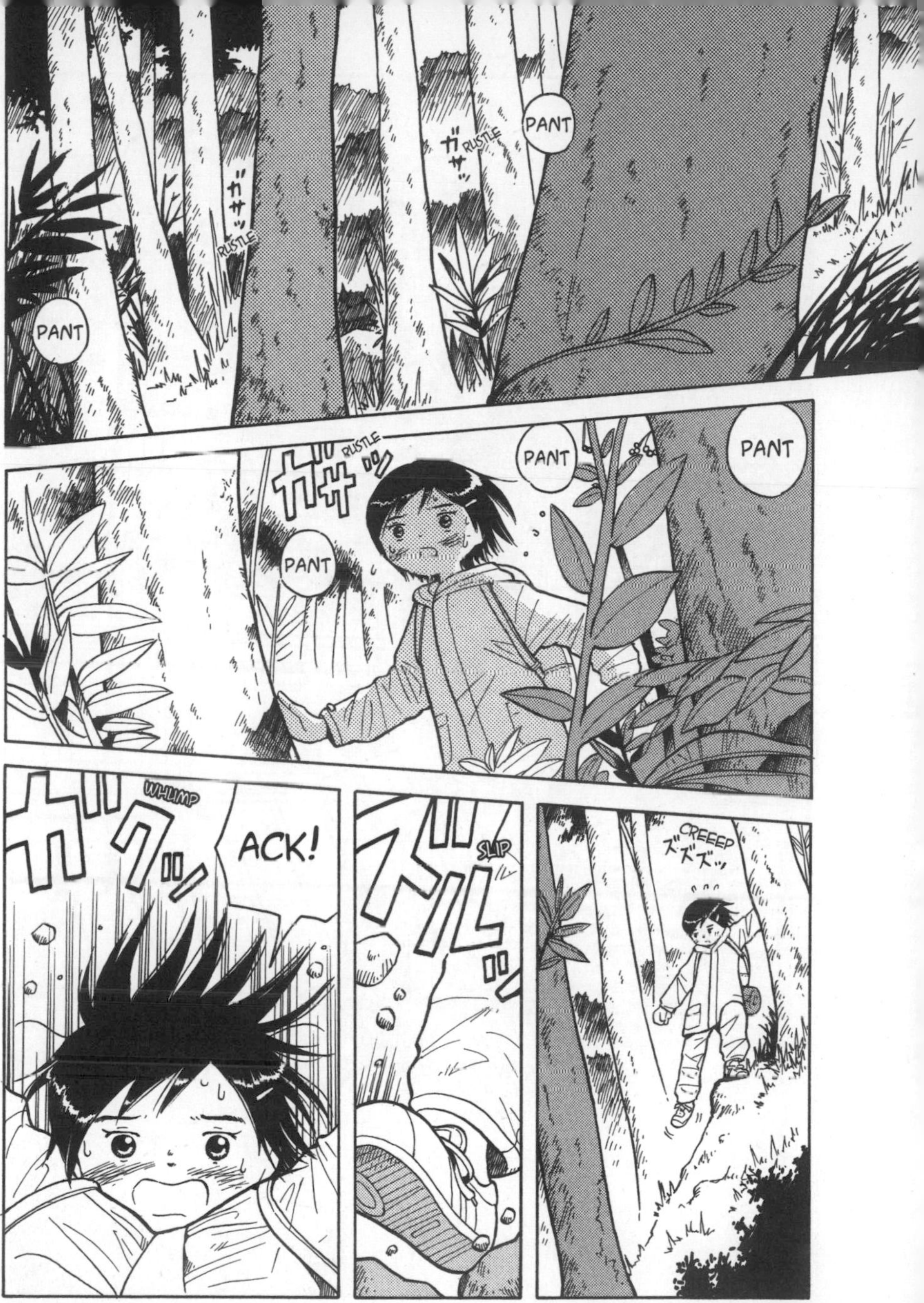
PANT
ガサッ RUSTLE
ガサッ RUSTLE
PANT
PANT
PANT
ガサッ RUSTLE
PANT
CREEEP ズズズッ
ズルッ SLIP
ACK!
ガクッ WHLIMP

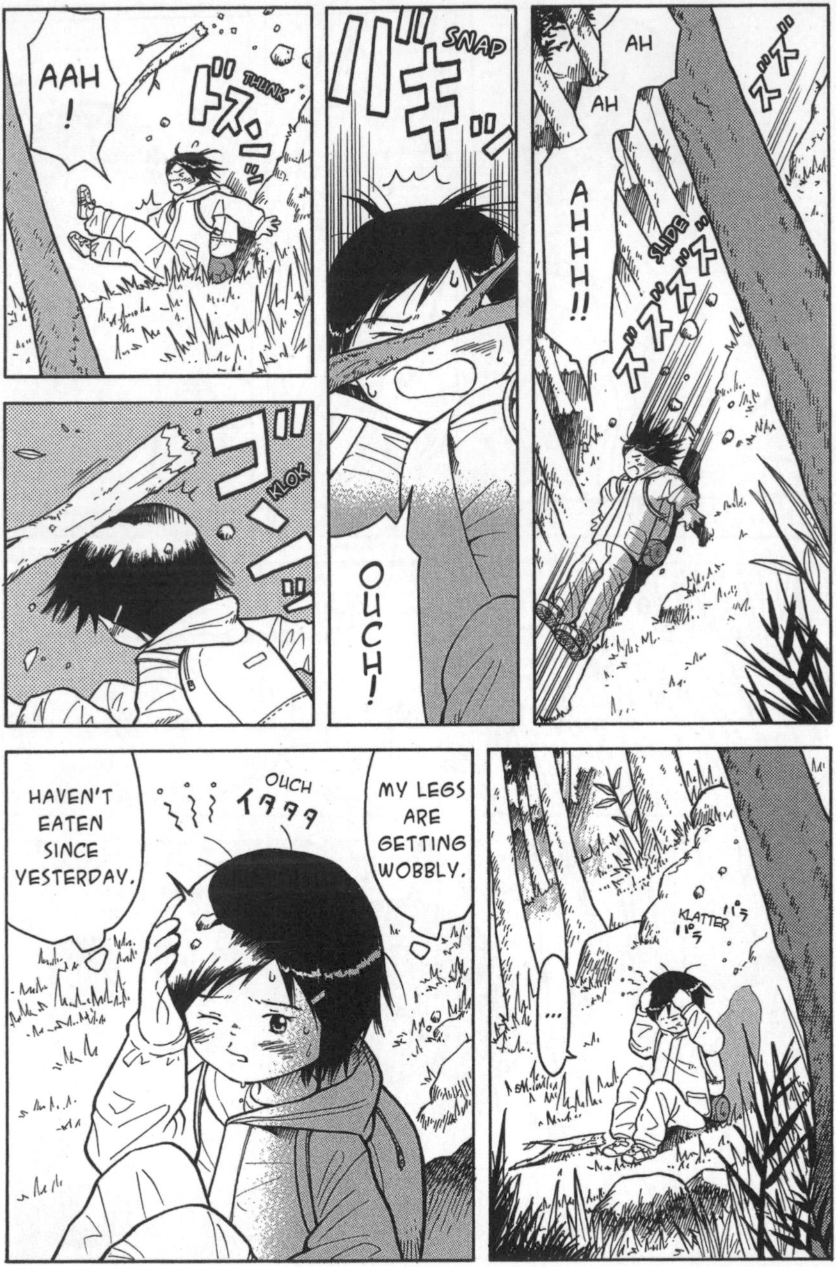
AH
AH
AHHHH!!
SLIDE
ズズズズ
バキッ
SNAP
OUCH!
AAH!
ドスッ
THINK
ゴンッ
KLOK
KLATTER
パラパラ
...
MY LEGS ARE GETTING WOBBLY.
OUCH
イタタタ
HAVEN'T EATEN SINCE YESTERDAY.

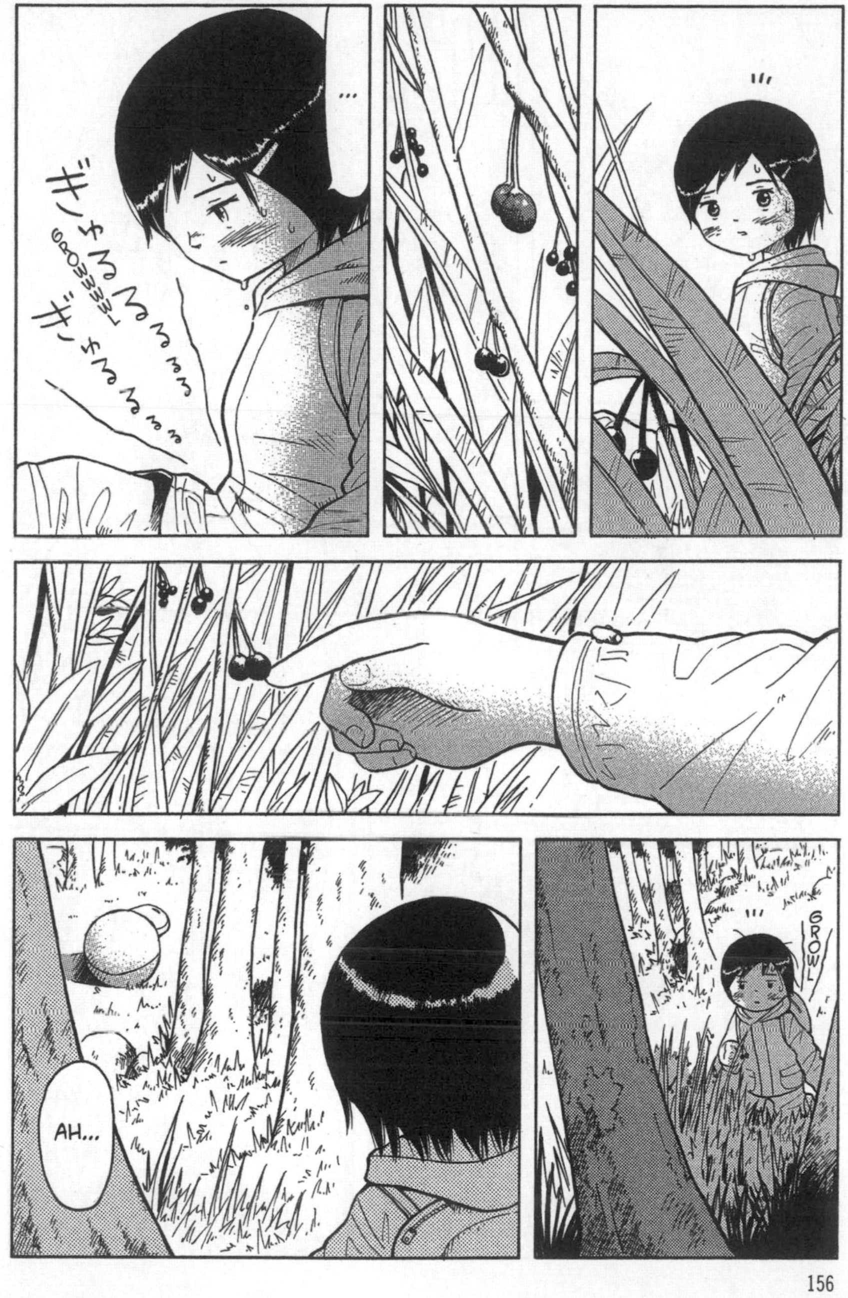
...
ギゅるるるるる
GROWWWWL
ギゅるるるるる
GROWL
AH...

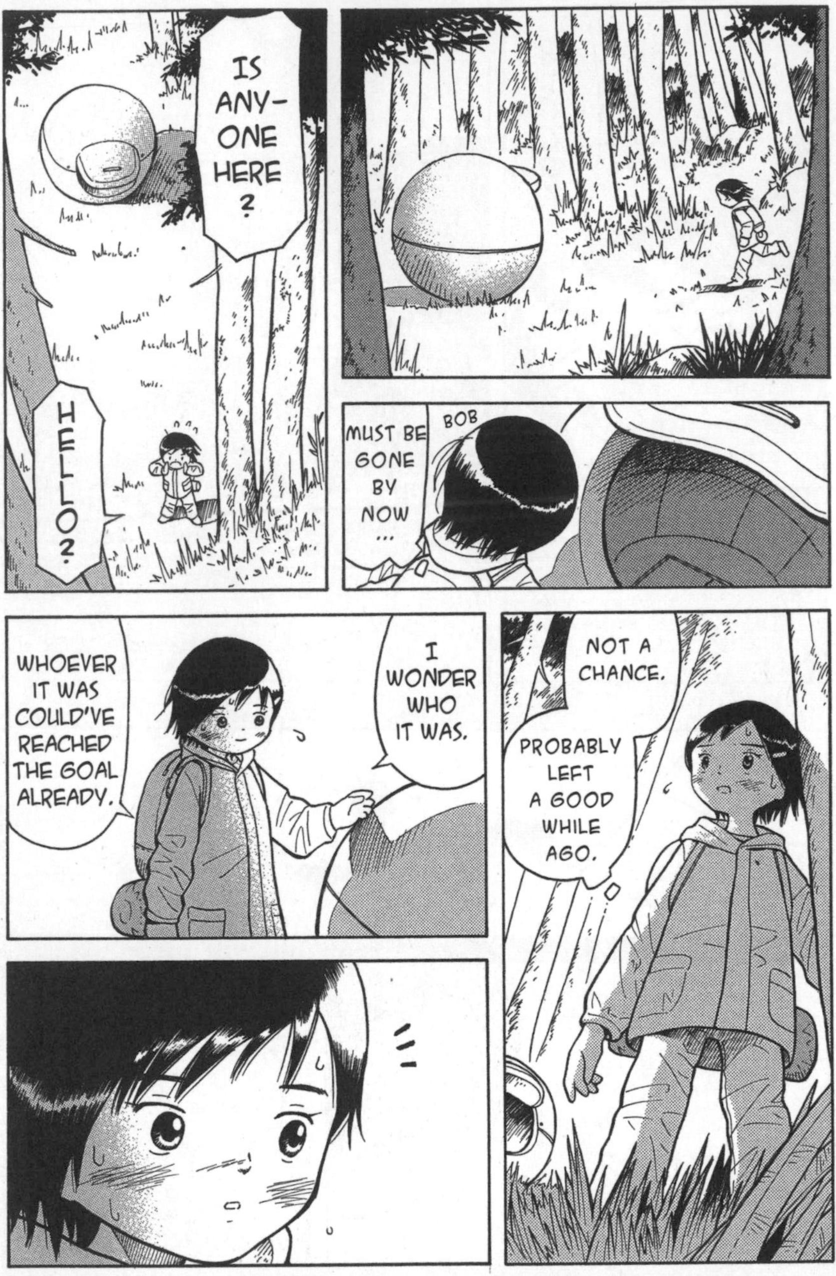
BOB
MUST BE GONE BY NOW ...
IS ANYONE HERE?
HELLO?
NOT A CHANCE.
PROBABLY LEFT A GOOD WHILE AGO.
I WONDER WHO IT WAS.
WHOEVER IT WAS COULD'VE REACHED THE GOAL ALREADY.

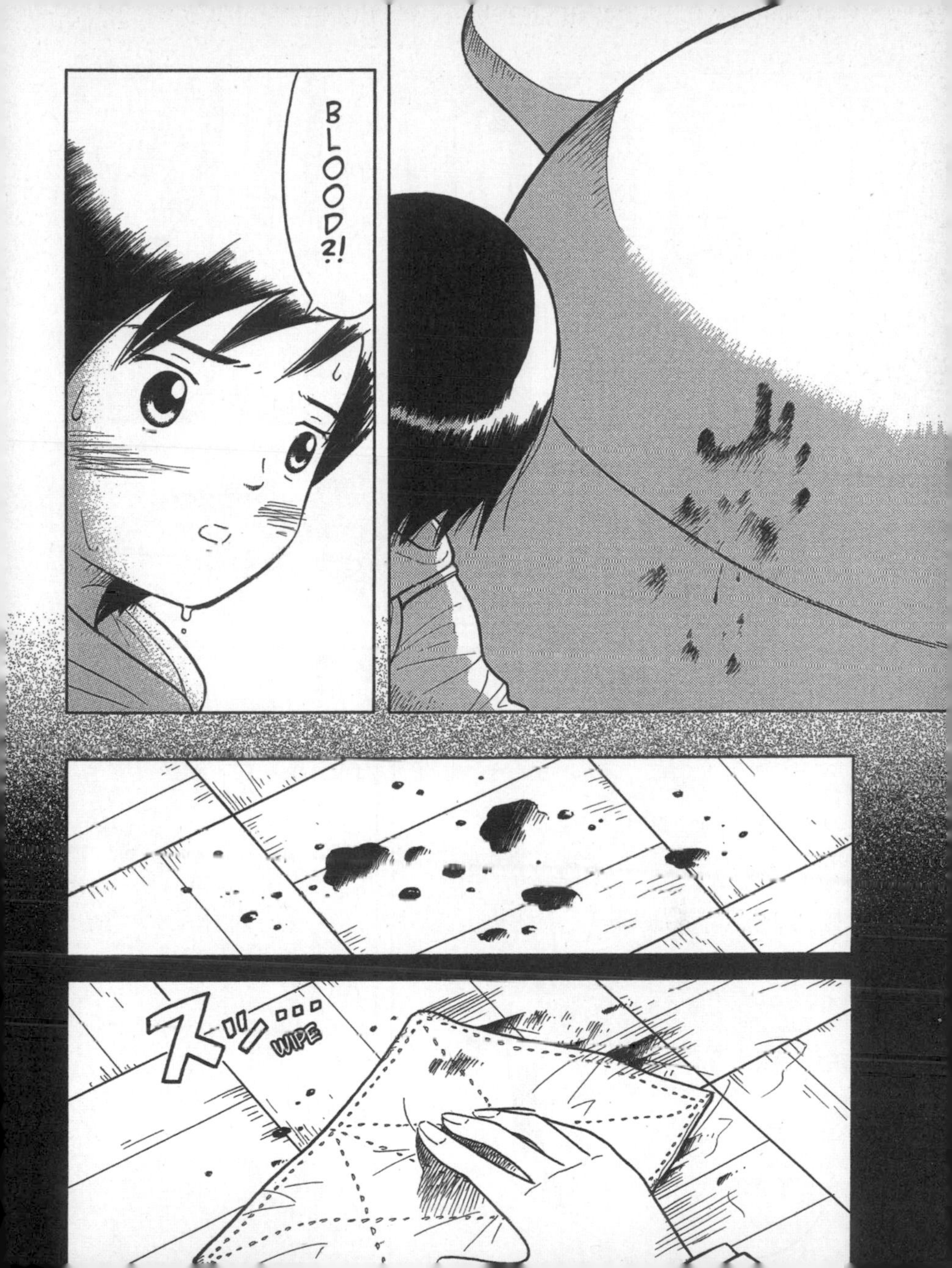
BLOOD?!
スー…
WIPE

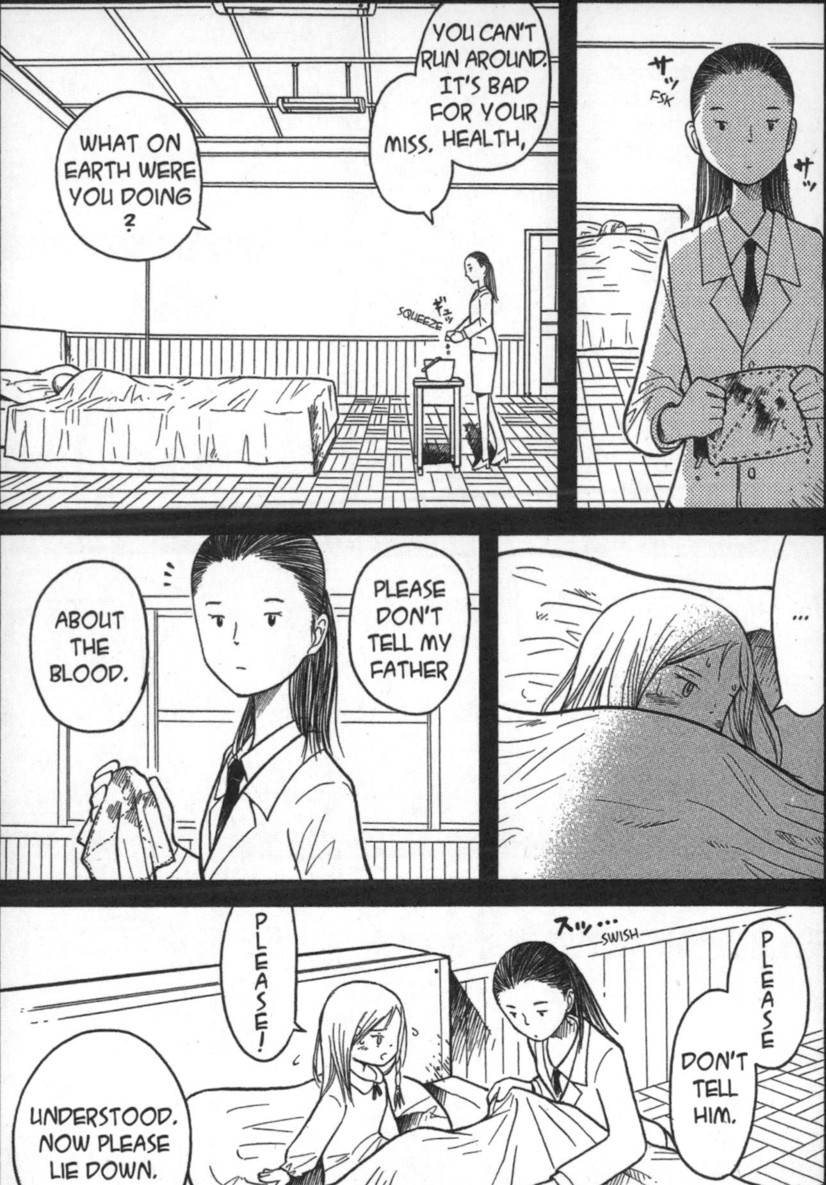
FSK
YOU CAN'T RUN AROUND. IT'S BAD FOR YOUR HEALTH, MISS.
WHAT ON EARTH WERE YOU DOING ?
SQUEEZE
...
PLEASE DON'T TELL MY FATHER
ABOUT THE BLOOD.
PLEASE DON'T TELL HIM.
SWISH
PLEASE!
UNDERSTOOD. NOW PLEASE LIE DOWN.

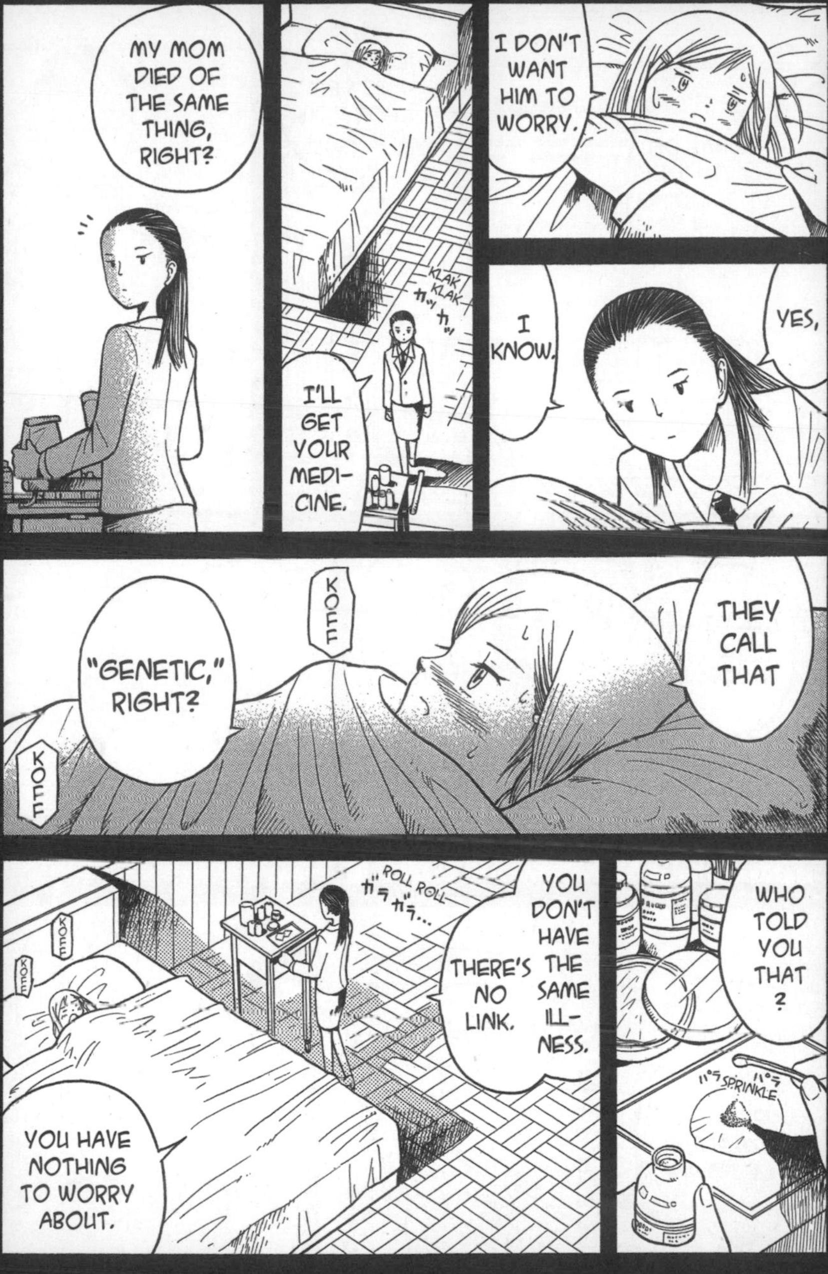
I DON'T WANT HIM TO WORRY.
YES,
I KNOW.
KLAK KLAK
I'LL GET YOUR MEDI-CINE.
MY MOM DIED OF THE SAME THING, RIGHT?
THEY CALL THAT
KOFF
"GENETIC," RIGHT?
KOFF
WHO TOLD YOU THAT?
SPRINKLE
YOU DON'T HAVE THE SAME ILL-NESS.
THERE'S NO LINK.
ROLL ROLL
KOFF
KOFF
YOU HAVE NOTHING TO WORRY ABOUT.

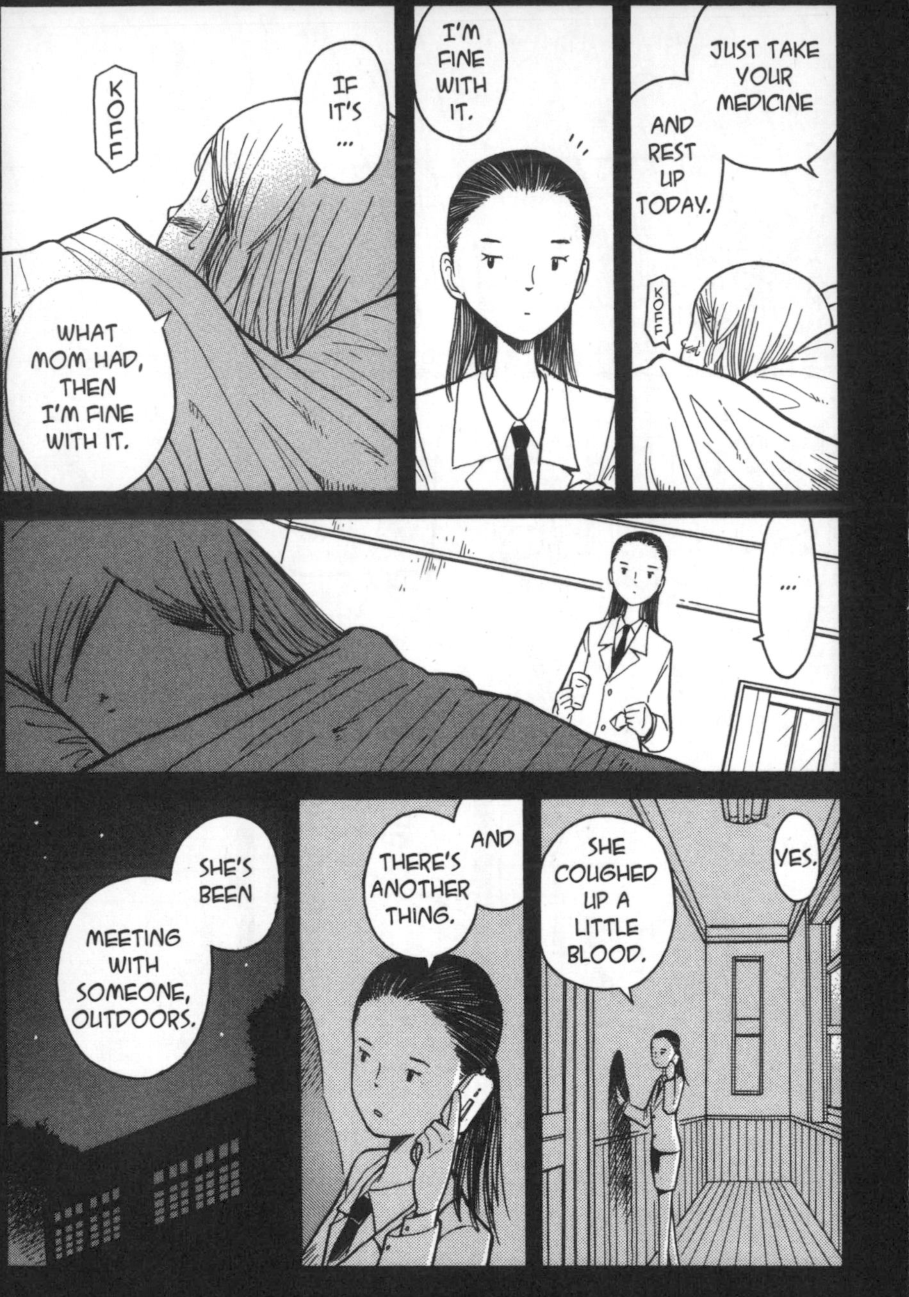
JUST TAKE YOUR MEDICINE
AND REST UP TODAY.
KOFF
I'M FINE WITH IT.
IF IT'S ...
KOFF
WHAT MOM HAD, THEN I'M FINE WITH IT.
...
YES.
SHE COUGHED UP A LITTLE BLOOD.
AND THERE'S ANOTHER THING.
SHE'S BEEN
MEETING WITH SOMEONE, OUTDOORS.

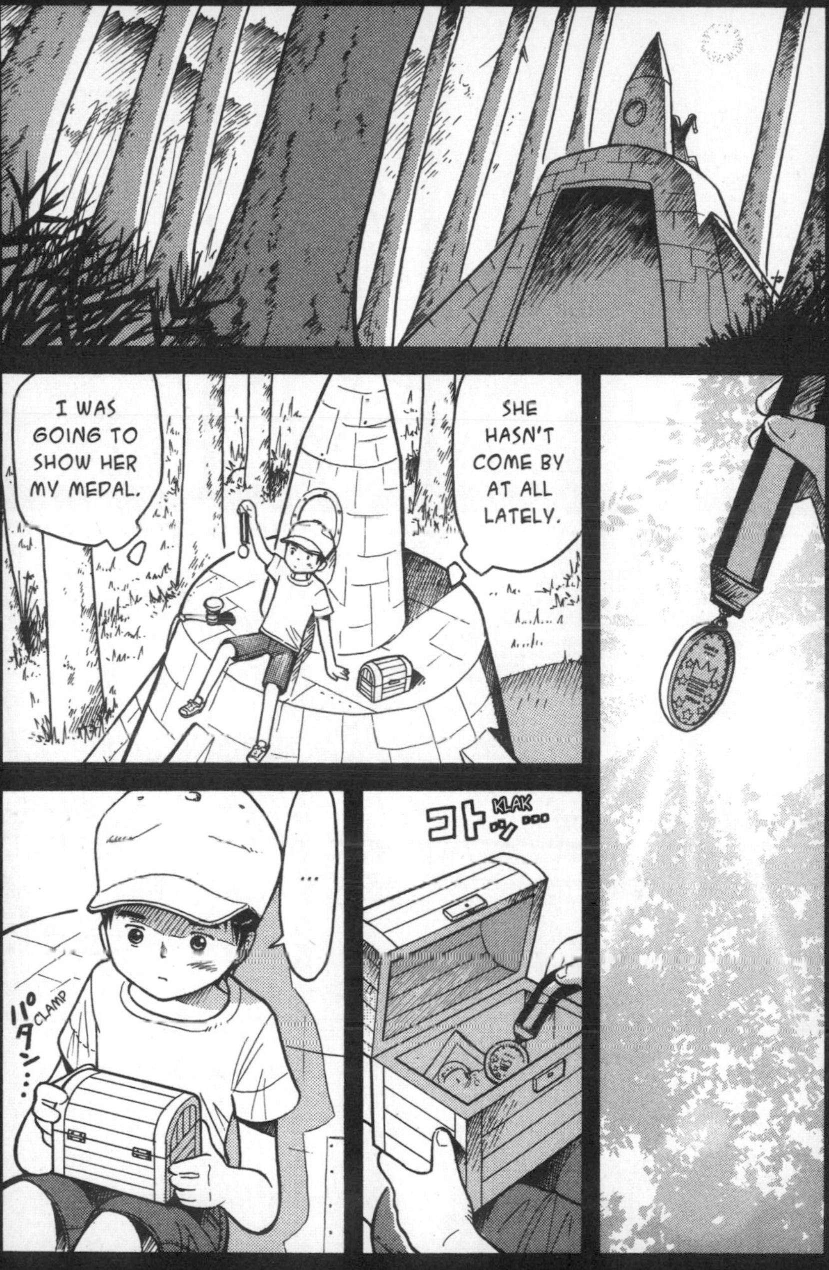
SHE HASN'T COME BY AT ALL LATELY.
I WAS GOING TO SHOW HER MY MEDAL.
コトッ...
KLAK
...
パタン...
CLAMP

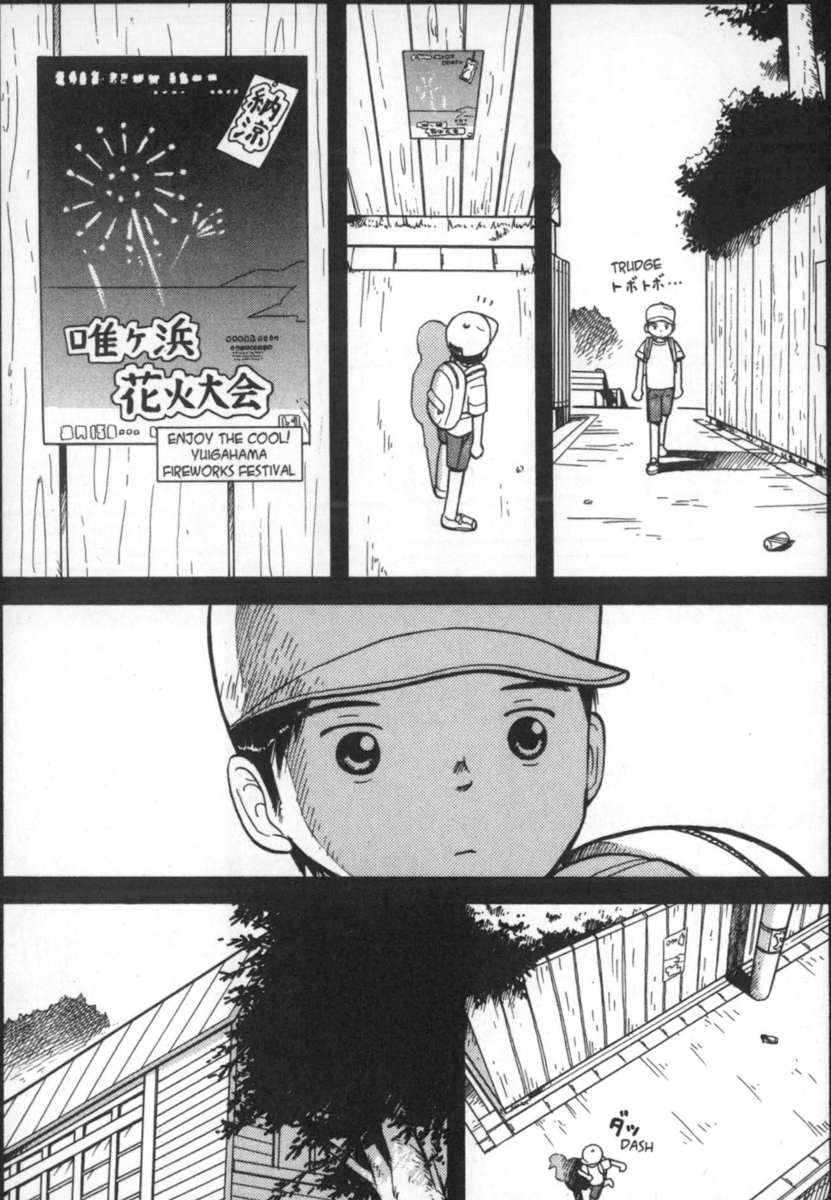
TRUDGE
トボトボ…
納涼
唯ヶ浜
花火大会
ENJOY THE COOL! YUIGAHAMA FIREWORKS FESTIVAL
ダッ
DASH

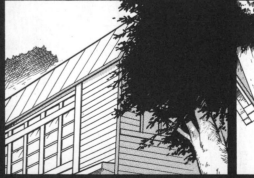

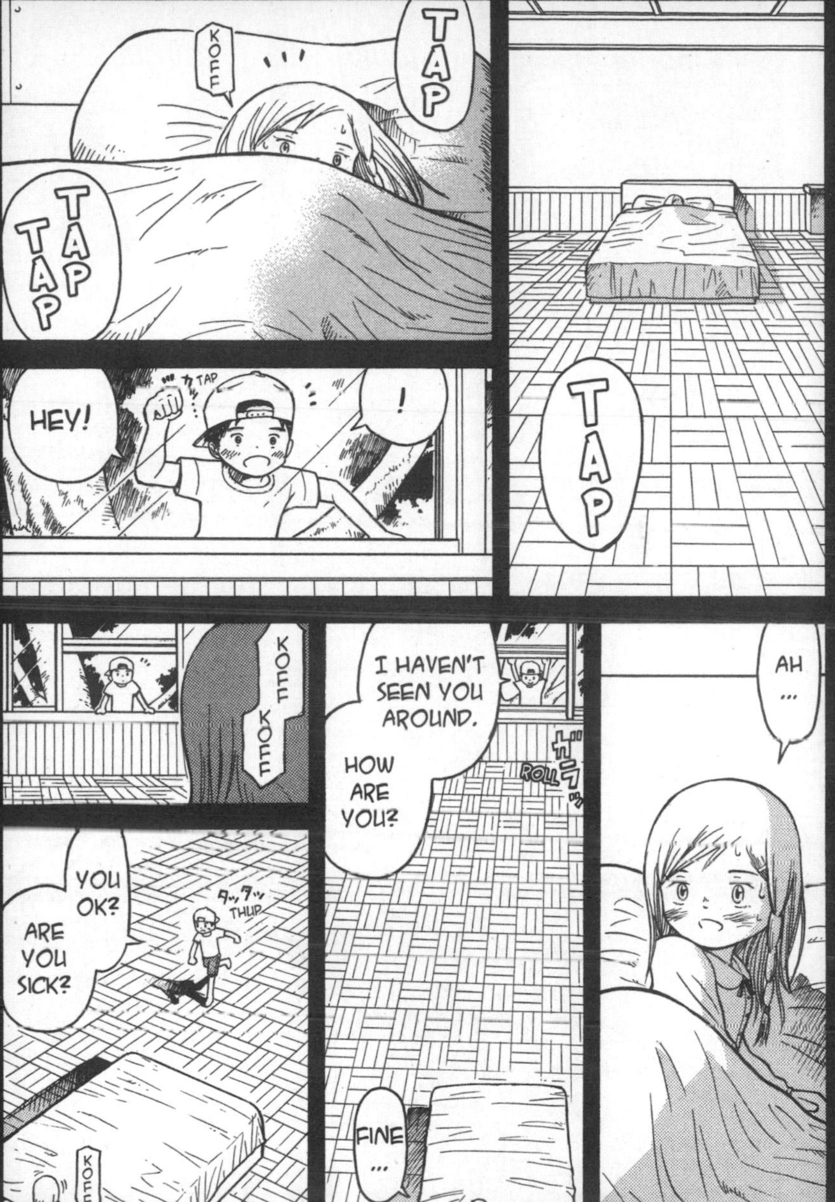
TAP
TAP
KOFF
TAP TAP TAP
!
TAP
HEY!
AH ...
I HAVEN'T SEEN YOU AROUND.
HOW ARE YOU?
ROLL
FINE ...
KOFF KOFF KOFF
YOU OK?
ARE YOU SICK?
THUP
KOFF

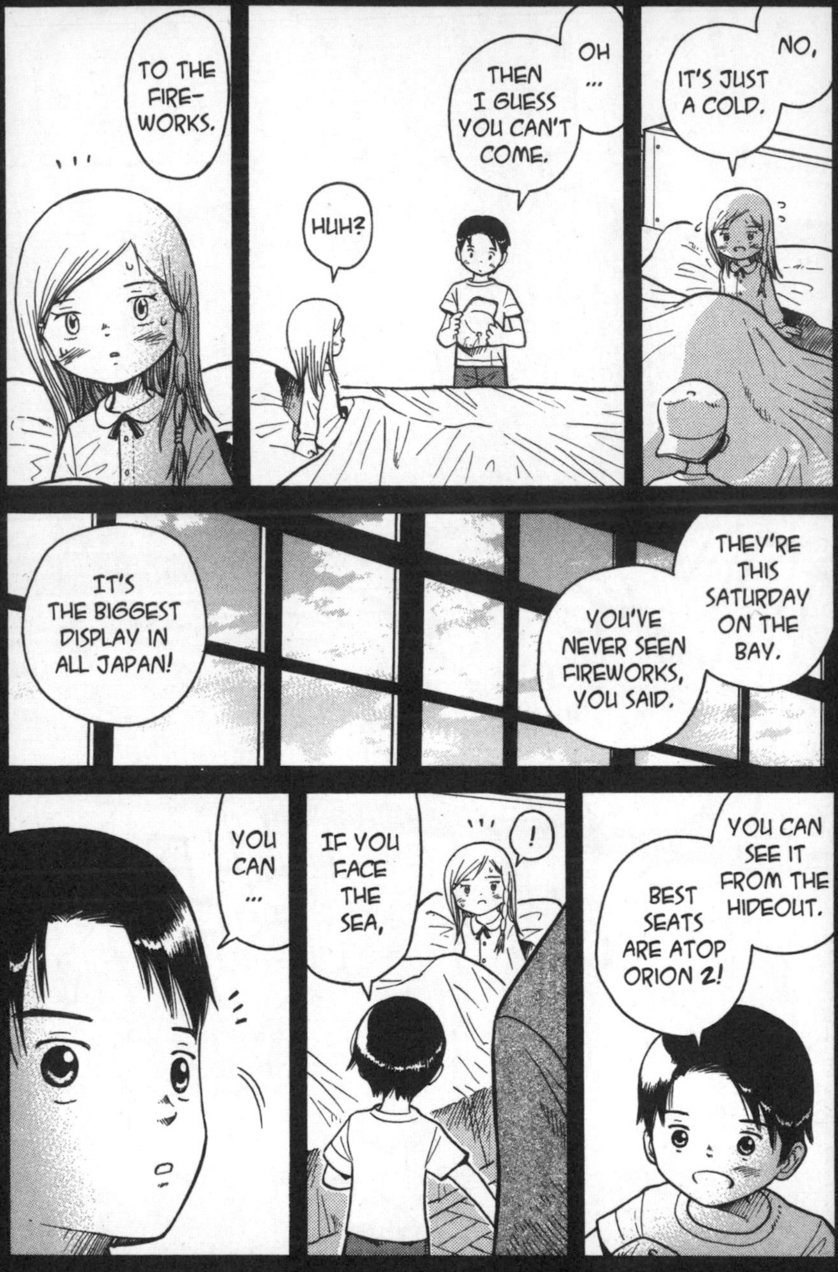
NO, IT'S JUST A COLD.
OH ...
THEN I GUESS YOU CAN'T COME.
HUH?
TO THE FIRE-WORKS.
THEY'RE THIS SATURDAY ON THE BAY.
YOU'VE NEVER SEEN FIREWORKS, YOU SAID.
IT'S THE BIGGEST DISPLAY IN ALL JAPAN!
YOU CAN SEE IT FROM THE HIDEOUT.
BEST SEATS ARE ATOP ORION 2!
!
IF YOU FACE THE SEA,
YOU CAN ...

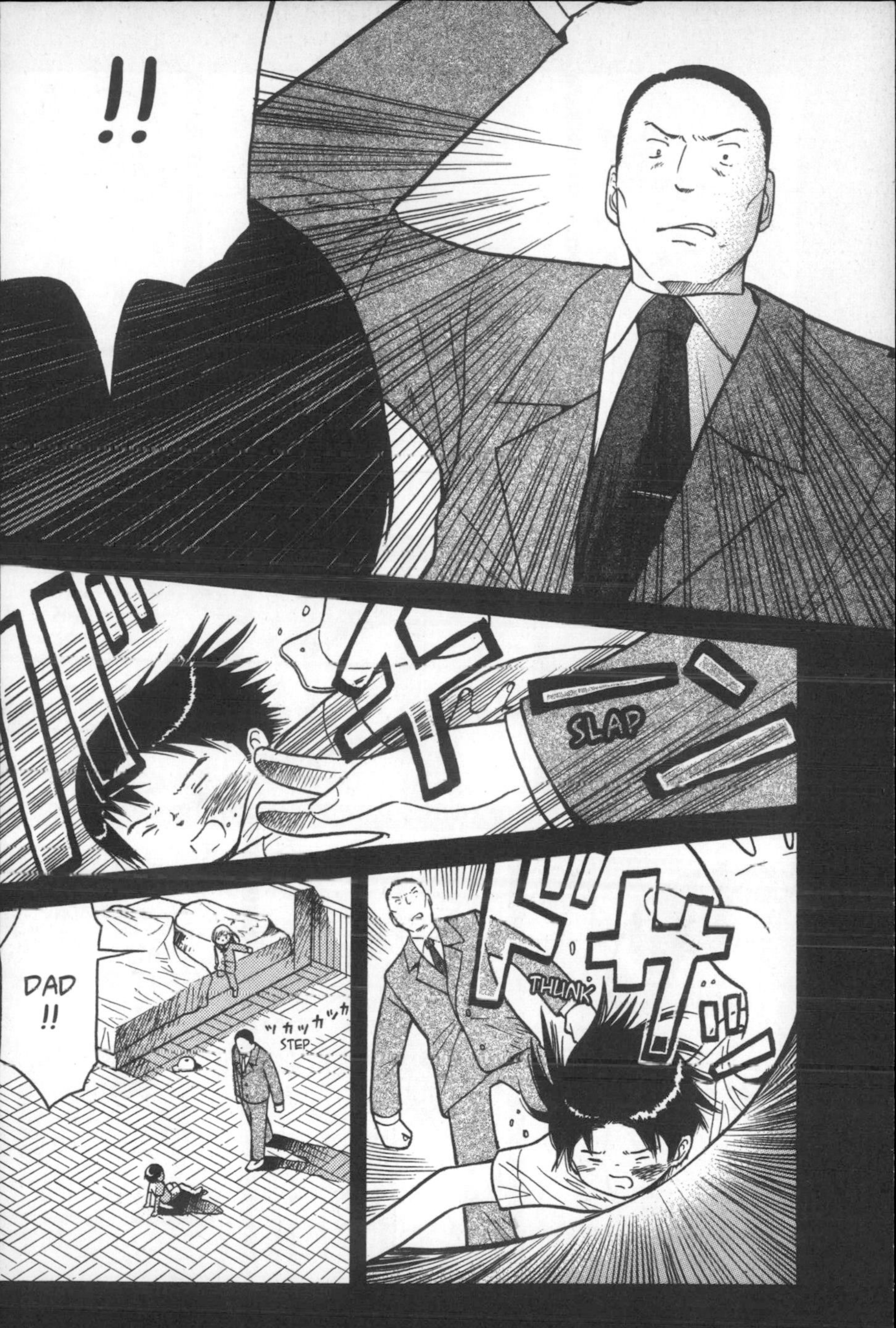
!!
SLAP
THUNK
ツカッカッカ
STEP
DAD !!

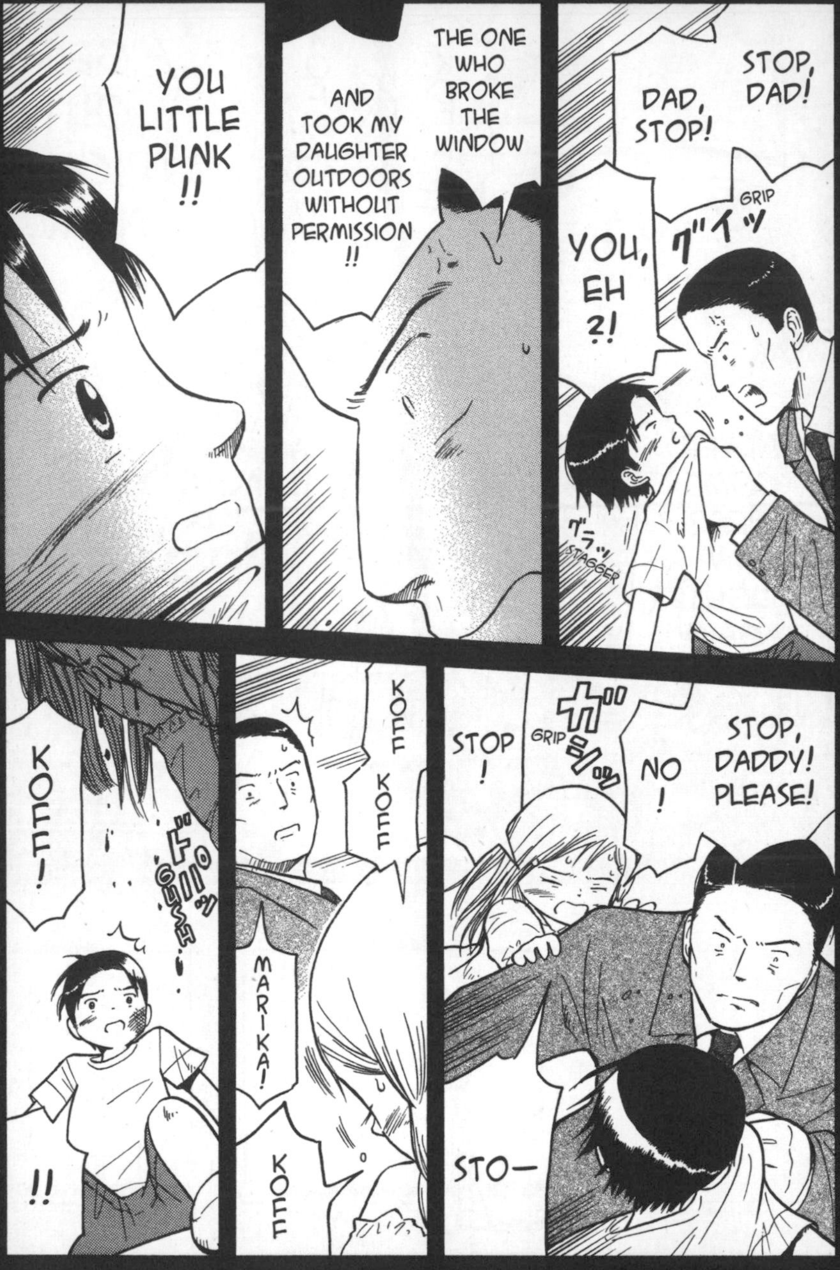
STOP, DAD!
DAD, STOP!
GRIP
グイッ
YOU, EH ?!
グラッ
STAGGER
THE ONE WHO BROKE THE WINDOW
AND TOOK MY DAUGHTER OUTDOORS WITHOUT PERMISSION !!
YOU LITTLE PUNK !!
STOP, DADDY! PLEASE!
NO !
ガシッ
GRIP
STOP !
STO—
KOFF KOFF
MARIKA!
KOFF
KOFF!
!!

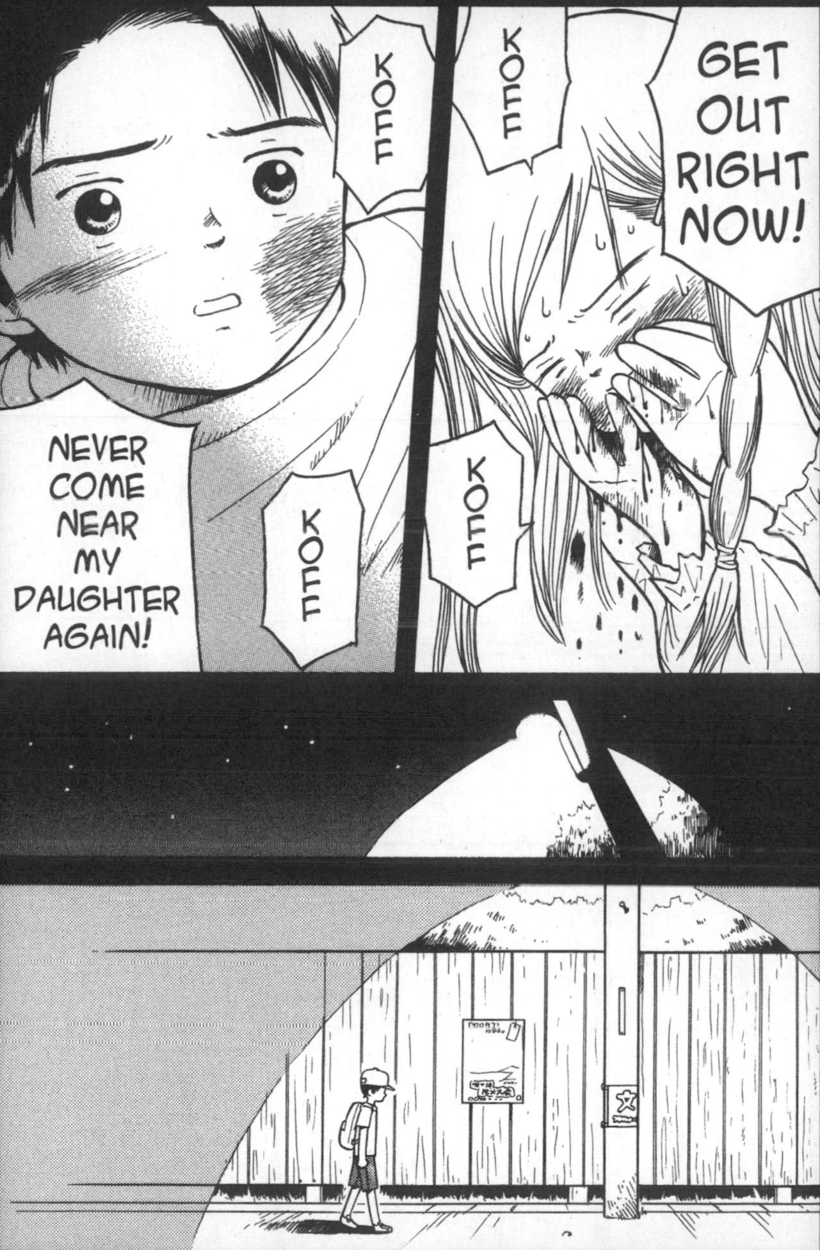
GET OUT RIGHT NOW!
KOFF
KOFF
KOFF
KOFF
NEVER COME NEAR MY DAUGHTER AGAIN!

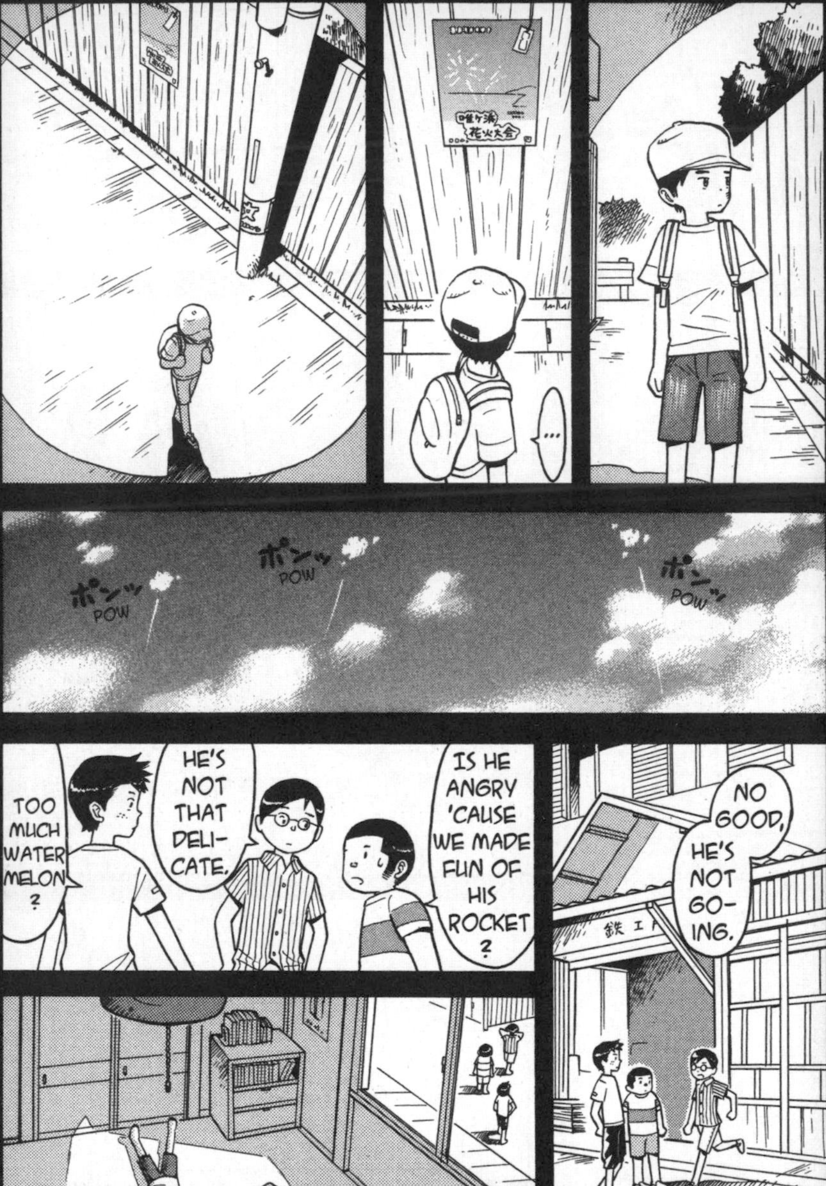
唯ケ浜
花火大会
...
ポンッ
POW
ポンッ
POW
ポンッ
POW
NO GOOD, HE'S NOT GO-ING.
鉄 工
IS HE ANGRY 'CAUSE WE MADE FUN OF HIS ROCKET?
HE'S NOT THAT DELI-CATE.
TOO MUCH WATER MELON?

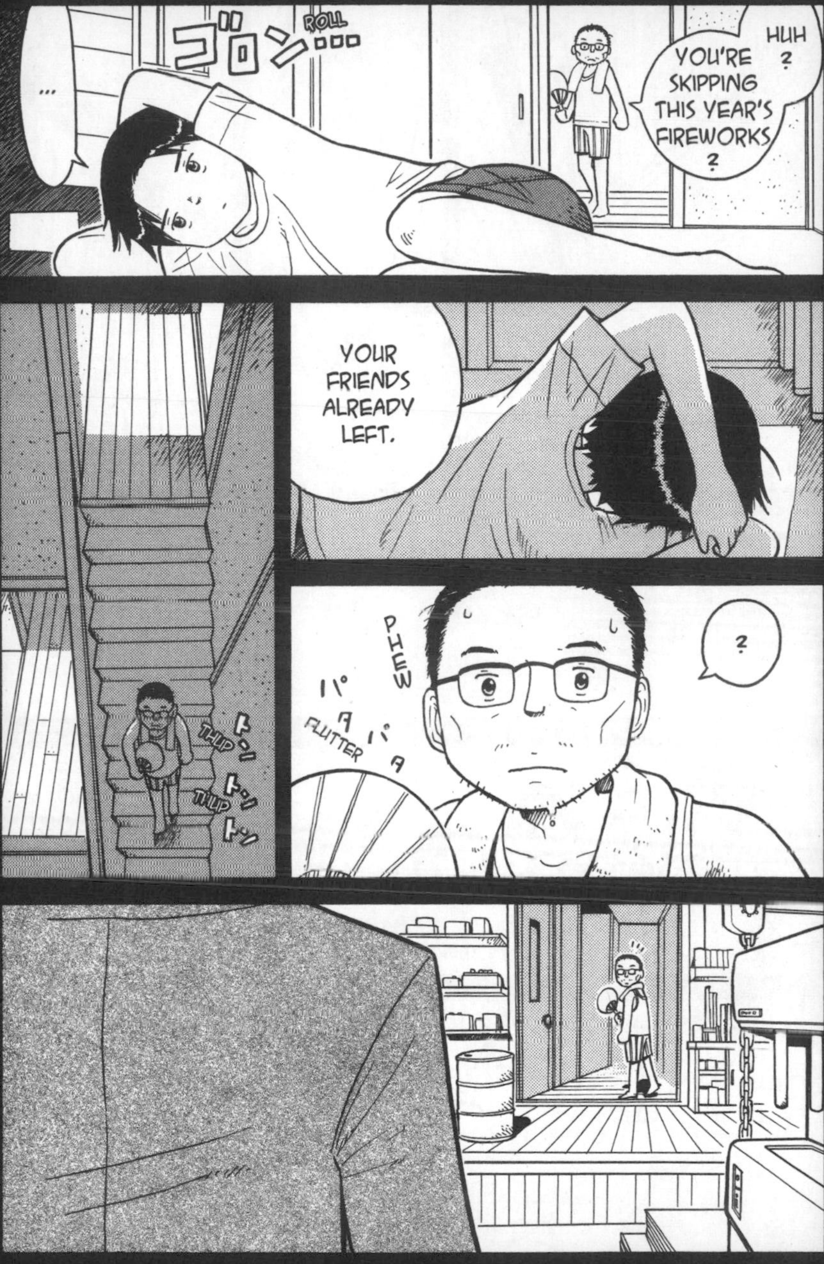
HUH? YOU'RE SKIPPING THIS YEAR'S FIREWORKS?
ゴロン… ROLL
…
YOUR FRIENDS ALREADY LEFT.
?
パタパタ PHEW FLUTTER
トッ トッ トッ THUP THUP

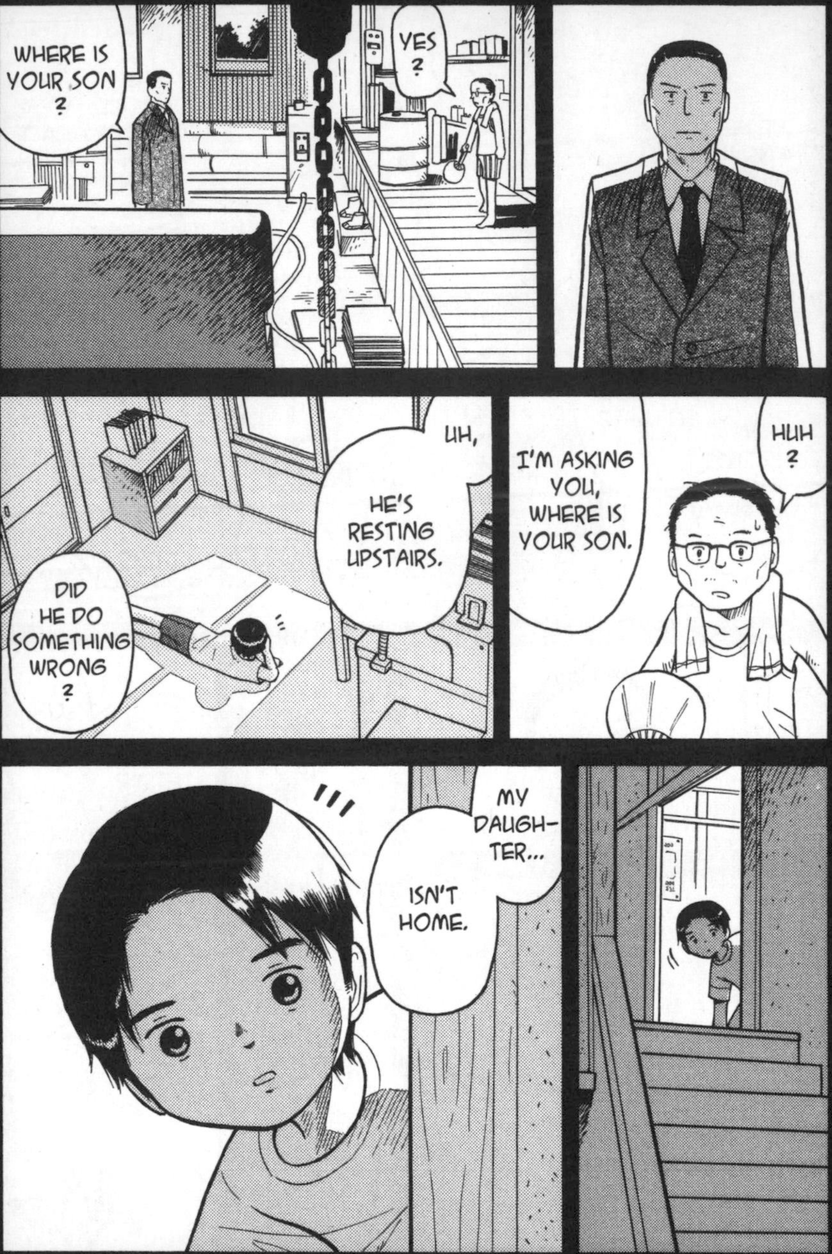
YES ?
WHERE IS YOUR SON ?
HUH ?
I'M ASKING YOU, WHERE IS YOUR SON.
UH,
HE'S RESTING UPSTAIRS.
DID HE DO SOMETHING WRONG ?
MY DAUGHTER...
ISN'T HOME.

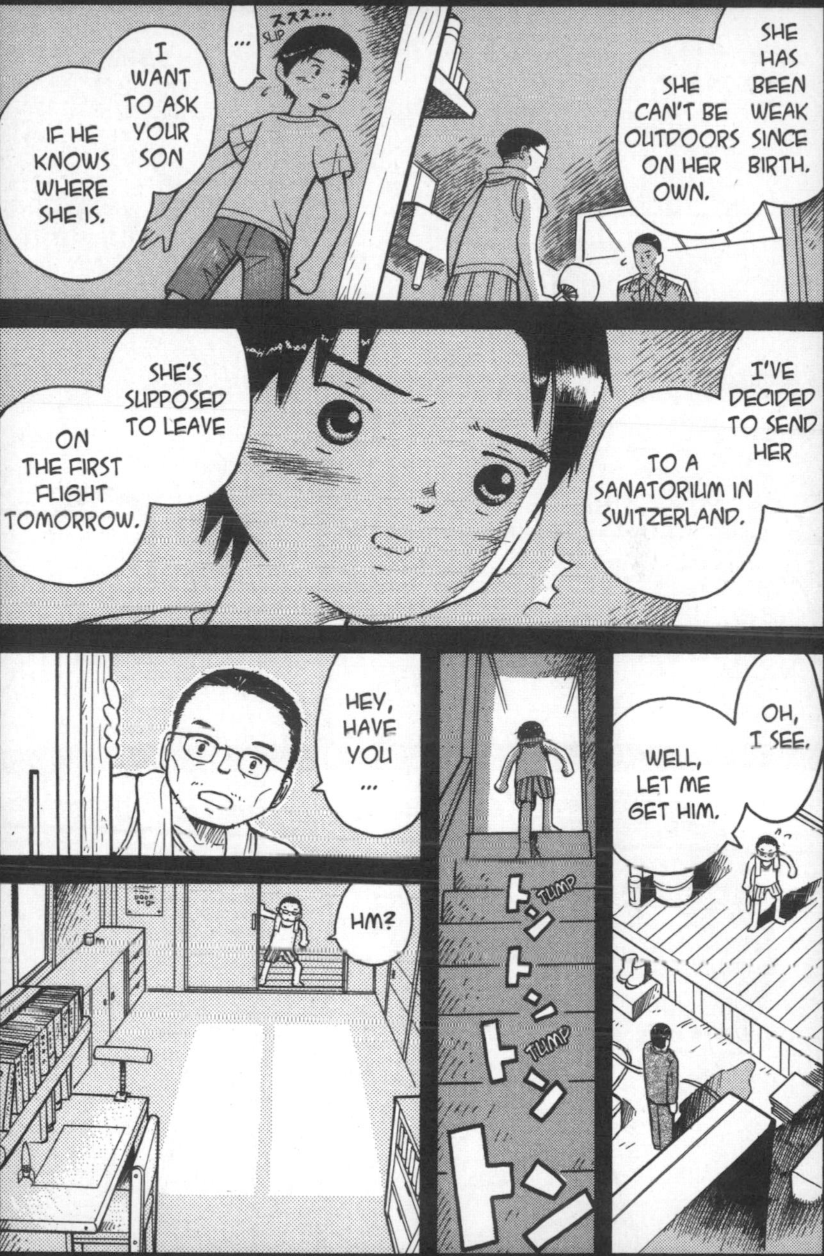
SHE HAS BEEN WEAK SINCE BIRTH.
SHE CAN'T BE OUTDOORS ON HER OWN.
...
ススス... SLIP
I WANT TO ASK YOUR SON
IF HE KNOWS WHERE SHE IS.
I'VE DECIDED TO SEND HER
TO A SANATORIUM IN SWITZERLAND.
SHE'S SUPPOSED TO LEAVE
ON THE FIRST FLIGHT TOMORROW.
OH, I SEE.
WELL, LET ME GET HIM.
トン TUMP
トン
トン TUMP
トン
HEY, HAVE YOU ...
HM?

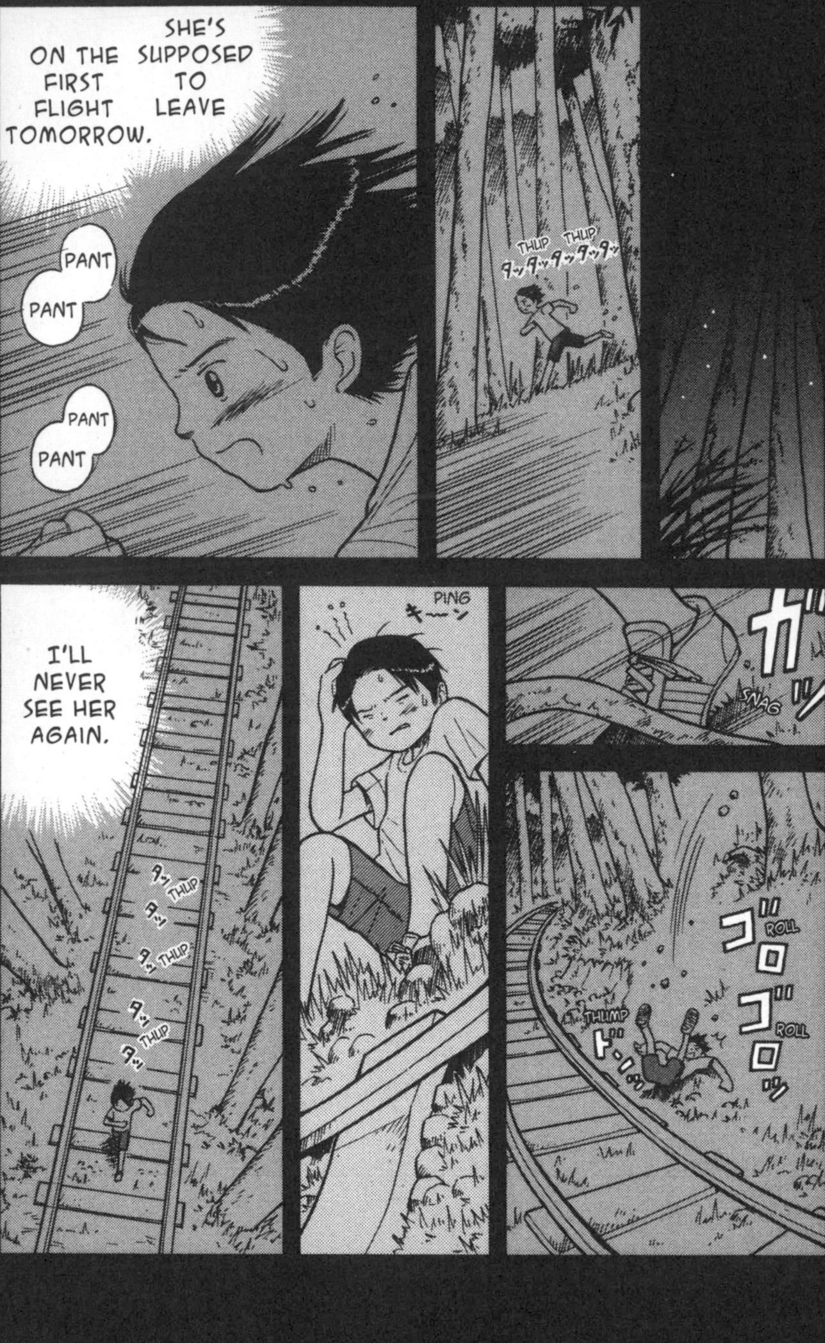
THUP THUP
タッタッタッタッタッ
SHE'S SUPPOSED TO LEAVE
ON THE FIRST FLIGHT TOMORROW.
PANT
PANT
PANT
PANT
ガッ
SNAG
ゴロ
ROLL
ゴロッ
ROLL
THUMP
PING
キーン
I'LL NEVER SEE HER AGAIN.
タッ
THUP
タッ
タッ
THUP
タッ
THUP
タッ

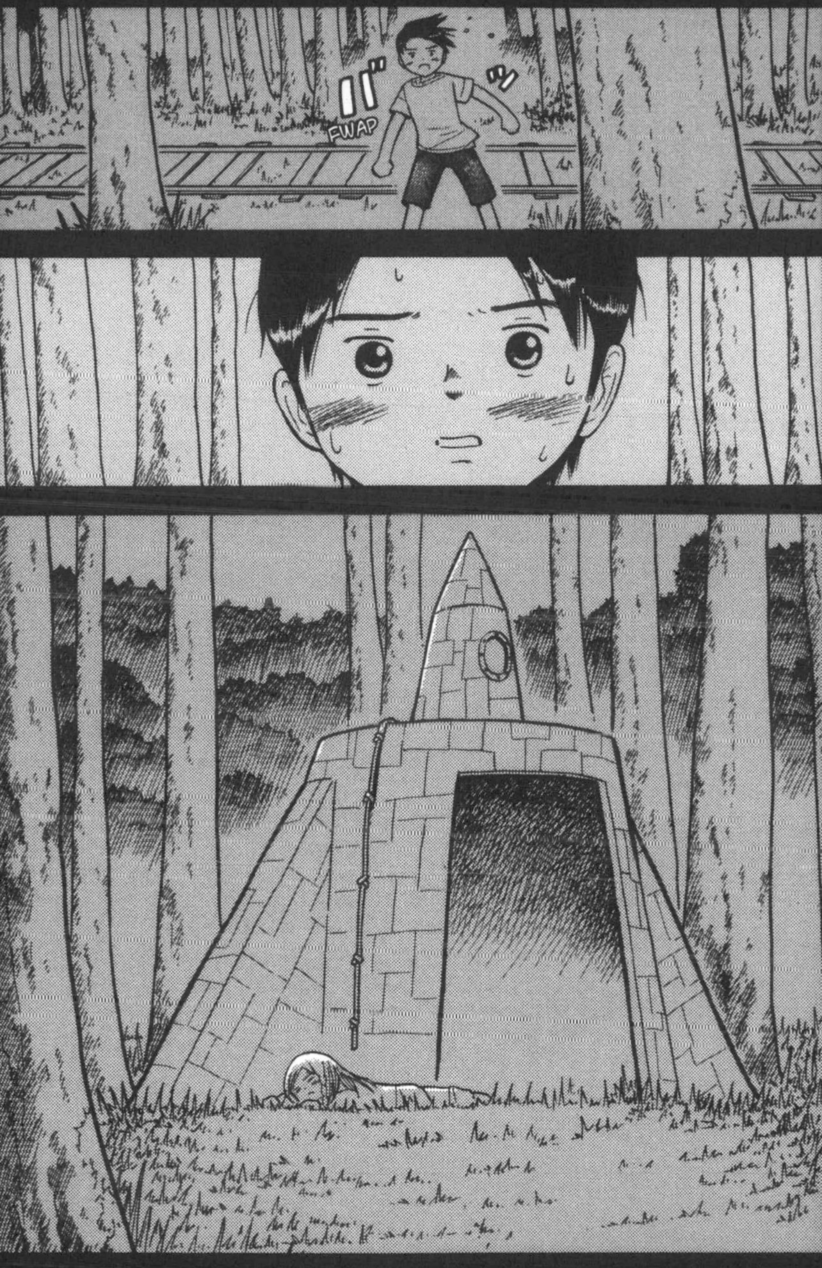
FWAP

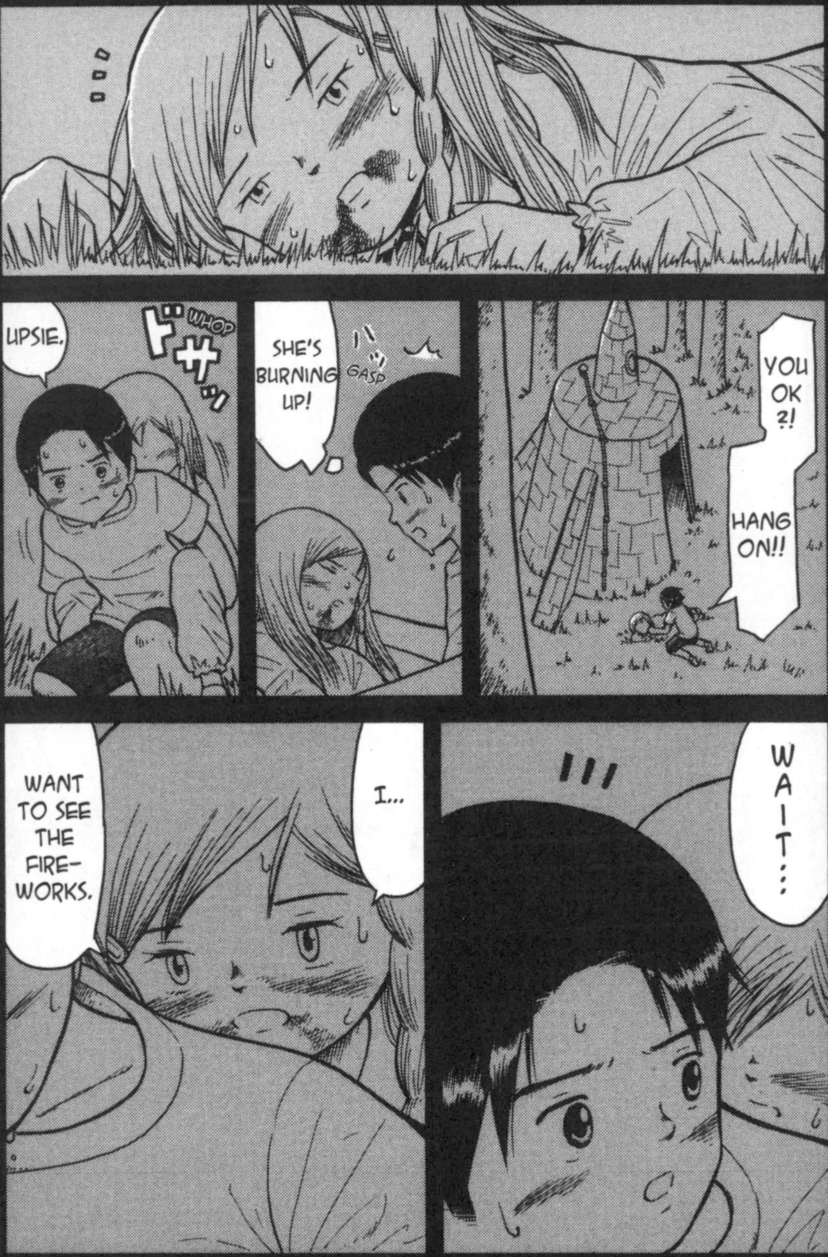
YOU OK?!
HANG ON!!
SHE'S BURNING UP!
GASP
UPSIE.
WHOP
WAIT...
I...
WANT TO SEE THE FIRE-WORKS.

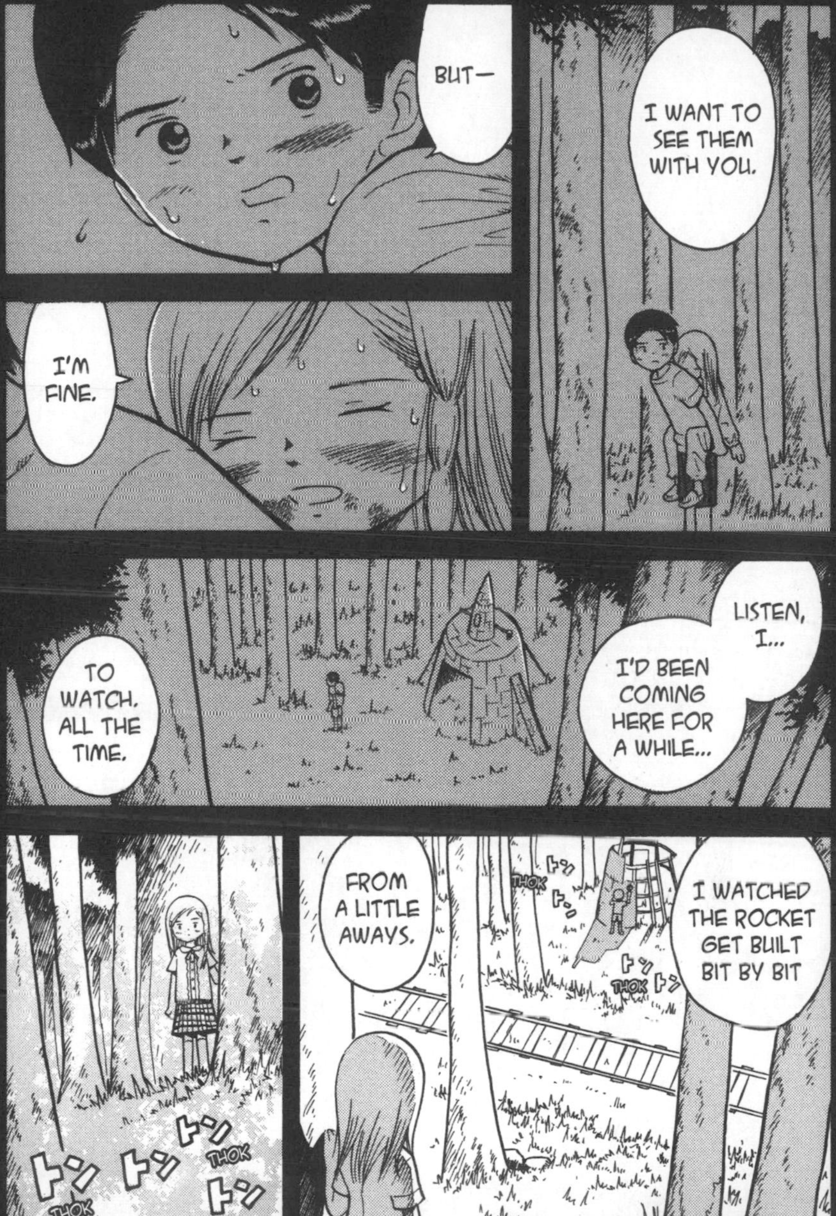
I WANT TO SEE THEM WITH YOU.
BUT—
I'M FINE.
LISTEN, I...
I'D BEEN COMING HERE FOR A WHILE...
TO WATCH. ALL THE TIME.
I WATCHED THE ROCKET GET BUILT BIT BY BIT
FROM A LITTLE AWAYS.
トン THOK トン
トン THOK トン
トン THOK トン
トン トン THOK

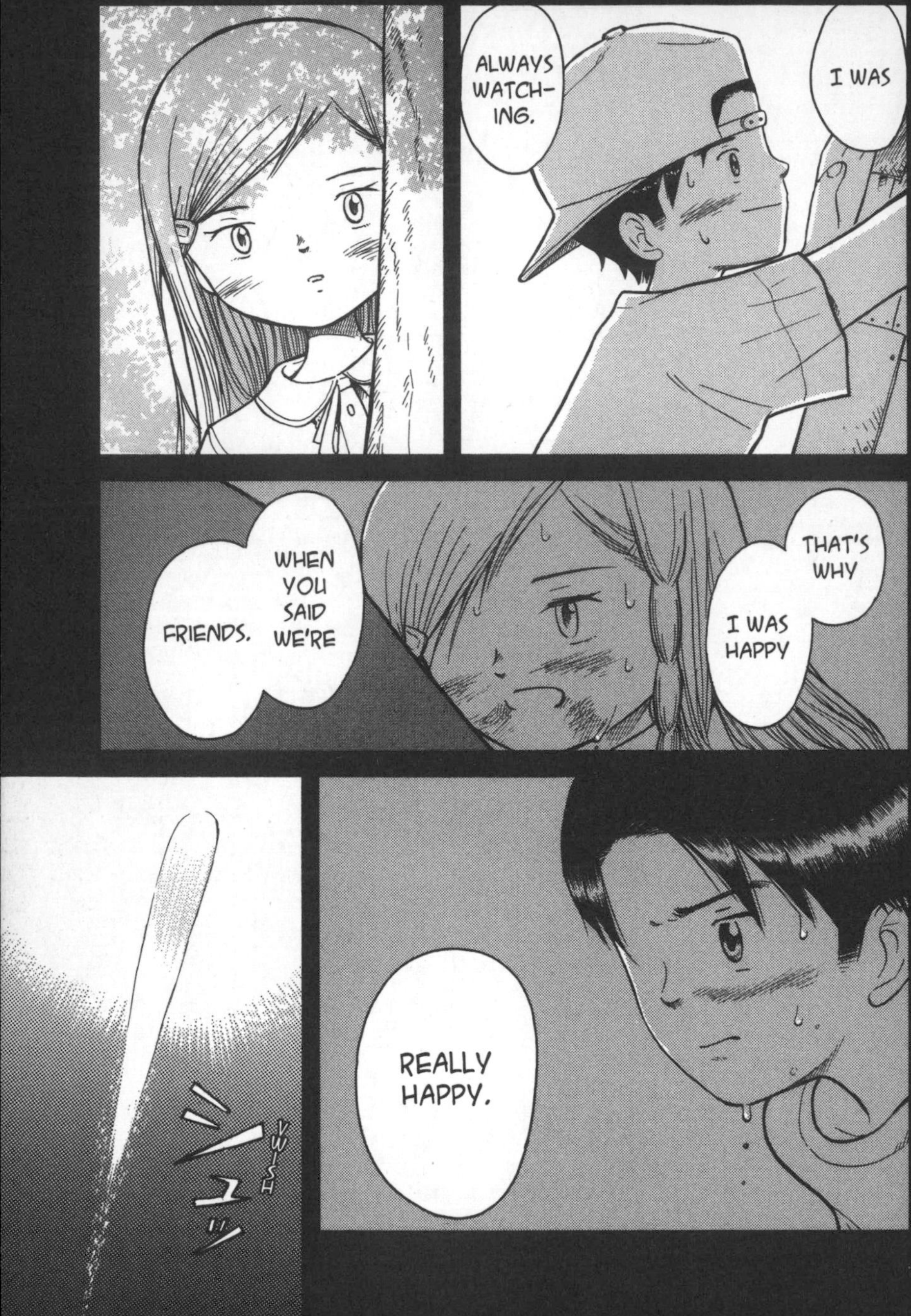
I WAS
ALWAYS WATCHING.
THAT'S WHY I WAS HAPPY
WHEN YOU SAID WE'RE FRIENDS.
REALLY HAPPY.
VWISH

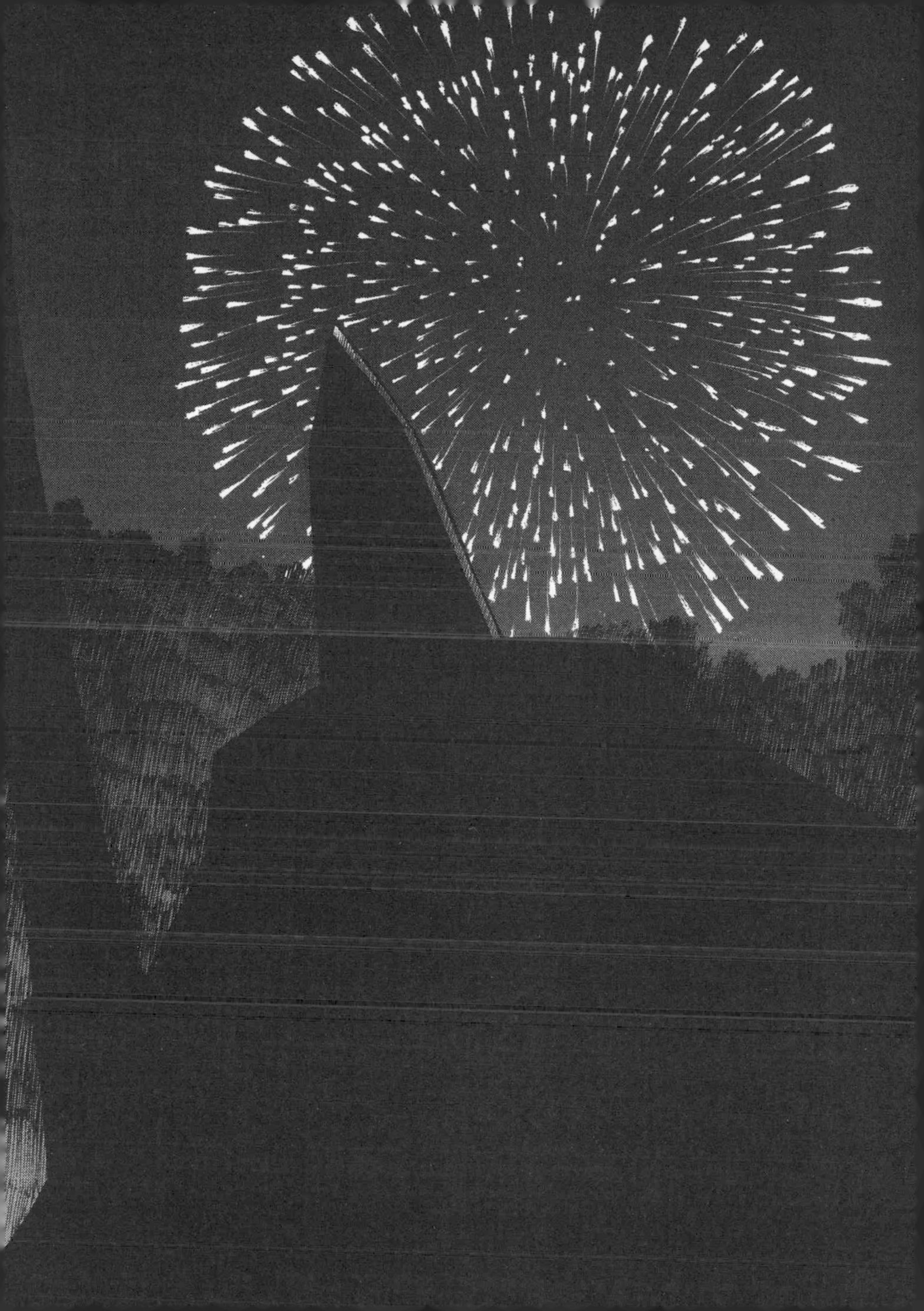

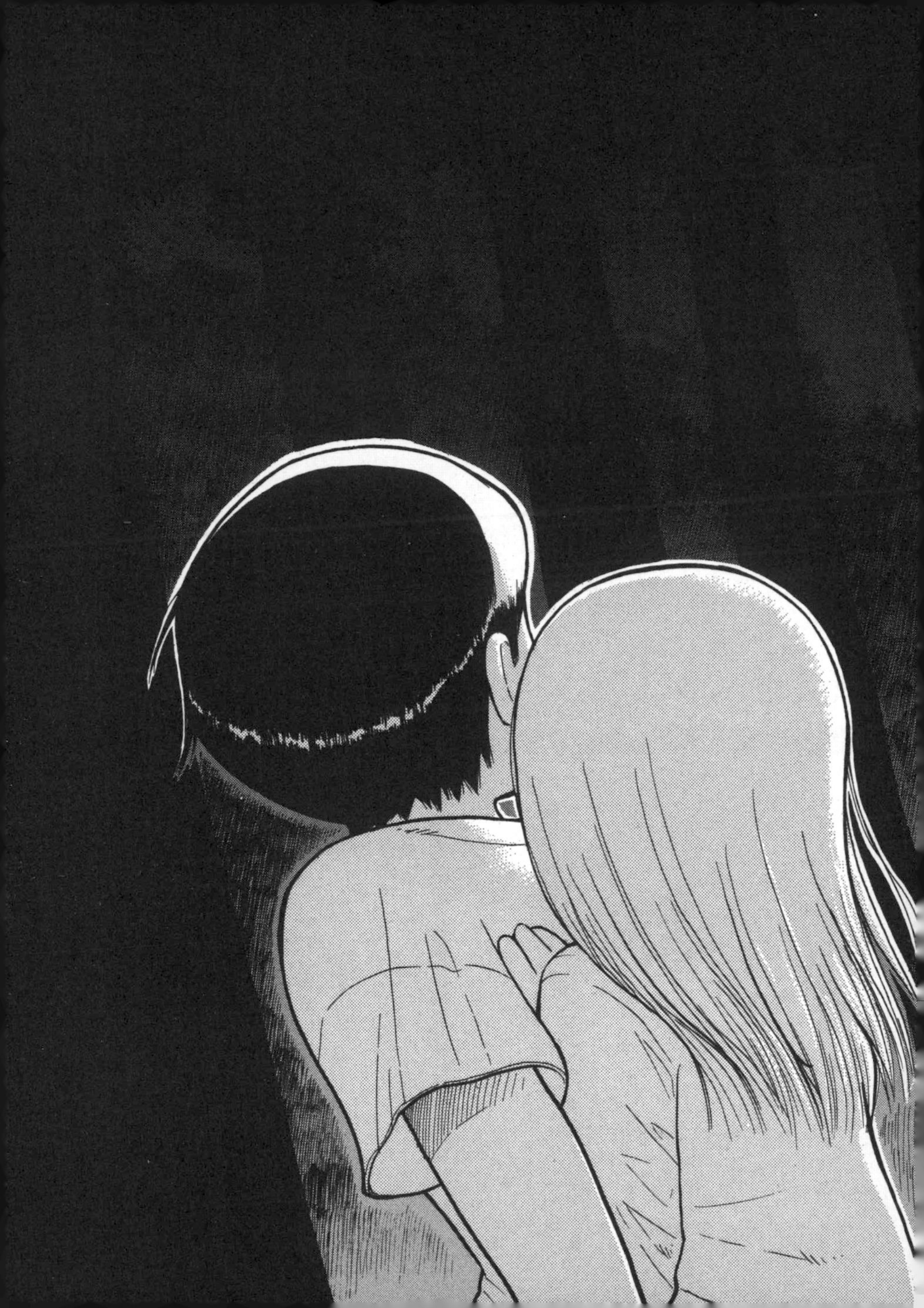

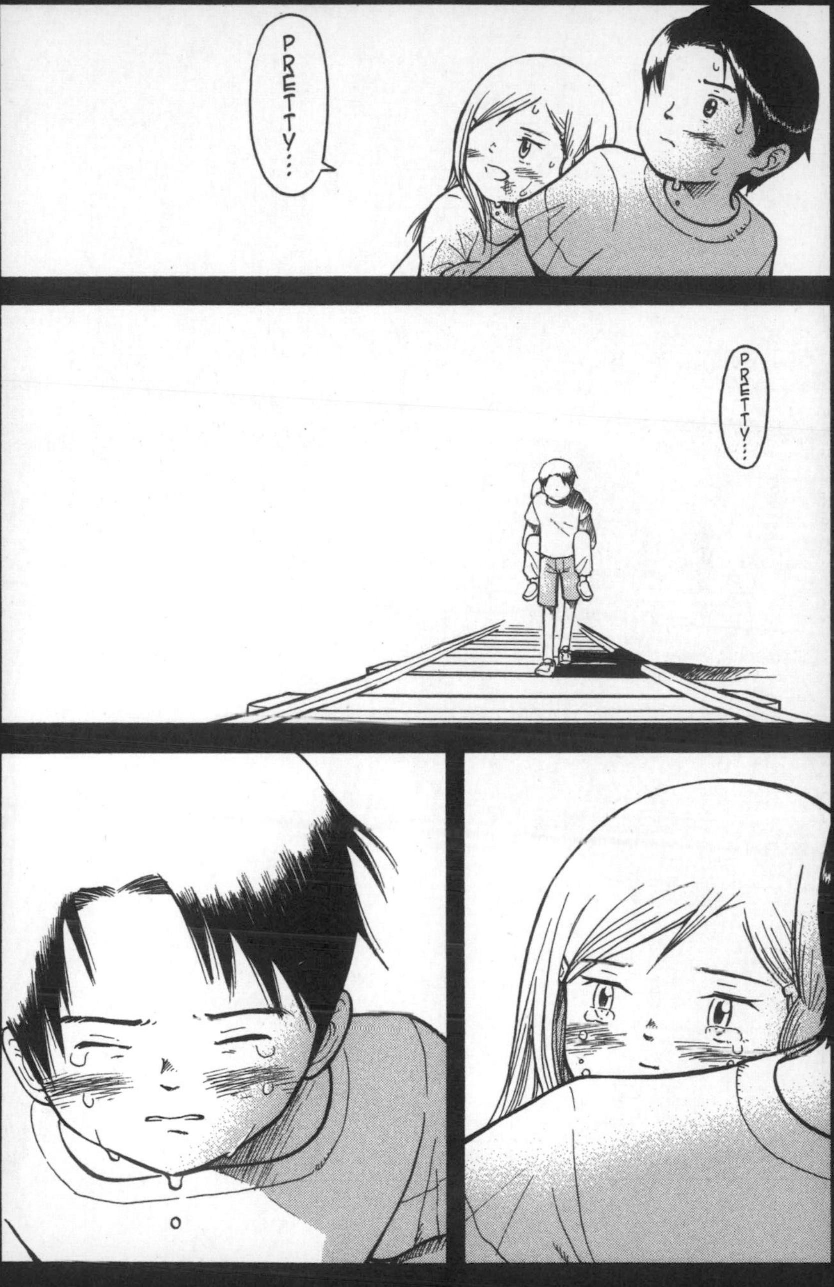
PRETTY...
PRETTY...

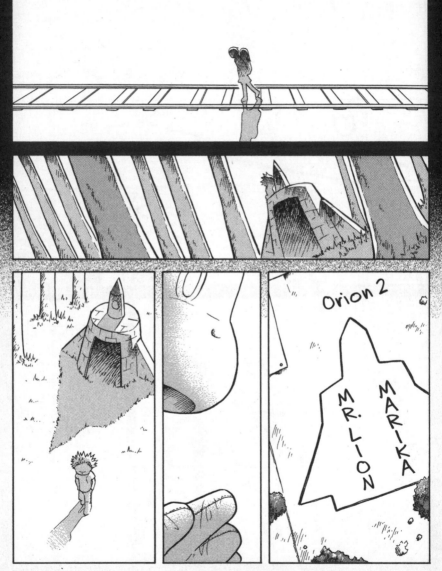

Orion 2

MR. LION

MARIKA

KAON
TO SPACE
TO SPACE—
TO SPACE—

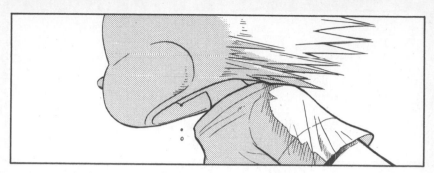

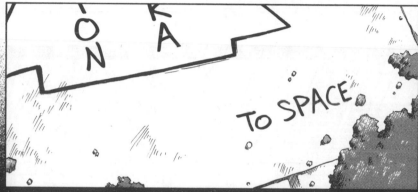

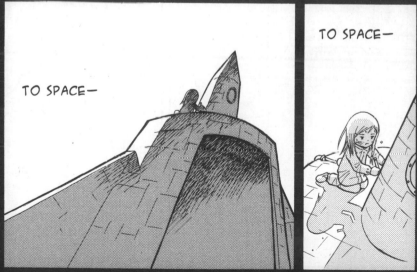

CONTINUED IN TWIN SPICA VOL. 6

ANOTHER SPICA

KOU YAGINUMA

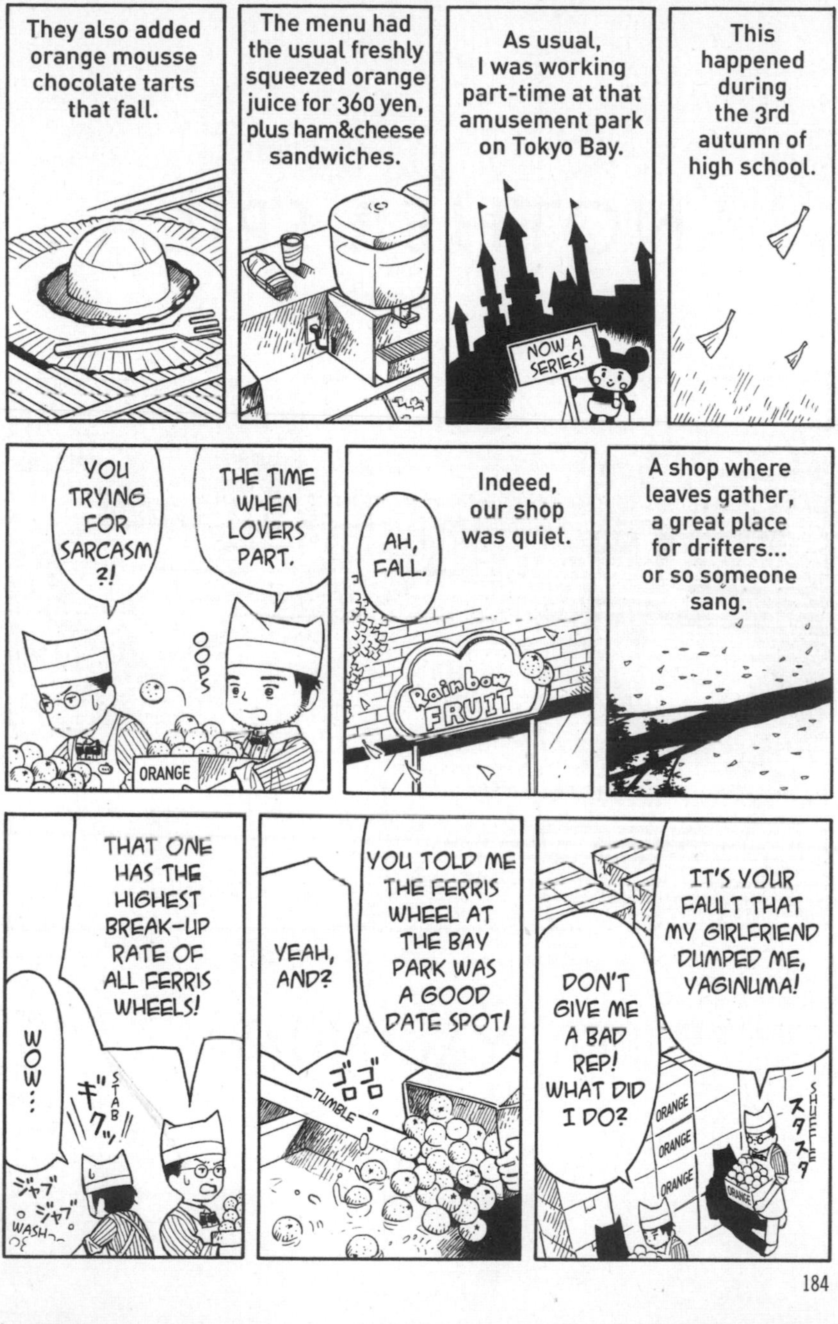
This happened during the 3rd autumn of high school.
As usual, I was working part-time at that amusement park on Tokyo Bay.
NOW A SERIES!
The menu had the usual freshly squeezed orange juice for 360 yen, plus ham&cheese sandwiches.
They also added orange mousse chocolate tarts that fall.
A shop where leaves gather, a great place for drifters... or so someone sang.
Indeed, our shop was quiet.
AH, FALL.
Rainbow FRUIT
THE TIME WHEN LOVERS PART.
YOU TRYING FOR SARCASM?!
OOPS
ORANGE
IT'S YOUR FAULT THAT MY GIRLFRIEND DUMPED ME, YAGINUMA!
DON'T GIVE ME A BAD REP! WHAT DID I DO?
スタスタ SHUFFLE
ORANGE
ORANGE
ORANGE
ORANGE
YOU TOLD ME THE FERRIS WHEEL AT THE BAY PARK WAS A GOOD DATE SPOT!
YEAH, AND?
ゴロゴロ TUMBLE
THAT ONE HAS THE HIGHEST BREAK-UP RATE OF ALL FERRIS WHEELS!
WOW...
ギクッ STAB
ジャブジャブ WASH

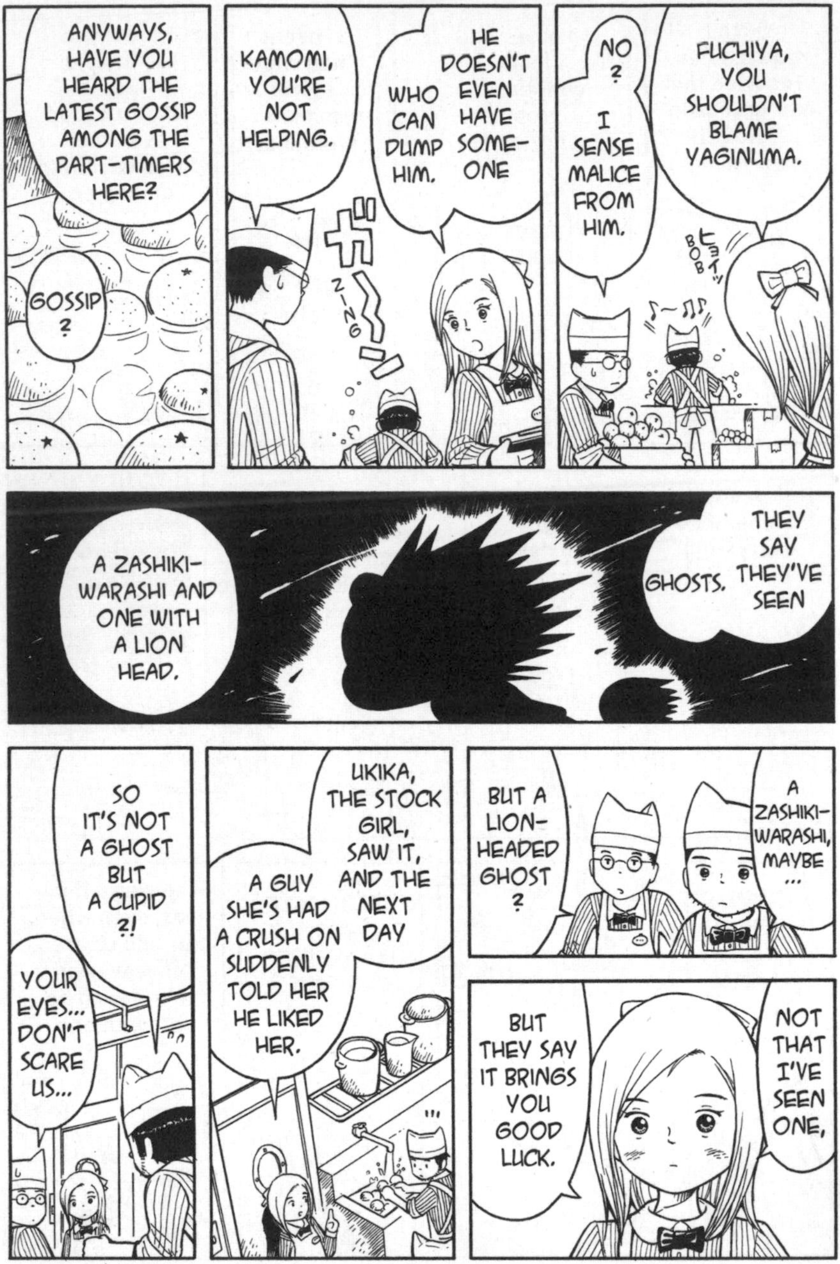
FUCHIYA, YOU SHOULDN'T BLAME YAGINUMA.
NO? I SENSE MALICE FROM HIM.
BOB
HE DOESN'T EVEN HAVE SOME-ONE WHO CAN DUMP HIM.
KAMOMI, YOU'RE NOT HELPING.
ZING
ANYWAYS, HAVE YOU HEARD THE LATEST GOSSIP AMONG THE PART-TIMERS HERE?
GOSSIP?
THEY SAY THEY'VE SEEN GHOSTS.
A ZASHIKI-WARASHI AND ONE WITH A LION HEAD.
A ZASHIKI-WARASHI, MAYBE...
BUT A LION-HEADED GHOST?
NOT THAT I'VE SEEN ONE,
BUT THEY SAY IT BRINGS YOU GOOD LUCK.
UKIKA, THE STOCK GIRL, SAW IT, AND THE NEXT DAY
A GUY SHE'S HAD A CRUSH ON SUDDENLY TOLD HER HE LIKED HER.
SO IT'S NOT A GHOST BUT A CUPID?!
YOUR EYES... DON'T SCARE US...

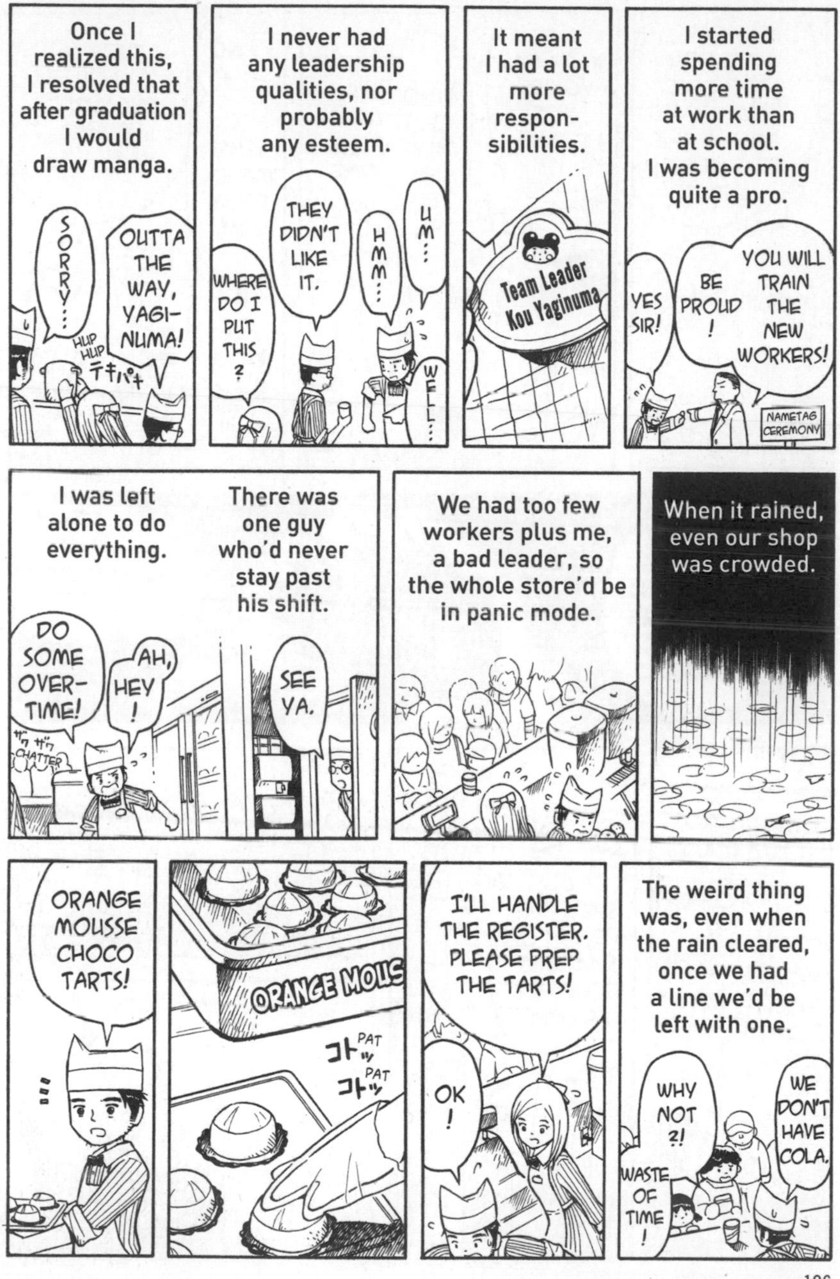
I started spending more time at work than at school. I was becoming quite a pro.
YOU WILL TRAIN THE NEW WORKERS!
BE PROUD!
YES SIR!
NAMETAG CEREMONY
It meant I had a lot more respon-sibilities.
Team Leader Kou Yaginuma
I never had any leadership qualities, nor probably any esteem.
UM...
HMM...
THEY DIDN'T LIKE IT.
WHERE DO I PUT THIS?
WELL...
Once I realized this, I resolved that after graduation I would draw manga.
OUTTA THE WAY, YAGI-NUMA!
SORRY...
HUP HUP テキパキ
When it rained, even our shop was crowded.
We had too few workers plus me, a bad leader, so the whole store'd be in panic mode.
There was one guy who'd never stay past his shift.
SEE YA.
I was left alone to do everything.
AH, HEY!
DO SOME OVER-TIME!
ザワザワ CHATTER
The weird thing was, even when the rain cleared, once we had a line we'd be left with one.
WE DON'T HAVE COLA.
WHY NOT?!
WASTE OF TIME!
I'LL HANDLE THE REGISTER. PLEASE PREP THE TARTS!
OK!
ORANGE MOUS
コトッ PAT
コトッ PAT
ORANGE MOUSSE CHOCO TARTS!

AH YES
ONE ORANGE TART.
...
?
HUB ガヤ
BUB ガヤ
WHAT'S WRONG?
UH, NOTHIN'.
YOU SAID TEN TARTS?
NO, ONE!
No matter how busy we were, at the sound of fireworks everyone cleared out.
That sound was our closing bell.
ドパーン POW
ドドド PA-PA-POW
WHEW.
THEY'RE GONE.
THE STORE'S EMPTY. CAN WE CLOSE?
KLACH ガチャッ
ジャーッ SPLUSH
...

ジャーッ
SPLUSH
DON'T WASTE WATER, PLEASE.
AH ...
DID YOU KNOW THAT GIRL?
HUH?
N-NO ...
ジャブジャブ
SPLISH
Whenever I see someone that looks like her, my chest aches.
The target of my unrequited love had sat 2 rows ahead of me in middle school.
I hadn't had the courage to tell her how I felt.
All I managed was to watch her walk away after graduation until I couldn't see her.
...
ジャブジャブジャブ
SPLISH
YAGI-NUMA, ARE YOU MAD ABOUT WHAT I SAID?
HUH?
THAT YOU DON'T HAVE SOMEONE TO DUMP YOU.
ジャバジャブ
SPLISH
NO!!
WHY WOULD I LET THAT BOTHER ME?!
TRUE, I'VE BEEN DUMPED A BUNCH OF TIMES.
AH,
KNEW IT.
SAVE WATER!
SNIF
トホホ

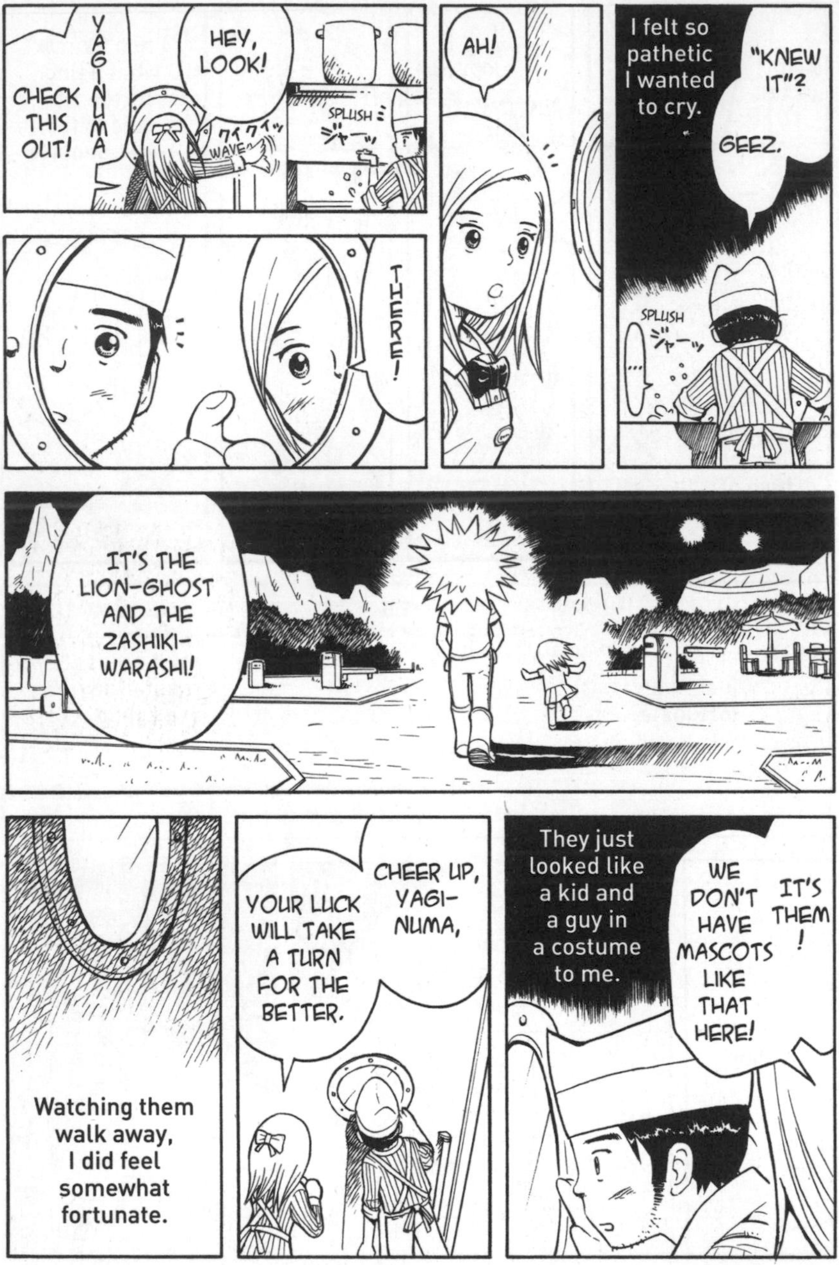
I felt so pathetic I wanted to cry.
"KNEW IT"?
GEEZ.
SPLUSH
ジャーッ
...
AH!
HEY, LOOK!
SPLUSH
ジャーッ
クイクイッ
WAVE
YAGINUMA
CHECK THIS OUT!
THERE!
IT'S THE LION-GHOST AND THE ZASHIKI-WARASHI!
IT'S THEM!
WE DON'T HAVE MASCOTS LIKE THAT HERE!
They just looked like a kid and a guy in a costume to me.
CHEER UP, YAGI-NUMA,
YOUR LUCK WILL TAKE A TURN FOR THE BETTER.
Watching them walk away, I did feel somewhat fortunate.

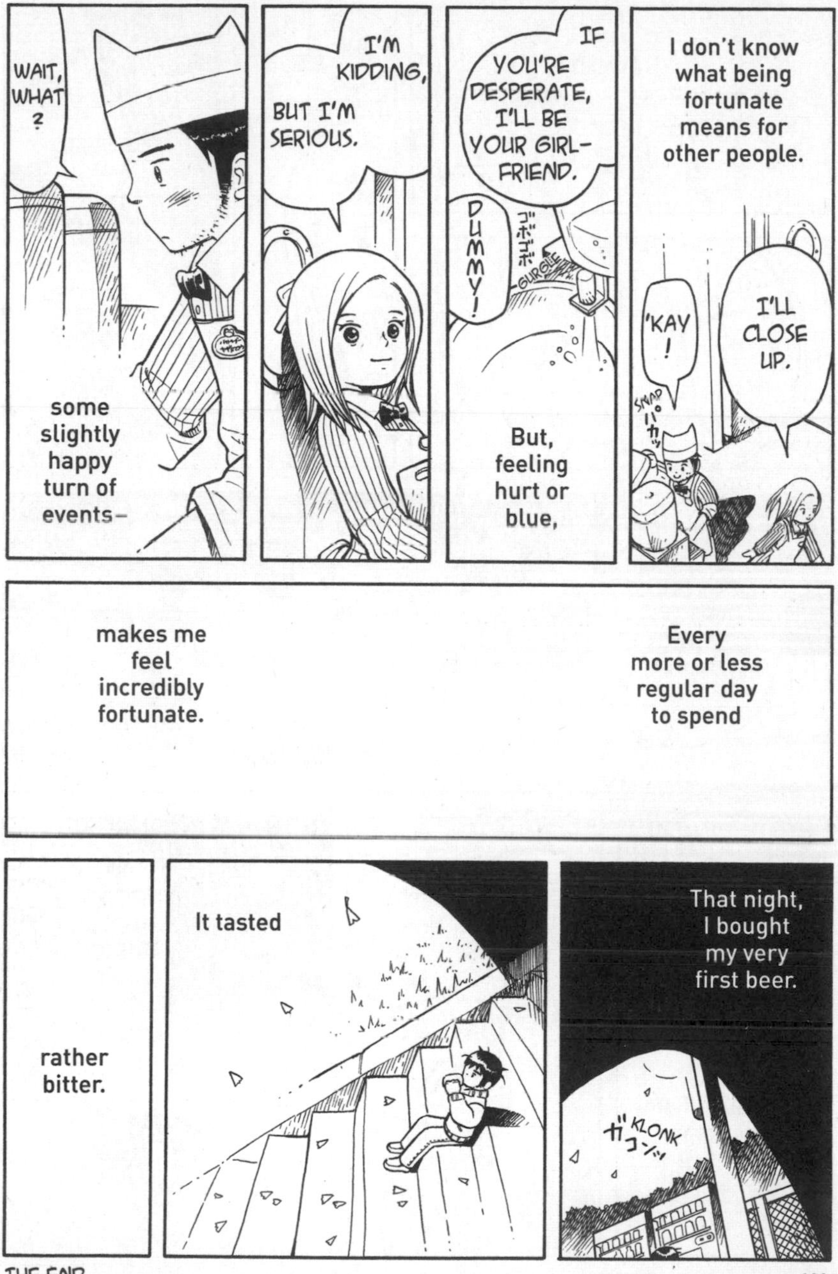
I don't know what being fortunate means for other people.
I'LL CLOSE UP.
'KAY!
SNAP
IF YOU'RE DESPERATE, I'LL BE YOUR GIRL-FRIEND.
DUMMY!
GURGLE
But, feeling hurt or blue,
I'M KIDDING,
BUT I'M SERIOUS.
WAIT, WHAT?
some slightly happy turn of events–
Every more or less regular day to spend
makes me feel incredibly fortunate.
That night, I bought my very first beer.
KLONK
It tasted
rather bitter.

THE END

Notes on the Translation

P. 43

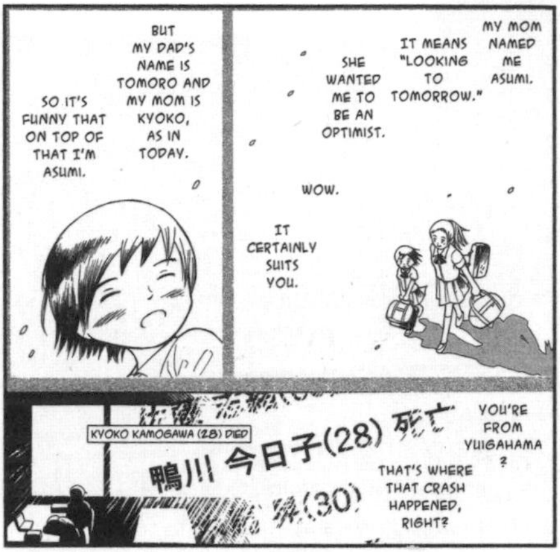
MY MOM NAMED ME ASUMI.
IT MEANS "LOOKING TO TOMORROW."
SHE WANTED ME TO BE AN OPTIMIST.
WOW.
IT CERTAINLY SUITS YOU.
BUT MY DAD'S NAME IS TOMORO AND MY MOM IS KYOKO, AS IN TODAY.
SO IT'S FUNNY THAT ON TOP OF THAT I'M ASUMI.
YOU'RE FROM YUIGAHAMA?
THAT'S WHERE THAT CRASH HAPPENED, RIGHT?
KYOKO KAMOGAWA (28) DIED
鴨川 今日子(28) 死亡

Mr. Kamogawa's first name, a fairly common one in Japan, happens to sound like the English word "tomorrow," which is Asumi's punning observation in the original. Incidentally, the *Kamogawa* is a stream that runs through Kyoto and does not evoke time or outer space in any blunt manner; the *kanji* characters mean "duck" (the bird) and "river."

P. 133

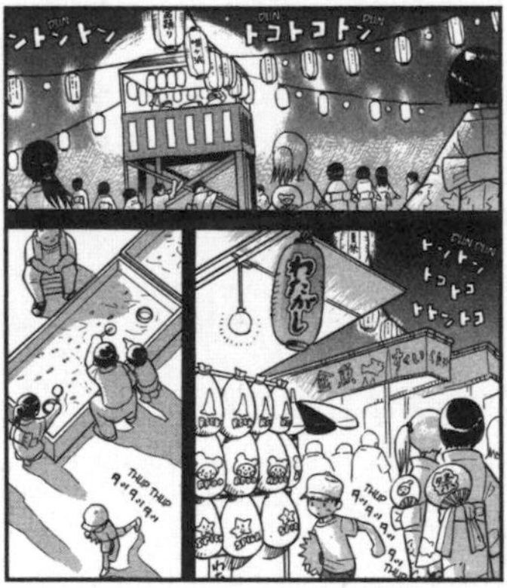

The characters on the lanterns in the top panel say "Bon Dance" and "Yuigahama." Festivals have been traditionally held across Japan during the summer *o-bon* period to honor the dead. Apart from the dancing, the festivities include food and amusement booths. In the bottom panel, the large lantern advertises *watagashi* or cotton candy, below which is an awning for *kingyo sukui* or goldfish scooping, pictured in the subsequent panel.

Production - Hiroko Mizuno
Tomoe Tsutsumi
Rina Nakayama

Published by Vertical, Inc., New York

Originally published in Japanese as *Futatsu no Supika*
by MEDIA FACTORY, Inc., Tokyo 2003
Futatsu no Supika first serialized in Gekkan Comic Flapper,
MEDIA FACTORY, Inc., 2001-2009

This is a work of fiction.

ISBN: 978-1-935654-02-5

Manufactured in Canada

First Edition

Vertical, Inc.
1185 Avenue of the Americas, 32nd Floor
New York, NY 10036
www.vertical-inc.com

[redacted]

[redacted]